Cross-Border Terrorism

Cross-Border Terrorism

Focus on Pakistan

Jayanta Kumar Ray

Maulana Abul Kalam Azad Institute of Asian Studies

SHIPRA

ISBN: 978-81-7541-842-4

First Published in India in 2016

Cross-Border Terrorism: Focus on Pakistan

Published by:
SHIPRA PUBLICATIONS
LG 18-19, Pankaj Central Market, I.P. Ext.
Patparganj, Delhi-110092, India
Tel: 91-11-2223 5152, 2223 6152
E-mail: info@shiprapublication.com
www.shiprapublication.com

For
My granddaughter
Anumegha

Preface

There is no better way to prepare the Preface to this book than to rely extensively on an April 1946 interview with Maulana Abul Kalam Azad by Shorish Kashmiri for *Chattan*, a Urdu magazine published from Lahore. Arif Mohammed Khan, a former Cabinet Minister of India, devoted many years to look for a book on Maulana Abul Kalam Azad by Kashmiri, which contained the April 1946 interview. This was published only once by a Lahore-based publisher, Matbooat Chattan, which subsequently went out of existence. In 2009, Arif Mohammed Khan published an authoritative English translation of the abovenoted interview.[1]

Azad (who opposed Partition consistently) brilliantly contested the view of advocates of Partition of British India that Hindus and Muslims were two different nations. In the Koran, said Azad, 'the term qaum has been used not only for the community of believers but has also been used for distinct human groupings generally. What do we wish to achieve by raising this debate about the etymological scope of terms like millat [community], qaum [nation] and ummat [group]? In religious terms,' Azad reminded Indian Muslims, 'India is home to many people—the Hindus, Muslims, Christians, Parsis, Sikhs, etc. The differences between Hindu religion and Islam are vast in scope. But these differences cannot be allowed to become an obstacle in the path of India gaining her freedom nor do the two distinct and different systems of faith negate the idea of unity of India. The issue is of our national independence and how we can secure it. Freedom is a blessing and is the right of every human being. It cannot be divided on the basis of religion.'[2]

Azad stressed that Muslims 'are not a racial or regional grouping in whose territory others cannot enter.' He added: 'Strictly speaking, Muslims in India are not one community; they are divided among many well-entrenched sects. You can unite them by arousing their anti-Hindu sentiment but you cannot unite them in the name of Islam. To them Islam means undiluted loyalty to their own sect. Apart from Wahabi, Sunni and Shia there are innumerable groups who owe allegiance to different saints and divines. Small issues like raising hands during the prayer and saying amen loudly have created disputes that defy solution.' Azad complains about the Ulama, because they 'used the instrument of takfeer [fatwas declaring someone as infidel] liberally. Earlier, they used to take Islam to the disbelievers; now they take away Islam from the believers. Islamic history is full of instances of how good and pious Muslims are branded Kafirs.' Actually, Azad maintained, this meant fossilisation of attitudes, and abandonment of 'reason and intelligence'.[3]

One major contention of Azad about Partition and the creation of Pakistan deserves special mention. According to him, 'Pakistan has nothing to do with Islam; it is a political demand that is projected by Muslim League as the national goal of Indian Muslims. I feel it is not the solution to the problems Muslims are facing. In fact it is bound to create more problems.'[4] Azad rightly stressed the economic problems of Muslims.

Azad made some specific predictions about what would happen in Pakistan after the Partition of British India. These predictions turned out to be correct. For example, about East Pakistan, Azad said: 'I feel it will not be possible for East Pakistan to stay with West Pakistan for any considerable period of time. There is nothing common between the two regions except that they call themselves Muslims.' Azad emphasised that 'the language, customs and way of life of East Pakistan, are totally different from West Pakistan. The moment the creative warmth of Pakistan cools down, the contradictions will emerge and will acquire assertive overtones. These will be fuelled by the clash of interests of international powers and consequently both wings will separate.'[5] Chapter one of this book has analysed in detail this painful process of violent separation, and the emergence of East Pakistan as the independent country of Bangladesh on 16 December 1971.

As to West Pakistan, Azad predicted: 'After the separation of East Pakistan, whenever it happens, West Pakistan will become the battleground of regional contradictions and disputes. The assertion of sub-national identities of Punjab, Sind, Frontier and Balochistan will open the doors for outside interference.'[6] Several chapters of this book can confirm the validity of these observations by Azad on West Pakistan.

A few other prophetic observations by Azad may be noted here. According to him, 'right from its inception' Pakistan was going to 'face some very serious problems.' One problem was the incompetence of political leaders, which would 'pave the way for military dictatorship as it has happened in many Muslim countries.'[7] Actually, since 1958, Pakistan has suffered from military rule, direct or indirect, visible or invisible.

Another problem to be faced by Pakistan, in Azad's view, was the 'absence of friendly relationship with neighbours and the possibility of armed conflict.'[8] As several chapters of this book illustrate, Pakistani rulers have never hesitated to start hostilities not only with India but also with Afghanistan, although in varying degrees.

In the April 1946 interview, Azad also underlined 'the dissatisfaction and alienation of the youth from religion and the collapse of the theory of Pakistan.'[9] In fact, Azad went further and said: 'Pakistan, when it comes into existence, will face conflicts of religious nature. As far as I can see, the people who will hold the reins of power will cause serious damage to Islam. Their behaviour may result in the total alienation of the Pakistani youth who may become a part of non-religious movements.'[10] It is pertinent to speculate whether all these words of Azad contain the seeds of emergence of acute Shia-Sunni conflict in twentyfirst century Pakistan, as also of the operations of non-state actors like the LET attracting the youth to the terrorist path.

Perhaps some of the most farsighted comments by Azad in the April 1946 interview relate to Arab countries. In order to highlight the futility of Partition of British India on the basis of religion and the creation of a new state of Pakistan, Azad pointed out that 'the fact of being Muslim has never created durable political unity anywhere in the world. The Arab World is before us; they subscribe to a common religion, a common civilisation and culture and speak a common language. In fact they acknowledge even territorial unity. But there is no political unity among them. Their systems of government are different and they are often engaged in mutual recrimination and hostility.'[11]

This 'mutual recrimination and hostility' appears to have reached a peak with the emergence of IS, which has a deleterious impact on non-Arab as also Arab countries, e.g. Iran, Iraq and Syria, and which is gradually expanding its operations in south Asia, especially Pakistan, which has a fertile ground for sectarianism and terrorism. The IS-run caliphate, wedded to totalitarianism, utilises the services of highly trained intelligence and military officers of Saddam Hussain's regime, who became the victims of expulsion after the Anglo-US invasion of Iraq. With the near-complete disengagement of the US from Iraq and Afghanistan, the IS senses a heaven-sent opportunity for employing Sunni Salafist militants to play havoc in an expanding number of countries, e.g. Iraq, Syria, Libya, Yemen. etc. IS has provoked resistance from a large number of countries, viz. Syria, Saudi Arabia, Iraq, Turkey, Iran, Jordan, as also some European countries. But these countries do not have common interests or mutual trust. Their intelligence agencies are also not known for extensive cooperation. There is some coordination when the US exercises leadership in air strikes on the IS, and US partners join these strikes. Taking advantage of these air strikes, Kurdish peshmerga forces probably offer the stiffest military resistance to IS. Nevertheless, the IS derives great advantage from acute rivalries between Iran (the leader of Shias) and Saudi Arabia (the leader of Sunnis), as also from differences between states who support Syria's rulers and those who do not.[12]

An opportunity seemed to have arisen in early February 2015 for transcending the rivalries and disagreements among the opponents of IS. In December 2014, the plane of a Jordanian pilot, who was part of the US-led coalition force striking at the IS, came down. The pilot was taken captive by the IS. In January 2015, the pilot was reportedly torched alive in a cage. But the video of this horrendous atrocity was circulated in the first week of February 2015. The aim was to scare away the actual or probable participants in the US-led air strike missions against the IS. But the impact was exactly the reverse. Protests against the IS were loud and widespread in West

Asia, North Africa and Europe, even though similar atrocities committed by the IS against Syrian soldiers in the past had been simply ignored. Arab countries began to exhibit a rare unity. Jordan became far more active than in the past in launching air strikes against the IS. Another opportunity for resolution of disunity among anti-IS forces arose in mid-February, when the IS beheaded twentyone Egyptian Coptic Christians in Libya, and circulated the video on this killing. Immediately, and for the first time, Egypt started direct anti-IS military action by bombing IS strongholds. A complex question arises: can the US and some European countries take a diplomatic initiative to bridge differences between Iran and Saudi Arabia, as also between pro-Syrian and anti-Syrian countries, and prompt Syria's ruling circle to achieve reconciliation between rebels and the government? The answer lies in the future—probably the distant future—and the IS can continue and spread its depredations till then, while Pakistan (the focus of this book) may not be spared.[13] For, IS leaders must be happy that Shias in Pakistan are butchered at brief intervals even when they are holding prayers in a mosque. Not to speak of Pakistan, the IS does not even leave Japan alone. It beheaded two Japanese journalist hostages in February 2015. Signals are ominous. Perhaps things have to get worse before they can get better.

References

1. http://newageislam.com/books-and-documents/maulana-abulkalam-azad-the-man-who-knew-the-future-of-Pakistan-before-its-creation/d/2139
2. *Ibid.*, p. 4.
3. *Ibid.*
4. *Ibid.*, p. 3. Anwar Shaikh, *Islam: The Arab Imperialism*, Cardiff: Principality Publishers, 1998, p. 94.
5. *Ibid.*, p. 2.
6. *Ibid.*
7. *Ibid*
8. *Ibid.*
9. *Ibid.*
10. *Ibid.*, p. 1.
11. *Ibid.*
12. For some insightful analysis of problems discussed in this paragraph, see an article by Moazzam Husain in *Dawn*, reproduced in *The Statesman*, 7 February 2015.

13. Editorial, *The Statesman*, 6 February 2015; AFP report, *Ibid.*, 7 February 2015; article by Robert Fisk in *The Independent,* reproduced *Ibid.*; PTI reports from Karachi and Peshawar on attack by suicide bombers in Shia mosques, *The Statesman*, 31 January and 14 February 2015; on the slaughter of Japanese journalists, see AFP report, *Ibid.*, 2 February 2015, AP report and editorial, *Ibid.*, 3 February 2015; AFP/PTI reports from Cairo and commentary in *The Independent*, *Ibid.*, 16 February 2015; as to how IS-sponsored butchery in Paris and Copenhagen in 2015 can reinforce solidarity among anti-IS Western countries, see reports by Agencies from Copenhagen, and an editorial, *Ibid.*, 16 and 18 February 2015 respectively; see article by Matin Haider in *Dawn*, reproduced *Ibid.*, 24 February 2015.

Acknowledgements

A number of years have gone into the preparation of this book. In course of these years, I have received invaluable support from some individuals and institutions. In case there is any omission, which is rather unlikely, I tender an abject apology. The support, I must add, is sometimes direct and measurable, sometimes indirect and inspirational.

Initially, I list names of some persons alphabetically in accordance with the first name: Ajai Sahni, Amiya Kumar Chaudhury, Anirban Ganguly, Bimal Pramanik, Durgadas Roy, Mukesh Mishra, Saradindu Mukherjee, Shatarupa Dutta Majumdar, and Swapna Bhattacharya.

I am indebted to two institutions for infrastructural aid. One is the Maulana Abul Kalam Azad Institute of Asian Studies, Kolkata. I built up this Institute for a decade in various capacities, viz. Honorary Chairman/Director. Subsequently, Professor Hari Shankar Vasudevan, the Director of the Institute, appointed me as Maulana Azad Fellow in 2011, and extended all possible facilities to me. I served this Institute as Maulana Azad Fellow for three years till early October 2014. I wanted to complete the writing of this book at this Institute. But I could not, because of the complexity of the topic; I had to spend a little more time; therefore, I moved to Calcutta University, the second institution to provide me with infrastructural aid. At the Azad Institute, I received generous cooperation from Chairman, Shri Sitaram Sharma (Honorary Consul of Belarus), Dr. Sreeradha Dutta, Director, and Ms. Anjum Katiyal, Publications Consultant. I also received unstinted help from some members of the library and administrative staff, especially from Sandip Sarkar, the librarian, and Sushanta Banerjee.

Amrita Basu and Putul Ghosh of the Maulana Azad Museum provided ungrudging assistance to me in the preparation of the manuscript.

At the University of Calcutta, Vice Chancellor Suranjan Das (subsequently the Vice Chancellor of Jadavpur University), Professor Hari Shankar Vasudevan, Coordinator, China Centre, and Professor Shantanu Chakrabarty, Head, Department of History, and Convener, Institute of Foreign Policy Studies, extended inestimable assistance to me, and they are still doing so in my current assignment as National Research Professor, Ministry of Human Resource Development, Government of India. Ms. Saptadeepa Banerjee, Ms. Shreya Banerjee, and Shri Mintu Barua of the Institute of Foreign Policy Studies have helped me enormously as Research Associates.

At a crucial stage of preparation of this book, in the house of my son Suryadeep and Susmita, daughter-in-law – initially at Houston and later at Richmond, Texas, U.S.A. – Rampada Duari, Susmita's father, devoted a lot of his valuable time and earned my gratitude.

Above all, as in all my academic activities, my wife, Krishna, has enabled me to write this book by cheerfully bearing all the onerous responsibilities of managing a family.

Contents

Abbreviations

ABC : American Broadcasting Corporation
AISHF : All India Shia Husaini Fund
AKA : Amanki Asha
ANF : Al Nusrah Front
ANP : Awami National Party
ANSF : Afghan National Security Force
APC : All Parties Conference
APHC : All Party Hurriyat Conference
AQAP : Al Qaeda in the Arabian Peninsula
ARC : Administrative Reforms Commission
ASWJ : Ahl E Sunnat Wal Jamat
ATC : Air Traffic Controller
ATS : Anti-Terrorist Squad
AWT : Army Welfare Trust
BLA : Baloch Liberation Army
BOP : Border Outpost
BSA : Bilateral Security Agreement
CAPPS : Computer Assisted Passenger Prescreening System
CAR : Central African Republic
CDA : Capital Development Authority
CDP : Council for the Defence of Pakistan
CEO : Chief Executive Officer
CIA : Central Intelligence Agency
CM : Chief Minister
COAS : Chief of Army Staff
CST : Chhatrapati Shivaji rail terminus
CTC : Counterterrorism Centre
CTF : Composite Task Force
CTIRU : Counter Terrorism Internet Referral Unit
BCCI : Board of Control for Cricket in India
DCI : Director of Central Intelligence
DCP : Deputy Commissioner of Police
DEA : Drug Enforcement Authority
DEP : Difa E Pakistan
DFI : Defence Field Intelligence
DGFI : Directorate General of Forces Intelligence
DGP : Director General of Police
EIJ : Egyptian Islamic Jihad

EPR : East Pakistan Rifle
FAA : Federal Aviation Administration
FATA : Federally Administered Tribal Areas
FBI : Federal Bureau of Intelligence
FF : Fauji Foundation
FTF : Foreign Terrorist Fighter
FY : Financial Year
GCHQ : Government Communications Headquarter
G8 : Group of Eight
HIM : Hubris Ignorance and Mismanagement
HUA : Harkat Ul Ansar
HUJI : Harkat Ul Jihad Al Islami
HUJI-B : Harkat Ul Jihad Al Islami Bangladesh
HUM : Harkat Ul Mujahidin
HVT : High Value Target
IB : Intelligence Bureau
ICJ : International Court of Justice
IDP : Internally Displaced Person
IDP : Islamic Democratic Party
IM : Indian Mujahideen
IMU : Islamic Movement of Uzbekistan
INS : Immigration and Naturalisation Service
IOR : Indian Ocean Rim
IPC : Indian Penal Code
IS : Islamic State
ISAF : International Security Assistance Force
ISI : Inter Services Intelligence
ISIL : Islamic State of Iraq and Levant
ISIS : Islamic State of Iraq and Syria
JEI : Jamaat E Islami
JIM : Jaish I Muhammad
J&K : Jammu and Kashmir
JUD : Jamat Ud Dawa
JUI : Jamiat E Ulama Islam
KPK : Khyber Pakhtunkhwa
LET : Lashkar E Taiyaba
L J : Lashkar I Jhangvi / Lashkar E Jhangvi (LEJ)
MCOCA : Maharashtra Control of Organized Crime Act
MFN : Most-favoured-nation
MHA : Ministry of Home Affairs
MQM : Muttahid Quami Movement
MSR : Maritime Silk Route
NAP : National Awami Party
NATO : North Atlantic Treaty Organisation
NCTA : National Counter Terrorism Authority
NDA : National Democratic Alliance
NEADS : North East Air Defence Sector

NHRC : National Human Rights Commission
NIC : National Integration Council
NMCC : National Military Command Centre
NORAD : North American Aerospace Defence Command
NSC : National Security Council
NSG : National Security Guard
NWA : North Waziristan Agency
NWFP : North West Frontier Province
OBL : Osama Bin Laden
OMB : Office of Management and Budget
PAF : Pakistan Air Force
PDB : President's Daily Brief
PIFPD : Pakistan-India Forum for Peace and Democracy
PILDAT : Pakistan Institute for Legislative Development and Transparency
PME : Private Military Enterprise
PMO : Prime Minister's Office
POK : Pakistan-Occupied Kashmir
POTA : Prevention of Terrorist Activities Act
PPP : Pakistan People's Party
PRT : Provincial Reconstruction Team
PTI : Pakistan Tehreek I Insaf
RAW : Research and Analysis Wing
RJD : Rashtriya Janata Dal
RPG : Rocket-Propelled Grenade
SAFMA : South Asia Free Media Association
SEIB : Senior Executive Intelligence Brief
SF : Shaheen Foundation
SP : Samajwadi Party
SSG : Special Service Group
SSP : Sipah I Sahabe I Pakistan
TET : Tehrik E Taliban
TNSM : Tehrik E Nifaz E Shariat E Mohammadi or Tehrik I Nifaz I Shariat I Mohammadi
TTP : Tehrik E Taliban Pakistan
UAE : United Arab Emirates
UAV : Unmanned Aerial Vehicles
ULFA : United Liberation Front of Assam
UN : United Nations
UNAMA : United Nations Assistance Mission in Afghanistan
UNGA : United Nations General Assembly
UNSC : UN Security Council
UP : Uttar Pradesh
UPA : United Progressive Alliance
VBIED : Vehicle-borne improvised explosive devices
WMD : Weapons of Mass Destruction
WTC : World Trade Centre

ONE

Introduction

This author has probably chosen an inappropriate title for this volume. The appropriate title should have been 'Islamist Terrorism', or, better still, 'Jihadi Terrorism'. For, since 1947, India has been the most prominent, consistent, and ceaseless victim of such terrorism launched by Pakistan. An elaborate enunciation of the Indian experience of what can also be designated as a variant of Pakistan-sponsored Wahabism and/or Salafism should probably await a brief analysis of its first successful practice in modern history inside the Arabian Peninsula.

This analysis, again, ought to be preceded by a brief apology or alibi for the choice of this volume's title by the author. Evidently, although a large part of the volume deals with terrorism emanating from India's Muslim neighbourhood and afflicting India severely, the author feels shy of using Jihadi terrorism or Islamist Terrorism in the title. The first reason for this is that he is nurtured and trained in a country (India) and a religion (viz. Hinduism), both of which take pride in their philosophical foundation of human unity and tradition of religious tolerance. Therefore, he hesitates to hurt (even if unwittingly) the sentiments of persons belonging to other religions. Moreover, despite certain lasting implications of the mega event of 11 September 2001 and the consequent (apparently never-ending) war on terror in India's Muslim neighbourhood, this author fondly imagines that the majority of Muslims may be devout practitioners of their religion, but they do not endorse Islamist Terrorism or Jihadi Terrorism.[1] One may now proceed to the story of the Arabian Peninsula in the 20th century.

In 1932, Ibn Saud (Abdul Aziz bin Abdul Rahman-al-Saud) formally established the Kingdom of Saudi Arabia. He could do so by launching a jihad that lasted for about two-and-a-half decades in the course of which he conquered the Muslim territories, which were incorporated subsequently in his Kingdom. Undoubtedly, his success reflected the strength of Wahabism (of which he was the patron and practitioner) as also the religious zeal of Bedwin villagers. Wahabism sanctioned a jihad not only against infidels (non-Muslims), but also against apostates, i.e., Muslims, especially Shia Muslims, who did not subscribe to Wahabism. (This jihad is to be sharply distinguished from the jihad that a number of Muslims equate to an incessant struggle for self-purification). Designated as brothers (Ikhwan), King Ibn Saud's rural recruits enjoyed the authorisation of Wahabi mullahs to molest enemy women, misappropriate enemy properties and murder all prisoners of war. If they died in the midst of a holy war (jihad), they were assured of a place in heaven in the company of seventy-two women of exquisite beauty.[2]

Ironically, by the end of the 1920s, the Saudi ruler had to slaughter the Ikhwan, who had laid the foundation of his Kingdom. For, in 1927, the Ikhwan became highly adventurous and invaded Iraq (whose people were mostly Shias). But British infidels were then ruling Iraq and their air force pounced upon the Ikhwan. Ibn Saud concluded that the carriers of jihad ceased to be profitable. He raised a new army with recruits from urban areas, who were not as much infected by religious bigotry as the Ikhwan. In 1929, Ibn Said employed this new army (with modern weapons) to crush the Ikhwan, some of whom survived to flee to Kuwait. The British arrested them and deported them to Saudi Arabia, where they were killed without any hesitation.[3]

The alliance between Saudi monarchy and Wahabi religious leaders imparted a sort of stability to the regime—despite some dangerous in-built contradictions. Whereas thousands of rich Saudi princes lived a life of luxury (if not dissipation), Wahabis looked upon the use of even such modern gadgets as radio and television as sinful. For, they derived their inspiration from an eighteenth century movement that preached restoration of the purity and perfection of an Islamic society in the days of the Prophet, i.e., seventh century Arabia. Contradictions between Wahabi mullahs and monarchy tended to deepen and widen in course of the twentieth century as Salafism became the dominant creed of Sunni Muslims in different parts of the world. For, unlike Wahabis, who would confine their jihad to the purification of only the Arab world, Salafis were determined to purify the whole world, making jihad the collective as also the individual responsibility of Sunni Muslims. If, therefore, in the past, the Saudi royal family could sometimes use money power to win over angry mullahs, it became more and more difficult over the years. Thus, in September 1965, even a young Saudi prince and his lieutenants staged an onslaught on the television centres in Riyadh. Although security forces killed the attackers, the danger signal was clear and present: the contradictions between the opulent and licentious life styles of the royal family and religious zealots could no longer be ignored.[4]

The 1970s witnessed deterioration in Saudi Arabia's security situation due to a complex combination of events outside this country. For example, in 1970, King Hussein of Jordan, an American ally, faced a rebellion by Palestinians. The Syrian Air Force was ready to intervene in favour of Palestinians. Israel neutralised Syria. But, in 1973, Syria and Egypt launched a surprise attack against Israel. Israel was in deep trouble, but it could override the crisis by a deft use of American weapons. This was a signal for America to step up the diplomatic campaign, which led, with active mediation by Jimmy Carter, the American President, to the landmark peace accord between Israel and Egypt at Camp David in 1979.[5]

This accord aggravated the hostility of religious bigots (who were anti-Israel) towards a staunch American ally, viz. Saudi Arabia. The Saudi monarch lost confidence in his citizens. He recruited Pakistani soldiers to guard himself. Pakistan secured a huge sum as economic assistance. But Saudi Arabia took care to dispatch a large number of religious bigots and preachers (Wahabis/Salafis) to Pakistan. The vigorous activities of these proselytisers could not but intensify religious fanaticism and the spirit of jihad in Pakistan.[6]

Undoubtedly, the efforts of Saudi zealots took place in the immensely fertile ground of Pakistan where Muslims could look back to centuries of successful practice of jihad much before the Partition of British-ruled India into India and Pakistan in 1947. An important component of jihad launched by Muslim invaders of India was the practice of slavery. 'The concept of jihad against unbelievers, the share of every Muslim in the loot from war including slaves, and the profit obtained through the sale of slaves added new zest in Islam for practising and profiting from slavery,' writes K.S. Lal.[7] 'Indeed from the days of Muhammad bin Qasim in the eighth century to those of Ahmed Shah Abdali in the eighteenth, enslavement, distribution, and sale of Hindu prisoners was systematically practised by Muslim invaders and rulers of India,'adds K.S. Lal.[8] Emperor Akbar did not recommend the enslavement of women and children due to a victory in war, but his commanders did not necessarily respect his desire.[9]

To give some examples, when Muhammad Bin Qasim, an Arab commander, invaded Sindh in 712, he had to carry out strictly the instructions from his superior authority in the land of the Caliph (Khalifa) to kill all infidels except women and children, who were to be enslaved. Those captives, who did not belong to upper classes, were distributed among soldiers.[10] Commencing in the year 1000, Sultan Mahmud of Ghazni, to take another example, invaded India as many as seventeen times. The general rule was to massacre the men and enslave women and children—as attested by contemporary Muslim chroniclers and historians of the modern era. Mahmud of Ghazni, it should be stressed, claimed that he carried out jihad to convert non-Muslims to Islam.[11] Slave-taking was the easiest way to such conversion by which a Muslim ruler could prove that he was adding to the Muslim population, and thereby promoting the cause of Islam.[12] It is advisable to cut short this long story of the conduct of jihad by Muslim rulers in medieval India with a reference to an interesting episode during the reign of Sultan Iltutmish from 1210 to 1236. A number of Ulama pleaded with this Sultan that he should govern his territory in accordance with the Sharia and subject Hindus to the choice between Islam and death. Actually, this plea of the Ulama was superfluous because, in practice, whenever a Muslim commander was victorious in a war, he would slaughter the Hindu soldiers, whose dependents became slaves and subsequently they had to embrace Islam.[13] This was a hard reality in medieval India—till the arrival of British rulers.

The British established their rule in India gradually in the eighteenth century. In the twentieth century, the Muslim League, led by Muhammad Ali Jinnah, launched an agitation for the Partition of British India, so that it could create the state of Pakistan, which, along with India, became independent on 14-15 August 1947. This story has been elaborately discussed elsewhere by numerous writers (including the present one). What in this book the present author has to stress, however, is the ill-concealed jihadi streak in the agitation for Pakistan. After all, the use of the word jihad might have scared the British rulers whose support, indistinguishable from collusion, was essential to ensure the emergence of Pakistan. The preferred word was Direct Action, which would be directed against non-Muslims, provoke retaliation and generate an environment of hate compatible with the basic Islamist distinction between believers and non-believers, which could sustain jihad against non-Muslims. Whereas Partition took place on 14-15 August 1947, the Working Committee of the All-India Muslim League had decided upon Direct Action in 1938. At about the same time, in Punjab, for example, the Muslim League raised a private militia. Its operations were secret. Known as Muslim National Guards, its strength grew over the years. There was a renewed call for Direct Action by the Muslim League on 27 July 1946. The seriousness of this threat could be perceived by noting the strength of the Muslim National Guards, which reached nearly 39,000 in Punjab by April 1947, i.e., a few months before Partition.[14]

Muslim National Guard volunteers played an important part in the Direct Action Day programme in Calcutta on 16 August 1946. Jinnah, the President of the All India Muslim League, declared on 29 July 1946 that 16 August 1946 would be a public holiday, because it was the Direct Action Day, when the Muslim League would abandon all methods of constitutional politics. The Muslim League Government of Bengal too announced on 15 August 1946 at the Bengal Assembly that 16 August would be a public holiday. The propaganda department of the Muslim League circulated a pamphlet that urged upon Muslims to learn how to murder by the use of knives, guns, etc. and form suicide squads to slaughter not only Hindu leaders, but also Muslims, who did not belong to the Muslim League. All this signified a spirit of jihad, the permission for which, as a Bengali leaflet of the Muslim League issued on 14 August argued, was obtained by Muslims from Allah in the holy month of Ramzan. Coincidentally, 16 August 1946 was a part of the Ramzan month.[15]

To cut short a long and familiar story, the short-term and long-term consequences of Partition were disastrous. Around two million people had to die, and about eighteen million had to suffer from forced migration, in the short run. Not even one murderer was tried and punished by any national or international court.[16] In the long run, Partition produced, and continued to multiply, such ghastly consequences as involuntary migration and conversions, which have been clearly noticeable in, e.g., East Bengal/East Pakistan/Bangladesh till the second decade of the twenty-first century. Nevertheless, the climactic and traumatic long-term result of Partition has been the transmutation of the antagonism of Pakistan's Muslim rulers towards India's Hindus into jihadi terrorism. Significantly, the United States did not advocate Partition, and, as late as 3 December 1946, the Secretary of State, Dean Acheson warned of the perilous consequences of Partition when he observed that 'Actions [viz. the creation of Pakistan] at this moment in history may directly affect world peace and prosperity for generations to come.'[17] A glaring and early evidence of post-Partition jihad came to the fore on 20-21 October 1947, when regular Pakistani soldiers led tribesmen to invade Jammu-Kashmir and start a war with India. But for a spirit of jihad (reinforced by British connivance), the Pakistani ruling circle could not have militarily challenged India at a time when India's military superiority was unquestionable and incontestable, as attested by some leading members of the Pakistani ruling circle.[18]

For example, according to Mohammad Ayub Khan, who was the most powerful figure in Pakistani politics during 1958-69, Pakistan's Army was 'badly equipped and terribly disorganized' at the time of Partition. For, 'there was no complete Muslim unit of battalion size in the British Indian Army'. And 'men from units in India began to trickle back to Pakistan in small groups'. Because they were 'untrained, half trained and highly trained', and because these men 'came from different units and different areas', 'they had all to be welded into fighting and ancillary units, divisions and corps'.[19] Mohammad Ayub Khan, a Field Marshal, further testified that as late as 1951, Pakistan did not have more than 'thirteen tanks with about forty to fifty hour' engine life in them'.[20] Similarly, Chaudhri Muhammad Ali, the Secretary General to the Government of Pakistan during 1947-51, the Finance Minister during 1951-55, and the Prime Minister during 1955-56, confessed that 'shortages in the technical arms, such as artillery, and in engineers, were very great, and even in the infantry, the number of senior officers with staff and command experience was limited'.[21] One can, therefore, reiterate that, despite British collusion, Pakistan's ruling circle would not have commenced a war in October 1947, unless they had a jihadi mindset.

Muhammad Ali Jinnah, the chief architect of Pakistan, created a temporary confusion about the prevalence of this jihadi mindset among Pakistan's rulers on 11 August 1947, when, at the Constituent Assembly of Pakistan, he talked eloquently of religious freedom, which was antithetical to the very concept of Pakistan, not to speak of a high consistency in the terribly hostile behaviour of the Pakistani rulers not only towards non-Muslims, but also towards minorities among Muslims, e.g., Ahmadis and Shias.[22] After all, a year back, on 16 August 1946, Jinnah gave a ferocious call for Direct Action (a euphemism for jihad) in Calcutta (now Kolkata). This led to unprovoked, premeditated and surprise attacks on non-Muslims (who naturally retaliated afterwards).[23]

Remarkably, Jinnah's official biographies took care to banish Jinnah's talk of religious freedom.[24] Officially, Jinnah was portrayed as an advocate of Islamic state. In January 1948, Jinnah delivered an address to the Sindh Bar Association at Karachi, where he affirmed that, in order to become 'a truly great Islamic state', Pakistan should base its Constitution on the Sharia.[25] The Objectives Resolution of the Constituent Assembly of Pakistan (adopted in March 1949) had patently Islamic provisions, which could strike fear in the minds of minorities, although the Resolution referred to principles of toleration underlying Islam.[26] A Basic Principles Committee was set up on the day the Objectives Resolution was passed.[27] Prime Minister Liaquat Ali Khan, while considering an Interim Report of the Basic Principles Committee, agreed with those, who would like to infuse more Islam into this Report, making it more in consonance with the Objectives Resolution. Liaquat, thus, strengthened, even if indirectly, those jihadi elements, which would aggrandise themselves at the expense of minority groups.[28]

The Objectives Resolution held out the ideal of a state where Muslims would be enabled to regulate their individual and collective living in accordance with the requirements of Islam set forth in the Koran and Sunna. The Basic Principles Committee set up a Talimat-i-Islami Board to help it in infusing Islam into the basic principles of the Constitution for Pakistan. A Report of the Basic Principles

Committee, presented to the Constituent Assembly in December 1952, significantly recommended that no laws repugnant to the Koran and Sunna should be enacted. In order to implement this recommendation, the Report prescribed the establishment of an Ulama Board to which all proposed laws should be referred. All these fanned the fanaticism of many Muslims including the Ulama at one extreme and the lawless adventurers at the other. They also inflamed the lust for political power in the Ulama.[29]

Muslim masses of Pakistan, dreaming of the splendid achievements of Islam during the 150 years after its birth, would always be enthralled by an appeal to the ideal of an Islamic state, without realizing that, in the context of modern democratic ideals, the ideal of an Islamic state was simply a menace to their rights. Again, they could interpret, or be incited by political bosses and the ambitious Ulama to interpret, the ideal of an Islamic state as permitting them to maltreat non-Muslims or minority Muslim sects in any way they liked for self-aggrandisement—without always calling for jihad or Direct Action openly or secretly. Such an interpretation might make it tremendously difficult to maintain law and order. The Objectives Resolution of the Constituent Assembly of Pakistan conformed to the Koran and the Sunna as it vested sovereignty in God. Quite inconsistently, however, it prescribed that Pakistan would be a sovereign state and observe democratic principles enjoined by Islam. According to Islamic political theory, the Islamic state embraced the entire community of Muslims in the world, and Pakistan did not have within its boundaries all the Muslims. Nor could it have the Caliph (Khalifa) to whom the heads of other Muslim states would pay their allegiance. An Islamic state can never claim to possess sovereignty, because it does not have the power to repeal any injunction of the Koran and the Sunna. Islamic political thought looks upon God as the Legislator, and rules out the role of any lawmaking body set up by ordinary human beings. Sharia, i.e., the Islamic law fixing up the code of conduct for the Muslims, did not evolve after the death of Muhammad, the Prophet, as his death snapped the line of communication between God and man. Sharia has no place for various individual liberties, which are the sine qua non of a modern democratic state. The doctrine of Siyasa in Sharia, again, is a negation of rights conferred on citizens by a modern democracy. This doctrine vests enormous discretionary powers in the ruler of an Islamic state, which would arbitrarily nullify the individual rights sanctioned by a modern democracy.[30]

The Objectives Resolution of 12 March 1949 was a virtual negation of Jinnah's speech of 11 August 1947. Brigands were encouraged to join hands with religious fanatics, who got a tremendous boost from the Objectives Resolution and the frequent announcements by leading politicians on Pakistan being or becoming an Islamic state. The upshot was a regular victimisation of the Muslim as well as non-Muslim minorities, including Ahmadis (also called Ahmadiyas or Qadianis) as also Buddhists, Christians and Hindus, which sometimes reached a climax, as in the holocaust of February 1950 (in the eastern wing of Pakistan or East Bengal), or of March-April 1953 in Punjab (which demands discussion at this point). Thousands of Ahmadis, a minority sect professing Islam, were slaughtered in Punjab during March-April 1953. The gravity of the failure of Pakistani leaders, who did not make any attempt to roll back the tide of anti-Ahmadi agitation, becomes all the more apparent when one notes that the jihadi persecution of Ahmadis, an insignificant minority among the Muslims, by the dominant Muslim sects, was not a new occurrence. It took place even during the British days when the majority sects took all possible measures to oppress the Ahmadis, e.g., boycotting them and forcing them to evacuate from areas, where they had been living for long, dismissing them from various jobs simply because they happened to be Ahmadis, and carrying on a campaign of vilification against Ahmadis. Even a poet and philosopher like Sir Muhammad Iqbal got very much agitated over this issue and suggested that the British Government should treat the founder of the Ahmadi sect in the same way as the Roman Government had treated Jesus Christ; on second thought, he calmed down and recommended that the Government should declare Ahmadis as non-Muslims. It was not surprising, therefore, although it was surely unwarranted by any notion of fairplay and decency, loyalty and discipline, expected of government functionaries, that members of the Board of Talimat-i-Islami backed the anti-Ahmadi agitation of 1953. None of them resigned from the government job, and none announced that he disapproved the massacre of Ahmadis.[31]

Evidences recorded by the Court of Inquiry on the anti-Ahmadi disturbances of 1953 vividly revealed the explosive potentialities of a jihadi mindset. The Objectives Resolution of the Constituent Assembly of Pakistan failed to satisfy the Ulama, who found, for instance, the provisions with regard to fundamental rights of citizens a direct violation of the concept of an Islamic state. The Ulama unequivocally rejected the concept of a modern democracy, while they failed to cite an agreed model of an Islamic state. Most of the Ulama referred the Court of Inquiry to the Islamic Republic operative during 632-661 A.D. Some of them cited the regime of such an intolerant ruler as Aurangzeb in medieval India, although none preferred the regime of Akbar, who, in contrast to Aurangzeb, advocated toleration. No two Ulama agreed upon the definition of a Muslim, although all of them were quite emphatic on the point that a Muslim, who changed his views during his lifetime, for instance, if he is born a Shia and becomes a Sunni or vice versa, is to be punished by death penalty. Anybody, who is a Shia or a Sunni, a Barelvi or a Deobandi, condemns everybody else as beyond the pale of Islam, a Kafir. In their testimonies to the Court of Inquiry, the Ulama were similarly emphatic on the position of non-Muslims in Pakistan as an Islamic state. Non-Muslims of countries conquered by an Islamic state earn the status of Zimmies; they are entitled to some rights although they are not full citizens. Non-Muslims, who are already inhabitants of an Islamic state, can claim certain rights of citizenship only if the Islamic state has entered into an agreement with them and conferred on them the status of mu'ahids. In the absence of such an agreement, they do not possess any rights of citizenship. In other words, the non-Muslims of Pakistan as an Islamic state would not be granted the status of even Zimmies or mu'ahids, not to speak of the status of a citizen.[32] The Inquiry Report of 1954 on the anti-Ahmadi disturbances in Punjab in 1953 made it abundantly clear that Pakistan's leaders were playing with fire, and damaging the social fabric of the state they were entrusted to build up when they strengthened the hands of the religious fanatics (or jihadis) by persistently preaching the notion of Pakistan as an Islamic state. But, instead of learning from what happened in Punjab in 1953, and advocating secular democracy, Pakistan's leaders did not correct course when they gave the country its first Constitution. On 23 March 1956, they inaugurated the

Constitution of the Islamic Republic of Pakistan. Interestingly, in the course of debates on this Constitution (which changed the name of the east wing of Pakistan from East Bengal to East Pakistan), some east wing members of the Constituent Assembly of Pakistan criticised the proclamation of the Islamic Republic. For example, they ridiculed the idea of an Islamic Constitution that would include only the Muslims in Pakistan, and exclude millions of Muslims living in many other countries of the world. They warned against a repetition of the 1953 Punjab carnage, which could easily flare up because of the nearly insoluble difficulty of defining a Muslim. These members of the Constituent Assembly of Pakistan from East Bengal further argued that the makers of the Constitution were trying to win over the Mullahs (the religious preachers) by using the slogan of an Islamic constitution, whereas for years, they were known to exploit the ordinary people of Pakistan, i.e., to deceive them in the name of Islam.[33] It is probably needless to add that Pakistan's first Constitution did not hesitate to stipulate, in the most undemocratic manner, that the Head of the State must be a Muslim.

By 1958, Pakistan's 1956 Constitution was buried under military dictatorship. General Ayub Khan became the supreme ruler, making himself the President and promoting himself to the rank of Field Marshal.[34] Ayub Khan emulated Pakistani politicians and used Islam to buttress his own influence, although one could claim that he was, thus, strengthening Pakistan's national solidarity. In 1959, he ensured that the Ministry of Religious Trusts would exercise control over all Muslim religious establishments. Ayub, furthermore, decided to dictate what students of primary and secondary schools should study, and how they should think. Therefore, official patronage was showered to generate textbooks, which paraded the emergence of Pakistan as the climactic point of the march of Islam from Arabia to India, and Hindu-Muslim antagonism was portrayed as permanent. The virtues of Muslim conquerors of India were proclaimed to be boundless. But it was not quite certain whether their supposed progenies, the people of Pakistan, were fit for a democratic government. Again, Ayub took great care of the religious sentiments of soldiers. He ensured that preachers attached to the army had qualifications superior to those engaged in the civil sector.[35]

Undoubtedly, the abovenoted textbooks aggravated religious fanaticism (or the jihadi orientation) in Pakistan. That Ayub Khan was not perturbed by this possibility, and that he was ready to foster such fanaticism, became evident when he was preparing to contest an election to the post of President of Pakistan. His opponent was Fatima Jinnah, the sister of Muhammad Ali Jinnah, the creator of Pakistan. The presidential election was scheduled for 2 January 1965. On 26 September 1964, obviously at the behest of Ayub, twenty-three prominent theologians issued a statement declaring that no woman could become a head of the state in accordance with Islamic law. Whereas Ayub won the presidential contest, it must be added that there was nothing in the dictionary of election manoeuvres that Ayub did not carry out, e.g., arbitrary reconstruction of electoral districts with awkward and unrealistic boundaries, tampering with voters' lists, misuse of radio and television, illegal deployment of officers, fixing the time for voting on weekdays at office hours, etc.[36]

In the same year, viz. 1965, when Pakistan launched an aggression upon India on 1 September, the Pakistani ruling circle (including Ayub) revealed a jihadi mindset in no uncertain terms.[37] Thus, on 29 August 1965, Ayub issued a 'top secret order' to General Mohammad Musa, the Commander-in-Chief of the Pakistan Army, which included the following observation: 'As a general rule, Hindu morale would not stand more than a couple of hard blows at the right time and place'.[38] In his book on the 1965 War, Musa, who headed the Pakistan Army during this War, pleaded for the nurturing of a 'spirit of jihad' in Pakistani soldiers. He wrote: 'In the war, the real motivating force for the superb performance of the armed forces was their spirit of jihad. In the final analysis, Islam and the concept of "Ghazi" or "Shaheed" provides the motivation, the esprit de corps, the elan and the fighting spirit for the Pakistani soldier and this concept must be nurtured and preserved.'[39] No wonder that a young Pakistani officer, wounded in the 1965 War and captured by India, rejected the offer of blood transfusion for normal medical treatment, because he preferred death to donation of blood by an infidel.[40]

The jihadi mindset of Pakistan's ruling circle had a macabre demonstration in 1971, when, barring exceptions, the civil-military bureaucracy of Pakistan decided to impose a military solution upon a political problem arising out of the results of the December 1970 election—the first-ever nationwide election held in Pakistan since its birth in 1947. The Awami League, under the leadership of Sheikh Mujibur Rahman, the most charismatic and popular politician of East Pakistan, secured majority of seats at the National Assembly of Pakistan as a result of the 1970 general election. The Awami League was determined to put an end to the cultural-economic-political domination of East Pakistan by the ruling circle of West Pakistani bureaucrats (civilian and military). That the military ruler of Pakistan, President Yahya Khan, was trying to explore an extra-parliamentary solution to this essentially political problem became obvious when he first put off the meeting of the National Assembly till 3 March 1971 without any valid reason, and then on 1 March 1971, indefinitely postponed the Assembly session. The 14,000-16,000 West Pakistani troops in East Pakistan were, soon after the postponement of the National Assembly session, strengthened by nearly 18,000 more. In fact, even before the postponement was announced, troops had started flying from the western to the eastern wing of Pakistan.[41]

It must be appreciatively recalled that in East Pakistan at that time Admiral S.M. Ahsan was the Governor, and Lieut. Gen. SahabzadaYaqub Khan was the topranking military officer. Both of them opposed military measures to reverse the popular verdict of the 1970 general election. They advocated a political solution.[42] Nevertheless, after the midnight of 25 March 1971, there could be no doubt about the decision of the Yahya regime to carry out genocide for the purpose of destroying the outcome of the 1970 election.[43] Like Admiral Ahsan and General Yaqub Khan, Air Marshal Mohammad Asghar Khan too was an exception. Both before and after 25 March 1971, Asghar Khan denounced the use of military force in East Pakistan.[44]

Such exceptions proved the rule, viz. the jihadi mindset of Islamabad's ruling circle, which appeared to mould the behaviour of Pakistani troops (as also their collaborators) in East Pakistan. East Pakistan witnessed this behaviour from 25 March to 16 December 1971, when, with the surrender of nearly 93,000 Pakistani soldiers and officers, Bangladesh emerged as an independent country. In defence of Islam and Pakistan's unity, all sorts of atrocities were committed on the people of East Pakistan—including mass murder, torture and rape. In the midnight of 25 March 1971, Pakistani jihadis pounced upon persons, who were unarmed and asleep. In the capital city of Dhaka, they first raided the headquarters of the police and East Pakistan Rifles (EPR), as also the residences of teachers, employees and students inside the Dhaka University campus. Afterwards, they destroyed the markets and slums, while they attacked the localities inhabited by the Hindu (minority) community. They set on fire the slums and markets and put to death by machine guns all those who sought to escape from fire. University teachers, students and employees were either killed inside their homes, or dragged out for slaughter. Most of these people were not even aware of why they were being killed in the course of what the Pakistani military designated as Operation Searchlight. At least 50-60,000 persons were killed in Dhaka on the night of 25 March 1971.[45]

The abovenoted operations in Dhaka were repeated by Pakistani forces in nearly all the towns of the country throughout the period of nine months. What merits attention in this context is the combination of indiscriminate murder with selective slaughter of some categories of persons following their planned identification. Dhaka University teachers, killed on 25 March 1971, belonged to this category. In the first and the second week of December 1971, when it became transparent that the defeat of Pakistan was inevitable, Pakistani marauders and their local associates (popularly called Rajakars) prepared a long list of topranking artists, litterateurs, educationists, journalists, lawyers, doctors, scientists and engineers, and massacred them.[46]

In order to measure the intensity of the jihadi mindset in Pakistani marauders, which naturally varied from person to person, one has to note the exact ways of torture and murder. Some of these ways were: to set a person on fire, allowing him to die; to bury a person alive; to fit a grenade in the body of a potential victim after removal of the pin, and rejoice at the immediate explosion of the human grenade; to tie a man to the back of a jeep running at a high speed, so that the man dies of multiple injuries; to push an iron rod through the anus of a man, and impart electric shocks; and to urinate on the face of a man pining for drinking water.[47]

Probably, in the case of women, the nature of violence crossed all limits of depravity. Testimonies of sweepers of Dhaka municipality on this point cannot but cause benumbing shocks. Dead bodies of most women—irrespective of age—were all naked. Breasts of many of them had been extracted. Sticks were found penetrating the vaginas of some. Some young ladies had been shot dead after tying their hands, feet, and eyes, and yet their breasts and vaginas were severely wounded and bloody.[48]

Geoffrey Davis, an Australian surgeon, visited Bangladesh in 1972. He engaged in treating women (in different age groups), who had been raped from March to December 1971. Government officers arrived at a rough estimate of 2,00,000 women, who had been raped in 1971. This was based on the average daily disappearance of two girls from 480 police station areas over a period of 270 days, when these areas were under the occupation of Pakistani troops. But Geoffrey Davis considers the government estimate of the number of raped girls as inaccurate and far lower than the actual number. His estimate stood between 4,00,000 to 4,30,000, for, the number of pregnant women stood at 2,00,000. A clinic to treat raped women was set up in Dhaka in February 1972. Even before treatment started, 1,50,000-1,70,000 carried out abortions. A large number of them committed suicide. By the time Davis arrived in Dhaka, raped women had been pregnant for at least eighteen weeks. Since abortions had been conducted by untrained or half-trained doctors and village midwives, women continued to suffer from serious problems despite the clinical termination of pregnancy. A large number of girls, subjected to sexual assaults despite being too immature for sexual union, began to suffer from complex diseases. Many, including 12-13 year-old girls, were raped after the removal of their saris, and they, while kept in confinement, were never supplied with saris in order to guard against the possibilities of suicides by the use of saris.[49]

Remarkably, officers and soldiers of the Pakistan army took great care to remove badges (with their names and designations) before they began to commit horrendous atrocities on men and women. Therefore, most of the survivors of attempts at massacre and molestation failed to reveal the exact identity of the perpetrators of war crimes. Nevertheless, strenuous researches by selfless members of the Committee to Eliminate the Murderers and Collaborators of 1971, as also exercises following the discovery of two killing fields as late as the 1990s, led to the identification of two hundred Pakistani military officers accused of war crimes. Whereas a large number of them were Captains and Majors, there was no dearth of Lieutenant Colonels, Colonels, Brigadiers, Major Generals, and there was at least one Lieutenant General in this list.[50] The Pakistan army's brutality derived a lot of impetus from the assessment that East Pakistanis (Bengalis) were anti-Islam as well as anti-Pakistani, and that their major lapse was religious/moral rather than political.[51]

The local associates of Pakistani marauders did not lag much behind in the perpetration of horrible atrocities in 1971—whether by way of actual commission or collusion. These local associates have been placed in various categories in terms of their major activities like addiction to violence, and preference of target groups. For example, a number of political leaders, businessmen, journalists, teachers, etc. came to be identified as collaborators, because they supported the Pakistani military without directly participating in violence against freedom fighters (Muktijoddhas). In contrast, the Government of Pakistan itself set up a force of Rajakars (a distorted version of the original Farsi word Rejakar, meaning a volunteer) by means of an ordinance in June 1971. Armed by the Pakistani military, Rajakars assisted Pakistani soldiers in trying to subjugate the freedom fighters. Al-Badr was formed soon after Rajakars began to operate. One major distinction between Al-Badrs and Rajakars was that Al-Badrs concentrated on slaughtering members of the Bengali intelligentsia, because they were suspected to be the principal opponents of Islamist fanaticism embraced by the Pakistani military. Matiur Rahman Nizami, the chief of Al-Badr, declared on 5 August 1971 that Allah entrusted the task of saving Pakistan, and thereby saving Islam, to the Pakistan Army when Muslims failed to devise a political solution to the problem facing Pakistan, and Pakistan confronted a liberation war. Another death squad, comparable to Al-Badr, was Al-Shams. Peace Committees, set up in different parts of the country immediately after the outbreak of the freedom struggle, did not take part in violence, but continuously collaborated with the Pakistani military in such tasks as the maintenance of law and order.[52]

An extremely pertinent question is: how were all these jihadi activities viewed on the other side of the fence—i.e. by high ranking military and civil officers, who were decision makers and evidently responsible for the Pakistani defeat in 1971? It is advisable to start with an exception, viz. Major General Tojammal Hussain Malik.[53] In his autobiography, he has not recorded any adverse comment on freedom fighters, although, after 16 December 1971, he spent some time as a prisoner of war in India. In the assessment of Malik, the military coup of 1958 obstructed the growth of democratic institutions in Pakistan, and military rulers could not possibly imagine that they were sowing the seeds of dismemberment of Pakistan. For, military rulers placed personal greed and lust for power above the interests of the country. To Malik, Sheikh Mujib was a patriot, and not a traitor. He acknowledged that he heard on the radio the call to jihad by Yahya Khan on 3 December 1971.[54] In the context of Yahya's call for jihad, one is reminded of another exceptional Pakistani observer of the events in East Pakistan in 1971. He is a civil administrator, viz. Alamdar Raja, the last Pakistani Commissioner of Dhaka. In his view, Pakistan made itself a laughing stock of the world by failing to punish those guilty of serious crimes in 1971. In an incident of barbarity narrated by him, some Pakistani soldiers attacked a house, killing a few, but keeping alive a lady for rape. The lady tried her utmost to dissuade the soldiers from rape. She argued that, like the soldiers, she was also a Muslim. How can a Muslim rape a Muslim lady, she asked. The lady then placed a copy of the Holy Koran on the bed, and pleaded that anyone trying to rape her would initially have to remove the holy book. Pakistani soldiers precisely did that, putting away the Holy Koran, and raping the lady, as Alamdar Raja narrated.[55]

Pakistanis thus ignored religious considerations while conducting jihad in East Pakistan in 1971. No less reprehensible was the widespread tendency of Pakistanis to refuse even to acknowledge the occurrence of mass murder or genocide in East Pakistan in 1971. This was one of the most remarkable findings of Muntassir Mamoon and Mohiuddin Ahmad, who visited Karachi, Lahore, Islamabad and Rawalpindi for three weeks in February-March 1998. They interviewed thirty-five persons, including a number of Pakistani Generals, who suffered from defeat in 1971. The explanation of their denial is not far to seek. They wanted to evade any responsibility for wrongdoing, which naturally aggravated the agony of defeat.[56]

Major General Ghulam Umar was the member secretary of Pakistan's National Security Council as also the principal political adviser to General Yahya Khan. Umar was present in Dhaka on the crucial date of 25 March 1971, and visited Dhaka several times during March-December 1971. When Muntassir Mamoon and Mohiuddin Ahmad met him in Karachi in 1998, Umar blandly denied any knowledge of what happened on 25 March 1971. He also denied knowing anything about what happened in the months following 25 March 1971. Like Umar, Roedad Khan, the Information Secretary of Pakistan, was present in Dhaka on 25 March 1971, and visited Dhaka a number of times from March to December 1971. Muntassir Mamoon and Mohiuddin Ahmad met him in Islamabad in 1998. Roedad not only denied what happened on 25 March 1971, but added that from twelve midnight to four in the morning, he did not hear any noise of gunfire.[57]

Major General Rao Farman Ali Khan wrote *How Pakistan Got Divided* (Lahore:1992). When Muntassir Mamoon and Mohiuddin Ahmad met him in 1998, and inquired about the genocide in East Pakistan in 1971, Farman Ali refused to admit the occurrence of genocide. He conceded that some people were killed, and, on repeated queries, admitted casually that fifty thousand persons could have died. But Farman Ali refused to reply when asked whether fifty thousand deaths amounted to genocide. After the fall of Dhaka in mid-December 1971, a list of intellectuals (who were massacred on 14 December 1971) was discovered on Farman Ali's office table at the Governor's residence. Confronted with this tell-tale evidence of his responsibility for this massacre, Farman Ali offered the flimsy explanation that many people met him, and reported activities of various persons, and he merely noted the names of these persons.[58]

The jihadi mindset of the Pakistani decisionmakers derived enormous justification from the jaundiced view that the conflict of 1971 was a Pakistan-India or Muslim-Hindu conflict, and, therefore, a war between infidels (Kafirs) and Muslims. The Awami League was India's agent. It was as much a threat to Islam as India, which provided leadership to the freedom struggle directed against Pakistan, the citadel of Islam. It was anti-Islamic to accuse the Pakistan army, engaged in jihad against Kafirs and agents of Kafirs, of genocidal activities. Actually, in the opinion of a former Pakistani Minister for Kashmir affairs, such an accusation would also be an affront to the patriotism of those who conducted this jihad in 1971 in East Pakistan.[59]

It is instructive in this context to quote a Pakistani journalist/ researcher: Muhammad Shehzad. He supplies the acronym TNT for the Two Nation Theory propounded by the advocates for the establishment of Pakistan in the pre-1947 days. Shehzad refers to religious divisions and fratricide in Pakistan in the second decade of the twenty-first century, and writes: 'The TNT was a highly biased, spiteful and malicious theory that preached nothing but hatred. Pakistan is reaping today what its leaders sowed yesterday. After getting rid of the Hindus, they subjected the Bengalis—who were Muslims and in the majority in the state of undivided Pakistan—to such torture and repression that they had to split away from Pakistan and have their own state. Unaffected by such reverses, Pakistan continued to follow the tenets of such a pernicious worldview, even until today.'[60]

The jihadi mindset of Pakistani decisionmakers was reinforced by extraordinary conspiracy theories. One theory was that Hindu teachers, who worked in East Pakistan, were determined to dismember Pakistan by preaching animosities between the two wings of Pakistan. Another theory was that Ahmadis, branded as non-Muslims, had a longstanding plan to break up Pakistan. Major General Ghulam Umar, the Member Secretary of Pakistan's National Security Council and a close associate of General Yahya Khan, clearly affirmed (when interviewed by Muntassir Mamoon and Mohiuddin Ahmad) that Ahmadis, who dominated Pakistan's military headquarters in 1965, tried, by means of the war against India in that year, to disrupt the unity of Pakistan, but failed, whereas they succeeded in their design in 1971.[51]

Some Pakistanis, who appear to be in an insignificant minority in 1971-72 or in 2016 (the expected date of publication of this book), because they do not subscribe to the jihadi mindset, can look upon the 1971 experience/outcome as a glorious opportunity to transcend this mindset. For example, an eminent Pakistani journalist, I.A. Rehman, has argued that Pakistan had probably an option to supplant the culture of intolerance by tolerance, fratricide by fraternity, in subsequent decades of its turbulent history—if it had cared to apologise or express regret for what it did to the people of East Pakistan (Bangladesh) in 1971. In 1998, he wrote almost prophetically: 'If we sincerely believe that in 1971, a great tragedy befell us, then a catharsis of the same order is necessary for the restoration of our mental health and our perceptions of justice and equity. So long as we believe, and continue to teach our children, that we were not responsible for killing our own innocent people in Bengal, we will never be able to understand what actually happened.... We will never comprehend the nature of the Yahya regime and the total collapse of the Pakistani mind it represented. Had we reflected on these matters, we might not have been deceived by Zia-ul-Haq or his apologists to the extent we were. If we had not killed fellow Pakistanis in Bengal, we might not have found the courage to kill fellow Pakistanis in Baluchistan and in Sindh or even Punjab. The operation in Bengal elevated a pre-existing streak of intolerance in our make-up to the level of a virtuous duty and convinced us that it was right to kill anyone, who did not accept our political prescription or did not share our ethnic goals or personal beliefs.... The present level of intolerance and fratricidal madness in our society may be older than 50 years, but these tendencies were greatly consolidated by what we did or allowed to be done in our name in 1971.'[62]

It is a matter of profound concern for Bangladeshi protagonists of democracy, including freedom from religious fanaticism and from military domination over the polity, that the mindset of Bangladeshi military Generals (barring exceptions) is not much different from that of their Pakistani counterparts. Muntassir Mamoon's book on this subject is an eye-opener.[63] He has thoroughly examined thirty books (and some essays) by twenty-one Bangladeshi Generals. Only one of them was trained in Bangladesh: he was the dominant figure behind the Caretaker Government of 2006-08, viz. Moinuddin Ahmed. All others, including Ziaur Rahman and H.M. Ershad, who played a paramount part in Bangladesh during 1975-90, were all trained in Pakistan. The military coup of 1975 (the climactic point of which was the assassination of Sheikh Mujibur Rahman) was staged by a handful of junior military officers. But, barring exceptions, all the top ranking Bangladeshi Generals seemed to welcome this removal of civilian control over the military, which highlighted their Pakistani mindset.[64] They were all for narrow religious sectarianism, Islamisation of the polity, and maximisation of economic opportunities for armed services, with or without the use of such misleading phrases as welfare of soldiers (as in Pakistan).[65]

Mujib's murder was planned by Pakistan's ISI, which used the services of some junior military officers of Bangladesh. Remarkably, in the Pakistani days, ISI assignments were given to only those Bengali military officers, who were endowed with a genuine Pakistani mindset, e.g., Ziaur Rahman and H.M. Ershad. Actually, Ershad appeared to be a special favourite of the Pakistan government. For example, from April to December 1971, a number of Bengali military officers, posted in West Pakistan, visited East Pakistan on leave and then went back to West Pakistan. Fifty such officers were dismissed from service by the Pakistan government. Ershad, too, came on leave to East Pakistan during the abovenoted period. But he remained in service. Again, during 1972-73, Ershad's personal possessions were dispatched from Pakistan by air to his home town in East Pakistan at least on four occasions. No wonder, when Ershad was the President of Bangladesh, he prohibited (by an unwritten directive) the appointment to the officer corps of the military of all children and near-relatives of the freedom fighters of 1971. Furthermore, an ISI idol like Ziaur Rahman exhibited his pro-Pakistan mentality most unabashedly in 1977, when, shortly after the Dhaka visit of Lt. Gen. Gholam Zilani Khan, the Director General of Pakistan's ISI, he replaced Bangladesh's Defence Field Intelligence (DFI) by the Directorate General of Forces Intelligence (DGFI). Many officers of the DGFI, modelled on Pakistan's ISI, received training at the ISI training centre in Islamabad.[66]

The impact of this ISI linkage was so pervasive and durable as to become glaring even in 2006-08, when Bangladesh had a Caretaker Government, but, invisibly, General Moinuddin Khan, the Army Chief, wielded supreme power, and went so far as to exhibit a jihadi mindset. Under his leadership, the Caretaker Government tried to expand the influence of Islamist militants. The DGFI presided over the establishment of a new political party, the Islamic Democratic Party (IDP). Composed of members of the Harkat Ul Jihad Al Islami Bangladesh (HUJI-B), the IDP, remained committed to a programme aimed at the transformation of Bangladesh into an Islamic state under the benign supervision of the DGFI. This jihadi project of the Bangladesh army proved abortive, because, by March 2008, the United States listed HUJI-B as a terrorist organisation.[67]

It is now advisable to resume the story of Pakistan (viz. old West Pakistan, following the emergence of East Pakistan as the independent state of Bangladesh on 16 December 1971). Pakistani rulers, including the civilian political leader, Zulfikar Ali Bhutto, who ruled Pakistan as President during 1971-73, and as Prime Minister during 1973-77, failed to draw appropriate lessons from the events of 1971. Bhutto appointed a Commission of Inquiry under Hamoodur Rahman, the Chief Justice of Pakistan. Rahman's report, withheld from public circulation till 2000, accused senior military officials of 'lust for wine, and women and greed for land and houses', which vitiated their decisionmaking capabilities as also their capacity to fight.[68] Lt. Gen. Tikka Khan became Pakistan's Eastern Command Commander in early March 1971. 'Military action ordered by Tikka Khan in March 1971 was the beginning of the end.... General Tikka Khan's military crackdown achieved some success, but at a heavy political price.... The people of East Pakistan suffered terribly.'[69] In early September 1971, Lt. Gen. A.A.K. Niazi replaced Tikka Khan. Hamoodur Rahman Commission's observations on Niazi are revealing: Niazi 'came to acquire a stinking reputation owing to his association with women of bad repute, and his nocturnal visits to places also frequented by several junior officers under his command.'[70] In the assessment of a Pakistani publicist, Mahir Ali, 'war crime trials in relation to the atrocities in East Pakistan ought to have been conducted in Pakistan, with the primary perpetrators in the dock.... In fact, quite to the contrary, the General internationally derided as "the butcher of Bengal" became the Army Chief in what remained of Pakistan and received a carte blanche, barely a couple of years after his exploits on Bangladeshi territory to deal with "miscreants" in Balochistan.'[71]

In the abovenoted statement, Mahir Ali refers to General Tikka Khan, whom Bhutto appointed as the Army Chief. Subsequently, Bhutto utilised Tikka's services in Balochistan for the restoration of law and order in an authoritarian manner by army deployment. Ironically, Bhutto, a civilian head of the state, failed to bring about normalcy in Balochistan, whereas his successor, General Zia-ul Haq succeeded, because 'Zia ended military operations in Balochistan, withdrew troops from the area, and granted general amnesty to all dissidents.'[72] Bhutto's authoritarian disposition had extraordinary manifestations. Bhutto thought that probably he could get away by doing anything, while stating or pretending anything else to the contrary. Bhutto wanted to be all things to all men. 'Talented politicians often excel as masters of deceit,'[73] and Bhutto regularly exhibited that before and after he attained supreme power in Pakistan. When, for instance, he founded the Pakistan People's Party (PPP), he proclaimed himself to be a socialist, a democrat, and yet an Islamist, harping upon jihad against India.[74]

Bhutto was inclined to parade his secularism.[75] But that was a mere rhetoric. He took the initiative to declare Islam as the state religion under the 1973 Constitution of Pakistan. This Constitution not only prescribed that only a Muslim could be the President or Prime Minister of Pakistan, but also that the government should actively encourage the teaching of Islam. Bhutto did not care to conceal his addiction to alcohol, but, in order to placate the Islamists, he prohibited the sale of alcohol as also night clubs and gambling. Friday, a holy day for Muslims, became the weekly holiday. Above all, Bhutto's pretence to secularism was punctured by his persecution of Ahmadis. Since the early 1950s, Islamists had been demanding that Ahmadis be declared non-Muslims. Military rulers like Ayub Khan and Yahya Khan did not yield. But Bhutto yielded, amending the Constitution in 1974 to declare Ahmadis as non-Muslims.[76] He thereby not only brought infamy to civilian political leadership, but also paved the way to a profound Islamisation of the polity by General Zia-ul Haq in the coming years, which, again, could be regarded as laying the foundation of what, in the second decade of the twenty-first century, appears as uncontrollable religious fanaticism and factionalism.

It was usual for Saudi Arabia to extend generous economic assistance to Pakistan. But Bhutto's ability to declare Ahmadis as non-Muslims (or Kafirs) made Pakistan even more deserving for such assistance. At the time of the anti-Ahmadi agitation, Shias joined hands with Sunnis. Little could Shias anticipate that this feeling of unity with Sunnis would prove to be short-lived. For, Sunni militants, encouraged by the victory against Ahmadis, began subsequently to target the Shia minority too, denouncing Shias as Kafirs.[77] Bhutto did not seem to bother about it, because he imagined that he would continue to enjoy the support of a majority of extremists among Muslims (i.e. Sunnis), and because he preferred to pursue his despotic preoccupations. He refused to tolerate dissent, whether among politicians or journalists. A number of his political adversaries were imprisoned under flimsy charges. Some of them even disappeared. Bhutto's opponents among journalists too were detained. A number of journals and newspapers were forced to cease publication.[78]

Bhutto's despotic behaviour appeared to cross all limits. Bhutto maintained a state of emergency for the entire period of five years that he ruled Pakistan (till the imposition of martial law in 1977 by General Zia-ul Haq). He set up a Federal Force, a sort of political army, to destablise and terrorise political opponents, breaking up their meetings and keeping them under surveillance. Despite having a majority of support in the national legislature, Bhutto preferred ordinances to laws, promulgating one ordinance (but not a law) per week on an average. He enacted eight Constitutional Amendment Bills in the National Assembly, five of them being passed in the course of only one day, or on the second day. All these aimed at curtailing the independence of the judiciary and the fundamental rights of the individual.[79]

Religious fanaticism and political despotism are often good companions. Bhutto promoted religious militancy, failing to put a restraint upon it in time. He also failed to curb his own despotic temperament. He manipulated the 1977 elections so flagrantly that the people of Pakistan revolted, mixing political disdain with religious denunciation provoked partially by Bhutto's socialist slogans, which did not bring much benefit to the ordinary people. Army Chief Zia-ul Haq, whom Bhutto had chosen in 1976, following Tikka Khan's retirement and superseding seven Lieutenant Generals, failed to preserve his loyalty to Bhutto. He proclaimed Martial Law on 5 July 1977. Eventually, on charges that could not be easily defended, Bhutto was hanged on 4 April 1979.[80]

'Unlike the earlier generation of Pakistani military dictators, Zia was an Islamist.'[81] 'A radical Islamist, Zia was obsessed with propagating Islam.'[82] By 1988, the number of official madrasas (Islamic schools) stood at 8000, whereas the number of nonofficial (or non-registered) ones was as high as 25,000, even though in the early 1970s registered madrasas were only 900 in number.[83] The military carried the signature of Islamisation in diverse ways. All soldiers and officers had no option but to join prayers, especially because their commanders were expected to lead the daily prayers. Religious teaching, moreover, formed an important component of military training. Military establishments had to provide for prayer halls.[84]

'The alliance between the military, led by Zia, and the religious parties was soon to open a new, much darker phase in Pakistani politics in which sectarian differences emerged.'[85] Zia prescribed only that line of interpretation of Islam, which carried the endorsement of Deobandis in the Hanafi school of Sunnis, which, however, did not enjoy the support of the majority of Sunnis in Pakistan. Not to speak of Shias, Barelvis among Sunnis did not accept this interpretation. As a result, religious tensions rose. But Zia believed that his way of Islamisation was essential to reverse the trend of moral decay set by Z.A. Bhutto's secular socialist regime. Moreover, it would reinforce Pakistan's identity as a Muslim state. Critics of Zia, however, could argue that Zia thus tried (even if without success) to supply a sort of legitimacy to his military rule. He passed the Hudood Ordinances to restrict the rights and demean the status of women. Zia won over the followers of Jamaat-i-Islami by providing them with government assignments, including the coveted ones of civil servants and judges.[86]

Such behaviour on the part of Zia should have provoked opprobrium in the West. But Zia's jihadi mindset became an asset as the Soviet Union moved into Afghanistan in 1979. For, the western powers, especially the United States, began to use Pakistan as a frontline state in the undeclared war against the Soviets in Afghanistan. Many Muslim countries sent thousands of mujahids to Afghanistan. Students in Pakistani madrasas too were trained and armed to fight the Soviets in Afghanistan. Zia did not miss the opportunity to proclaim jihad against Soviet invaders in Afghanistan. This led to a rapid rise in religious militancy in Pakistan throughout the 1980s. Zia capitalised this to enhance his personal authority—especially among religious extremists inhabiting the Pakistan-Afghanistan border, who were to play an important part in the war against the Soviets in Afghanistan. Soviet troops proved to be the greatest political benefactors of a jihadist military dictator in Pakistan.[87]

Shias denounced Zia's efforts to shower patronage on Sunnis. For, this was not merely a matter of religious favouritism. It was a matter of how political dividends could flow from religious partisanship.[88] Zia surpassed Bhutto's anti-Ahmadi moves by an Ordinance of 1984. This Ordinance (No. 20) threatened Ahmadis with criminal prosecution if they declared themselves as Muslims and described their places of worship as mosques. Moreover, this

Ordinance of 1984 stipulated that the evidence of an Ahmadi in a law court could not be treated as equal to that of a person enjoying constitutional recognition as a Muslim. Thus, civil rights of Ahmadis were demonstrably curbed.[89] No wonder that fanatics among Sunnis felt encouraged by such religious bigotry of Zia to try to assert their hegemonism. In 1985, they set up the Sipah-i–Sahaba-i-Pakistan (SSP), which clamoured for the recognition of Sunni Islam as Pakistan's official religion.[90]

Zia's Islamic radicalism could not but aggravate pre-existing religious divisions inside Pakistan. In the 1980s, for example, there were tremendous tensions in Sindh, for, the gulf between the humanist approach of Sufis in Sindh and the jihadi mindset of Sunnis was unbridgeable. Again, this was also the time when Sunnis felt puffed up by support from Saudi Arabia, which enabled them to exercise a sort of guardianship over the anti-Soviet jihad in Afghanistan. Coincidentally, in 1979, when Soviet troops moved into Afghanistan, Iran, too experienced a revolution, which enhanced the self-confidence of Shias in Pakistan. The long-standing rivalry between Sunni-ruled Saudi Arabia and Shia-ruled Iran had its repercussions in Afghanistan as also in Pakistan during the 1980s.[91]

Religious tensions in Pakistan assumed peculiar dimensions in the 1980s. For example, Sunni migrants from Indian Punjab confronted Shias in the post-1947 Pakistani Punjab. For, steeped in the Deobandi ideology and nursing political ambitions, they inevitably clashed with Shia landlords enjoying traditional domination.[92] To take another example, there were violent conflicts in the 1980s between Shia tribes among Pashtuns in certain localities of Federally Administered Tribal Areas (FATA) on one side and, on the other, Afghan Sunni refugees as also other Pakistani Sunnis arriving in these localities.[93] Moreover, in the 1980s, there were murderous clashes between Shias in the so-called Northern Areas, i.e., parts of Pakistan-occupied Kashmir (POK), with Sunnis from other parts of Pakistan migrating to these Areas in quest of profitable commerce after the construction (with China's aid) of the Karakoram Highway.[94]

It may be pertinent to argue that such sectarian outbursts have their roots in the jihadi mindset, which can generate a variety of tensions transcending mere religious differences, and overlapping political-ethnic disputes. Such tensions, moreover, are aggravated by an interaction of domestic misgovernance with international crises. A unique amalgam of domestic and international circumstances struck Pakistan in the 1980s, and Zia-ul Haq utilised them fully to preserve and strengthen his autocracy. Bhutto's execution generated a lot of unrest, especially in Sindh, which provoked Zia to unleash military repression causing hundreds of deaths.[95] Moreover, the Soviet invasion of Afghanistan drove hundreds of thousands of Pashtun refugees to Pakistan, especially to big cities like Karachi. A large number of Pashtuns cornered a big slice of arms and money coming from America to Pakistan for the jihad against Soviets in Afghanistan. The wealth and influence of Pashtuns became all the more visible as many of them, with police collusion, developed heroin smuggling networks. All this could not but alienate the Urdu-speaking migrants from India, who came to Karachi in the post-1947 years (called Mohajirs) as also those who came in the years following the creation of Bangladesh in 1971 (known as Biharis). Whereas Pashtuns did not bother to distinguish between Mohajirs and Biharis, the explosion of Mohajir-Pashtun tensions into bloody conflagration in the long-prevalent atmosphere of many-sided sectarianism in Pakistan was predictable. What was not predictable was probably the scale of such conflagration. Actually, in 1985 and again in 1986, the scale and brutality of Mohajir-Pashtun clashes could not but shock liberal observers.[96]

Into this cauldron of sectarian violence, the ISI poured its own brand of jihad. It sequestered a substantial part of immense resources supplied by the United States to conduct anti-Soviet jihad in Afghanistan, so that the ISI could boost its own power in Pakistan as well as Afghanistan. For this purpose, the ISI used two major instruments. One was Gulbuddin Hekmatyar's Hezb-i-Islami, even though ordinary Afghans did not have much respect for Gulbuddin. The ISI used another instrument to consolidate its own authority, viz., radical Sunni outfits inside Pakistan. In this process, however, the ISI (on the pretext of anti-Soviet jihad in Afghanistan) infected the Pakistani society with a sort of Kalashnikov culture. For, when it operated among around three million Afghan refugees in Pakistan by the end of 1980s, disseminating ideas and weapons for jihad, the larger Pakistani society (not to speak of the ISI-backed Sunni radical bodies) could not remain unaffected. American arms, meant for anti-

Soviet jihad in Afghanistan, would reach wrong hands, being used for personal aggrandisement in diverse ways, e.g., in arms or drug smuggling. The ISI (or the Pakistan Army) did not seem to bother much about the resultant moral erosion of the Pakistani society in this fashion.[97]

President Zia-ul Haq died in a mysterious plane crash in August 1988. The Soviet Union collapsed in 1989. The Soviet-backed Kabul regime perished in April 1992. Meanwhile, from the late 1970s, America supplied arms worth US$ 68 billion, which created tens of thousands of jihadis (Pakistanis as well as Arabs and Afghans) trained in madrasas, and made Pakistan a victim of Kalashnikov culture. The Soviet war in Afghanistan came to an end, but the global war of Mujahids (including the arch-terrorist outfit Al Qaeda) just commenced.[98]

Endnote

1. For some relevant observations, see Carl Hammer, *Tide of Terror: America, Islamic Extremism and the War on Terror*, Boulder, Colorado: Paladin Press, 2003, p. 39. Robin Wright, 'The Struggle Within Islam,' *Smithsonian*, Vol. 42, No. 5, September 2011, pp. 1-2 of 5.
2. Jonathan Randal, *Osama: The Making of a Terrorist*, London: I.B. Tauris, 2006, pp. 48-49. For contrasting views of jihad, see M.A. Khan, *Islamic Jihad: A Legacy of Forced Conversion, Imperialism and Slavery*, USA, no city mentioned: Felibri.com, 2008, pp. 2-4. There is a distinction between jihad-e-akbar, greater jihad, which is a constant endeavour to purify one's personal life, and jihad-e-asgar, lesser jihad, which stands for fighting: see an article by Mohammed Nasimul Ghani, *The Statesman*, 6 December 2014. Hammer, *Tide of Terror*, pp. 9-12.
3. Hammer, *Ibid*., pp. 12-13.
4. *Ibid*., pp. 35-36, 45-46.
5. Priya Singh, 'Reflections on Domestic Politics and Foreign Policy in Israel', in Kingshuk Chatterjee, (ed.), *India and the Middle East: Problems and Prospects*, New Delhi: Knowledge World and the University of Calcutta, 2012, p. 142.
6. Hammer, *Tide of Terror*, p. 46.
7. K.S. Lal, *Muslim Slave System in Medieval India*, New Delhi: Aditya Prakashan, 1994, p. 7. For some illustrations of the practice of slavery by Muslims in medieval India, see Khan, *Islamic Jihad*, pp. 212-15.
8. Lal, *Muslim Slave System in Medieval India*, p. 17.
9. *Ibid*., pp. 72-73. Also see Khan, *Islamic Jihad*, p. 216.

10. Lal, *Muslim Slave System in Medieval India*, p. 19.
11. *Ibid*., pp. 19-24.
12. *Ibid*., p. 69.
13. *Ibid*., p. 46. For some details about the practice of slavery by Muhammad Bin Qasim and Sultan Mahmud, see M.A. Khan, *Islamic Jihad*, pp. 209, 222-23, 228.
14. S. Gurbachan Singh Talib, *Muslim League Attack on Sikhs and Hindus in the Punjab1947*, New Delhi: Voice of India, 1991, pp. 11-23. M.A. Khan, *Islamic Jihad*, p. 185; Khan unequivocally equates the call of the Muslim League for Direct Action to jihad.
15. Annwesa Roy, 'Anatomy of a Riot: The Great Calcutta Killing: August 1946', *Bengal Past and Present*, Kolkata: Vol. 128, Year 2009, esp. pp. 83-89.
16. Madhav Godbole, *The Holocaust of Indian Partition: An Inquest*, New Delhi: Rupa, 2006, pp. 425-27.
17. Jayanta Kumar Ray, *India's Foreign Relations, 1947-2007*, New Delhi: Routledge, 2011, p. 2. Nicholas Mansergh and Penderel Moon, eds., *Transfer of Power, 1942-47, Vol. 9, The Fixing of a Time Limit 4 Nov. 1946-22 March 1947 Constitutional Relations Between Britain and India,* London: Her Majesty's Stationery Office, 1980, p. 251.
18. For evidence of persistent British collusion with Pakistan, as also Indian incompetence, which led eventually to the seizure of about one-third of Jammu-Kashmir, see various chapters of Lt. Gen. L.P. Sen, *Slender was the Thread*, New Delhi: Sangam/Orient Longman, 1973, and C. Dasgupta, *War and Diplomacy in Kashmir: 1947-48*, New Delhi: Sage, 2002.
19. Mohammad Ayub Khan, *Friends Not Masters: A Political Biography*, London: Oxford University Press, 1967, p. 20.
20. *Ibid*., p. 40.
21. Chaudhri Muhammad Ali, *The Emergence of Pakistan*, New York: Columbia University Press, 1967, p. 376.
22. For an impressive representation of Jinnah's 11 August 1947 speech, see http:// *www.youtube.com*
23. For the most authoritative and elaborate account of the Great Calcutta Killings and an aftermath in the eastern Bengal district of Noakhali, where Hindus suffered from a genocide signifying jihad, see Dinesh Chandra Sinha and Ashok Dasgupta, *1946: The Great Calcutta Killings And Noakhali Genocide: A Historical Study*, Kolkata: Tuhina Prakashani, 2011. There are 21 chapters and an annexure comprising 349 pages.
24. Dilip Hiro, *Jihad on Two Fronts*, New Delhi: Harper Collins, 2011, p. 188.
25. *Ibid*., p. 187.
26. Jayanta Kumar Ray, *Democracy and Nationalism on Trial: A Study of East Pakistan*, Simla (now Shimla): Indian Institute of Advanced Study, 1968, p. 16.
27. *Ibid*., p. 41.

28. *Ibid.*, p. 51.
29. Leonard Binder, *Religion and Politics in Pakistan*, Berkeley: University of California, 1963, pp. 142-43, 155-56.
30. H.A.R. Gibb, 'Constitutional Organisation', in Majid Khadduri and Herbert J. Liebesny, eds., *Law in the Middle East*, Washington D.C: The Middle East Institute, 1955, p. 3. Noel J. Coulson, 'The State and the Individual in Islamic Law', *International and Comparative Law Quarterly*, Vol. 6, No. 1, January 1957, pp. 50-52. Noel J. Coulson, 'The Concept of Progress and Islamic Law', in Robert N. Bellah, (ed.), *Religion and Progress in Modern Asia*, New York: Free Press, 1965, pp. 74-75. For an ingenious, though unconvincing, interpretation of an Islamic state as the repository of justice, see W.C. Smith, *Pakistan as an Islamic State*, Lahore: Shaikh Muhammad Ashraf, 1951.
31. Maulana Muhammad Ali, 'Sir Muhammad Iqbal's Statement re the Qadianis', *The Ahmadiyya Anjuman Isha'at-i-Islam Tract Series*, Vol. 1, No. 2, October 1935, Lahore, pp. 24-26, 28-29, 31. *Report of the Court of Inquiry constituted under Punjab Act II of 1954 to inquire into the Punjab disturbances of 1953*, Lahore: Government Printing, Punjab, 1954, pp. 242-43.
32. *Report of the Court of Inquiry*, pp. 203, 212-15, 218-19. Also see Allen McGrath, *The Destruction of Pakistan's Democracy*, Karachi: Oxford University Press, 1998, pp. 189-92.
33. *Constituent Assembly of Pakistan Debates*, 21 January 1956, Vol. 1, No. 53, pp. 1890-91, 1903-04, 2116-17.
34. Jayanta Kumar Ray, *Democracy and Nationalism on Trial*, pp. 185-87.
35. Dilip Hiro, *Jihad on Two Fronts*, pp. 188-89.
36. Ray, *Democracy and Nationalism on Trial*, pp. 305-08.
37. For some details about the 1965 India-Pakistan war, see Ray, *India's Foreign Relations, 1947-2007*, pp. 139-47.
38. Stanley Wolpert, *Zulfi Bhutto of Pakistan: His Life and Times*, Delhi: Oxford University Press, 1993, p. 90.
39. General Mohammad Musa, *My Version: India-Pakistan War, 1965*, New Delhi: ABC Publishing House, 1983, p. 111.
40. Kuldip Nayar, *India: The Critical Years*, Delhi: Vikas, 1971, p. 186.
41. Harald Munthe-Kaas, *The Far Eastern Economic Review*, 20 March 1971, p. 5. *The Working People's Daily*, Rangoon (Yangon), 7 March 1971. For details about the Awami League's longstanding tussle with the Central Government of Pakistan, see Jayanta Kumar Ray, *Democracy and Nationalism on Trial*, and Anthony Mascarenhas, *The Rape of Bangladesh*, Delhi: Vikas, 1971.
42. Muntassir Mamoon, *Parajito Pakistani Generalder Dristite Mukti Juddha*, i.e., *Freedom Struggle in the Eyes of the Defeated Pakistani Generals*, Dhaka: Somoy Prakashan, 1999, pp. 202-08.
43. Jayanta Kumar Ray, *Public Policy and Global Reality*, New Delhi: Radiant Publishers, 1977, p. 112.

44. For details see Air Marshal Mohammad Asghar Khan, *Generals in Politics: Pakistan, 1958-1982*, Dhaka: The University Press Limited, 1983, pp. 1-51.
45. Shahriar Kabir, ed., *Ekattorer Dussaha Smriti*, i.e. *Unbearable Memories of 1971*, Dhaka: Ekattorer Ghatak Dalal Nirmul Committee, i.e., Committee to Eliminate the Murderers and Collaborators of 1971, 1999, pp. 9-10.
46. Kabir, ed., *Ekattorer Dussaha Smriti*, p. 10.
47. *Ibid.*, pp. 10-11.
48. Hasan Hafizur Rahman, ed., *Bangladesher Swadhinatar Juddho Dalilpatra,* i.e., *Documents of Bangladesh Freedom Struggle*, Dhaka: Ministry of Information, Government of the People's Democratic Republic of Bangladesh, Volume eight, 1984, pp. 51-52.
49. *Banglar Bani*, Genocide Special Number, December 1972 (Bengali daily of Dhaka).
50. Kabir, ed., *Ekatorrer Dussaha Smriti*, pp. 8-9, 199-208.
51. Stephen P. Cohen, *The Idea of Pakistan*, Washington DC: The Brookings Institution, 2004, p. 169.
52. Muntassir Mamoon, *Rajakarer Mon*, i.e. *The Mind of the Rajakar*, Dhaka: Mowla Brothers, 2000, pp. 9-11, 14-16; *Dainik Pakistan*, 26 April 1971, a Bengali daily of Dhaka; *Dainik Sangram*, 14 November 1971, a Bengali daily of Dhaka; for a horrifying compilation of jihadi statements by men like Matiur Rahman Nizami, which appeared in course of 1971 in *Dainik Sangram*, see *Prothom Alo*, a Bengali daily of Dhaka, 11 January 2012.
53. See Major General Tajammal Hussain Malik, *The Story of My Struggle*, Lahore: Jang Publishers, 1991.
54. Mamoon, *Parajito Pakistani Generalder Dristite Mukti Juddha*, i.e. *Freedom Struggle in the Eyes of Defeated Pakistani Generals*, pp. 151-57.
55. *Ibid.*, pp. 26-27.
56. *Ibid.*, pp. 5-7.
57. *Ibid.*, pp. 23-26.
58. *Ibid.*, pp. 24-25, 100, 103-04.
59. *Ibid.*, pp. 35, 43-44, 199-200.
60. Mohammad Shehzad, 'The State of Islamic Radicalism in Pakistan', *Strategic Analysis*, New Delhi: Volume 37, Number 2, March-April 2013, p. 186.
61. Muntassir Mamoon and Mohiuddin Ahmad, eds., *Pakistanider Dristite Ekattar,* i.e. *Bangladesh Liberation War: Views from Pakistan*, Dhaka: The University Press Limited, 2005, pp. 78, 172-74, 183-84.
62. Newsline, March 1998, Reproduced in Muntassir Mamoon, *Parajito Pakistani Generalder Dristite Mukti Juddha*, pp. 212-13. For a recent exposure by a Western writer of the 1971 genocide in East Pakistan, ignored by the US, see an article by Gary J. Brass in *National Post*, 7 November 2014—http://news.bbc.co.uk/2/hi/4633263stm

63. Muntassir Mamoon, *Bangladeshi Generalder Mon,* i.e. *Psyche of Bangladeshi Generals*, Dhaka: Somoy Prakashan, 2013.
64. *Ibid.*, p. 444.
65. *Ibid.*, pp. 185-86, 200-03, 454.
66. *Ibid.*, pp. 439-43, 520-21.
67. *Ibid.*, pp. 180-83, 520-21.
68. Eamon Murphy, *The Making of Terrorism in Pakistan: Historical and social roots of extremism*, Abingdon, Oxon: Routledge, 2013, p. 73.
69. General K.M. Arif, *Khaki Shadows: Pakistan 1947-1997*, Karachi: Oxford University Press, 2001, p. 127.
70. Murphy, *The Making of Terrorism in Pakistan*, p. 74.
71. Mahir Ali, 'A partial reckoning', *Dawn*, reproduced in *The Statesman*, 21 February 2013.
72. Arif, *Khaki Shadows*, p. 283.
73. James P. Farwell, *The Pakistan Cauldron: Conspiracy, Assassination & Instability*, New Delhi: Pentagon Press, 2012, p. 58.
74. *Ibid.*
75. Farzana Shaikh, *Making Sense of Pakistan*, London: Hurst, 2009, p. 63.
76. Farwell, *The Pakistan Cauldron*, pp. 79-81.
77. *Ibid.*, pp. 82-83.
78. Pervez Musharraf, *In the Line of Fire*, New York: Free Press, 2006, pp. 60, 159.
79. Arif, *Khaki Shadows*, pp. 218-87.
80. *Ibid.*, pp. 151-52, 332-33, 345-46. Seyyed Vali Reza Nasr, *The Vanguard of the Islamic Revolution: The Jama'at-i-Islami of Pakistan*, Berkeley: University of California Press, 1994, p. 189.
81. Bruce Riedel, *Deadly Embrace: Pakistan, America and the Future of the Global Jihad*, New Delhi: Harper Collins, 2011, p. 20.
82. Farwell, *The Pakistan Cauldron,* p. 60.
83. Steve Coll, *Ghost Wars: The Secret History of the CIA, Afghanistan and Bin Laden, from the Soviet Invasion to September 10, 2011*, New York: Penguin, 2004, p. 180.
84. Husain Haqqani, *Pakistan: Between Mosque and Military*, Washington DC: Carnegie Endowment for International Peace, 2005, p. 113.
85. Murphy, *The Making of Terrorism in Pakistan*, p. 83.
86. *Ibid.*, pp. 87-88. Mohammad Waseem, 'Origins and growth patterns of Islamic Organizations in Pakistan', in Satu P. Limaye, Mohan Malik and Robert Wirsingh (eds.), *Religious Radicalism and Security in South Asia*, Honolulu: University of Hawaii Press, 2004, p. 31.
87. Pervez Musharraf, *In the Line of Fire: A Memoir*, pp. 274-75.
88. S.V.R. Nasr, 'International Politics, domestic imperatives and identity mobilization: sectarianism in Pakistan, 1979-1998', *Comparative Politics*, Vol. 32, No. 2, January 2000, pp. 171-90.

89. Yohanan Friedmann, *Prophecy Continuous: Aspects of Ahmedi religious thought and its medieval background*, Berkeley: University of California Press, 1989, pp. 42-43.
90. S.V.R. Nasr, 'International Politics, domestic imperatives and identity mobilization', p. 176.
91. Muhammad Amir Rana, 'The militants' landscape: Pakistan's Islamist organizations and their impact on the body politic', in Ashutosh Misra and Michael E. Clarke (eds.), *Pakistan's Stability Paradox,* London: Routledge, 2011, p. 79; Mariam Abou Zahab, 'The regional sectarian conflicts in Pakistan', in Christophe Jaffrelot (ed.), *Pakistan: nationalism without a nation?* London: Zed Books, 2002, pp. 115-28.
92. Muhammad Qasim Zaman, 'Sectarianism in Pakistan: the Radicalisation of Shia–Sunni identities', *Modern Asian Studies*, Vol. 32, No. 3, 1998, p. 691.
93. Farzana Shaikh, *Making Sense of Pakistan*, p. 66.
94. Ian Talbot, *Pakistan: A Modern History*, London: Hurst, 2005, pp. 117-18.
95. T. Rahman, *Language and Politics in Pakistan*, Karachi: Oxford University Press, 1997, p. 127.
96. F. Shaheed, 'The Pakhtun Muhajir Conflicts 1985-1986: A National perspective', in V. Das (ed.), *Mirrors of Violence: Communities, Riots, and Survivors*, New Delhi: Oxford University Press, 1990, p. 204; A. Hussain, 'The Karachi Riots of December 1986', in V. Das (ed.), *Ibid.*, p. 192.
97. Susanne Schmeidl and William Maley, 'The Case of the Afghan Refugee Population: Finding Durable Solutions in Contested Transitions', in Howard Adelman (ed.), *Protracted Displacement in Asia: No place to call home*, Aldershot: Ashgate, 2008, pp. 131-79; Svante E. Cornell, 'Pakistan's Foreign Policy: Islamic or Pragmatic?' in Brenda Shaffer (ed.), *The Limits of Culture: Islam and Foreign Policy*, Cambridge, Mass: The MIT Press, 2006, pp. 313-14; Barnett E. Rubin, *The Fragmentation of Afghanistan: State formation and collapse in the international system*, New Haven: Yale University Press, 2002, p. 201; Larry Goodson, 'Foreign Policy Gone Awry: The Kalashnikovization and Talibanization of Pakistan', in Craig Baxter and Charles H. Kennedy (eds.), *Pakistan 2000, Karachi*: Oxford University Press, 2001, p. 159.
98. Khalid Aziz, 'Causes of Rebellion in Waziristan', in *Policy Report*, Peshawar: Regional Institute of Policy Research and Training, 2007, p. 22; Sumit Ganguly, 'Putting South Asia Back Together Again', *Current History*, Vol. 100, Issue 650, December 2001, p. 41; Amina Mahmood, 'US-Pakistan Relations During Reagan Presidency: Pakistan's Perspective', *Regional Studies*, Vol. XXI, No. 2, Spring 2003, pp. 89, 94, 97.

Two

Paving the Way to 9/11

In the 1990s, Pakistan had civilian governments headed by Prime Ministers Nawaz Sharif and Benazir Bhutto. The Pakistan army (as also the ISI), however, continued to patronise the jihadis trained in madrasas. The Jamiat-e-Ulema Islam (JUI) exercised control over by far the largest number of these madrasas. The architects of the Taliban movement of the 1990s had their education in these madrasas. Benazir Bhutto was the Prime Minister of Pakistan during 1993-96. Her Interior Minister was Naseerullah Babar, a retired army officer with the rank of Major General. He ensured the growth of the Taliban movement into a mighty military machine by arranging the flow of abundant resources from government agencies (including the ISI) as also from businessmen (some of whom could be heroin dealers).[1]

The Taliban could dominate its rivals inside Afghanistan, and establish its ascendancy by the middle of 1990s. For, it received from the Pakistan government an ample supply of military equipment and training, financial and diplomatic support, and it even obtained direct participation (whenever needed) in combat operations by Pakistani soldiers.[2] Actually, in the middle 1990s, Pakistan witnessed a significant swing of its military (especially the ISI under the headship of General Hamid Gul and General Javed Nasir) towards Islamist extremism, which undoubtedly helped the Taliban in expanding its authority in Afghanistan. Hamid Gul not only wanted to liberate Pakistan from the cultural contagion of the West, but also bring about an Islamic revolution.[3] Hamid Gul and Javed Nasir advocated the establishment of the pan-Islamic headquarters in Pakistan. Javed Nasir impelled the ISI to support Islamist rebels in Bosnia, the Philippines,

Xinjiang and Central Asia.[4] In September 1995, a number of military officers in Pakistan tried, but failed to carry out a coup for the establishment of an Islamic state with a radical Sunni bias and pan-Islamic aims as advocated by Harkat-ul-Jihad-al-Islami (HUJI).[5] Within a year (in September 1996), however, the Taliban (which shared these aims) captured power in Afghanistan. Their excessively cruel treatment of women made the Taliban a target of international contempt.[6]

Significantly, the impact on Pakistan of the Taliban's growing power inside Afghanistan was much more serious. Whereas the Taliban would feel proud and assertive about its increasing links with the Al Qaeda and Saudi Arabia, which was the principal patron of Sunni Muslims, the radical Sunnis within Pakistan began to receive arms, sanctuaries and instigation from the Taliban. For example, the Sipah-i-Sahaba-i-Pakistan (SSP) and the Lashkar-i–Jhangvi (LJ) received an enormous support from the Taliban, because they advocated the inauguration of a Sunni state in Pakistan.[7]

This meant that, in the 1990s, Pakistan experienced an explosion of sectarian violence, especially because non-Sunnis, e.g., Shias, could be branded as less-than-genuine Muslims. The Pakistan government (virtually the Army and the ISI), hesitated to do much to curb this sectarianism, for, it had to rely on these very sectarian forces to pursue the aims of enhancing its authority in Afghanistan as also its reach in India's J&K. To encourage one form of jihad in Afghanistan and J&K could not but force the Pakistan government to look away (at least partially) from another form of sectarian jihad inside Pakistan. The so-called Talibanisation appeared to infect the whole of Pakistan, while the government could draw comfort from the employment of foreign jihadis in J&K, even if that required the use of illicit drug money. Whereas an agency like the Jaish-i–Muhammad (JIM) under Masood Azhar's leadership tended to concentrate on jihad in J&K, another like Harkat-ul-Ansar (HUA) was more dedicated to the cause of global jihad. But all this coexisted with large scale sectarian violence inside Pakistan. The Pakistan government tried to exercise control over jihadi organisations, e.g., the Taliban, but did not succeed. In 1991, for example, Pakistan tried to respond to a (post-Soviet) Russian government request for the release of a few Russian prisoners held by leaders, who received enormous support from Pakistan in the days of anti-Soviet jihad. Their release would have significantly helped Pakistan in improving relations with the new Russian government at a time when America was getting somewhat aloof. But the leaders of Afghan jihad rebuffed and embarrassed Pakistan on this matter.[8]

At any rate, keeping jihadi agencies under control was hardly the major preoccupation of the Pakistan military, which preferred to concentrate on innovative and adventurous ways and means to expand the economic fortunes of its members, in service or retired. It set up organisations like the Army Welfare Trust (AWT), Fauji Foundation (FF) or Shaheen Foundation (SF) to engage in a mind-boggling variety of enterprises, e.g., real estate development, banking, insurance, ship breaking, aviation, etc. Military officers did not hesitate to use links with Afghanistan, and engage in the illegal drug business, e.g., conversion of smuggled opium into costly heroin.[9] In the course of the 1990s, moreover, the private security companies set up by military-sponsored bodies experienced a boom because of a marked deterioration in the law and order situation in the wake of arrival of a huge mass of refugees from Afghanistan, which the Pakistan government appeared to welcome in order to justify its demands for CIA money.[10] When in 1999, the civil government of Prime Minister Nawaz Sharif made an attempt to curb the financial depredations of military-backed business agencies, like the AWT, it was simply rebuffed.[11] Afterwards, in October 1999, General Pervez Musharraf captured political power by means of a coup, and any further question of curbing the money-making orgies of the military could not arise. Musharraf's government, for example, 'provided about 4000-5000 jobs to military officers and officials in various departments and ministries of the government.'[12]

Meanwhile, the Taliban under the leadership of Mullah Muhammad Omar grew from strength to strength in Afghanistan. There was a substantial accretion to this strength in 1996, when Osama Bin Laden came to Afghanistan, and Arabs from a number of countries followed him. Soon afterwards, Muslims from a large number of countries, viz. America, Australia, Bangladesh, China, Chechnya, Europe, India and Pakistan reached Afghanistan to reinforce the authority of the Taliban. But the Taliban, probably drunk with power, had clashes with its principal protagonists, i.e., Pakistan and Saudi

Arabia. For, once, they burnt the Pakistani embassy in Kabul, attacking physically even the ambassador of Pakistan. In 1998, after the Al Qaeda failed to bomb the American Consulate in Jeddah, but succeeded in bombing the American embassies in Kenya and Tanzania, Omar was asked by Saudi Arabia to deliver Laden to Saudi Arabia, or, at least, to turn him out of Afghanistan. But Omar not only refused, he, like Laden, denounced the presence of American troops on the sacred soil of Saudi Arabia. Omar even pleaded that Muslims in various countries should join hands to liberate Saudi Arabia. Moreover, the Taliban did not accede to the Pakistani request that the centuries-old Buddha statues in Bamiyan should not be destroyed. Evidently, Omar was too dogmatic to practise moderation.[13]

A unique aspect of Omar-Laden relationship–perhaps unbelievable to persons who do not belong to countries like Afghanistan or Saudi Arabia–deserves a special mention. Political loyalties were boosted by ties of marriage. Laden 'reportedly married one of his daughters to Mullah Muhammad Omar.'[14] Laden, too, reciprocated, and married a daughter of Omar.[15]

The worldwide Islamist terror was looming large. But the United States remained guilty of utter mismanagement of this threat after the Soviet withdrawal from Afghanistan. Islamist radicals within Afghanistan and Pakistan (including the military establishment) became more powerful as the United States began abruptly to disengage itself economically and militarily after the Soviets withdrew from Afghanistan.[16] General Mirza Aslam Beg, who succeeded Zia-ul Haq as Pakistan's Army Chief, was a radical Islamist;so was his ISI chief, General Hamid Gul. American indifference (or incompetence) in dealing with them was somewhat incredible. On one occasion, Beg and Gul even tried to remove from office the civil Prime Minister, Benazir Bhutto, by using Laden to assassinate her, although the plot fizzled out.[17]

Such indifference might account for the lack of even rudimentary safeguards against the attack upon the World Trade Center in America taking place on 11 September 2001. In 1993, Ramzi Yousef, a Pakistani trained by the ISI, tried to demolish the World Trade Center. Yet, the Americans remained incapable of forewarning themselves about another future attack on the World Trade Center, a symbol of American power, and, therefore, an attractive target for publicity-crazy terrorists. Years of close interaction with Pakistanis, Afghans and Arabs could not enlighten Americans on the complexities of the jihadi mindset, which they themselves fostered during the anti-Soviet jihad in Afghanistan. Not long after the termination of this jihad, in course of the Iraq-Kuwait war, as American troops stationed themselves on the sacred soil of Saudi Arabia, they certainly reinforced the zeal for global jihad in persons like Laden.[18] The callousness of the United States towards coping with the jihad appeared to cross all limits when at some stage it was revealed that it failed even to pre-empt the recruitment of jihadis in the United States Army.[19]

The United States apathy towards putting in place appropriate measures to cope with Islamist terror survived the bombing of its East African embassies in 1998 by Al Qaeda (more on these bombings will appear later in this chapter). The United States Navy failed to prevent the explosion on its ship, Cole, at Aden in 2000. It is possible to trace the root of this apathy to the first presidential term of Bill Clinton when the CIA appeared to suffer from serious problems of leadership and management. As to the Federal Bureau of Investigation, it earned notoriety for its inefficiency even in rescuing the victims of bombing in American embassies in 1998. Moreover, the FBI remained averse to sharing of information on terrorists (e.g. Laden's Egyptian ally Ayman Zawahiri) with other government agencies in the country, and thereby impeded the fight against Islamist terrorism. CIA Director George Tenet identified Al Qaeda as the most formidable and immediate threat to America's security. Yet, George Bush (Bush II), commencing his presidential term in 2001, failed to comprehend the nature and intensity of Islamist terrorism emerging in the course of the 1990s. The Bush Administration, in early 2001, remained impervious to the need for adequate funding of counter-terrorist operations. Nor could it tame intra-administration rivalries on the deployment of unmanned aerial vehicles for directing missiles towards terrorist bases, although it was aware of how zealously Laden was circulating videos of explosion in American embassies and on Cole for the training of terrorists. If again the government proved to be irresponsible in permitting the training of potential terrorists in the country's flying academies, no less irresponsible were the American media persons, who, at one stage of Clinton presidency, appeared to pay far more attention to the scandal centring on Clinton's relationship with Monica Lewinsky, than to the overwhelming threat from Islamist terrorism.[20]

The adverse impact of domestic politics upon American capabilities for dealing with Islamist terrorism has been discussed in such a masterly fashion in some reports of the United States House of Representatives Republican Research Committee that one should insert a few quotations here. 'After the Watergate era, Congress established oversight committees to ensure that the CIA did not undertake covert action contrary to basic American law. Case officers in the CIA's Clandestine Service interpreted legislation, such as the Hughes-Ryan Amendment requiring that the president approve and report to Congress any covert action, as sending a message to them that covert action often leads to trouble and can severely damage one's career. ... During the 1990s, tension sometimes arose, as it did in the effort against Al Qaeda, between the policymakers, who wanted the CIA to undertake more aggressive covert action and wary CIA leaders, who counselled prudence and making sure that the legal basis and presidential authorization for their actions were undeniably clear. The Clandestine Service felt the impact of the post-cold war peace dividend, with cuts beginning in 1992. ... Inevitably, some parts of the world and some collection targets were not fully covered, or not covered at all. ... The nadir for the Clandestine Service was in 1995, when only 25 trainees became new officers.'[21]

The stage was thus set for the 1998 East African bombings as also the Armageddon, viz. 9/11. Future generations of Americans may be inclined to look back to 9/11 as another testimony to the unpardonable failure of their government to use its enormous resources to deter or stop an aggression that was not beyond the pale of anticipation and normal intelligence operations, i.e., another Pearl Harbour.[22]

Hubris, ignorance and mismanagement (HIM) formed a vicious cocktail that inhibited America from forestalling 9/11. How deep and widespread were the roots of HIM in the United States Administration could be comprehended at the very commencement of the anti-Soviet jihad in Afghanistan. The United States failed to take a long term view of the implications of what it was about to do. It overlooked a primary and obvious guideline about what it was planning: solutions of today must not be problems of tomorrow.

The United States, moreover, made two cardinal errors: it failed to identify the principal long term global enemy, as also the territory where to fight the enemy.

When the Soviet Union positioned its troops in Afghanistan in late December 1979, it was already a decayed debilitated state. The United States had to calculate coolly whether the Soviet Union posed a greater threat to South Asia, the United States and the world than the jihadi terrorism emerging in Pakistan in Zulfikar Ali Bhutto's regime and consolidating itself in the regime of Zia-ul Haq.[23] Inside Pakistan, Ahmadis and Shias became the easily identifiable victims of jihadi terrorism.[24] Outside Pakistan, Indians remained the regular victims. The communist regime in Kabul was far from being the promoter of jihadi terrorism; so was its patron the Soviet Union.[25] America failed dismally to identify the principal enemy, viz. jihadi terrorism, and immeasurably strengthened this enemy by the measures it adopted to fight Kabul and Moscow.

In order to assess the impact of this failure on the part of America upon Pakistan, as also its stunning relevance in the second decade of the twenty-first century, it is advisable to quote what Mehmood Khan Achakzai, leader of the Milli Awami Party of Baluchistan, said in Pakistan's National Assembly on 17 June 2013. "The year 1979 was the turning point when Zia-ul Haq threw us in an unwanted war in Afghanistan. ISI's late Colonel Imam confessed that the agency trained 95,000 Pakistanis in sabotage activity, who are now out to destroy Pakistan. It's a volcano where everybody is now armed to the teeth."[26] But if General Zia is to be denounced, America cannot escape blame for its own blunder, because without massive American support, Zia and his Pakistani successors would not have been able to do what they actually did in the years of anti-Soviet jihad in Afghanistan. Significantly, the recent history of international relations provides several examples of America's propensity to commit grave blunders. In China in the 1940s, for example, America defended the indefensible regime of Chiang Kai-shek. From the late 1940s to the early 1970s, America refused to recognise the reality in China.[27] In Vietnam, too, in the 1960s and 1970s, America remained blind to realities. Subsequent events confirmed the veracity of these allegations against America, as America developed extraordinarily close relations with China and Vietnam by substitution of realism for dogmatism.

In Afghanistan and Pakistan, throughout the 1980s, America looked away from realities as it proceeded to launch the anti-Soviet jihad in the manner it did. To re-emphasise what merits re-emphasis, it outsourced the venture to Pakistan's ISI, which used it as a heaven-sent opportunity to multiply its already existing capabilities for conducting jihad. Americans imagined, somewhat childishly, that such outsourcing would enable them to conceal their paramount role in the anti-Soviet jihad in Afghanistan. Whereas America supplied arms and money for the anti-Soviet Mujahideen (Mujahids), the ISI exercised strict control over their distribution.[28] It preferred to distribute weapons and funds to those groups of Mujahids, who were more fanatical than others, and this had long term implications for the spread of jihadi terrorism, especially in the post-Soviet era.[29]

Counter-productive American policy harmed South Asia, America and the entire world in another significant way. The production of poppy and the number of laboratories processing opium into heroin registered a phenomenal increase in the course of the anti-Soviet jihad. Whereas poppy production is normal in Afghanistan, because it is far more profitable to produce poppy than other crops, what happened in course of the anti-Soviet jihad was remarkable in other ways. Even if some farmers occasionally preferred other crops to opium, they would be compelled by leaders of jihadi factions to produce opium, because these leaders developed a vested interest in the production of opium. Their incomes rose sharply, as also the capacity to procure additional weapons. Pakistan's ISI, the army, police and various jihadi factions developed an intricate network of enormously profitable smuggling operations. American weapons would land in the Pakistani port of Karachi, get transported in army-controlled trucks to Afghanistan, and the trucks would carry hashish, heroin, etc. from Afghanistan in their return journey to Pakistan. Heroin was then dispatched to Western countries, or sold to the growing number of addicts in Pakistan. It was thus possible to adapt Dan Brown's term to depict jihadis as hassassins.[30]

The United States did not appear to study, and/or learn from the Soviet intervention in Afghanistan, which the United States tried to terminate by means of a proxy war. The Soviets faced a ferocious resistance from a large and growing number of Afghans inspired by Islamist fanaticism. The Soviets were guided by political fanaticism, and propped up a communist regime in Kabul, and, for that purpose, did not hesitate to kill even Prime Minister Hafizullah Amin, who had invited the Soviets to march into Afghanistan. The United States consciously backed the Islamists to conduct a jihad against the Soviets in Afghanistan. Thus, America sowed the wind of Islamist terrorism, and reaped the whirlwind in the last decade of the twentieth century, and has continued to do so in the twenty-first century. After all, the Soviet Union confronted a situation of unmanageable complexity in which its supporters as also opponents suffered from acute and chronic factionalism; and the current United States experience in the same region has not been different.[31]

Despite factionalism, however, Islamist fanaticism remained the dominant force in Afghanistan in the decade of Soviet occupation. The American recipe of Islamism as an antidote to Soviet communism, and Saudi Arabia's continuing support for the same recipe before and during the Soviet occupation of Afghanistan, enabled Pakistan to strengthen itself militarily vis-a-vis India, although the Taliban and the Al Qaeda grew enormously in the Pakistan-Afghanistan border.[32] It is, however, doubtful whether Pakistan could thus serve the longterm interests of itself, the United States and the world. For, in the 1980s, as already stated, Pakistan transformed itself into a global hub of international terrorism, while its madrasas trained and armed tens of thousands of jihadis representing forty-three Islamic countries.[33] Moreover, the United States could hardly imagine that its success in the anti-Soviet jihad in Afghanistan would enable Laden to 'present himself and his allies as victorious warriors in the one great successful experience for Islamic militancy in the 1980s: the Afghan jihad against the Soviet occupation.'[34]

The Soviet Union withdrew its forces from Afghanistan during 1988-1989. The United States, however, committed crucial blunders in the mid-1980s to take a proverbial jump from a frying pan into the fire—from a fight against a shaky Soviet-backed regime in Kabul to an unending war against partly invisible, but ubiquitous Islamist terrorists with a global outreach. In mid-1980s, Mikhail Gorbachev was in power in the Soviet Union, which was economically weak and militarily demoralised. Gorbachev was bent upon the introduction of democratic reforms in the Soviet Union and a dignified disengagement from Afghanistan, where Soviet troops were undoubtedly guilty of atrocities, but were themselves victims of unspeakable atrocities; for instance, many Soviet soldiers were burnt alive or had their genitals mutilated. But American policymakers, headed by Ronald Reagan, were not interested in negotiations with Gorbachev for a planned Soviet withdrawal from Afghanistan. They did not bother about the high probability of terrible chaos following an unplanned Soviet withdrawal. American policymakers had a peculiar mindset: they were afraid that deliberations on what would happen after the Soviet withdrawal might distract from the main goal of inflicting a patent defeat on the Soviet forces. Americans were arrogantly aware of their superiority in military technology, and took the short-sighted step of equipping Afghan militants with surface-to-air missiles and advanced sniper rifles, to which Soviet troops had no answer. In this way, American decisionmakers paved the way to what they imagined to be a triumphant end to the Cold War by expediting unplanned Soviet withdrawal from Afghanistan. But, in this process, to state a hard truth that bears reiteration, they also gave birth to a far more deadly global enemy: an army of Islamist terrorists equipped with highly sophisticated Washington-gifted weapons and led by the Taliban and Al Qaeda.[35]

As has been already noted, Muslims from a large number of countries assembled in Afghanistan to reinforce the anti-Soviet jihad. West Asian (Middle Eastern) countries, including Saudi Arabia, supplied the maximum number. Laden, belonging to an exceptionally rich family of Saudi Arabia, came to Afghanistan, and liberally financed the anti-Soviet jihad. It is generally recognised that American funds and weapons substantially helped Laden in amassing influence inside Afghanistan. Nevertheless, in view of his role in organising 9/11, American officials appear to be shy of acknowledging any close link with Laden during the anti-Soviet jihad in Afghanistan.[36] An interesting, though, significant sidelight of the anti-Soviet jihad in Afghanistan was the defection of young Muslim recruits to the Soviet army from Central Asian Republics, who joined the jihad against the Soviet Union.[37]

An important by-product of the anti-Soviet jihad in Afghanistan, to repeat what deserves repetition, was the emergence of the Taliban. Afghan refugees in Pakistan, trained in madrasas, which infected them with Sunni militancy, formed the Taliban.[38] If the conscious support by America of these Islamist terrorists in the 1980s was perplexing, no less so was America's abrupt disengagement from Afghanistan after the Soviet withdrawal. Probably, America (and Europe) were too enthralled by the fall of the Berlin Wall and the dismantling of the Soviet Union to think seriously about the fierce contest among blood-thirsty warlords and rival anti-Soviet Mujahid groups in Afghanistan.[39]

In this labyrinth of chaos, the Al Qaeda and Taliban got ample opportunities to grow into a global threat. *The 9/11 Commission Report* traces, for example, the evolution of Al Qaeda with admirable clarity. It notes that in the 1980s, Laden not only conceived Al Qaeda as a worldwide jihadi organisation, but sent his representatives to different parts of the world for such sensitive missions as procurement of arms. It was also in the 1980s that Omar Abdel Rahman (better known as the Blind Sheikh), an intellectual preceptor of Laden, who spent some time in Egypt's jails for being a motivator of Egyptian President Anwar Sadat's assassin, succeeded in building a shelter in Jersey City of the United States, from where he went on broadcasting jihadi messages. After April 1988, when the Soviet Union announced the decision to leave Afghanistan in the following nine months, Laden accelerated the pace of Al Qaeda's emergence as a global jihadi outfit.[40] The question is if all this was known to American decisionmakers (including intelligence officers), why did they not pre-empt the march of Al Qaeda during and after the anti-Soviet jihad in Afghanistan? If not, will it be pertinent to observe that the competence of these decisionmakers has been overrated?

Whereas the Al Qaeda was more interested in global jihad than in jihad inside the South Asian region, the Taliban concentrated on the latter. The Soviet Union finally withdrew its troops from Afghanistan on 15 February 1989. Around this time (probably as a matter of pure coincidence), the Pakistan government, under Prime Minister Benazir Bhutto, brought about a substantial change in the conduct of Afghan operations. General Mirza Aslam Beg, the Army Chief, took over these operations, although in the past the ISI was in charge.[41] It was open to debate whether this change added further complexity to an already intricate situation in Afghanistan. In order to gauge this complexity, one has to remember that, before the departure of the Soviet army, the Mujahid militias in Afghanistan, despite inevitable factional rivalries, had at least one common enemy—the Soviet Union. But, after Soviet withdrawal, there was an aggravation of multi-level hostilities. Pashtuns formed the bulk of the Taliban, and clashed with Tajiks and Uzbeks. Pashtuns advocated the establishment of a Sunni fundamentalist state in Afghanistan. Therefore, they also fought Hazaras, who were Shias.[42] Pakistan, again, fostered Sunni militancy among the Pashtun Taliban in order to keep dormant the old demand of Pashtuns on both sides of the Pakistan-Afghanistan border for a separate independent Pashtunistan, or for the inclusion of all Pashtun majority territories within Afghanistan. Needless to add that Pakistan could also use the Taliban for its proxy war in India's J&K.[43]

In the period following the near-simultaneous disengagement from Afghanistan of the Soviet Union and the United States (till 9/11 at any rate), the United States appeared to behave with incredible ineptitude, and virtually paved the way to 9/11. In contrast, Pakistan, although suffering from a sense of being abandoned by its patron, the United States, tried to make the most of the situation. As stressed previously, it enabled the Taliban to establish its sway over nearly the whole of Afghanistan. Pakistan undoubtedly retained a little control over the Taliban. But the relationship between the two was so close (perhaps symbiotic) that the Taliban, too, irrespective of the Pakistan government's desire or design, succeeded in stepping out of its original habitat in the Pakistan-Afghanistan border, and establishing its influence over large parts of Pakistan, in a sort of continuation of activities commencing in the decade of anti-Soviet jihad. It could be argued that Pakistan appeared to lose in the rear what it seemed to gain in the front. If Pakistan imagined that, with the help of the Taliban, it would gain a strategic depth in Afghanistan in case of a conflict with India, the Taliban, in turn, seemed to succeed in gaining a sort of strategic depth by spreading its extremist thought over vast tracts of Pakistan. As Mohammad Shahzad puts it: 'The jihadis and the sectarian terrorists are the products of the Afghan jihad. They are being used as "cheap labour" to pursue self-defeating security policies of the state like "bleed India" or "strategic depth" in Afghanistan.'[44]

American policy remained vitiated by contradictions and misjudgements. In 1990, on account of irrefutable intelligence assessment that Pakistan was acquiring nuclear weapons, the Administration of President George H.W. Bush (Bush I) had no option but to abide by the Congressional mandate of 1985 (The PresslerAmendment to the Foreign Assistance Act of 1961), and stop all assistance to Pakistan.[45] Nevertheless, even after the Soviets left Afghanistan, for a period of about two years, America continued to supply weapons to Mujahids. Yet, in 1994, when Mujahids had already turned into a so-called students' movement or the Taliban, which succeeded in gaining control over Kandahar, the CIA was reportedly surprised. In 1995, America obtained a new mandate from Congress (the Brown Amendment), and supplied a limited quantity of military and economic assistance to Pakistan. In the same year, the Taliban (with Pakistan's active support) marched into western Afghanistan, and in 1996, captured Kabul. The Taliban established the Islamic Emirate of Afghanistan, and Pakistan dreamt of using Taliban-ruled Afghanistan to expand Pakistan's influence from Central Asia on one side to the Arabian Sea on the other.[46]

At this point, it is worthwhile trying briefly to remind oneself of the meaning of Taliban, while it may not be practicable to provide an accurate definition of Taliban. Students of madrasas, which have existed for centuries to provide Islamist instruction (or, better still, indoctrination), are Talibs. But, at the time of the anti-Soviet jihad in Afghanistan, the Taliban assumed the role of Mujhahids. Pashtuns (as already noted) formed the majority of the Taliban, but some Pashtun tribes refused to subscribe to the hardline Islamism of the Taliban. Many Pakistanis (e.g. Punjabis), who joined the anti-Soviet jihad in Afghanistan, returned to Pakistan after the end of the Soviet occupation, but continued to count themselves as belonging to the Taliban. Many Pakistanis, again, moved to Afghanistan to reinforce the efforts of the Taliban to consolidate its authority in trouble-torn Afghanistan following the departure of the Soviet army. After they came to power in Afghanistan, the Taliban, under the leadership of Mullah Omar, began to apply strictly the Islamic law of Sharia. For example, if a man did not have a beard, if a woman went to school, or took up some work outside the home, or even went out of the home without a male relative as escort, they would all be severely punished. The Taliban prohibited kite flying, and stoned women to death in public for adultery. There could be a debate on which country was more responsible—Pakistan or America—for creating a situation in which about ninety percent of Afghanistan became a victim of domestic Islamist terrorism. But America, a superpower, could not be pardoned for mindless apathy to the not-unpredictable consequences of deliberately deserting the hapless ordinary Afghans after the Soviet withdrawal.[47]

After the Soviet army left Afghanistan, Osama Bin Laden went back to his own country, Saudi Arabia. But Laden and the pro-American Saudi government did not take long to develop deep mutual antagonism.[48] Laden was forced to flee in 1991 to Sudan where he enjoyed excellent relations with a powerful and staunchly Islamist political leader, Hassan Al Turabi. Laden promised to assist Turabi by drawing upon his skills in construction business, in which his family built a vast empire in Saudi Arabia. Although he was no longer able to utilise his family wealth in Sudan, Laden could capitalise his own business talents inherited from the family. Turabi ensured complete freedom for Laden to carry on his operations. Being an exceptionally meritorious person, Laden built up a huge transcontinental business within a short period of time. Success in business generated for some years at any rate abundant funds for creating, training and equipping a large army of Islamist terrorists, who hailed from an impressive number of countries, and were capable of launching jihadi operations at places and times of their choice.

The 9/11 Commission Report is a brilliant narrative. It records the multifarious activities of Laden in stunningly diverse parts of the world. Unbelievably, Laden established numerous cells of Islamist terrorists in Africa (e.g. in Mali, Nigeria, Uganda, etc.), Asia (e.g. in Algeria, Iraq, Lebanon, Libya, Saudi Arabia, Somalia, Sudan, Philippines, Indonesia, etc.), Europe (e.g. in Baku, Croatia, Cyprus, Serbia, etc.), and even in the United States (e.g. in Boston, Chicago, New York, etc.). The nagging question is—as has been rightly and repeatedly raised in this study—what was America (especially the CIA or FBI) doing when Laden was raising an army that had no parallel in history. The American Administration—an enormous reservoir of capabilities—appeared to be incorrigibly incompetent in safeguarding national interests. If this is the message of *The 9/11 Commission Report*, this was also the message of such epoch making studies as *The China White Paper* of 1949 and the *The Pentagon Papers* of 1971.[49]

It is indeed amazing that even when America made some efforts in the 1990s to enlist the help of its decades-old ally, Pakistan, to tame Islamist terrorists, it did not succeed. For example, the terrorist, who tried to demolish New York's World Trade Center in 1993, i.e. Ramzi Yousef (more about him later), was a Pakistani. The ISI trained him in one of the many training camps managed by the ISI, and situated inside Pakistan. Nawaz Sharif was the Prime Minister of Pakistan, whom America pressed to close down these camps. It must be admitted that Nawaz made an attempt to restrain the ISI. But the ISI proved to be too tricky for the Pakistani Prime Minister as well as the American government. The camps for training terrorists disappeared from Pakistan only to reappear in Afghanistan's eastern region.[50]

In 1995, again, the ISI-backed Harkat Ul Ansar (HUA) abducted a number of Western tourists in J&K. Nevertheless, there was no accessible evidence on whether subsequently America reprimanded Pakistan for this incident. After all, the HUA happened to be one of the thirty foreign entities categorised as terrorist groups in accordance with America's Anti-Terrorism and Effective Death Penalty Act of 1996.[51]

Pakistan also acted visibly against American interests when it reportedly helped Osama Bin Laden in rebuilding a sanctuary in Afghanistan, where he returned from Sudan (in 1996 as already noted). There was, however, no published information on whether America tried to counteract Pakistan's lenience towards Laden. Significantly, Laden had to leave Sudan, because he and his patron, Turabi, lost their influence while America and a number of regional powers (e.g. Egypt, Jordan and Saudi Arabia) prevailed upon the Sudanese government to withhold support from terrorist outfits, including obviously the ones managed by Laden.[52]

Laden issued a fatwa in February 1997. He proclaimed in this fatwa that Muslims were duty-bound to murder Americans and their associates in whichever country it was feasible to do so, and that the murderers did not have to observe any distinction between military and civilian personnel. Strikingly, even though a fatwa should properly be issued by a religious authority, Laden did not pretend to exercise any such authority. In a year, in February 1998, together with Zawahiri,

Laden put out another fatwa. The title of this fatwa was significant: World Islamic Front for Jihad against Jews and Crusaders.[53]

In May 1998, ABC News interviewed Laden, who reiterated his previous fatwa, refusing to discriminate between civilian and military targets in the holy war against Americans and other enemies of Muslims. In a few weeks in the course of another interview, Laden went a step further to announce that, in situations where even execution of Muslims was unavoidable for extermination of Americans, such executions conformed to the teachings of Islam. This interview took place following the Al Qaeda's truck bomb attacks on the American embassies in Nairobi and Dar-es-Salaam on 7 August 1998 (these attacks have earlier been briefly noted in this study). Nairobi witnessed the death of 12 Americans, and of an additional number of 201 persons (mostly Kenyans), whereas the number of injured stood at 5000. In Dar-es-Salaam, 11 persons died, but there were no Americans among them. In the course of the same interview, Laden said that these bombings in two African capitals complied with the fatwa issued by the World Islamic Front for Jihad against Jews and Crusaders. Laden added that he was ready to be called a criminal if this jihad was viewed as a crime.[54] Bombings in Kenya and Tanzania proved Laden to be 'the prototype of a new breed of terrorist—the private entrepreneur, who puts modern enterprise at the service of a global terrorist network.'[55]

These incidents in Kenya and Tanzania underline some chronic infirmities of American policy makers—a theme recurrently and regretfully stressed in this study. American embassies in these two countries did not yet attain the requisite standards of security. What was much more important was that these embassy bombings illustrated the validity of some findings of a 1993 report—*Terror 2000*—prepared by forty-one experts working for the Pentagon's secretive Office on Special Operations and Low Intensity Conflict. These experts were former officials of not only the CIA, FBI, Rand Corporation and the State Department, but also of Israel's intelligence agency and even the KGB. "In one uncannily accurate prediction," wrote Robin Wright, "*Terror 2000* warned that extremists may try to maximize their impact by moving beyond one-at-a-time attacks to multiple, simultaneous targeting, thus demonstrating their reach and taxing governments' ability to respond. That's exactly what happened in Africa, when the two car bombs exploded within minutes of each other in cities about 400 miles apart." Americans were certainly the real targets—or 'the head of the snake' in Laden's words—but African civilians formed 95 per cent of the casualties. But, how did the United States Administration treat *Terror 2000*? Instead of obtaining appropriate guidance from this report and planning apposite actions, the Administration decided to entomb it unceremoniously.[56]

A few years before the African bombings of 1998—on 26 February 1993, to be specific—mainland America narrowly escaped a far more devastating attack. That was the handiwork of Ramzi Yousef, whose name has already appeared in this study, but some additional details may be noted now. Yousef probably heralded the advent of that era of highly educated Islamist terrorists, who could eventually stage as sophisticated an assault as 9/11. An engineering graduate of a British university, Yousef, headed what he called the Liberation Army. 'Moreover by acting independently, the small self-contained cell led by Yousef prevented authorities from linking it to an established terrorist organization, such as its suspected coordinating group, Osama bin Laden's al-Qaida, or a possible state sponsor.'[57] Yousef and his group committed a small mistake in their plan of where to locate the bomb for demolition of New York's World Trade Center (WTC) in 1993. If this mistake was avoided, approximately 50,000 persons would have perished.[58]

In the literature on terrorism, the 1993 WTC attack has not apparently received as much attention as it deserves. More than one thousand persons received injuries, the number of deaths stood at six, but the explosion of the truck bomb was so enormous as to create a cavity covering seven storeys. The depravity of a terrorist's mind could be determined by what Ramzi Yousef said subsequently: Yousef said that he expected the number of deaths to reach 2,50,000. Mohammad Salameh, an accomplice of Yousef, made a critical blunder that probably facilitated his arrest. He rented the truck that was used for WTC bombing. He furnished a deposit of US$ 400 for renting the truck. He was so anxious to recover this deposit that he made repeated calls to the renting agency. The FBI, therefore, did not have much difficulty in arresting Mohammad Salameh. Also arrested soon by the FBI were an engineer, Nidal Ayyad, and Mahmoud (Mahmud) Abouhalima.[59]

There was a plot to bomb the Holland and Lincoln tunnels of New York, which were highly significant transport links of this city. The mastermind of this plot was a resident of the Farouk mosque in Brooklyn, Sheikh Omar Abdel Rahman (better known as the Blind Sheikh, whose name has already appeared in this study). The arrest of the Blind Sheikh by the FBI in June 1993 (upsetting this plot) was undoubtedly expedited by the previous arrests of Salameh, Ayyad and Abouhalima. Arresting Ramzi Yousef, however, proved to be much more difficult. Yousef had an excellent record of deceiving American security agencies. In 1992, he entered America with a forged passport, clamoured for political asylum, and even obtained it. Immediately after the 1993 WTC bombing, he took shelter in Pakistan, and could not be caught for about two years. Yousef (in Pakistan) and his uncle, Khalid Sheikh Mohammed (in Qatar), conspired to blow up airlines in Manila. The uncle escaped arrest, because America could not overcome the obstruction by a Qatari official and, eventually, Khalid Sheikh Mohammed performed a critical role in the 9/11 assault. But Yousef was arrested in Pakistan in 1995. He, like other conspirators of the 1993 WTC bombing, as also the Blind Sheikh, were successfully prosecuted in America.[60]

It was a hard-earned success under the American legal process. 'The process was meant, by its very nature, to mark for the public the events as finished—case solved, justice done. It was not designed to ask if the events might be harbingers of worse to come. Nor did it allow for aggregating and analysing facts to see if they could provide clues to terrorist tactics more generally—methods of entry and finance, and mode of operation inside the United States...successful prosecutions contributed to widespread underestimation of the threat. The government's attorneys stressed the seriousness of the crimes, and put forward evidence of Yousef's technical ingenuity. Yet the public image that persisted was not of clever Yousef, but of stupid Salameh going back again and again to reclaim his $400 truck rental receipt.'[61] Thus, remarkable success generated fatal failures.

Remarkably, Louis Freeh, the FBI Director from 1993 to mid-2001, appeared to comprehend that terrorism was a principal threat to American security. He raised the number of foreign offices of his Bureau, and advised his field officers to act before—rather than after—the occurrence of a terrorist event. After the 1993 WTC bombing, while presenting his request for funds to Congress, Freeh pleaded that the FBI should prevent future acts of terror, and not confine itself merely to successful investigation of a past terrorist act. Nevertheless, attempts by Freeh to boost counter-terrorism operations did not succeed. There was the usual intra-administration blame game. Officers of the Justice Department and the Office of Management and Budget (OMB) argued that topranking FBI officers were reluctant to transfer resources from conventional crimes (including violation of drug laws) to counter-terrorism, whereas FBI leaders accused the OMB and Congress of remissness in realising FBI's requirements of additional resources for counter-terrorism operations.[62]

As already mentioned in this study, though briefly, the CIA did not appear to fare better than the FBI in terms of empowerment for counter-terrorist operations needed urgently in the 1990s. For, mainly because of intra-administration power rivalries, the CIA was deprived of authority to deal with any threat to domestic security, even though as Islamist terrorists can easily demonstrate, internal and external dimensions of security are inextricably linked up. 'This structure built in tensions between the CIA and the Defence Department's intelligence agencies, and between the CIA and the FBI.'[63]

Throughout the 1990-1996 fiscal years, America's external intelligence operations suffered from budget decreases. Next, during the 1996-2000 fiscal years, expenditure on these operations remained largely static. No wonder that American intelligence officials confessed to inadequacies of resources for meeting the threats from Al Qaeda and Laden. As late as 2004, George Tenet (who was the Director of Central Intelligence during 1997-2004) had to testify that the clandestine service of the CIA required a minimum of five years to prepare itself fully for counter-terrorism operations.[64] This was indeed unfortunate, because—as predicted by the *Terror 2000* report of 1993 and confirmed, e.g., by the East African bombings of 1998—'Whether motivated by ideological hatred, financial greed or religious passions, terrorists have moved further and faster in devising imaginative new targets and tactics than government counter-terrorism officials can keep up with.'[65]

The American government failed even to devise adequately restrictions on travel to and from its mainland, and enabled, therefore, an arch-terrorist like the Blind Sheikh to enter into, and depart from, America whenever he wanted. America's Immigration and Naturalization Service (INS) had a substantial number of staffers to launch effective counter-terrorism operations. For, it had about 2000 special immigration agents, 4500 persons in the rank of inspectors, as also 9000 agents engaged in border patrol. But, even in the middle 1990s, the INS staffers suffered from technological obsolescence. For example, inspectors in entry ports had to cope with the problem of unlawful entrants by means of watch lists preserved in ordinary papers; and border patrol agents could not replace their manual typewriters by electronic ones. On three occasions—in 1986, 1995 and 1997—some INS staffers submitted elaborate counter-terrorism schemes to superior authorities without any response. Terrorists took advantage of Canada's relatively liberal immigration laws to enter into America from Canada. Yet, in the late 1990s (for instance), there was only one border patrol agent for every 13.25 miles at America's border with Canada.[66]

It was only around late 1990s that the State Department of the United States could establish an electronically accessible watch list of terrorists for such purposes as enforcement of laws, issuance of visas, and admission in various ports of entry. Yet, at entry ports, there were no instructions for inspectors to concentrate their attention on terrorists. As a result, while scrutinising watch lists electronically, inspectors did not even know that they should look for terrorists. The number of persons, who were refused admission at American entry ports because of being suspected to be terrorists, stood at 97 by the year 1998.[67]

This chapter may properly end with a survey of aviation safety and security in America before 9/11—the mega terrorist event in the country's twenty-first century history. It was far from easy for the Federal Aviation Administration (FAA) to ensure the safety and security of commercial aviation, as also to minimise the inevitable restrictions upon the civil aviation industry for protection against all sorts of criminal and terrorist activities. Interestingly, whereas the 9/11 episode epitomised hijacking of aircraft, before 9/11, for about a decade, Americans did not witness hijacking on their territory. So, explosives were dreaded more than hijacking. Vice President Al Gore, the Chairman of a presidential commission on safety and security of aviation, did not express any concern for hijacking by any suicide mission in the final report that he submitted in 1997. The Gore Commission report stressed the threats from explosives, sabotage and surface-to-air missiles. This was only about four years before 9/11.[68]

The FAA undoubtedly had comprehensive security devices. But each component had deficiencies, and, therefore, 9/11 could not be averted. The first component, naturally, was intelligence. There were forty intelligence personnel in the FAA. They received information from various authorities (e.g. the FBI, CIA, etc.) about probable threats to security. Nevertheless, there was negligible information about terrorist activities inside America. In 1998, for instance, the FBI tried to ascertain whether potential terrorists were in a position to avail of training facilities for pilots offered inside the country, but, amazingly, did not transmit any information to FAA.[69]

The second component of the FAA security system was the usual pre-screening of passengers. Before 9/11, there were about 60,000 persons known or suspected to be terrorists in the watch list of the Department of State. Surprisingly, however, there were only twelve suspected terrorists, who were barred from flights, in accordance with the FAA's own list. There was also a Computer Assisted Passenger Pre-screening System (CAPPS) since1997. But, only the checked-in bags of CAPPS-chosen travellers—but not those carried inside the cabin—were subjected to additional search. Loopholes in the FAA security system were thus obvious.[70]

The third component of the FAA security package was screening at checkpoints by means of metal detectors and X-ray machines. But the performance of the equipment in the pre-9/11 era was poor. For instance, metal detectors failed to identify many hazardous materials carried by passengers, and X-ray machines were sometimes unable to distinguish between harmful and harmless objects. The operations manuals of the airlines, again, were slipshod, allowing passengers to carry knives, which had blades that were less than four inches in length. In the years before 9/11, again, airlines had some special responsibility for security lapses. For, they cared more for aircraft and passenger movements than for security. Airlines were so much interested in reducing expenses on security that they remained probably unaware of whether and how this would affect security adversely.[71]

On board security comprised the fourth and final bundle of FAA security measures. But as late as the 9/11 episode, the domestic flights of commercial aircrafts did not normally have air marshals on board. The training manual of the FAA did not provide instructions for airlines personnel on how to cope with violent assaults on board. The fact that since 1986, American commercial aircraft did not witness hijacking by terrorists, minimised the concern for security planning, and maximised that for improvements of services to passengers. Above all, there was a lackadaisical approach to enforcement of restrictions upon access to the cockpit.[72]

It is worthwhile measuring the success of America's counter-terrorism operations by means of extraditions and renditions during 1993-1999. For example, in the case of the 1993 World Trade Centre bombing, America succeeded in securing the extradition of two terrorists: Mahmoud Abuhalima and Ramzi Yousef. Both were sentenced to 24 years of imprisonment. As to the 1998 East African bombings, there was extradition in the case of Mamdouh Mahmud Salim, and rendition in the cases of Mohamed Rashed Daoud Al Owhali, Mohamed Sadek Odeh, and Khalfan Khamis Mohamed.[73]

It may be interesting to review what happened in the year 2000—the last year before the episode of 9/11. Evidently, America remained the leader of counter-terrorism operations. This was logical because Afghanistan, under Taliban control, was the nerve centre of the so-called 'Afghan Alumni', i.e., those militants, who took part in the jihad against the Soviet Union in the 1980s, and who received arms and training mainly because America provided the necessary support. The nexus of these militants was powerful and widespread, even if informal and flexible. But, in an irony of history, they now treated America as the principal target of their jihad, and America too, focused its counter-terrorism operations on them. The centrality of the Afghan sanctuary for Islamist terrorists was demonstrated anew after the attack upon the USS Cole (already mentioned in this study) in Aden in October 2000, for, some of the culprits took refuge in Afghanistan.[74]

America's counter-terrorism policy—as of 2000—had four major planks. In the first place, no concessions were to be granted to, and no deal was to be struck with terrorists. Secondly, terrorists were to be brought to justice for their criminal activities. Thirdly, pressures for change of behaviour were to be applied against those states, which sponsored terrorism. Lastly, America was ready to help those states, which wanted to enhance their capacity for anti-terrorist operations. Success of American policy could be measured by, e.g., the efforts of Central Asian states to strengthen their vigilance against terrorists, especially those with bases in Afghanistan. In June 2000, five Central Asian states joined a conference sponsored by America, and promised to adopt measures to deprive terrorists of physical shelter and economic succour.[75]

Along with other partners in the G-8, America signed an International Convention for the Suppression of Terrorist Financing in January 2000. The aim was to deprive terrorists of the opportunity to use already available funds, and of access to new funds. Soon afterwards, thirty-five countries (including G-8 countries) signed this convention. In order to carry out detection, detention, arraignment/ arrest of financiers of terrorist activities, this convention laid down an international framework of laws. It further stipulated steps for recognition and obstruction of sources, as also cross-border flows of finances for terrorists.[76]

Nevertheless, as of 2000, parts of Afghanistan (which were under Taliban sway) continued to provide a safe shelter to Osama Bin Laden and his followers. The Taliban, thus, persisted in defiance of the United Nations Security Council Resolution 1267 of November 1999, which prohibited the grant of any sanctuary to Laden. In December 2000, therefore, the UN Security Council adopted Resolution 1333, which required the Taliban to carry out resolution 1267, to stop assisting and training international terrorists, to hand over Laden for subjecting him to legal prosecution, and to wind up (within 30 days) all encampments of militants in Afghanistan. The UN members must in case of Taliban's non-compliance with Resolutions 1267 and 1333, enforce a number of measures. For example, they were to keep Laden's financial assets frozen, impose an arms embargo upon the Taliban, prohibit the export to Afghanistan of acetic anhydride needed for heroin production, wind up all offices of the Taliban in foreign countries, etc. Such sanctions, prescribed by the UN Security Council Resolutions 1267 and 1333, were called 'smart' or 'targeted' sanctions, for, unlike general, especially economic sanctions, those would not cause hardship to the ordinary people of Afghanistan. Thus, private trade in consumer goods, medicine and food were exempted from these sanctions.[77]

Despite a public pledge of compliance with the UN Security Council Resolution1333, Pakistan provided military/material/technical support to the Taliban, and also supplied military advisers. Madrasas in Pakistan persisted in recruiting terrorists for operations in Afghanistan. America continued negotiations with the Taliban, and warned that, as long as Laden stayed in Afghanistan, America would fix responsibility on the Taliban for any terrorist assault upon America. The Taliban ignored UN sanctions, and carried on training and motivation work for Islamist militants assembling in Afghanistan from various parts of Africa, Asia, Europe and North America. Pakistan's military ruler, Pervez Musharraf, stuck to the policy of previous governments of his country in the matter of encouraging such organizations as Harkat-ul-Mujahidin and Lashkar-e-Taiyaba (LET) to subject India's J&K to terrorist onslaughts. America could do very little beyond remaining concerned about all these.[78]

On 12 October 2000 (as already mentioned in this study), an American destroyer, USS Cole, on a journey to the Persian Gulf, had a fuel stop at the Aden harbour in Yemen. Explosives loaded in a vessel lying next to this destroyer, detonated and seventeen American sailors lost their lives. Terrorists did not receive any support from Yemen's government, but its border control machinery was not strong enough to pre-empt the entry of terrorists in Yemen with forged documents. Yemen fully cooperated with America in investigations, which generated the interesting suggestions that the attack on Cole might have originated in Afghanistan, where some of the terrorists associated with this attack received their training.[79]

'As 2001 began, counter-terrorism officials were receiving frequent, but fragmentary reports about threats. Indeed, there appeared possible threats almost everywhere the United States had interests—including at home.'[80] Evidently, there was a massive volume of intelligence reports about terrorist threats based on human sources or signals. The President and senior officials (viz. the Vice President and the National Security Adviser) received only a small portion as briefs. For instance, George Tenet, the Director of Central Intelligence (DCI), met President Bush daily. President's Daily Brief (PDB), comprising 6-8 relatively brief essays, formed the most sensitive and important intelligence items supplied to a few top-level officials. In the period from 20 January to 10 September 2001, Osama Bin Laden was the subject of 40 articles in PDBs. Next in importance to the PDB was the SEIB (Senior Executive Intelligence Brief). The Attorney General, the FBI Director and the National Security Council (NSC) counter-terrorism coordinator (i.e. Richard Clarke) got the SEIB, but not the PDB.[81]

In late March 2001, Clarke informed Condoleezza Rice, the National Security Adviser, that Al Qaeda and some other terrorist groups were known to run their cells inside America. In subsequent weeks, the CIA warned repeatedly that Abu Zubaydah, a close lieutenant of Laden, planned to attack India, Israel or Saudi Arabia. In May 2001, the FBI reported that attacks on Boston, London, New York were being planned. Late in the same month, the FAA issued a circular to commercial airlines, warning a hijack attempt to bargain for the release of terrorists detained in America. On 24 May 2001, there were reports of possible terrorist attacks in Italy, Yemen and even America. On 29 May, Clarke urged upon Rice to inquire from DCI Tenet what America could do to prevent Abu Zubaydah from staging attacks on targets in Israel, including American facilities. At the same time, curiously, Clarke wrote to Rice and Stephen Hadley (the deputy to Rice), 'When these attacks occur, as they likely will, we will wonder what more we would have done to stop them.' Again, in May 2001, Cofer Black, the Chief of CIA Counter-terrorism Centre (CTC) informed Rice that the level of current terrorist threat stood at 7 on a scale of 1 to 10.[82]

Reports of terrorist threats to America rose intensely in June and July 2001. On 21 June, for instance, America's Fifth Fleet sailed out of its Bahrain base for fear of an attack by Laden's followers. Americans closed their embassy in Yemen. Again, on 25 June, Clarke informed Rice and Hadley of as many as six reports on a probable Al Qaeda assault. Clarke further referred to an Al Qaeda tape that ominously talked of recruitment of new cadres and procurement of fresh funds. This, according to Clarke, was not merely an attempt to apply psychological pressure upon America. For, a number of intelligence reports pointed to catastrophic attacks being planned. Moreover, in the same month, one report on Al Qaeda indicated an impending attack that could be 'very, very, very, very' devastating. Next, on 30 June, an intelligence report warned of an attack by Laden's men, which might cause a calamity, even though there might be some delay in its occurrence due to pre-emptive measures by Washington.[83]

In July 2001, America and its friends coordinated steps to deactivate groups connected with Al Qaeda in as many as 20 countries. Later in that month, Italy launched massive operations in order to stave off threats to the G-8 Summit to be attended by the American President, and to be held at Genoa, closing the air space over the city, positioning anti-aircraft guns, etc. On 31 July, again, the FAA issued a circular, cautioning airliners against a possible operation by known terrorist agencies, which had the expertise to hide explosives in luggages and consumer goods, and which were engaged in training hijackers.[84]

In the run-up to 9/11, an extraordinarily important date was 6 August 2001. 'Bin Laden Determined to Strike in US' was the title of an article in the PDB submitted on that date. This was prepared by two CIA analysts in response to orders by President Bush in the summer and spring of 2001, which focused on an inquiry into the specificity of any terrorist threat to America. The 6 August article was significant in a number of ways. First, it referred to 70 Laden-related investigations being conducted by the FBI. Secondly, it drew attention to 1997/1998 interviews of Laden by American television, which lauded the example of Ramzi Yousef, who bombed the World Trade Center in 1993, as worthy of emulation so that a war could be launched in mainland America. Thirdly, the 6 August PDB article referred to American citizens, who were Al Qaeda operatives, and who resided/travelled in America for years. Two of them, along with a member of Egyptian Islamic Jihad (EIJ) were found guilty of plotting to bomb the American embassies in Nairobi and Dar-es-Salam in 1998. Fourthly, the 6 August article stressed that Laden engaged in longterm planning for any attack. For instance, his followers carried out a surveillance of the American embassies in Kenya and Tanzania in 1993, whereas the actual bombing took place in 1998.[85] This was indeed alarming in view of a multiplicity of unavoidably opaque intelligence reports of possible assaults by an invisible worldwide army of terrorists.

In the summer of 2001, top level leaders of America's intelligence establishment suffered from a sense of desperation about how to prevent what seemed to be an imminent and cataclysmic attack upon

America. For, reports of terrorist threats were excessively large in number and uncharacteristically alarming. Yet, as to the target, time, location and mode of attack, information was far from specific. Moreover, a majority of reports spoke of targets outside America, including those vaguely representing American interests. What happened in the 11 September 2001 attacks upon the US challenged the ability of intelligence agencies to provide specific information. For, these attacks belonged to an extraordinary category, having neither exclusively domestic nor exclusively foreign origin. Domestic intelligence agencies of the US focused their attention on indigenous terrorist threats, including those planned by secret cells. Foreign intelligence agencies of the US were preoccupied with foreign threats with targets comprising US interests abroad or at home. But 9/11 eluded all these agencies partly because it was unique: it was planned/ executed by foreigners, who had bases inside the US.

It may now be instructive to refer again to the prophetic 1993 report—*Terror 2000*—which was suppressed by the American government. The report talked of transformation of terrorist assaults from having selected targets to mass targets, and constructed the scenario of a chemical attack inside the subway system of New York City. The aim could be to maximise the psychological impact of a terrorist strike by a multiplication of casualties. The advent of the Internet Age facilitated such attacks. For, there were sites purveying details of advanced plastic explosives. For instance, readers could gain online access to guide books not only for the preparation of bombs, but also on how bombs could be concealed in books, for example. Easily available elements, e.g., fertiliser or ink, can be used for manufacturing explosives. Moreover, numerous American libraries hold *The Merck Index: An Encyclopaedia of Chemicals and Drugs*, which offers formulas for poisonous gases that can be used as chemical weapons.[86]

What, however, *Terror 2000* failed to predict, and what happened on 9/11, was the use of hijacked commercial aircraft as missiles for mass destruction. North American Aerospace Defence Command (NORAD), too, could not foresee such an innovative use of commercial airliners. Along with the FAA, NORAD certainly worked on probable responses in case an aeroplane was hijacked. But, before 9/11, the FAA had to pursue highly complex procedures for the procurement of military support from NORAD. It had to notify a number of government agencies at the highest level, and solicit their approval.[87]

As of 9/11, the FAA and NORAD continued to remain burdened with a number of wrong assumptions about how to react to a probable hijacking. These assumptions were: first, it was possible to identify promptly the hijacked aircraft and the hijacked airplane would not try any vanishing trick. Secondly, there would be enough time to avail of the normal FAA and NORAD chains of command. Thirdly, nobody anticipated that hijackers could undertake a suicide mission, and, therefore, could deploy the captured aircraft as a missile.[88]

These assumptions proved to be wrong around 8:14 in the morning of 9/11, when the American Airlines Boston-Los Angeles Flight was hijacked. The Air Traffic Controller (ATC) at the Boston Centre, however, failed to understand initially that it was a case of hijacking, although the flight did not carry out the instruction to ascend to a height of 35,000 feet. The ATC imagined that there was a radio failure. Subsequently, due to a change of route by the airliner and some incomprehensible transmission of messages, the ATC realised that a hijacking had occurred.[89]

Boston Centre acted in accordance with the usual FAA protocol. It issued notifications, between 8:25 and 8:32, to the normal chain of command. Thus, at 8:28, it informed the Herndon Command Centre of the movement of the hijacked American Airlines Flight 11 towards New York City. FAA headquarters received the hijacking report and began to follow the usual procedures. It did not get in touch with the National Military Command Centre (NMCC), which could have planned the dispatch of combat aircraft. As late as 8:37:52, Boston Centre informed NORAD's North East Air Defence Sector (NEADS) of the hijacking. But NEADS had no knowledge of where to send the fighter aircraft. Still, F-15 combat aircraft scrambled at 8:46 from the Otis Air Force Base, which happened to be 153 miles away from New York City. But that was the precise moment when the hijacked American Airlines Flight 11 ravaged the North Tower of New York's World Trade Center. Nine minutes' notice proved inadequate for NEADS to pre-empt this strike.[90]

There were three more flights hijacked in the morning of 9/11. But it is hardly necessary to deal with each of them elaborately. The abovenoted account of the hijacked American Airlines Flight 11 is enough to demonstrate the deficiencies in America's counter-terrorism apparatus. These, again, can be brought to a sharper focus if we briefly review the immediate responses of top level national leaders to 9/11. For instance, President Bush was informed at about 9:00 that a small twin-engine plane struck the World Trade Center, and the President observed that a mistake by the pilot might have led to this accident. When the President spoke to Condoleezza Rice, the National Security Adviser, she also first reported that a twin-engine plane—and then a commercial airliner—crashed into the World Trade Center. Vice President Dick Cheney was at the White House, when an assistant informed him that a plane crashed into the North Tower of the World Trade Center, and asked him to watch the television. When Dick Cheney looked at the television, a second plane crashed into the South Tower. But the White House staff carried on their normal meetings, commencing at 9:00, as they imagined that these were all freak incidents. The FAA administrator, too, first knew about the crash from television.[91]

Richard Clarke, a special assistant to President Bush, who dealt with counter-terrorism operations, organised a video teleconference in the White house Situation Room at 9:25. Hijackers rammed an aircraft in the Pentagon at 9:37. But the NMCC, which was itself conducting a voice conference, did not receive any information, for at least an hour, from the video conference in the White House. In an emergency, thus, rather disturbingly, decisionmaking and command/control operations took place in a fragmented fashion. The NMCC, moreover, while commencing its teleconference at 9:29, failed to establish communications with the FAA before 10:17. But the representative of the FAA was not even aware of the hijackings. Meanwhile, at about 10:03, another hijacked aircraft, United Airlines Flight 93, exploded at Pennsylvania.[92]

Bold and selfless resistance by passengers led to this explosion. Otherwise, United Airlines Flight 93 might have reached Washington D.C. and destroyed the White House or the Capitol. For, there was no possibility of a military response from NORAD, which learnt about the hijacking of this flight only after it crashed. It should, however, be observed, in a mild defence of NORAD and the FAA, that in the past, they never witnessed a challenge of the type of 9/11, nor did they ever receive any training to cope with such a hazard. It was, after all, a war of a unique genre.[93]

Even at the risk of repetition, one has to inquire whether the suicide mission of hijackers on 9/11—a totally unprecedented event—could be foreseen even partially, and forestalled, even if at a big cost, e.g., by use of missiles, or combat aircraft. *The 9/11 Commission Report*—a wonderful narrative—provides some vital clues to facilitate this inquiry. The Report confesses to the application of hindsight,[94] without succumbing to it, and without hesitating to indulge in self-criticism. It admits that imagination is not deemed to be a virtue of bureaucracy.[95] Yet, in the 1996 Atlanta Olympics, Richard Clarke apprehended an attack from the air, and requested the Defence Department for countermeasures. Being refused, Clarke turned to the Treasury Department, and collected resources to cope with a possible threat from the air in the Olympics.[96] In 1998, a group of experts, with Clarke as the chairperson, met and debated how to deal with a situation in which an aircraft, seized by some terrorists, and packed with explosives, could try to hit a target in Washington D.C. Officials from the FAA, the Secret Service and the Pentagon participated in this meeting. But the conclusion was tentative and dissatisfactory. Actually, in August 1998, there was an intelligence report that some Libyans might try to batter the World Trade Center with an aircraft.[97] In September that year, again, there was an intelligence report of a conspiracy to smash a plane (full of explosives) into an American city. Subsequently, on one occasion, the Counter-terrorism Security Group, with Clarke in the chair, even analysed the possibility of an aircraft being hijacked by Al Qaeda.[98]

Therefore, 9/11 could not be assessed as unforeseen or unforeseeable. Richard Clarke, for instance, was evidently worried about a terrorist assault from the air. 'But he attributed his awareness more to Tom Clancy novels than to warnings from the intelligence community. He did not, or could not, press the government to work on the systematic issues of how to strengthen the layered security defences to protect aircrafts against hijackings or put the adequacy of air defences against suicide hijackers on the national policy agenda.'[99] Over a number of decades, since the Pearl Harbour surprise attack of 1941, American officials steadily worked on and refined elaborate techniques on how to track down and warn against a surprise attack. The efficacy of these techniques could not be tested before the occurrence of 9/11, because, remarkably, 'they were not really tried.'[100]

It is easy to criticize a government—any government—for failure to cope with the Al Qaeda, which has a loose worldwide organization without any identifiable assets, territory or cadres/supporters.[101] No task can be conceivably more difficult, and no criticism for failure can be deemed to be absolutely accurate. Moreover, 'America stood out as an object for admiration, envy and blame. This created a kind of cultural asymmetry. To us, Afghanistan seemed very far away. To members of Al Qaeda, America seemed very close. In a sense, they were more globalised than we were,' observes *The 9/11 Commission Report*.[102]

Yet, Richard Clarke cannot but be praised for stressing the threat from Al Qaeda. For instance, on 25 January 2001, in a note to Condoleezza Rice, Clarke urged that top level decisionmakers should no longer avoid a recommendation on whether the threat from Al Qaeda was a 'first order threat'. Obviously, there was no response to this memo sent by Clarke. Therefore, on 4 September 2001 (a few days before Al Qaeda's 9/11 attack), he forwarded another memo in which he convincingly (even if ominously) analysed two prevalent currents of thought about Al Qaeda. One view was that Al Qaeda's 'terrorist network was a nuisance that killed a score of Americans every 18-24 months. If that view was credited, the current policies might be proportionate. Another school saw Al Qaeda as the "point of the spear of radical Islam".' Clarke's 4 September 2001 memo launched a 'blistering protest about foot dragging in the Pentagon and at the CIA'. 'But,' as *The 9/11 Commission Report* acknowledges, 'no one forced the argument into the open by calling for a national estimate or a broader discussion of the threat. The issue was never joined as a collective debate by the U.S. government, including the Congress, before 9/11.'[103]

There was thus a touch of tragic inevitability to the 9/11 catastrophe. An outsider (like this author), however, can exercise the privilege to hazard a few hunches. There was no dearth of information with the American government; probably, there was a blinding surfeit. There seemed to be much more of intellectual exercise and analysis than of attempt at profound perception. There was recognisably a labyrinthine compartmentalisation of intelligence collection/ processing, which precluded patient coordination because of normal bureaucratic jealousies. The people of America certainly deserved better.

Endnotes

1. Anthony Davis, 'How the Taliban Became a Military Force', in William Maley (ed.), *Fundamentalism Reborn?: Afghanistan and the Taliban*, London: Hurst, 1998, pp. 43-71; Ahmed Rashid, *Taliban: Militant Islam, oil and fundamentalism in central Asia*, New Haven: Yale University Press, 2010, pp. 183-95; S. IftikharMurshed, *Afghanistan: The Taliban Years*, London: Bennett and Bloom, 2006, p. 45.
2. *Afghanistan—Crisis of Impunity: The role of Pakistan, Russia and Iran in fuelling the civil war*, New York: Human Rights Watch, 2001, p. 23. Daniel Byman, *Deadly Connections: States that sponsor terrorism*, Cambridge: Cambridge University Press, 2005, p. 195.
3. Zahid Hussain, *Frontline Pakistan: the struggle with militant Islam*, London: I.B. Tauris, 2007, p. 21.
4. Hassan Abbas, *Pakistan's drift into extremism: Allah, the army, and America's war on terror*, Armonk, NY: M.E. Sharpe, 2005, p. 148.
5. Hussain, *Frontline Pakistan*, pp. 73-74.
6. William Maley's *The Foreign Policy of the Taliban*, New York: Council on Foreign Relations, 2000, pp. 6, 11-14.
7. Oliver Roy, 'Islam and foreign policy: central Asia and the Arab Persian World', in Christophe Jaffrelot (ed.), *A History of Pakistan and its origins*, London: Anthem Press, 2002, p. 145; Ahmed Rashid, *Taliban: the story of the Afghan warlords*, London: Pan Books, 2001, p. 187.
8. Abbas, *Pakistan's drift into extremism*, p. 148; Muhammad Amir Rana, *A to Z of Jehadi organisations in Pakistan*, Lahore: Machal Books, 2004, pp. 24-45; S.V.R. Nasr, 'Islam, the state and the rise of sectarian militancy in Pakistan', in Christophe Jaffrelot (ed.), *Pakistan: nationalism without a nation?* London: Zed Books, 2002, p. 94; Hussain, *Pakistan and the Emergence of Islamic Militancy in Afghanistan*, pp. 219-24; Nasr, 'Islam, the state and the rise of sectarian militancy', p. 96; Musharraf, *In the Line of Fire*, pp. 210-11; K. Warikoo, 'Islamist Mercenaries and Terrorism in Kashmir,' *Himalayan and Central Asian Studies*, Vol. 2, No. 2, April-June 1998, pp. 36-37; Riaz Mohammad Khan, *Afghanistan and Pakistan: Conflict, Extremism, and Resistance to Modernity*, New Delhi: Oxford University Press, 2011, pp. 34-36. It is instructive in this context to quote Husain Haqqani: 'Declassified State Department documents and secret cables made public by Wikileaks show that in the 1990s, as now, Pakistan

claimed it had contact with the Taliban but no control over them.' See Husain Haqqani, *The New York Times*, reprinted in the *The Indian Express*, 29 June 2013.

9. Alexander Cockburn and Jeffrey St. Clair, *Whiteout: The CIA, drugs and the Press*, London: Verso, 1998, p. 257. Ayesha Siddiqa, *Military Inc.: Inside Pakistan's Military Economy*, London: Pluto Press, 2007, pp. 112-28.
10. Louis Dupree, 'Pakistan and the Afghan Problem', in Craig Baxter and Syed Raza Wasti, *Pakistan Authoritarianism in the 1980s*, Lahore: Vanguard, 1991, p. 59.
11. Ahmed Murad, 'Army Welfare Trust: vested Khaki interests and double standards of business accountability', *The Friday Times*, 14-20 December 2001.
12. Siddiqa, *Military Inc.*, p. 127.
13. Musharraf, *In the Line of Fire*, pp. 212-16. Bruce Riedel, *Deadly Embrace*, New Delhi: Harper Collins, 2011, p. 56.
14. Arshi Saleem Hashmi, 'Five years on: Resurgence of Taliban and the Fate of Afghanistan', *Regional Studies*, Islamabad, Vol. XXV, No. 1, Winter 2006-07, p. 34.
15. Gilles Dorrowsoro, *Revolution Unending: Afghanistan, 1979 to the Present*, New York: Columbia University Press, 2005, p. 305.
16. Hasan-Askari Rizvi, *Military, State and Society in Pakistan*, London: Macmillan, 2000, pp. 246-47.
17. Adrian Levy and Catherine Scott-Clark, *Deception: Pakistan, the United States and the Global Nuclear Weapons Conspiracy*, London: Atlantic Books, 2007, pp. 193-94.
18. Charles Allen, *God's Terrorists: The Wahabi Cult and the Hidden Roots of Modern Jihad*, London: Little Brown, 2006, p. 288. Daniel Benjamin and Steven Simon, *The Age of Sacred Terror: Radical Islam's War Against America*, New York: Random House Trade Paperbacks, 2003, p. 463.
19. Benjamin and Simon, *Ibid.*, pp. 123-24.
20. Benjamin and Simon, *Ibid.*, pp. 239-41, 258, 296-307, 323-25, 334, 336-40, 346-48, 389-96.
21. United States. House Republican Research Committee. Task Force on Terrorism and Unconventional Warfare reports 1989-1994, Hoover Institution Archives, Stanford, California. No page number. *National Commission on Terrorist Attacks upon the United States*- http://govinfo.library.unt.edu/911/report/911Report_Ch3.htm.bak (no page number).
22. Jonathan Randal, *Osama: the Making of a Terrorist*, London: I.B. Tauris, 2006, p. 18.
23. Muhammad Amir Rana, 'Pakistan's Islamist Organisations', p. 79.
24. Muhammad Qasim Zaman, 'Sectarianism in Pakistan: The Radicalisation of Shi'i and Sunni Identities', *Modern Asian Studies*, Vol. 32, No. 3, 1998, pp. 689-716; Arshad M. Abbasi, 'An Islamic Perspective on Conflict

Resolution and the Spectre of Religious Militancy in Pakistan: The Missing Link,' in Shantanu Chakrabarti (ed.), *Searching for Non-Western Roots of Conflict Resolution: Discourses, Norms and Case Studies*, New Delhi: Knowledge World, 2013, p. 75.

25. Murphy, *The Making of Terrorism in Pakistan*, p. 104.
26. Quoted in Khaled Ahmed, *The Indian Express*, 29 June 2013.
27. Jayanta Kumar Ray, *Public Policy and Global Polity*, New Delhi: Radiant, 1977, esp. pp. 57-65. See *Ibid*., pp. 127, 134, for samples of somewhat illogical mindsets of American policymakers on this issue. For astonishing, at times incredible, evidence of such blindness, see Chapter 4, *Ibid*., pp. 143-77.
28. Mohammad Yousaf and Mark Adkin, *The Bear Trap: Afghanistan's Untold Story*, London: Leo Cooper, 1992, p. 97; Robert M. Gates, *From the Shadows: The Ultimate Insider's Story of Five Presidents and How They Won the Cold War*, New York: Simon and Schuster, 1996, p. 321; Gretchen Peters, *The Seeds of Terror: The Taliban, the ISI and the New Opium Wars*, New Delhi: Hachette, 2010, p. 29.
29. John Prados, 'Notes on the CIA's secret war in Afghanistan', *The Journal of American History*, Vol. 89, No. 2, 2002, pp. 467-68; A.Z. Hilali, *US-Pakistan Relationship: Soviet Invasion of Afghanistan*, Hampshire: Ashgate Publishing, 2005, p. 104.
30. Peters, *The Seeds of Terror*, pp. 28, 31-32, 37-38; Dan Brown, *Angels and Demons*, London: Corgi Books, 2001, p. 32.
31. Shahmahmood Miakhel, 'Military Withdrawal: Prospective Scenario for the Region', in Arpita Basu Roy, Binoda Kumar Mishra, and Aliva Mishra (eds.), *International Intervention in Afghanistan: Motives and Approaches*, Delhi: Shipra, 2012, pp. 78-81.
32. Michael Cohen, 'No Win Policy for Afghanistan,' *Dissent*, Vol. 57, No. 2, Spring 2010, p. 8; Allen, *God's Terrorists*, p. 282.
33. Ahmed Rashid, *Descent into Chaos*, New Delhi: Allen Lane, 2008, pp. 38-39.
34. *The 9/11 Commission Report*, New York: Norton, 2004, p. 54.
35. Steve Coll, *Ghost Wars: The Secret History of the CIA, Afghanistan, and Bin Laden, from the Soviet Invasion to September 10, 2001*, New York: Penguin, 2004, pp. 158-59; Rafael Reuveny and Aseem Prakash, 'The Afghanistan war and the breakdown of the Soviet Union', *Review of International Studies*, Vol. 25, No. 4, 1999, pp. 693-708; Artemy Kalinovsky, *A Long Goodbye: Soviet Withdrawal from Afghanistan*, Cambridge: Harvard University Press, 2011; the entire book deserves a thorough reading for imbibing a proper perception of the Soviet retreat from Afghanistan. 'By conservative estimates,' writes Riaz Mohammad Khan, 'over one million Soviet soldiers were exposed to the war and more than fourteen thousand lost their lives.' See Riaz Mohammad Khan, *Afghanistan and Pakistan: Conflict, Extremism and Resistance to Modernity*, New Delhi: Oxford University Press, 2011, p. 30.

36. *The 9/11 Commission Report*, pp. 55-56 and 467; Andrew Hartman, '"The red template": US policy in Soviet occupied Afghanistan', *Third World Quarterly*, Vol. 23, No. 3, 2002, p. 480.
37. Benjamin and Simon, *The Age of Sacred Terror*, pp. 205-06.
38. Murphy, *The Making of Terrorism in Pakistan*, p. 113.
39. Musharraf, *In the Line of Fire*, p. 275. Khan, *Afghanistan and Pakistan: Conflict, Extremism and Resistance to Modernity*, p. 30.
40. *The 9/11 Commission Report*, pp. 55-57.
41. Arif, *Khaki Shadows*, p. 359.
42. Nazif M. Shahrani, 'Factionalism, and the state in Afghanistan', *American Anthropologist*, New Series, Vol. 104, No. 3, 2002, p. 719.
43. Barnett R. Rubin and Abubakar Siddique, 'Resolving the Pakistan-Afghanistan Stalemate,' *Special Report*, United States Institute of Peace, Washington DC, October 2006, p. 9; Adeel Khan, 'Pakhtun Nationalism: From Separation to Integration,' *Asian Ethnicity*, Vol. 14, No. 1, February 2003, pp. 67-83. Humera Iqbal, 'Pak-Afghan Ties in the Light of Pak-US Strategic Dialogue', *Regional Studies*, Islamabad, Vol. XXIX, No. 1, p. 7.
44. Shehzad, 'The State of Islamic Radicalism in Pakistan', p. 190. Also see Hassan Abbas, *Pakistan's Drift into Extremism: Allah, the Army and America's War on Terror*, New York: M.E. Sharpe, 2005, p. 155. Also see Riaz Mohammad Khan for the following comment: 'The idea of Pakistan seeking strategic depth on its western border made little sense by any measure, when its threat perception was almost entirely linked to India.' Khan, *Afghanistan and Pakistan*, p. 54.
45. Although in 1990, Afghanistan was 'in a state of ruin and civil war', Pakistan's plight was 'even worse', because Pakistan 'was left largely on its own to deal with over three million refugees and the deteriorating situation next door.' See Khan, *Afghanistan and Pakistan*, p. 30.
46. Murphy, *The Making of Terrorism in Pakistan*, p. 113; Riedel, *Deadly Embrace*, pp. 41, 47-49, 54; Kamal Matinuddin, *The Taliban Phenomenon, Afghanistan 1994-1997*, Karachi: Oxford University Press, 1999, pp. 20-24; Mohsen M. Milani, 'Iran's Policy Towards Afghanistan', *Middle East Journal*, Vol. 60, No. 2, Spring 2006, p. 239.
47. Arsi Saleem Hashmi, 'Five Years On: Resurgence of Taliban and the Fate of Afghanistan', pp. 31-32; Riedel, *Deadly Embrace*, p. 57; Seth G. Jones, 'The Rise of Afghanistan's Insurgency, State Failure and Jihad', *International Security*, Vol. 32, No. 4, Spring 2008, pp. 11-12; Coll, *Ghost Wars*, p. 239; Allen, *God's Terrorists*, p. 292; Ashok K. Behuria, 'The Rise of Pakistani Taliban and the Response of the State', *Strategic Analysis*, Vol. 31, No. 5, September 2007, p. 702.
48. Allen, *God's Terrorists*, p. 287.
49. *The 9/11 Commission Report*, pp. 57-59. Also see Allen, *God's Terrorists*, p. 287, and Rex A. Hudson, *The Sociology and Psychology of Terrorism: Who Becomes a Terrorist And Why?* Federal Research Division, Library of Congress: Washington, DC, 1999, p. 116. *The China White PaperAugust*

1949, Vols. I & II, Stanford: Stanford University Press, 1967 (a re-issue of an original publication of the United States State Department); Neil Sheehan & others, *The Pentagon Papers*, New York: Bantam Books, 1971.
50. Farwell, *The Pakistan Cauldron*, p. 84.
51. P.R. Rajeshwari, 'US Policy on Terrorism—Part I Case of Harkat Ul Ansar', *Strategic Analysis*, Vol. XXII, No. 7, October 1998, pp. 1060-63.
52. *The 9/11 Commission Report*, pp. 62-65.
53. Allen, *God's Terrorists*, pp. 293-94.
54. *The 9/11 Commission Report*, pp. 69-70.
55. Hudson, *The Sociology And Psychology of Terrorism*, p. 6.
56. Robin Wright, *Los Angeles Times*, 9 August 1998; *The 9/11 Commission Report*, p. 67.
57. Hudson, *The Sociology And Psychology of Terrorism*, pp. 3-4.
58. *Ibid.*, p. 4.
59. Abouhalima was red-haired, and called 'Mahmud the Red': *Ibid.*, p. 78; *National Commission on Terrorist Attacks upon the United States*, Ch. 3 (no page number).
60. *Ibid*; for some interesting biographical details about the Blind Sheikh, Yousef and Salameh, see Hudson, *The Sociology and Psychology of Terrorism*, pp. 78-82.
61. *National Commission on Terrorist Attacks upon the United States*, Ch. 3, (no page number).
62. *Ibid.*
63. *Ibid.*
64. *Ibid.*
65. Wright, *Los Angeles Times*, 9 August 1998.
66. *National Commission on Terrorist Attacks upon the United States*, Ch. 3 (no page number).
67. *Ibid.*
68. *Ibid.*
69. *Ibid.*
70. *Ibid.*
71. *Ibid.*
72. *Ibid.*
73. United States Department of State, *Patterns of Global Terrorism 2000 Report*, Washington DC, 2001, Appendix E; *http://www.state.gov/j/ct/rls/crt/2000/2466.htm* Also see Hudson, *The Sociology and Psychology of Terrorism*, pp. 78, 82.
74. United States Department of State, Patterns of Global Terrorism 2000 Report; *http://www.state.gov/j/ct/rls/crt/2000/*
75. *Ibid.*
76. *Ibid.*
77. *Ibid. http://www.state.gov/j/ct/rls/crt/2000/2432.htm*
78. *Ibid.*
79. *Ibid. http://www.state.gov/j/ct/rls/crt/2000/2438.htm*

80. *The 9/11 Commission Report*, p. 254.
81. *Ibid.*, pp. 254-55.
82. *Ibid.*, pp. 255-56.
83. *Ibid.*, pp. 257-58.
84. *Ibid.*, pp. 258-59.
85. *Ibid.*, pp. 260-62.
86. Wright, *Los Angeles Times*, 9 August 1998.
87. *The 9/11 Commission Report*, p. 17.
88. *Ibid.*, p. 18.
89. *Ibid.*, pp. 18-19.
90. *Ibid.*, pp. 19-21.
91. *Ibid.*, p. 35.
92. *Ibid.*, pp. 36-38.
93. *Ibid.*, pp. 44-46.
94. *Ibid.*, p. 339.
95. *Ibid.*, p. 344.
96. *Ibid.*, p. 345.
97. *Ibid.*, p. 344.
98. *Ibid.*, p. 345.
99. *Ibid.*, p. 347.
100. *Ibid.*, p. 348.
101. *Ibid.*
102. *Ibid.*, p. 340.
103. *Ibid.*, p. 343.

Three

From 9/11 to 5/1

Nine Eleven occurred at a time when Pakistan's relationship with America was far from cordial. For example, when President Bill Clinton had to avail of a brief stopover in Islamabad in 2000, he declined to have a photograph with President Pervez Musharraf. Actually, Clinton was disturbed about Pakistan's nuclear weapons mission, as also about Pakistan's support for jihadis in India's Kashmir. The Clinton government seriously considered a proposal to brand Pakistan as a state sponsor of terrorism. In December 1999, a Pakistani terrorist agency, Harkat-ul-Mujahideen (HUM) was accused of hijacking an Indian commercial aircraft. In the early part of 2000, the American government alerted the Pakistan government that it was worried about the connection between the HUM and the ISI.[1]

Immediately after he learnt about 9/11, Musharraf was deeply perturbed that in case the Al Qaeda had carried out the 9/11 attack, America would not spare Pakistan. For, Al Qaeda had a sanctuary in Taliban-dominated Afghanistan, and Pakistan was the only state having diplomatic relations with the Taliban led by Mullah Omar. Musharraf was presiding over a meeting in Karachi, when he received a phone call from General Colin Powell, the American Secretary of State. Powell rejected Musharraf's request that he would phone Powell later. Musharraf had to get out of the meeting immediately, and talk to Powell, who gave a clear warning as he said: 'You are either with us or against us'. Musharraf 'took this as a blatant ultimatum'. A much more blatant warning, however, was delivered by Richard Armitage, the Deputy Secretary of State, to the Director General of Pakistan's ISI, who was then in Washington, D.C. Armitage repeated

Powell's message that after 9/11, Pakistan had to choose between terrorists and America. But Armitage added, in 'the most undiplomatic statement ever made', that in case Pakistan opted for the terrorists, it 'should be prepared to be bombed back to the Stone Age'.[2]

In response to the American warning, Musharraf claimed to make 'a dispassionate, military-style analysis' of his options, but, as his memoir reveals, this analysis sometimes verged on a ridiculous over-simplification. For example, Musharraf weighed the option of confronting America (!), and concluded that confrontation was not feasible, because Pakistan would be unable to cope with an American offensive militarily, economically and socially. Nevertheless, Musharraf was pragmatic when he brought in the India factor. He was apprehensive that if Pakistan did not join America, India would, and create difficulties for Pakistan, especially on the Kashmir issue. Moreover, Musharraf was fearful that, in case of a confrontation, America would grab the opportunity to eliminate Pakistan's nuclear weapons capability, because America was never 'comfortable with a Muslim country acquiring nuclear weapons.' Musharraf was further worried, that in this process, the hard-earned parity with India gained by Pakistan due to the possession of a nuclear armoury would be decimated. Nuclear tests by Pakistan, again, had resulted in 1998 in an isolation of Pakistan from the international community. This could be dissolved if Pakistan joined America after 9/11.[3]

An alliance with America—inescapable though it was after 9/11—posed severe domestic problems for Musharraf. Extremist/ terrorist groups (which were also anti-American) were gaining ground in Pakistan (as already noted in this study) for decades, especially since the time of General Zia-ul Haq. These groups were very powerful in the North West Frontier Province (NWFP—currently renamed Khyber Pakhtunkhwa). Taliban's domination over Afghanistan (as already mentioned in this study) spread extremism not only in Pakistan-Afghanistan borderlands, but also in other parts of Pakistan. Musharraf, therefore, had to prepare himself for a highly adverse domestic reaction to Pakistan's post 9/11 alliance with America. In the 1990s, Pakistan's extremist/terrorist forces were favourably disposed towards the government, because the Pakistan government systematically used these forces for anti-Indian operations in Kashmir as also for enhancement/consolidation of Pashtun control over

Afghanistan. Post 9/11, the situation changed dramatically, because Musharraf wanted to use American economic-technical support to curb terrorism inside his country, and shrewd observers in Taliban and Al Qaeda could not have been unaware of this.[4]

Remarkably, Laden did not fail to take precautionary steps against a probable American offensive in Afghanistan following 9/11. He aimed to build a sanctuary for himself and his followers among Pashtun tribesmen in the Pakistan-Afghanistan border areas, e.g., the Tora Bora mountains in Afghanistan, and Pakistan's Waziristan. He had plenty of money to win over the tribesmen. For instance, Laden paid as much as US$ 250 a month to tribal recruits to Al Qaeda—a fabulous sum in that inaccessible region of forests and mountains with negligible employment opportunities. Laden also paid handsomely high rents for compounds used as shelters by his followers fleeing Afghanistan. In the 1980s, the CIA contributed to the construction of caves in the Tora Bora mountains. Interestingly, these could serve as Laden's headquarters inside the sanctuary provided by Pashtuns. Whereas the American troops attacked Tora Bora in the early days of December 2001, and Al Qaeda's defence in Tora Bora collapsed on 16 December 2001, the number of invading American troops was so small—only 1300—that Laden and his followers could escape to Waziristan, especially with the solid support of Pakistani troops. In March 2002, again, America launched a major attack in the Shahi Kot Valley of Afghanistan, which led to the flight of a large number of terrorists (under Laden's command) to Waziristan. Subsequently, Laden relocated his headquarters in South Waziristan.[5]

Such success registered by America was, of course, facilitated by Pakistan. For, despite all the bluff and bluster in his *Memoir*, Musharraf had no option but to accede to America's demands in the wake of 9/11. It had to permit America, for instance, to use the Shamsi base in Balochistan, and the Jacobabad base in Sindh. Pakistan had to close down its embassy in the Taliban territory of Afghanistan, and the Taliban had to wind up its consulates in Pakistan. Also, Pakistan tried to persuade Taliban to extradite Laden to America. But it failed, just as previously Saudi Arabia failed to have Laden extradited to his birth place. Musharraf knew that this surrender of Laden to America would save death and destruction in Afghanistan as a result of an American invasion. But the thoughts of Taliban and

Al Qaeda were in a different realm. They imagined that God would defeat America in case it encroached upon Afghan territory, just as God punished America on 9/11. Musharraf worried that the Frankenstein created by Pakistan and America during the anti-Soviet jihad—the Mujahids, the Taliban and Al Qaeda—which had already contaminated the Pakistani polity and society, would further magnify instability in Pakistan by adding to the number of several million Afghan refugees already in Pakistan in case of an American offensive in Afghanistan. Moreover, in such a situation, hard core Taliban and Al Qaeda militants would swamp Pakistan. America set 7 October 2001 as the deadline for Laden's handover. On the expiry of this deadline, the inevitable took place: the carpet-bombing of Taliban territory in Afghanistan.[6]

As claimed by Musharraf in his *Memoir*, Pakistan 'did more than any other country to capture and kill members of Al Qaeda, and to destroy its infrastructure in our cities and mountains.'[7] For Pakistan, this also happened to be a profitable operation. The Government of Pakistan earned millions of dollars as rewards from America by arresting 689 Al Qaeda terrorists and by deporting 369 terrorists to America.[8] But Musharraf's claim was tainted by exaggeration. For, Al Qaeda continued to carry out atrocities in Pakistan. On 23 January 2002, for instance, Daniel Pearl, an American journalist, was kidnapped in Karachi, and on 21 February, a videotape of his gruesome slaughter was circulated. Subsequently, after his body was exhumed, it was found that his body had been sliced into ten pieces. On 17 March 2002, Al Qaeda showered hand grenades on worshippers at the Protestant International Church in Islamabad, killing six and injuring 42 persons (including the Ambassador from Sri Lanka). On 5 August 2002, Al Qaeda targeted a Christian school in Murree, but failed to kill anyone except the guard, whose alertness and self-sacrifice saved the children. Again, on 9 August 2002, Al Qaeda threw grenades at worshippers in a church inside a Christian hospital in Taxila, killing five and injuring 20.[9]

An important reason why Al Qaeda not only survived, but flourished despite onslaughts by America and Pakistan, who were allies in the war on terror following 9/11, was a sort of mini-mutiny in the Pakistani military provoked by this America-Pakistan alliance. A substantial number of Pakistani military officers and soldiers shared the belief that the 9/11 attacks were due to a conspiracy of Jews against Muslims, and not due to Al Qaeda manoeuvres. This was hardly a surprise. For, years later, on 11 September 2013, in a stunning testimony to the prevalent Pakistani mindset, Professor Mujahid Kamran, Vice Chancellor of Punjab University, Lahore, argued at the launch of his book, *9/11 and the New World Order*, that CIA used Al Qaeda as an asset of its own. He supported his argument by referring to 350 web-links and declassified documents. The Vice Chancellor made an extraordinary claim: a coterie of bankers controlled American and British governments, and they influenced the whole world by inserting microchips in the brains of human beings. No wonder that when Musharraf joined President Bush in fighting Al Qaeda, the above noted Pakistani military personnel went so far as to leave their jobs, departed for Afghanistan, and reinforced the anti-American resistance movement. Afghan militants benefited immensely from military assistance provided by former members of the Pakistani defence forces. Musharraf certainly fought Al Qaeda in collaboration with America. But, despite American pressure, he refrained from carrying out large scale military actions in territories inhabited by Al Qaeda operatives. By February 2003, however, the situation became rather intractable as America supplied to Pakistan a list of 53 Al Qaeda suspects allegedly residing in South Waziristan. America threatened that its forces would disregard the border to march into this territory, unless Pakistan visibly commenced a major armed operation there. Still, Musharraf failed to overcome his hesitation. He was indeed lucky. For, the situation was saved by the arrest from Rawalpindi of Al Qaeda's military chief, Khalid Sheikh Mohammed, who was number three in the Al Qaeda hierarchy, and who had supposedly planned 9/11.[10]

Another significant reason why Al Qaeda and Taliban continued to flourish in Afghanistan and Pakistan despite the war on terror launched by American and NATO forces was the invasion of Iraq by America and Britain in 2003. Even without being a policy maker, one is entitled to exercise common sense and ask the question about who benefited from this new war in Iraq in the midst of the old war in Afghanistan, which was not progressing well despite the quick expulsion of the Taliban from Kabul. One obvious explanation for this lack of adequate progress was Pakistan's half-hearted cooperation with America, which enabled the Taliban to preserve its organisation and wait for another day to regroup and take the offensive. As to the beneficiaries of the invasion of Iraq, the notable were the private military enterprises (PMEs), e.g. Brown & Root, DynCorps, Haliburton, etc. which participated on a large scale in this war. PMEs employed highly trained, but retired military personnel at emoluments much higher than those of regular military recruits. Their financial benefits were obvious. Not so obvious but easily comprehensible were the benefits of American legislators, who depended for their election expenses on companies linked to PMEs, and thriving on American government military contracts. To some American scholars, this interpretation may appear to be somewhat uncharitable, but this alone leads to an understanding of the rationale of the Second Gulf War in conformity with a minimum of common sense.[11]

Yet another major reason why Al Qaeda and (its ally) Taliban continued to function and grow in Afghanistan and Pakistan-Afghanistan borderlands was a serious diplomatic failure on the part of America and its allies engaged simultaneously in the war on terror and the establishment of an interim administration in Afghanistan conducive to a democratic evolution of the country. The exclusion of any Taliban representative from the process leading to the Bonn Agreement of 5 December 2001 underlined this diplomatic failure. For, the Bonn Agreement not only led to the installation of a transitional administration in Afghanistan (with Hamid Karzai as the Chairman) but also of an International Security Assistance Force (ISAF) sanctioned by the United Nations. What America and its allies failed to realise was that the military power of America and NATO would not be adequate to build enduring peace and stability in Afghanistan. For, ethnic fractures (e.g. Pashtuns vs Tajiks) as also tensions between a central government and regional authorities (especially warlords) persisted, despite the adoption of a democratic constitution on 4 January 2004, elections to a bicameral central legislature in September, and the presidential election of October 2004 (which Karzai won fairly and handsomely). Therefore, the Taliban and Al Qaeda continued to flourish, and the writ of Karzai's government did not seem to run much beyond Kabul. Corruption and maladministration appeared to be incurable. The promised economic support from the international community fell far short of requirements, and could hardly compensate for lack of governance. Moreover, the UN Security Council Resolutions 1267 and 1333 critically endangered any broad based quest for political stability in Afghanistan by equating the Taliban (confined more or less to Afghanistan and Afghanistan-Pakistan borderland) with Al Qaeda, which had a worldwide network, but profited immensely from Taliban support. The UN labelled both these groups as terrorist, froze their assets, and prohibited any political contacts with them, which could have been oriented towards long term peace-building in Afghanistan.[12]

Since Pakistan's ISI had developed extraordinarily close relations with the Taliban over a long period of time, it was not prepared to equate Taliban with Al Qaeda. Nor was it ready to assume that some sections of the Taliban should not be approached for mutually convenient diplomatic deals. The ISI, therefore, patronised a group called Jamiatul Khudamul Koran, which, the ISI believed, comprised those Taliban—the so-called good Taliban—who did not endorse Mullah Omar's grant of a sanctuary to Osama Bin Laden. Remarkably, some officers of America's CIA, too, set up Jaishul Muslim, consisting of a Taliban group, which was expected to rise above Mullah Omar's influence. Both these groups functioned for some time in Afghanistan. A third group of the supposed-to-be-good Taliban, headed by Mullah Abdul Razzaq and based in Quetta, carried on discussions with America on how to initiate a truce. All these groups received ample amounts of money and even training. But they all betrayed, and joined hands with the so-called bad Taliban or the blind followers of Mullah Omar.[13]

General Musharraf also tried conciliation with the Taliban in Pakistan's tribal areas on the border with Afghanistan. He had a meeting with tribal leaders, and requested them to stop sheltering Al Qaeda members, who were foreigners. Musharraf even proposed that foreigners would be granted amnesty, provided they desisted from attacking American and Afghan soldiers. As this proposal was not accepted, Musharraf had no alternative to an exercise of the military option in South Waziristan, which amounted to the deployment of 6,000 regular soldiers and paramilitary troops in mid-March 2004. On 16 March, however, these Pakistani forces suffered a huge setback in two places near Wana, the regional capital, i.e., in Kaloosha and Shin Warsak. A large number of regular soldiers died or got injured, whereas paramilitary troops sought safety in flight, without having the courage even to carry their weapons. Again, in a few days, on 22 March, militant tribals ambushed an army convoy, and slaughtered all the soldiers in a place near Wana, i.e., Sarwaki. In all these successful operations against Pakistani forces, Nek Mohammed (a Waziri) was the commander, ably supported by Tahir Yuldashev, who headed the Islamic Movement of Uzbekistan (IMU), but at that time, he was helping the Taliban in Pakistan's border area with Afghanistan. On 28 March, Pakistani soldiers withdrew from Kaloosha and Shin Warsak. Significantly, in Islamabad, the famous Lal Masjid's clerics declared that the fight against Pakistani forces in Waziristan was a jihad, and asked the parents of deceased soldiers not to offer Islamic burial to their sons. Parents obeyed the clerics, declining even to touch the bodies.[14]

On 24 April 2004, Pakistani authorities had to eat a humble pie, and enter into a peace deal. They reportedly tried to buy off militant tribals by a payment of fifty million rupees to be ostensibly used to repay the debt owed by these tribals to Al Qaeda. In return, tribals promised to renounce militancy, and opt for peaceful ways. But it was not possible for their leader, Nek Mohammed, who earned a lot of money from Al Qaeda by organising training camps for the Taliban, to honour this deal. In June 2004, he issued a proclamation of war against Pakistan. Perhaps coincidentally, on 10 June 2004, in a non-tribal area, Musharraf had to witness Lieutenant Governor General Ahsan Saleem Hayat, the Corps Commander in Karachi, becoming a target of attempted liquidation. He survived, but eight persons, including his driver, were killed. Hayat escaped by sheer luck. For example, the phone meant for triggering an explosive device did not work. But, on 18 June 2004, an American drone (reportedly with Pakistani collaboration) fired a missile to eliminate Nek Mohammed. Haji Omar, who succeeded him, extorted as much as US$ 540,000 from Pakistani authorities before he and his followers agreed to surrender. Nevertheless, Musharraf suffered a terrorist blow in a non-tribal area on 30 July 2004, when Pakistan's Finance Minister, Shaukat Aziz, escaped assassination by sheer chance as he turned inside the car to talk to another person and he was only hit by hot air, while a suicide bomber exploded himself to death. In early 2005, again, the Pakistani military concluded another financial deal, i.e., with Baitullah

Mehsud. By such payments, the Pakistan government ensured, more or less, the safety of South Waziristan from militant outbreaks.[15]

But, whether in tribal or non-tribal territories, nothing could stop the forward march of terrorism inside Pakistan. Musharraf himself was exposed to two unsuccessful assassination attempts—on 14 December 2003, and 25 December 2005. In North Waziristan, Pakistani forces confronted serious assaults by terrorist tribals, even though, as noted above, in South Waziristan, they seemed to win a respite by simply buying off militants. On 1 January 2006, for instance, terrorists in North Waziristan struck at a security outpost by way of retaliation against an American drone attack on a Muslim priest's residence. On 13 January, again, there was an unsuccessful American air attack upon a suspected hideout of Al Zawahiri, a top ranking Al Qaeda leader. On 1 March, helicopters of the Pakistan Army launched an attack upon a madarasa in North Waziristan, killing forty people and injuring many. Immediately afterwards, on 2 March 2006, there was a suicide assault upon the American embassy as a revenge. The story of retaliation and counter-retaliation was uninterrupted. On 9 March, a well-known rural madarasa in North Waziristan suffered an attack for sheltering militants. It was evident by early 2006 that Pakistani Taliban (as distinct from, though in alliance with, the Afghan Taliban) wielded enormous influence in tribal areas, even introducing a penal code in certain areas—for example, by way of prohibiting music. Actually, in mid-2006, the Taliban (including the Pakistani Taliban) appeared to be far more powerful than Al Qaeda, especially by availing of the services of retired military/intelligence personnel of Pakistan, who happened to be veterans of the 1979-89 anti-Soviet jihad.[16]

Meanwhile, in Afghanistan, despite apparently impressive international commitments, the situation continued to remain unstable at best. If the Taliban was getting more and more powerful in Pakistan, as noted above, so was it in Afghanistan. The elusiveness of effective central government in Afghanistan was nothing unfamiliar. Nor were chronic ethnic divisions and conflicts. But the torrent of global terror and the America-led war on terror constituted a historically unprecedented situation, as did the presence of the UN, especially the UNAMA (the United Nations Assistance Mission in Afghanistan). Even the creation of a semblance of stability required a proper utilisation of international economic aid on a very large scale, but assurances offered by the 2002 donors' conference in Tokyo, for example, were not fulfilled. Another donors' conference met in Berlin in 2004. Next, fifty one donors assembled in London in 2006, and formulated an Afghanistan Compact, which ambitiously attempted to harmonise development, governance and security. But the result was thoroughly dissatisfactory. Actual aid was much less than the promised amount. Reconstruction of the Afghan economy was the most urgent task before the world community. But it suffered mainly because of inadequacy of funds—despite allowances for corruption and malgovernance. A comparison of expenditure by America's Department of Defence from 2001 to 2009 (for instance) with assistance committed by donors for Afghanistan from 2002 to 2011 can make this glaring. The former stood at US$ 173 billion whereas the latter amounted to about US$ 25 billion.[17]

It is pertinent to refer at this point to the role of Pakistan in the first five years (2001-2006) of the America-led war on terrorism in Afghanistan. Remarkably, Pakistan avoided direct and comprehensive entanglement in this war, and yet continued to receive bounties from America. America had no option. It was apprehensive that any appreciable enlargement of Pakistan's participation in the war in Afghanistan might create too dangerous a political instability in Pakistan. For, Islamist radicals, who were (as noted above) already very powerful in Pakistan, might use the enhancement of Pakistani role in the Afghan war to portray its rulers as anti-Islam and try thereby to destabilise the government. Using the Pakistan-Afghanistan border region as their sanctuary, Islamist radicals might even succeed in this venture, and in a worst case scenario, gain access to the nuclear armoury. Moreover, America's military leaders had the firm belief that, without Pakistani support, however limited and grudging, military operations in Afghanistan had very little chance of success, especially because of safe havens enjoyed by the Taliban inside Pakistan.[18]

Remarkably, by 2006, American military operations in Afghanistan became more difficult because the Afghan warriors travelled from the Afghanistan-Pakistan border region to learn terrorist tactics from the Al Qaeda in Iraq, which emerged as a centre of Sunni insurgency led by Abu Musab Al Zarqawi. Starting his carrier as a roadside hooligan, Zarqawi transformed himself into an Al Qaeda chieftain to lead Sunni militants in Iraq. Zarqawi, interestingly, roused the battle-averse Iraqi Sunnis initially against Shias, and subsequently, incited them to attack Americans, who then discovered a new rationale for their military role in Iraq. For, the old justification for this role, e.g., the possession of weapons of mass destruction (WMDs) by Iraq and enveloping the Middle East by a democratic cover, no longer attracted any support inside America or elsewhere. Zarqawi's macabre tactics, however, led to prolonged Shia-Sunni civil war in Iraq. Although there was an election in Iraq in January 2005, the new government was naturally dominated by the Shias, who also had their terrorist groups to fight Sunnis, who happened to be numerically in a minority in Iraq. Al Qaeda, it must be noted, attracted Sunni militants from other countries, e.g., Saudi Arabia and Libya, to Iraq, and perfected the technique of suicide bombing. Eventually, they even succeeded in enlisting women and children in the suicide squads. Al Qaeda used to launch attacks on Shia religious places and clerics as a matter of routine. But the spectacular attack in February 2006 on the most famous Shia shrine in the world, i.e. the Golden Mosque of Samarra, was a turning point. For, after this episode, the Shia-Sunni civil war developed an irreversible momentum. The American military presence merely added fuel to the fire, because insurgents had the burning desire to emancipate Iraq from the clutches of non-Muslim invaders. Iraq experienced, by far, the largest number of suicide missions in current history during the first decade of the twenty-first century, and Afghan insurgents undoubtedly learned a trick or two from Al Qaeda trainers before they returned to their home territory.[19]

A question that should haunt policy makers and researchers for a long time is why, for instance, in the FY (financial year) 2007 and FY 2008, America was planning to spend as much as (even though the final figures would naturally vary) US$ 564 billion for the war on terror in Iraq, and only US$ 155 billion in Afghanistan.[20] Inadequacy of funds (as already mentioned above) was the primary cause of lack of economic development in Afghanistan, which could not but hinder nation building, and delay (if not frustrate) the attainment of political normalcy (not to speak of stability). The same reason stalled the prevention of use of drug money by Afghan terrorists.[21] This grant of priority to Iraq—at the expense of Afghanistan—could be explained (at least partially) by the interest of American corporations in Iraq's vital natural resource, i.e., oil.[22] But Afghanistan too was rich in natural resources, e.g., copper and iron. The relative (though evident) downgrading of Afghanistan, the original site of America's war on terror, may therefore need an explanation that can be deemed to be less than charitable. Perhaps, America did not mind Afghanistan remaining submerged in its historically chronic ethnic rivalries and political instability (aggravated by jihad), so that terrorists would tend to pay less and less attention to the American homeland. At any rate, such an explanation can be traced to the following observation by President Bush: 'We are fighting these terrorists with our military in Afghanistan and Iraq and beyond so we do not have to face them in the streets of our own cities.'[23]

If America failed to register appreciable progress in nation building activities inside Afghanistan, its principal partner in the war on terror in Afghanistan, i.e., Pakistan itself appeared to be unable to curb militancy on the home ground. The basic cause for this was the failure of the Pakistani ruling elite, especially the military, to distinguish between the promotion of short term apparent interests and long term real interests of the country. In order to take care of real long term interests (including the development of a democratic culture), the Pakistan government had to curb Taliban activities, especially in the FATA, where Pakistani Taliban not only shielded the Afghan Taliban, but also took part in the war against ISAF inside Afghanistan, and gradually spread its network beyond FATA to non-tribal areas of Pakistan. A large number of Pakistan's civilian decision makers and a few military leaders wanted to subdue the Taliban, but their voices were weaker than the voices of those, who wanted to court the Taliban not only for retaining/enhancing influence in Afghanistan, but also for using the Taliban in the proxy war against India. Even America failed as early as 1998 to activate the Pakistan government to prevail upon the Taliban and Al Qaeda to refrain from launching an imminent attack upon America. But, as documents declassified in 2013 reveal, the Pakistan government confessed that its efforts at persuasion did not normally suffice to overcome the obstinate tendency of these militant outfits to reject any call for cooperation.[24] What was true in the late 1990s was also true in the first decade of the twenty-first century. The Pakistan government failed even to prompt itself to checkmate the Taliban, despite obvious signs of infectious intensification of militancy inside the Pakistani homeland.[25]

The government failed to propel itself to act sternly against Pakistani Taliban, which proved itself to be capable of committing greater atrocities than the Afghan Taliban. For example, Pashtuns had great respect for some holy places, which were monuments to Sufi saints. But the Pakistani Taliban destroyed them. They diminished the authority of the government by slaughtering a large number of police officers, and forcing many police and other government officials to leave their jobs. The efficiency that the Pakistan government under Musharraf demonstrated at the commencement of America's war on terror by capturing a number of Al Qaeda leaders stood in sharp contrast to its subsequent acquiescence in the ruthless activities of the Pakistani Taliban. Instead of using security agencies to wipe out the Pakistani Taliban, Musharraf deployed them to persecute rebels in Balochistan, including highly educated persons, many of whom disappeared never to return to their families. Relatives of such persons urged upon the Supreme Court of Pakistan for remedial action. When Chief Justice Iftikhar Mohammed Chaudhry began to plead for an end to gross violation of human rights, Musharraf summoned him to his office in March 2007, forced him to resign, and appointed a new Chief Justice.[26]

The unwarranted dismissal of Chief Justice Chaudhry created a political crisis for Musharraf, who confronted an agitation for the restoration of democracy by means of installation of a civilian government based on free elections. The agitation, spearheaded by lawyers that rocked important cities of Pakistan, took place at a time when, unluckily for Musharraf, the country was already facing a predicament brought about by Islamist radicals under the influence of Al Qaeda as also Afghan and Pakistani Taliban. In his memoir, published in 2006, Musharraf boasted that, since 9/11, he succeeded in sapping the military and organisational strength of Al Qaeda.[27] But events in the central locality of Islamabad in 2007 belied this tall claim. These events took place in and around Lal Masjid (Red Mosque), which virtually grew up along with the new capital city of Islamabad since the middle of 1960s. President Zia showered patronage on the chief priest of Lal Masjid, Maulana Muhammad

Abdullah, who recruited Mujahids for the anti-Soviet jihad in Afghanistan. Abdullah also recruited jihadis for operations in Kashmir. With Saudi as well as Pakistani financial support, Abdullah established two madrasas, one for boys (Jamia Fareedia), and another for girls (Jamia Hafsa). They were built on the land belonging to the Capital Development Authority (CDA) of Islamabad, which ignored the encroachment till 2007, when, as noted below, the situation took a serious turn. Gradually, Lal Masjid emerged as a centre of Islamist radicals, including female activists. The death of Abdullah in 1998 (in the hands of suspected Shia assassins) saw his sons Abdul Aziz and Abdul Rashid Gazi running the mosque with equal religious fervour. In fact, after Musharraf joined America in the post-9/11 war on terror, Aziz and Rashid turned Lal Masjid into a centre of resistance against Musharraf, who was dubbed as a puppet of America. The two brothers propagated and planned the replacement of the existing Pakistani political system by a Sharia-ruled system.[28]

A few weeks before the ruthless removal of Chief Justice Chaudhry and the resultant mass protests, militants staying inside the Lal Masjid complex (including women wearing burkas, but carrying clubs) rushed out to nearby streets. They ransacked shops which, they thought, engaged in un-Islamic activities, e.g., sale of video cassettes. This happened in February 2007. In the following months, due to Musharraf government's indecision, despite criticisms by liberals (including media persons), the mosque-bred Islamists went so far as to attack government offices and kidnapped police functionaries; thus, translating into action their oft-repeated calls for jihad. The Lal Masjid trained suicide bombers (including women), and the Musharraf regime worried that any tough action against rampaging militants might provoke suicide squads, and produce incalculable chaos. Although the government (including the military) patronised the entire Lal Masjid establishment in the past, their patience broke down in the first week of July 2007, because they became afraid that Lal Masjid militants might succeed in acquiring in popular eyes a position of dominance in Islamabad. So, on 3 July 2007, the military surrounded the Masjid with barbed wire, imposed curfew, and shut off electricity and gas supplies. The military had no option, because even the intervention of the Imam of Ka'aba in Mecca, who came to Islamabad for persuading the Lal

Masjid clerics to abandon confrontation with the government, did not succeed.[29]

In the night of 3 July 2007, the Pakistan army launched a limited attack, but faced a stout resistance from the Masjid's militants, who, after all, had training as guerrilla fighters in Afghanistan and Kashmir. They used sand bags and even bunkers. Pakistani commandos could create fissures in the boundary walls of the Masjid, but postponed the final assault because of the expectation that, simultaneously with the use of force, announcements for surrender broadcast by loudspeakers might be fruitful. Actually, the announcements appeared to succeed in securing the surrender of all the female inmates of the mosque (as also many of male inmates). As burka-clad women surrendered, one of them, curiously, happened to be Abdul Aziz, who was arrested on 4 July. In course of the limited encounters, some soldiers lost their lives. This strengthened the case for final showdown, which took place on 7-9 July 2007, climaxing a week of continuous firing by militants from inside the mosque, who succeeded in killing one and injuring two officers on 9 July. Deadly onslaughts by Pakistan's commando brigade led to many deaths (the exact figure was not revealed by the government) and reduced large parts of Lal Masjid to rubble. But a military cordon prevented the public from having any glimpse. Amidst the rubble lay petrol bombs, machine guns, suicide vests, antitank mines, rocket propelled grenade launchers, etc. Preparations for jihad were indeed comprehensive. Its collapse in Lal Masjid marked a turning point as Al Qaeda leader, Osama Bin Laden, vowed retaliation against Musharraf and the Pakistan government for the first time and openly. Laden's deputy, Ayman Al Zawahiri revealed the true character of the jihad when he directed that the first target of jihad should be un-Islamic Muslim states like Musharraf's Pakistan. The next target would be the military of non-Islamic states.[30]

If the response of Al Qaeda to the Lal Masjid skirmishes highlighted the fearsome international implications, the domestic ones were no less serious. These clashes upset a lot of the wishful thinking of Pakistan's ruling elite (as also of Americans) about the Pakistan Taliban (with manifold links to Al Qaeda). First, the patronage (or at any rate acquiescence) extended invisibly to the Pakistani Taliban (which escaped any official ban) failed to keep it confined to the

FATA. Irrespective of how much influence was exercised by lack of development and/or democracy in FATA on the growth of militancy among the youth, the fact that students from the FATA formed a majority of Lal Masjid militants, who did not hesitate to sacrifice their lives for infecting even the capital city of Islamabad with Talibanisation, was indeed striking. Secondly, Musharraf should have probably permitted some mainstream political parties to operate in FATA and try to curb religious fanaticism. Instead, Musharraf looked away hoping that the rest of Pakistan would remain immune, despite the experiences at the end of anti-Soviet jihad in Afghanistan (which has been previously noted in this study), when the Pakistani Taliban leaders set up their separate (though small) spheres of Sharia rule. Disunity of these leaders, and the absence of any central command structure, did not prevent the spread of Islamist governance in their own fiefdoms (however tiny). Thirdly, the fond belief that the Pakistan government would be able to take advantage of unsettled times, and use the Pakistani Taliban to consolidate its influence in FATA as also Afghanistan, without affecting the larger Pakistani polity adversely, proved to be illusory. Three peace deals between Pakistani security forces and the militants—the first in 2004 with the Ahmadzai Wazir militants in South Waziristan, the second with Baitullah Mehsud in 2005, and the third with North Waziristan's Haqqani network and Al-Qaeda in 2006—turned out to be infructuous. They gave a free rein to militants, who expanded their influence so much as to bring, by 2007, the capital of North West Frontier Province (NWFP) under a state of besiegement.[31]

In the aftermath of the Lal Masjid clashes, moreover, the Pakistan government realised how one can reap the whirlwind by sowing the wind. Pakistani Taliban leaders began to shed their disunity even though the process of formal unification of forty groups naturally took a few months. This move contributed to a tremendous rise in terrorism inside Pakistan. Tribal leaders in northwest Pakistan proclaimed a jihad against the Pakistan military and the government. As early as in two days following the final collision at Lal Masjid, on 12 July 2007, armed with deadly weapons, twenty thousand tribals staged a demonstration at Bajaur in northwest Pakistan. They shouted slogans calling for death to Musharraf and Americans. In NWFP alone in 2007, there were 460 terrorist attacks causing death to 1,096 persons and injuries to 1,593. Suicide bombers killed hundreds of people throughout Pakistan—including soldiers. Even high security areas in cities like Islamabad were not spared, and commandos specialising in counter-terrorism operations were killed. Apparently, retired Pakistan army officers helped the jihadis, who had the guts to circulate video cassettes of cases of successful slaughter by the Taliban, as also to appear on national television channels to declare the success of jihad. Again, despite a government ban, there was a large scale distribution of jihadi literature and radio transmissions urging upon the common men to join the jihad against the government.[32]

This was the time when Musharraf had to preserve mental steadiness and refrain from doing anything that could cause a setback to America's plans to advance democracy in Pakistan and other Muslim countries. But he did just the reverse. On 3 November 2007, Musharraf defied the Constitution and assumed Emergency powers. The military's reaction could not be assessed—clearly or immediately. After all, suicide strikes by militants left the armed forces in a state of demoralisation. The American response, again, left much to be desired. Condoleezza Rice, the US Secretary of State, depicted the imposition of Emergency as 'highly regrettable', but did not denounce it in a straightforward manner. Somewhat awkwardly, Rice even praised Musharraf for doing 'a lot' in the past to pave the way to 'democratic rule' in Pakistan. General Hamid Gul, a former ISI chief, already known for his opposition to Pakistan's participation in America's war on terror, condemned Musharraf for his attempt to save his own position while endangering that of the country. He did not mince words as he observed that Musharraf opted not for Emergency but actually for martial law. A large number of Judges of the Supreme Court of Pakistan, including Chief Justice Iftikhar M. Chaudhry issued an order overruling the declaration of Emergency. But they were removed from the Court by security forces, whereas Abdul Hamid Dogar, a new Chief Justice, annulled their order.[33]

Musharraf seemed to suffer from a sense of desperation. He did not hesitate to use the proclamation of Emergency to suspend a number of fundamental rights conferred by the Constitution of Pakistan upon citizens, e.g., rights to life and liberty, freedom of speech, equality before law, assembly in public, protection of property, etc. Moreover, anyone could be arrested without any information about his/her offence. Emergency rules restricted reporting by the media of militant activities, including suicide strikes. India expressed regret over the imposition of emergency. But Musharraf hardly bothered. He did not even care for the reaction of America, which had advised Musharraf several weeks back not to impose Emergency. Neither India nor America could probably think of a better alternative to Musharraf for the preservation of peace, however uneasy. Musharraf appeared to set arbitrary terms even in a state of desperation. He had the alibi that in order to cope with a virtual civil war, and launch effective military attacks upon the Al Qaeda and Taliban, he needed Emergency powers. To some extent, again, Emergency was Musharraf's riposte to pressures for the grant of permission to American and NATO forces to move from Afghanistan into Pakistan for the liquidation of Al Qaeda and Taliban.[34]

If the imposition of Emergency could be deemed to be a coup, its author, Pervez Musharraf, was probably not as confident as he was in October 1999, when he staged a coup to oust a duly elected Prime Minister. For, in the intervening eight years, Musharraf's principal prop, the army, became weak on account of a number of reasons. The army was mauled severely by terrorist groups, which alleged that the government was in collusion with anti-Islamist American forces. Some soldiers even capitulated before terrorist onslaughts. The army thus suffered from demoralisation and disunity. In such an unpropitious circumstance, Musharraf was trying to cling to two posts somewhat awkwardly: the posts of the President and the Army Chief. This required a political finesse, which was not expected from Musharraf with his military background and temperament. Perhaps, he could have avoided the political opprobrium of Emergency if he was able to muster the art of political adjustment with civilian stakeholders. He was not. Consequently, he alienated not only his Western patrons but also the ordinary people of Pakistan, who were victims of poverty and inflation, and who were not convinced by Musharraf's argument that he had to assume greater powers by means of Emergency to fight Islamist militants. For, the most visible effect of Emergency was the employment of security forces to arrest human rights campaigners and opposition leaders.[35]

Musharraf, like his military predecessors, left no stone unturned to cause the near-decimation of all other public institutions in the country, while preserving and enriching the military, which continued to enjoy unwarranted power and privileges. Whereas America relied on the military, the situation on the border was not at all compatible with what America wanted to achieve in the war on terror. In Khyber Pakhtunkhwa (the NWFP), Maulana Fazlur Rahman's JUI was the dominant partner in the ruling coalition. It had pronouncedly Islamist leanings, and the strength of terrorist groups showed no sign of diminution on the Pakistan-Afghanistan border. Following the declaration of Emergency, the Pakistan government asked three journalists from Britain to leave the country. Interestingly, the concerned newspaper labelled Musharraf as a 'son of a bitch'. It was not far different from a YouTube Video, posted by a Pakistani, which had the tantalising title 'Ek Sala General'. *The San Fransisco Chronicle*, however, went much further by using the facts supplied by two reputed authors: Adrian Levy and Catherine Scott-Clark. Their major contention was that Musharraf was a terrorist, who, in his earlier career as a commando leader, was responsible for spreading terrorism in such countries as Afghanistan and India.[36]

If the battle of Lal Masjid (July 2007) was looked upon as a jihad by the Masjid's inmates, it marked only the commencement of a much greater jihad in different parts of Pakistan. For, the leaders of Lal Masjid, Aziz and Rashid, had close contacts with such powerful militant leaders as Mullah Fazlullah of the Swat Valley, and Baitullah Mehsud of South Waziristan. Rashid died in the course of military action against Lal Masjid. This enraged Fazlullah, who decided to take revenge. In a radio address on 12 July 2007, Fazlullah declared jihad against the Pakistan government. A large number of soldiers were killed in a few days by direct attacks on a convoy, roadside bombs, as also suicide squads. In a few weeks, on 3 August 2007, Baitullah's men too took on an army convoy. They captured a huge assortment of arms, seventeen vehicles, and 260 soldiers, including nine officers, who, amazingly, did not even try to fight. They tamely surrendered, bringing deep humiliation to the mighty Pakistan army. The government further discredited itself by continuing negotiations for weeks to get the release of soldiers detained by Baitullah, whereas Baitullah himself did not order the stoppage of attacks, including suicide attacks. Eventually, the government acceded to all demands of Baitullah Mehsud, e.g. the release of thirty militants under government detention, and only then, soldiers (except a few already killed under detention) won their release on 4 November 2007. Soon afterwards, misreading the government's mind, Baitullah's men staged a large number of attacks upon military installations. This led to massive retaliation by the army and air force, which destroyed large areas of South Waziristan under Baitullah's domination. Although Baitullah could not be arrested, 200,000 people became internally displaced persons. But terrorism in Pakistan reached a sort of climax on 27 December 2007, when Benazir Bhutto (who had been the country's Prime Minister three times) was killed, although she survived another attack earlier in the same month.[37]

The month of December 2007 was extraordinarily important in the history of terrorism inside Pakistan. In this month, Baitullah Mehsud brought all Taliban factions under one command. He formed the Tehrik-e-Taliban Pakistan (TTP), making it very effective in FATA and NWFP. The coordination of the activities of numerous Taliban groups ensured that when, for example, armed forces started any campaign against one Taliban dominated area, Taliban forces from other strongholds would rush to the vulnerable area. Moreover, the TTP would be able to challenge the Pakistani security forces at different localities in a synchronised fashion.[38] In 2007, it is noteworthy, suicide attacks led to the death of 765 persons in Pakistan and injured 1677.[39] But deaths from other terrorist attacks in Pakistan in 2007 totalled 111 and injuries 185.[40] Indeed, one cannot accurately estimate how many of these terrorist incidents can be attributed to the TTP, and how many to the Al Qaeda against which Musharraf stepped up campaigns after Al Qaeda tried to assassinate Musharraf in 2003. Yet, as of 2007, Al Qaeda continued to flourish, and set up some training camps on the Pakistani soil contiguous to the border with Afghanistan.[41] Remarkably, Al Qaeda leaders in Pakistan were known to have links with terrorist cells in diverse parts of the world.[42]

But America, the sole superpower, did not mind being chastised by Pakistan. Musharraf, compelled by America to vacate the post of Army Chief on 28 November 2007, harshly denounced America in an interview to the ABC television on 30 November. He passed on to America the blame for Pakistan's failure to stamp out the Taliban and Al Qaeda by going back to the days after the end of anti-Soviet jihad in Afghanistan. After spending enormous amounts on the jihad,

America reduced its support for Pakistan when the jihad reached a successful conclusion. Musharraf found it convenient to identify this as the cause of Pakistan's failure to eliminate the Taliban and Al Qaeda, whereas he kept silent on the massive diversion by Pakistan of American funds for the Afghan jihad to another jihad in India's J&K, for which Pakistan narrowly escaped being branded by America as a state sponsor of international terrorism. Still, President Bush telephoned President Musharraf to pacify Musharraf's exasperation, and even praised Musharraf for his dedication to the anti-terrorist cause. America thus kept alive the myth of Pakistan's avid participation in the war on terror.[43]

This myth received a further boost when senior military and intelligence officials of America publicly acknowledged their happiness with the appointment of Ashfaq Parvez Kayani as Army Chief (in succession to Musharraf). Certainly, Kayani had attended as many as three high level training courses in America, but America overlooked the dismal fact that during his tenure as the ISI chief (2004-2007), Kayani permitted retired ISI officers to extend active support to the Taliban for launching attacks on American and Afghan soldiers. America was free to call Kayani 'a good guy', but there was hardly any evidence that he would be more compliant than Musharraf with America's dominant design that Pakistan should make more determined efforts to root out terrorists from the Pakistan-Afghanistan border. Musharraf was obviously responsible for the circulation of a rumour that his personal ties with Bush prompted direct and prolonged intervention by America in terrorist sanctuaries inside the FATA. Moreover, with his past record of being an enthusiastic abetter of terrorism in India's J&K, Kayani could not but maintain the habitual posture of the Pakistan military on preserving its undeserved privileges by persistence in confrontations with India and weakening India with a thousand cuts.[44]

Lashkar-e-Taiyaba (LeT) was one of the terrorist outfits deployed by Pakistan to bleed India. America was spending a huge amount of money for the war on terror. In Afghanistan, its annual appropriations for the FY 2007, for instance, stood at $5.5 billion. Unless America took punitive actions against agencies like the LeT, a lot of its investment in the war on terror was likely to be infructuous. But, for many years, somewhat unfairly, America refrained from taking any action against agencies like the LeT, even though it was fully aware of the LeT's depredations against India since 1993. It was as late as May 2008 that the United States Department of Treasury identified four top ranking LeT leaders, and banned any financial transaction with them. These leaders were: Hafiz Mohammed Sayid, the LeT founder; Zakiur Rahman Lakhvi, the chief of operations; Mahmoud Mohammad Ahmed Bahaziq, the financier; and Haji Mohammad Ashraf, the finance chief. America did this not because of LeT's activities against India, but because of its ties to Al Qaeda and participation in insurgencies inside Afghanistan (and Iraq).[45]

The TTP, as already noted, represented not merely the tribal areas of Pakistan, but also the settled regions adjoining the FATA. The TTP's aims were quite ambitious. It not only sought to promote solidarity among various factions of Pakistani Taliban, but also to continue assistance to the Afghan Taliban fighting the America-led coalition of international forces. Moreover, it wanted to Talibanise the government and society of Pakistan as also those in other countries, if possible. Following the assassination of Benazir Bhutto in December 2007, Pakistan's armed forces launched a massive attack against the followers of Baitullah Mehsud in South Waziristan, which compelled several hundred thousand Mehsud loyalists to escape from their residences. Mehsud had command over enormous financial resources procured through illegal opium trade and extortion from businessmen. In August 2008, the Pakistan government imposed a formal ban on the TTP, which enabled it to freeze TTP's bank accounts and suppress its propaganda pamphlets and other publicity materials. But Pakistan's military and intelligence agencies continued to suffer from a split. One section assisted the Taliban, whereas the other section even bombed civilians, whom militants tried to use as shields.[46]

Naturally, doubts arose in the minds of American legislators about the efficacy of their aid to Pakistan for counter-terrorism efforts in the FATA, and even about the existence of any appropriate plan for such efforts. Perhaps, in order to assuage these doubts, Pakistan began to raise private militias, who would fight the Taliban in the FATA. But tribal militias, supplied with small arms by the government, were no match for the Taliban warriors, who not only had much superior weapons, but also a more profound motivation. In the latter part of 2008, probably due to a secret meeting between Pakistan Army Chief

Parvez Ashfaq Kayani and Mike Mullen (America's Joint Chiefs of Staff Chairman) held in late August 2008, Pakistan appeared to extend greater cooperation to America in counter-terrorism efforts. In early September 2008, thus, American forces crossed the Afghan border to attack Taliban enclaves inside Pakistan (although Pakistan was prompt to protest). Americans later admitted that they not only fired shells at Taliban camps, but also sometimes pursued the militants for a short distance inside the Pakistani territory.[47]

Evidently, this reflected America's lack of faith in the sincerity and capability of Pakistan's military/intelligence agencies for conducting counter-terrorism operations, and confirmed the validity of President Bush's secret order of July 2008. This order permitted American forces to launch attacks inside Pakistani territory without advance authorisation from Pakistan. Americans were deeply aggrieved by the mounting evidence about Islamabad's intelligence agents giving prior warnings to and thereby protecting militants against imminent American raids. Therefore, the aforesaid order of President Bush also called upon America's Special Operations Forces (including the Navy Seals) to arrest/assassinate Al Qaeda agents. Sometimes, these forces allegedly committed blunders, killing women and children instead of Al Qaeda fighters. Pakistanis made loud protests. General Kayani met Admiral Mullen, and delivered a warning against any violation of Pakistan's sovereignty by American forces operating inside Pakistan.[48]

Kayani gave this warning in the latter part of September 2008. But America, probably, did not take this warning seriously before or after September 2008. America's hands were apparently strengthened by the results of the February 2008 parliamentary elections in Pakistan (shortly after Benazir Bhutto's assassination). These elections led to the emergence of Pakistan People's Party's (PPP) leader, Asif Ali Zardari (Benazir's husband), as the President of Pakistan, following Musharraf's resignation from the position of President in August 2008. Zardari (with his notorious record of corruption) was shrewd enough to realise that he should perhaps court America more than the Pakistan army. It certainly did not escape his attention—as also of Americans—that the ties between Afghan and Pakistani Taliban and a section of Pakistan's military/intelligence officials (in service or retired) being impregnable, the only way America could mark some visible achievements in the war on terror was by the use of pilotless aircrafts (drones). This may explain, why, in late September 2008, Zardari exhibited the guts to inform Americans that he had no objection to the use of drones by Americans without the constraint of prior Pakistani authorisation.[49]

This could be viewed as a turning point in America's war on terror. In the past, the Pakistani military approved a strictly limited number of drone strikes by Americans. The fear of public disapproval and a feeling of dilution of sovereignty enforced these limits. Actually, there was a sort of tug-of-war, continuous and prolonged, between Pakistanis and Americans on how to multiply the efficacy of the war on terror. Pakistanis pondered that America failed to comprehend the complexities of conducting this war on account of domestic terrorism, which naturally inhibited the capability of Pakistanis to contain international terrorism. American assessments, on the other hand, stressed the lack of sufficient return from billions of dollars disbursed to Pakistan for the war on international terrorism. When supplies for America and its allies passed through Pakistan to Afghanistan, Pakistan made a lot of money. Moreover, Pakistan received reimbursement from America for its expenses on military operations in counteracting international terrorism. America, moreover, had access to Pakistani bases (which facilitated, among other things, the drone attacks). Amidst this interminable America-Pakistan tug-of-war, Zardari's go-ahead to unrestricted American drone strikes was a sort of god-send, especially because America nurtured serious complaints about the waste and mismanagement by Pakistan of military funds provided by America.[50]

One wonders whether Zardari's audacious move (which must have displeased the army-ISI combine) reflected an exasperation of civilian rulers with their failure to restrain the military from retaining its decades-old political predominance. Pakistan's army/ISI wanted to have the best of different worlds—enjoying America's political-financial patronage as also commanding the loyalty of terrorist groups (even if partially injurious to Pakistan's interests and the power of the military). For, the combat operations of these terrorist groups enabled the Pakistani military (including the ISI) to preserve its capacity to browbeat (or blackmail) Afghanistan, India and even America in a state of limited antagonism. The Pakistani military revelled in this complex manoeuvre, which, undoubtedly, caused immeasurable irritation to America. Whereas the strength of Pakistani terrorist groups gradually acquired a strength that the Pakistani military did not have the capability to vanquish totally, this inability merely reinforced the military's ingrained intention not even to try to do so. It was a bizarre situation in which America too could not deal harshly with the Pakistani military for the latter's negligence towards counter-terrorism operations. Again, enhancing the authority of Pakistan's civilian rulers was an announced goal of American administrators. But America had the uneasy comprehension that any decisive attempt to consolidate civilian rule in Pakistan could have an unacceptably adverse impact upon the Pakistani military's already half-hearted counter-terrorism efforts.[51]

After Zardari became the President, there was a significant increase in drone attacks by America. Actually, to put this issue in a proper perspective, one should note that, following 9/11, there was a comprehensive agreement on collaboration between America and Pakistan. One component of this agreement related to the use of drones for surveillance and sharing of intelligence. But America was disappointed with Pakistan's failure, in general, to take appropriate counter-terrorism measures, as also with Pakistan's inability or unwillingness to act upon intelligence provided by drones to eliminate Al Qaeda or Taliban leaders. Therefore, America decided, without any consultation or understanding with Pakistan, to add missile attacks to mere surveillance work by drones. It was on 13 January 2006 that a drone was used for the first time as an offensive weapon inside Pakistan, although America's main suspect in this operation could escape. He was Zawahiri, second in command to Osama Bin Laden, the Al Qaeda chief. This drone attack, however, did not attract media attention and cause public outrage. But, on 30 October 2008, another drone attack resulted in the death of more than eighty persons, although, once again, the principal target, Zawahiri, was missed. This time media publicity and public outcry deeply embarrassed the Pakistan government, which lodged a protest with the American government. Subsequently, whenever there was a drone strike, Pakistan formally protested through diplomatic channels.[52]

America's frustrations about Islamabad's counter-terrorism efforts were easy to fathom, but extremely difficult to resolve. By 2008, the most urgent need, in the American perspective, was to eliminate the Pakistani Taliban leaders, who had near-complete freedom of operations inside the Pakistani territory. It appeared to be unlikely that American persuasion would have any serious impact upon Islamabad on this issue. America certainly continued to provide Pakistan with necessary support in terms of training and technology, but that did not have a fair chance to translate into greater Pakistani endeavour towards the liquidation of the Pakistani Taliban leadership. A much more complex task for America was to achieve simultaneously cooperation with the Pakistan army for counter-terrorism efforts as also the promotion of genuine democracy in Pakistan. For, any strengthening of democracy in Pakistan automatically alienated the Pakistan army long habituated to an experience of political ascendancy. An additional dimension to this complexity related to the query of how to prevent American encouragement to Pakistan's counter-terrorism efforts from being interpreted as unacceptable pressure, which might dash the hope about the Pakistan government renouncing Islamist extremism.[53]

Evidently, America could register a few significant successes in 2008 largely due to drone attacks. One such attack killed one of the topmost Al Qaeda leaders, Abu Laith Al Libbi, who was the accused in an unsuccessful assassination attempt upon America's Vice President Dick Cheney. The year 2008 also witnessed the death of not less than eight high ranking Al Qaeda operatives due to drone strikes. Yet, on the negative side, in late 2008, the Pakistani Taliban succeeded in establishing almost an unchallenged domination over the Swat Valley. Moreover (as already noted), because of the Iraq war, America could not allocate the minimum of military-economic resources needed for the achievement of even a visibly moderate level of military-economic-political stability in Afghanistan. Again, the task of finding resources for Kabul became more and more difficult on account of widespread corruption in the Karzai government publicised often in the Western media. The police force, for instance, easily rated as the most corrupt public institution in Afghanistan, was even known to collaborate actively with terrorists in regular narcotics smuggling.[54]

Actually, the elected government in Islamabad, headed by Prime Minister Yusouf Raza Gilani (which replaced Musharraf's government) failed to advance much beyond Musharraf's policy towards terrorist groups, although it talked of a new policy. One component of Gilani's policy was to use bullying/bribery/dialogue to push terrorist groups to concentrate their attacks on Afghanistan, sparing Pakistan. Another component was to reach a compromise with agencies like Jaish-e-Mohammed (JeM), headed by Maulana Masood Azhar, urging upon them to cease to assault Pakistani soldiers, and focus on raids against India. But all this could not protect Pakistan against onslaughts by the Frankenstein it created as early as 1994, i.e., the Taliban. The TTP leaders like Baitullah Mehsud were not ready to carry out fully the directives of the ISI or Gilani or of the pro-government Pakistani clerics. They dreamt of capturing Islamabad, which, on its part, hesitated to apply maximum force against the Taliban for fear of enraging Pashtuns. After all, Pashtuns formed 15 per cent of Pakistani population, but about 25 per cent of the army.[55]

In mid-2008, Pakistan's civilian rulers appeared (or pretended) to be interested in galvanising the peace process with the major target of their werewolf-type official-cum-nonofficial proxy war, viz. India. Shah Mahmood Qureshi, the Foreign Minister of Pakistan, declared in New Delhi on 28 June 2008 that India and Pakistan should follow the examples of ASEAN and European Union, and translate the enormous potentialities of dialogue into feasible measures. For, the time was ripe for such a dialogue in view of the prevalent mood of the people and politicians, as also the bonds of commonalities. Qureshi stressed that both the countries would be losers if they failed to seize this opportunity.[56]

An important reason behind this assertion by Pakistan's Foreign Minister could be the growing anti-Americanism among a large number of civilian political leaders (including the cricketer-turned-politician, Imran Khan). These leaders felt that America's war on terror was a thinly veiled war on Islam, and that Pashtuns living along the Durand Line were Pakistan's own people, who should not attract attacks by the Pakistani military acting on behalf of America. Such a view, however forcefully articulated, erred on several essential counts. It underplayed the domestic roots of militancy in Pakistan as illustrated by the growing strength of the TTP, which even the mighty Pakistani army learned to respect. To take an example, most victims of attacks by Sunni militants in FATA (averaging one hundred a month in the second half of 2007) were civilians. These militants, characteristically, did not spare barber shops, CD/music/video stores not only in FATA but also in NWFP, because these were un-Islamic. These terrorist activities continued in 2008 (to be elaborated below). Moreover, the above noted view of Pakistani politicians on America's war on terror ignored the ever present tendency of Pakistani militants to cross the border and harm India.[57]

It should be emphasised, though, that Pakistani Foreign Minister Qureshi, by his optimistic New Delhi statement, was probably misleading himself as also Indians. For, although Foreign Ministers of India and Pakistan decided to restart the peaceful dialogue in May 2008, they were facing thoroughly discouraging circumstances. Pakistan violated the ceasefire in Jammu and Kashmir—five years after it came into force in 2003. Moreover, on 13 May 2008, Pakistan-sponsored terrorists slaughtered 64 civilians, injuring about 200 persons and damaging a Hindu temple in Jaipur (Rajasthan) by means of nine IEDs. The Indian Mujahideen admitted responsibility. President Asif Ali Zardari might not have desired to sabotage the peace process. Even General Kayani might not have been interested in defeating the peace dialogue. But the collusion between a section of the Pakistani military and terrorists was too obvious to be missed. India's suffering could hardly be alleviated by the fact that some Pakistani army personnel—and not the entire military establishment—incited terrorist onslaughts upon India.[58]

It may be useful at this stage to remind Qureshi, the Pakistani Foreign Minister, of a number of terrorist blasts affecting India before and after the Jaipur explosion of May 2008, which hardly represented a situation conducive to the resumption of India-Pakistan peace process as claimed by Qureshi on 28 June 2008 in New Delhi. In October 2005, for instance, Delhi blasts claimed 67 lives, and an LeT commander died in the course of the encounter with the police. A terrorist attack in Varanasi in March 2006 liquidated 28 persons, although the police could kill an LeT leader in Lucknow. As many as 187 persons died in Mumbai train blasts in July 2006. One LeT leader and 15 SIMI members were arrested, whereas all Pakistani bombers, excepting one, could flee. Azzam Cheema masterminded the entire episode from the soil of Pakistan. In September 2006, 31 persons died of blasts at Malegaon. In February 2007, 68 people were killed in the Samjhauta Express blasts. One HUJI leader, Bilal, turned out to be the brain behind the Hyderabad blasts in May 2007, which took a toll of 11 persons. In August 2007, again, 43 persons died in Hyderabad, and again Bilal was the prime suspect. In November 2007, 15 persons were killed in the courts of Uttar Pradesh, and two HUJI suspects were arrested. In January 2008, eight persons were killed by terrorists at Rampur.[59]

The Jaipur blasts of May 2008 were followed by explosions in Ahmedabad on 26 July 2008. Alarmingly, on both the occasions, emails were sent to news channels along with proofs of authenticity in the form of photographs of IEDs described as weapons of mass destruction. Police and intelligence sources decoded the phrases used for email senders, and their suspicion fell on the members of IM, i.e., the Indian Mujahideen (which is sometimes indistinguishable from the SIMI). They could also trace connections to Pakistan's LeT and two Indian Muslims conducting their terrorist operations for a number of years from the soil of Saudi Arabia.[60]

The Ahmedabad blasts took place at seventeen congested areas, e.g., bus routes, hospitals, markets and residential locations. The number of civilians who died was 56. The number of injured stood at 200. The explosive devices used were of two types: VBIED (vehicle-borne improvised explosive devices) and IEDs. The spectacular character of the organisation, the management of terrorist plots and the expanding geographical coverage were clear from the fact that Ahmedabad was hit only a day after explosions in Bangladesh. Moreover, around this time, security forces fortunately stopped a truck carrying explosives to Kerala, and an impending attack on the American consulate in Chennai. In Surat, again, the lucky interception of a car carrying gadgets for triggering explosions in more than two dozen locations averted the remote-controlled bomb attacks. If successful, those attacks would have dealt a severe blow to the textile and jewellery industries in Surat. The courage and alertness of the local people helped in the identification of the explosive devices scattered over a large area.[61]

A question that came to the fore was whether the ruling circle in New Delhi lacked the political courage to stop the proliferation of secret terrorist cells with such nomenclatures as the IM or SIMI, set up in various parts of India by the ISI in collusion with Al Qaeda, LeJ, JeM, LeT as also India-bred local jihadi networks. For, otherwise, it was difficult to explain the scale of planned attacks (even if abortive) in Surat, or the dispatch of emails to television channels before or after the blasts in Jaipur and Ahmedabad (and, significantly, going back a bit, emails dispatched before explosions in three cities of Uttar Pradesh in November 2007). The legal machinery for checkmating Pakistan-backed terrorists inside India had to be substantially strengthened. Since the Prevention of Terrorist Activities Act (POTA) was not in force (from September 2005), the State governments needed new laws. Maharashtra, ruled by a party (the Congress Party) that was the dominant component of the ruling coalition in New Delhi, got ample substitute for POTA: the Maharashtra Control of Organized Crime Act (MCOCA). But, when the State governments of Rajasthan and Gujarat (ruled by an opposition party, viz., the BJP) drafted laws on similar lines, the government in New Delhi refused for years to provide concurrence. The then Union Home Minister Shivraj Patil even observed that the Union government decided not to permit the enactment of any new anti-terror law by a State. This was inexcusable, because the need for a new anti-terror legislation became apparent as the Union government's National Security Adviser, M.K. Narayanan, himself pointed out that local people were participating more and more in recent terrorist activities (unlike in previous years).[62]

It is worth serious exploration whether the ruling circle in New Delhi—more specifically, the United Progressive Alliance (UPA), which emerged as the ruling coalition in 2004—was more interested in protecting agencies like IM or SIMI for electoral dividends than in safeguarding national security and a democratic order. None could provide an accurate assessment of whether any appeasement of the IM or SIMI could yield such a dividend, and whether any community could fairly be treated as a vote bank. Yet, the UPA appeared to treat such appeasement as an article of faith. The National Democratic Alliance (NDA) government, with the BJP as the core component, imposed a ban on SIMI in September 2001, and extended it till September 2005. Meanwhile, in 2004, the UPA gained power in New Delhi, and it refused to grant any further extension to this ban beyond September 2005. Such political patronage, available even before the UPA came to power, ensured the growth of, for instance, the SIMI menace. The Institute of Conflict Management (New Delhi) brought out a study that listed one hundred terrorist incidents (from 2000 to July 2008) attributable to SIMI.[63]

In 2001, it may be useful to recall, the Congress Party had opposed the ban on SIMI enforced by the NDA. The President of the Uttar Pradesh Congress Committee, Salman Khurshid, went so far as to plead for the withdrawal of the ban upon SIMI in the High Court as also the Supreme Court. Paradoxically, in 2006, the Maharashtra government, headed by the Congress Party (which led the UPA in New Delhi), detected the role of SIMI in the train blasts in Mumbai. Therefore, the UPA was forced (perhaps not repentantly) to ban the SIMI. Astonishingly, in August 2008, a New Delhi Court revoked the ban on SIMI, deploring the lack of new evidence. But this was the time when the Gujarat Police not only discovered bombs in Surat, but also arrested a number of SIMI leaders, who had been the kingpins behind recent explosions in some States, including Gujarat and Rajasthan. Curiously, Samajwadi Party (SP) leader, Mulayam Singh Yadav, and Rashtriya Janata Dal (RJD) leader, Lalu Prasad Yadav, both aligned with the UPA, not only expressed pleasure over the withdrawal of the ban on SIMI in August 2008, but also declared that the ban had been unjustly imposed. But the exultation of Mulayam and Lalu was short-lived. For, the government appealed to the Supreme Court, which stayed the lifting of the ban on SIMI, which, above all, had been propagating jihad, quite openly and fearlessly, for more than three decades.[64]

Taken together, the above noted terrorist events in Ahmedabad, Bangalore and Jaipur signalled the emergence of one or more Indian jihadi organisations (with names designed to terrify and/or mislead), which could operate with or without the collaboration of Pakistani counterparts. Even if the culture of hate was conveyed by Pakistanis, some Indians began to establish terror outfits in unlikely places like Bangalore. The Islamist radicals could easily assemble in a variety of places in this city, including mosques. The forests of Karnataka hosted a properly equipped military training facility. Remarkably, explosives used in Bangalore were far more advanced than those employed in Jaipur and Ahmedabad. Whereas the ISI would certainly avail of the services of jihadis nurtured by Indians themselves, such local organisations as the Tablighi Jamaat and Ahle Hadees must be given due credit for recruitment and indoctrination of jihadis. In the years following 9/11, India tended to develop an illusion that this country could not probably prove to be a breeding ground of jihadis. This illusion had to fade away.[65]

Whereas the terrorist incidents in Jaipur, Bangalore, Ahmedabad and Surat pointed to serious lapses in intelligence operations and the counter-terrorism apparatus, the situation in J&K revealed a much more critical lapse, viz., the infirmity of political will. Thus, on 8 August 2008 (for instance), when three Indian soldiers (including a Colonel) sacrificed their lives to stop Pakistani terrorists from infiltrating into J&K, Indian political leaders did not react. Nor did the human rights protagonists. On 11 August 2008, a few J&K leaders, who had the reputation of not only killing Indian military personnel, but also proclaiming Independence (Azadi) for J&K, were about to organise an anti-Indian rally, when they were arrested. Immediately, accusations were showered upon security forces for taking repressive actions. One familiar accusation of civil society activists was repeated: India was guilty of militarily occupying J&K for about two decades. Curiously, the political leaders ruling J&K during this period (e.g. an Abdullah, a Mufti or an Azad) were not held accountable. As V.P. Malik, a former Chief of Army Staff of India wrote: 'I feel it is time to introspect India's nationhood and governance.' He added: 'Security forces personnel waiting in the bunkers for the next round of sentry duty or a quick reaction call ...wonder why the government is risking their lives defending the LoC and fighting terrorists.'[66]

The lack of will and accountability of J&K's political leaders became deplorably evident at a crucial moment, viz. when the escalation of Pakistan-sponsored terrorism in J&K after 1989 (in the wake of Soviet withdrawal from Afghanistan) was successfully counteracted by the Indian army in less than a decade. This success was achieved despite the frequent scapegoating of security forces as a cover for dismally weak governance in J&K, and despite the exemplary abstention by the Indian army from the use of tanks or heavy artillery or an air force cover. This was in sharp contrast to how the Pakistanis were fighting militants in the NWFP or FATA, Russians in Chechnya, and Americans in Iraq. Instead of lauding the Indian army for such self-restraint and encouraging it to give a finishing touch to counter-terrorist operations by some decisive measures, the J&K government put the clock back. 'With the first signs of normalcy, the Mufti administration put pressure on the security forces to scale down operations', wrote Gagandeep Bakshi, a retired Major General of the Indian army with extensive work experience in J&K. Bakshi added: 'Realising that the *tanzeems* have largely lost the military phase of the battle, it appears that there might have been a deft shift of strategy to exploit trivial local causes and generate mass hysteria over communal issues.'[67]

One such issue related to the obvious requirement of some land for Amarnath pilgrims. Separatists or Azadi advocates in the Valley worked up this issue in collusion with their Pakistani patrons, to try to nullify the impressive gains of counter-terrorist operations in J&K. After all, as General Deepak Kapoor, India's Army Chief, pointed out, although anti-terrorist measures decreased the number of Pakistani infiltrators into India during 2008 by 65 per cent, as of July 2008, in contrast to the corresponding number in 2007, there should be no complacency. For, Pakistan still had about 18 camps for training terrorists in POK, two in Gilgit-Baltistan (the Northern Areas), and 20 inside Pakistan. Significantly, as Kapoor disclosed, J&K had on its territory about 750-800 terrorists (in August 2008), 40 per cent of them being foreigners. In order to comprehend how easily these terrorists could receive assistance from Pakistan, one can do no better than to quote from the concluding observations in a book by Ahmed Rashid, a Pakistani. In the words of Rashid, 'Today, seven years after 9/11, Mullah Omar and the original Afghan Taliban Shura still live in Balochistan Province. Afghan and Pakistani Taliban leaders live farther north, in FATA, as do the militias of Jalaluddin Haqqani and Gulbuddin Hikmetyar. Al Qaeda has a safe haven in FATA, and along with them reside a plethora of Asian and Arab terrorist groups.'[68]

This massive terrorist infrastructure inside Pakistan was not expected to wallow in idleness. There were targets in not only J&K but the whole of India, and Indian associates of Pakistani jihadis were ready to oblige. The place and time of a terrorist outrage, however, could not be predicted before it actually occurred. So, on 13 September 2013, New Delhi suffered from the explosion of five low intensity bombs, which caused death to 31 civilians and injuries to around 100 persons. All the blasts took place in crowded markets between 6:07 pm and 6:38 pm, hitting shoppers, including their children. That the terrorists had a degenerate mindset became obvious when three bombs, including one at even a centrally located Childrens' Park, had to be defused. It may be useful to stress that ten minutes after the first blast in New Delhi, an email was sent by the Indian Mujahideen (IM) to media offices, reminding one of the emails sent before the UP court explosions as also before those in Jaipur and Ahmedabad. The IM email of New Delhi warned that this was a 'Message of Death', and that nobody could stop further attacks by the IM despite this message, because IM enjoyed the blessings of Allah. The defused IEDs had a story to tell. They revealed the use of timer devices, as also a mixture of ball bearings, chemicals, gun powder and nails—the same deadly ingredients as those identified in the recent explosions at Jaipur, Bangalore and Ahmedabad. The IM did not hesitate to own responsibility for the New Delhi blasts. Indian security agencies were of course aware that the IM acted as handmaids of Pakistan's JeM, LeT and HUJI. Following the arrest of a number of SIMI-IM activists by the Ahmedabad police, there was an expectation that the terrorist threat might subside. But this expectation was belied on 13 September 2008.[69]

It was legitimate to speculate on whether the incident of 13 September 2008 was a sort of frustrated reaction against American and NATO attacks on Pakistani territory in the month of September itself. On 3 September, American and NATO soldiers invaded a base of Al Qaeda and Taliban in South Waziristan. On 9 September, American drone attacks liquidated 20 persons, including some Al Qaeda leaders, who were inside a college for Muslim clerics. This college, significantly, was run by no less an Islamist militant leader than Jalaluddin Haqqani, who, in the past had masterminded an assault upon the Indian embassy in Kabul. Haqqani obtained the service of a Pakistani suicide bomber (belonging to the LeT) for this assault. The ISI of course was the principal instigator of this attack upon the Indian embassy in Kabul. On 12 September 2008, again, an American drone targeted a commander of Al Badr Mujahideen at Tul Khel in North Waziristan.[70] The terrorist attack in New Delhi on 13 September 2008, therefore, could be interpreted as an act of revenge (by proxy) directed against a near-ally of America at a time when negotiations on Indo-American civilian nuclear deal were at the final stage. While remaining in anguish about this nuclear deal (which was consummated in 2008),

Pakistanis forgot two things. One, America and other Western powers were thoroughly well-informed (though not happy) about China's clandestine but close nuclear ties with Pakistan culminating in a nuclear test conducted by China on behalf of Pakistan in 1990.[71] Two, America, its Western allies and Russia were respectful about India's determination (despite its impressive advances in nuclear technology) of not causing any proliferation, whereas China and Pakistan were in gross violation of the non-proliferation norms regime. Therefore, in the eyes of these powers, India was eligible for the membership of the non-proliferation regime sustained since the middle of 1970s by countries like America, Russia, Britain, etc. The India-America civilian agreement merely sanctified the process of conferment of this eligibility.[72] The terrorist attack in New Delhi failed to stall this process. But it was an indirect way of pacifying the sympathisers of militant Islamists among the Pakistani public, who were deeply aggrieved by American drone strikes.

The IM email of 13 September 2013 affirmed that the aim of the explosions was to stop India's heart-beat. It enclosed a manifesto as long as 13 pages. It also provided a video slide-show, which in a macabre fashion displayed pictures of victims of past explosions. This was a reflection of the gruesome Al Qaeda mode of terrifying potential victims. The manifesto was replete with warnings of infliction of harm upon policemen and media persons. It revealed the concern of IM for such global issues (considered to be extremely important by radical Islamists) as that of Palestine or Anglo-American intervention in Iraq, and also for the typical India-Pakistan issue of J&K.[73]

The IM electronic message of September 2008 launched clear political attacks on two national parties, viz. the Congress and the BJP. This had an ominous implication. In all probability, the IM used the titles SIMI and IM interchangeably to create confusion among policemen and other security forces. One influential section of the IM hailed from Azamgarh in eastern Uttar Pradesh (UP). One member of this IM/SIMI group—or the Azamgarh group—happened to be the son of a Samajwadi Party (SP) office bearer. The Congress Party at that time could have been worried about an impending spilt with the Left Front MPs on the India-America civilian nuclear deal, and, therefore, it was anxious to cultivate the SP. This might explain the imaginary accusation of the Congress spokesperson, Manish Tiwari, ventilated on 22 September 2008, that the Gujarat government (a non-Congress government) had not acted upon the available intelligence input to avert the Ahmedabad blasts of 26 July 2008. According to Tiwari, a specific input was provided by Safdar Nagori, the General Secretary of SIMI, to officers who interrogated him in detention. Actually, however, the officers revealed that no such input was provided by Nagori on Ahmedabad or subsequent New Delhi blasts. What was alarming, in terms of a threat to the country's security, was that national leaders did not hesitate to stoop to using an alleged failure of counter-terrorist measures as a political platform to outwit an opposition party (ruling Gujarat).[74]

In the period from 2005 to 2008, the IM carried out ten explosions in different parts of India. The Azamgarh group was responsible for as many as nine of these ten attacks. The IM, as directed by Pakistan's ISI, tried to propagate that it was an Indian, and not a Pakistan-sponsored outfit. It began to collect chemicals, etc. from the local markets for use in bombs. But it could not do without financial and logistical support from Pakistanis. It also received the help of smugglers to procure explosives from Bangladesh. Moreover, the leaders of the IM continued to preserve links with Pakistan, and obtain whatever assistance they could.[75]

The police, while investigating the New Delhi blasts of 13 September 2008, discovered a mobile phone number. Trying to trace the person, who used this phone, the police reached the Batla House on 19 September 2008 in New Delhi, which sheltered no fewer than 13 IM operatives. The police came across five of them, and engaged in an exchange of fire. Two militants, Atif Ameen and Mohammad Sajid, died. Two were detained, whereas one could flee. Investigators could collect so much information from the Batla House that the IM suffered from a series of arrests, and some prominent IM members had to escape to Pakistan.[76]

Some reactions to the Batla House episode revealed the enormity of problems facing the Indian police while trying to tackle the home-grown but foreign-assisted jihadis. M.C. Sharma, an Inspector of the Delhi Police, died of injuries sustained in the course of this episode. He was a brave officer with several gallantry awards to his credit. But his martyrdom in the cause of the country was denounced by some political leaders (e.g. central government ministers), media persons and social activists as the product of a fake encounter. There was hardly any evidence to justify this denunciation, which reflected a mindset vitiated by the virus of politics of religion. It was a sad demonstration of the failure to distinguish between a friend and an enemy, which could not but demoralise the police, and encourage terrorists to stick to their aggressive behaviour.[77]

The Batla House arrests did not deter terrorists from staging another explosion, even if of low intensity, at a crowded flower market of Delhi on 28 September 2008, which injured more than 20 persons but killed only one. Nevertheless, the Batla House episode, especially its aftermath, demands careful scrutiny. A number of media persons, politicians (including Digvijay Singh, a Congress leader) and human rights activists denounced the episode as a case of fake encounter without caring to supply a shred of evidence. One NGO clamoured for a judicial inquiry. The Delhi High Court, on 21 May 2009, asked the National Human Rights Commission (NHRC) to conduct a probe. Eventually, the NHRC endorsed the action taken by the Delhi police, and could not detect any foul play. On 26 August 2009, the High Court accepted the NHRC report. On 29 April 2010, the police submitted a chargesheet against only one of several accused (Shahzad) under various Indian Penal Code (IPC) provisions, including those for attempt to murder and for murder. The High Court framed charges against this accused on 15 February 2011, and on 25 July 2013, pronounced him guilty of murdering Inspector M.C. Sharma of Delhi Police. The Union Home Minister P C Chidambaram gave a clean chit to the Delhi police. But, evidently, terrorists were highly skilled in sowing confusion and disunity among some members of their target groups, which generated intense politicking linked to the nefarious enterprise of harvesting votes. Therefore, in a terrorist incident, occurring at daytime in a crowded place of Delhi (the national capital), it took as long as five years to reach a decisive verdict against only one of a number of accused. One wonders how such tardiness in counter-terrorism operations could reassure potential terror victims, especially at the level of States, where administrative capabilities and resources were expected to be at a lower level than in the national capital.[78]

Remarkably, a few weeks before the New Delhi blasts of 13 September 2008, Pakistan itself suffered terribly in the hands of terrorists nurtured by itself (and trained to attack India). Thus, to take one of many examples, in the morning of 25 August 2008, the Taliban launched an assault on the house of a brother of an Awami National Party (ANP) legislator in the NWFP (KPK from 15 April 2010). The terrorists used automatic weapons and even rockets. This legislator's brother, seven security personnel and two nephews of the legislator's brother were killed before the entire house was razed. The ANP led the coalition government in the NWFP, and it supported military operations against terrorists. Therefore, as a Taliban spokesman declared, this was a retaliatory onslaught, which could be repeated. Within a few hours after this incident, Pakistan imposed a ban on the TTP and several terrorist organisations accused of deadly attacks, including suicide strikes. Pakistan's interior ministry issued a notification for freezing the bank accounts of the Taliban. Whereas an Indian observer could not but depict this Pakistani move as too little too late, and (what subsequent events proved) as largely ineffective, it is worthwhile noting the names of the banned agencies in addition to the TTP. They were Lashkar-e-Islam, Ansar Ul Islam, and Amar Bil Maroof Wa Nahi Aneelmunkar (Force for the Promotion of Virtue and Prevention of Vice).[79]

After the New Delhi blasts of 13 September 2008, significantly, Lalu Prasad Yadav, the Union Railway Minister, deplored that the Union Home Ministry was unable to cope properly with the problem of internal security. Shivraj Patil was then the Home Minister. According to him, the existing laws of the country were adequate to deal with cases related to terrorism. But M. Veerappa Moily, who headed an Administrative Reforms Commission (ARC), disagreed with Home Minister Patil. In a report titled *Combating Terrorism*, Moily recommended that a new counter-terrorism law should be enacted. The ARC, moreover, suggested the establishment of a federal investigating agency. Whereas a debate on such issues was useful, inaction could be harmful.[80]

Actually, what was worse, the debate appeared to degenerate into a dangerous rivalry between the ruling coalition, the UPA, and the opposition NDA. In consequence, coping with terrorism by concrete measures became much less important for the UPA than appeasing coalition partners (e.g., the Samajwadi Party (SP). This became quite evident at a meeting of the National Integration Council (NIC) on 13 October 2008, where the Chief Ministers (CMs) of States run by the BJP (the leader of NDA) discussed terrorism seriously, and recommended a POTA-like legislation to tackle terrorism. They accused the UPA of the inability to muster necessary determination to confront terrorism. This accusation derived confirmation from the NIC meeting where an SP leader went so far to denounce the assessment of M.K. Narayanan, the National Security Adviser, that the Batla House encounter was genuine. According to this SP leader, somewhat amazingly, what appeared to be more important was that no Muslim believed that this encounter was genuine, even if it was really genuine. Lalu Prasad Yadav, the chief of RJD and a UPA Minister, sang a similar tune and even told media persons (by way of commenting on the NIC proceedings) that all members of SIMI should not be condemned as terrorists. Such a mindset about SIMI (which had been thoroughly probed by the judiciary and found to be a militant outfit deserving a ban) could not but encourage terrorists and pave the way to the attack upon Mumbai on 26 November 2008 (which will be discussed shortly in this chapter).[81]

The supine approach of India's ruling circle to Islamist terrorists contrasted sharply with the sophisticated duplicity of Pakistani rulers. In an interview to *The Wall Street Journal*, published on 4 October 2008, Asif Ali Zardari, who succeeded General Musharraf as the President of Pakistan, observed that India had never posed a threat to Pakistan, that the Islamist militants fighting in J&K were terrorists (and not freedom fighters as Musharraf had observed), and that Pakistan had to achieve better ties with India for sheer economic survival. Whereas Zardari belonged to the Pakistan People's Party (PPP), the ruling coalition in Pakistan had two other partners: the Muttahid Quami Movement (MQM) and the Awami National Party (ANP). All these three parties, according to Zardari, were secular parties ready to contest the alliance between the military and the mullahs.[82]

Evidently, Zardari was trying to win over western powers (especially America) at a time when Pakistan, with foreign currency reserves so low as to be adequate for the purchase of food and oil for only about two months, was facing an economic crisis. He wanted the international community to provide him with 100 billion US dollars. Otherwise, as Zardari attempted blackmail in a suave manner, his government might collapse, and terrorist agencies like the Al Qaeda might gain access to two hundred nuclear weapons in Pakistan's possession. He added that in case Pakistan failed to wipe out the menace of terrorism, the international community could not hope to do so. Zardari tried to make light of the growing tensions between Pakistan and America, especially the American complaint about military collaboration between the Taliban and Pakistan's intelligence officials, as also of the resistance of the Pakistan government to raids by NATO commanders upon the Taliban located inside Pakistan. He said, for example, that he had a few days back removed the chief of Pakistani intelligence service, and that American predator missiles operated within Pakistan territory with the consent of the Pakistani authorities.[83]

In his above noted interview with *The Wall Street Journal*, Zardari accused Musharraf of simultaneously attacking militant Islamists as also assisting them, whereas Zardari said that he himself was prepared to treat them as mere criminals. Zardari's Ambassador to America, Husain Haqqani, further claimed, in an interview to CNN, that civilians now exercised control over the military, and therefore, the army would have to fight religious extremists, so that secularism could prevail in Pakistan.[84] It was, however, ominous that Zardari's claim of being secular and liberal nearly echoed what Musharraf also claimed for the eight years when he ruled Pakistan. As to Haqqani's boast about the civilian control over the military (including, presumably, the ISI, as also the ISI-nurtured terrorists), it turned out very soon to be empty in practice, e.g., in the matter of Islamist terrorists slaughtering Indians as also Pakistanis. Haqqani, again, told Paul Richter of *The Los Angeles Times* (reported on 24 October 2008) that Zardari's government would perform better than Musharraf's government in tackling militants. He was also responsible for setting the tone of a speech delivered by Zardari at the UN General Assembly in late September 2008, which stressed that Pakistan was fighting militants not as an American surrogate, but on its own initiative in the interest of the country. Nevertheless, this contention was not yet convincing to Americans, who had to use commandos, e.g., in South Waziristan on 3 September, killing twenty persons. Haqqani told Paul

Richter that Pakistani public opinion was infuriated by such unilateral military actions on the part of America, and that this would be counterproductive in the ongoing war on terror. But this too was not yet credible to the Washington Administration.[85]

Not long after the Batla House episode, on 23 November 2008, ten Pakistani LeT terrorists slaughtered the captain of a trawler and four fishermen in order to hijack the trawler plying near Mumbai's coast line. They set the stage for a terrorist assault upon Mumbai on 26 November 2008, which ranked as the most stunning jihadi attack since 9/11. Between the late evening of 26 November and the early morning of 29 November, terrorists used IEDs and AK 47 rifles to kill 19 members of security forces (including 17 police officers) and 164 civilians, as also to cause injuries to 25 military functionaries, three police officers, and more than 300 civilians. Terrorists focussed on the most spectacular targets in the financial capital of India, viz., the Chhatrapati Shivaji Rail Terminus (CST), the Taj Hotel at the Gateway of India, the Oberoi Trident hotel at Nariman Point, the airport at Santa Cruz, two well-known hospitals near CST, a famous multiplex, a cafe, a Jewish cultural centre (Chabad House) and the Mazgaon Dockyard. The choice of these spots, some of them high favourites of rich Indian and foreign tourists, was designed to impair India's international prestige, and economic might. Six Americans, two Australians and one Briton were among the dead.[86]

The LeT could not have carried out the Mumbai attack of 2008 without years of research and surveillance. According to Bruce Riedel, a former CIA official, the LeT could do this with substantial help from Pakistan's ISI, Al Qaeda, and a Pakistani-turned/American, David Coleman Headley. Headley was the son of a Pakistani, his name at birth being Daood Sayed Gilani. America's Drug Enforcement Authority (DEA) detained him for a drug-related offence, and then recruited him for espionage against the illegal narcotics dealers of Pakistan. In 2002, however, during a visit to Pakistan, Gilani joined the LeT, which advised him to adopt the name, David Coleman Headley. From 2002 to 2005, Headley visited Pakistan on five occasions, and acquired the various skills of a terrorist, e.g. handling weapons, carrying out surveillance, collecting intelligence, etc. He received training from the ISI as well as LeT. From 2005 to 2008, Headley visited India five times in preparation for the Mumbai attack, e.g., by using GPS systems to record potential locations of attack. On each of the five occasions, Headley received instructions in Pakistan from the LeT and ISI before a trip to India and reported back to them at the end of each trip. He always had joint meetings with the LeT and ISI. The ISI supplied to Headley a handsome amount for his activities in India. He closely collaborated with Hafiz Saeed, the leader of LeT, in engineering the Mumbai conspiracy.[87]

The slackness of Americans and Indians in dealing with Headley was glaring. After all, Indian immigration officials failed to gauge the significance of Headley's repeated visits to India through Pakistan—not to speak of any follow-up action by police/intelligence agencies in Mumbai. For instance, Vishwas Patil, who joined as Deputy Commissioner of Police (DCP), South Mumbai, in June 2008, soon discovered that the police and intelligence agencies failed to pay proper attention to a large number of warnings from the CIA about potential attacks by terrorists upon such important hotels as the Taj and Trident-Oberoi. The state of apathy was such that a committee appointed by the Maharashtra government to study/investigate the terrorist strike of July 2006, went on delaying the submission of its report and recommendations even after the lapse of five years. Some intelligence alerts even suggested infiltration from the sea and attacks by suicide missions upon Mumbai. Yet, the coastal police failed to procure appropriate equipment for lack of funds.[88]

American officials, again, failed to exercise any restraint upon their agent, who metamorphosed into an agent of the LeT/ISI. Eventually, it was intelligence supplied by the British, which enabled the Americans to detain and convict Headley. In contrast, Pakistan could be credited with keeping a proper watch on Headley and his three wives. Whereas Headley was a mastermind of the Mumbai plot, along with Hafiz Saeed, the ISI and LeT did not disclose to Headley any detail about the final execution of the plot. They suspected Headley to be a double agent, transmitting intelligence to Americans, after they learnt about one of his wives visiting the American Embassy in Islamabad, and ventilating her misgivings about questionable activities by Headley. The American Embassy did not take seriously the warning from this wife of Headley about her suspicion that Headley could be a terrorist or an American agent. Even the National Security Team of President George W. Bush ignored messages from

European inquisitors about Sajid Mir, an LeT operative, who was raising funds and recruiting terrorists in a number of countries. Sajid Mir happened to be a handler of Headley.[89]

India and America subsequently engaged in a blame game. America affirmed that it gave India, during June-September 2008, advance warnings about LeT threats to targets in Mumbai. India argued that America should have passed on to India the information about Headley. America contended that before the Mumbai-26/11 attack, it did not have adequate information to connect Headley with the Mumbai terror plot. In fact, according to James R. Clapper, America's Director of National Intelligence, America would surely have shared with India, a partner to America in counter-terrorism operations, all reliable intelligence (including that on Headley) if the same was available before 26/11. It is noteworthy that M.K. Narayanan (who was the National Security Adviser at the time of 26/11) admitted on 20 January 2011 that the IB and the RAW had, to some extent, the information about the probable targets on 26/11, but the mode of operation of the LeT was so reckless as to put these Indian intelligence agencies in a fix.[90]

Significantly, P.C. Chidambaram, who replaced Shivraj Patil as Union Home Minister after 26/11, visited Mumbai, and tendered an apology to the people of Maharashtra, which implied deficiencies on the part of the Union government. Ram D. Pradhan, a former Union Home Secretary, and V. Balachandran, a retired IPS officer, were appointed by the Maharashtra government to probe 26/11. Pradhan was the head of the committee. It was not a judicial but an administrative committee. It, therefore, did not inquire into subjudice matters. Moreover, it did not meet non-officials, because, the collection of non-official inputs would have taken an indefinite period of time, whereas the Pradhan panel had to complete the probe in three months, and formulate recommendations for early action by the Maharashtra government. Therefore, it selected fifty police personnel (including some high-ranking IPS officers as also constables) for a thorough investigation. The committee drew up a report of 100 pages, which praised young officers of the Mumbai police for courageously and speedily coping with a crisis, which was a sort of a three-day war (26-29 November 2008). There was no police force in India (whether in Mumbai or elsewhere), which had the capacity to confront such an unprecedented contingency. The report expressed satisfaction over the performance of the police control room, as it noted that the Pradhan committee reached this conclusion after the verification, over a period of three days, of the log records of 5000 calls to and responses by the control room in the course of the crisis. The Maharashtra government did not have in its possession any direct intelligence about the terror attack. The Pradhan panel recommended that in order to face a similar crisis in future, the Maharashtra government should set up agencies for providing commando-type training to police personnel.[91]

The Ram Pradhan committee did not fail to register some severe lapses on the part of the Maharashtra State government. The processing of intelligence alerts from the Union government's Ministry of Home Affairs (MHA) exhibited utter confusion, according to the committee's report. The alerts were normally transmitted to the State's Home Department by the Chief Secretary. The Additional Chief Secretary and Principal Secretary of the State Home Department, however, informed the Pradhan committee that they had not received any intelligence alert from the Union MHA. But Maharashtra's Director General of Police (DGP) placed before the Pradhan committee some copies of important intelligence alerts supplied by the Union MHA to Maharashtra's Chief Secretary and Home Secretary. The Additional Chief Secretary (Home) had actually assigned the task of processing sensitive intelligence alerts and communications to a junior officer, while he refrained from doing the job himself. The report denounced the Police Commissioner of Mumbai for leadership lapses, whereas it praised the DGP for trying his best, although the Mumbai area lay beyond the DGP's administrative jurisdiction. Still, the committee criticised the officers of the DGP as also of the Anti-Terrorist Squad (ATS) and the State Home Department for the adoption of a mechanical and casual approach towards transmitting to operational units the intelligence inputs provided by the Union government. Moreover, the Pradhan panel noted that the infrastructural facilities of the Mumbai police were not only inadequate, but poor and the performance of the Mumbai police suffered also because of lack of proper supervision and coordination.[92]

It is worth providing a sample of an expectedly perverse view of 26/11 from Pakistan, where many people think that the 9/11 catastrophe represented a conspiracy by Americans and Jews. So, the Pakistani view was that the Indian intelligence establishment was the architect of the 26/11 episode. The terrorists, including Ajmal Kasab (who was captured by Indian forces), were agents of this establishment, which even liquidated Hemant Karkare, the head of the ATS of the Mumbai police. As to the Indians finding that Kasab hailed from the Faridkot village in the Punjab province of Pakistan, the Pakistani view was that Kasab had no training or inclination for recitations from the Holy Koran, or practising Islam, and there was a video clip in which he was heard appealing to a Hindu god for mercy. Proponents of such a Pakistani view of 26/11 further argued that Kasab had no idea of jihad, and that Pakistan's ISI would not launch this Mumbai-type attack because Pakistan's palpable losses could far exceed the probable gains.[93]

Even Pakistani President Asif Ali Zardari, in an interview to Larry King of CNN (published on 3 December 2008), stuck to the usual Pakistani mode of denial of involvement in the 26/11 episode. Normally, Pakistani officials talk of non-state actors committing terrorist acts against India. But, when talking about 26/11, Zardari went one step further and told Larry King that stateless actors (which was a category significantly different from non-state actors within the Pakistani state) were responsible for 26/11, and that they were a menace not only to India, but also to Pakistan and Afghanistan. When, again, he was reminded by Larry King of the American fear that Pakistan could be the springboard of the next massive terror attack on America, Zardari cleverly played the ball back to the American court. He argued that, in order to forestall any such attack, America (and the international community) should extend more assistance to Pakistan. They should look after Pakistan if Pakistan was to look after America (and the world) in the war on terror. This was a virtual reiteration of what (as already noted in this chapter) Zardari told *The Wall Street Journal* in October 2008. As to the Indian request to Pakistan for handing over to India the twenty terrorists (including Dawood Ibrahim) enjoying a sanctuary in Pakistan, Zardari repeated to Larry King the hackneyed Pakistani excuse (which was totally indefensible) that Pakistan needed and waited for proof of the terrorist activities of the persons named by India. Zardari furthermore argued that, despite possessing the fourth largest army in the world, Pakistan suffered every day from terrorist onslaughts (quietly forgetting that the ISI of Pakistan had itself created these terrorists).[94]

In support of Zardari's lament that Pakistan itself was a victim of terrorism, one could cite some instances from the month of November 2008 itself. On 6 November 2008, a meeting of tribal leaders at Batmali in the FATA suffered from an attack. IEDs strapped to the body of a suicide bomber killed 22 civilians and injured 51. The TTP owned responsibility. In a fortnight, on 21 November 2008, a funeral procession at Dera Ismail Khan in the NWFP encountered the detonation of IEDs. Ten civilians died, and 43 persons were injured, although there was no terrorist group claiming responsibility. Again at Bannu, in the NWFP, on 28 November 2008, six police officers and seven civilians (including two Afghans) died, and 13 civilians were wounded, when a vehicle carrying suicide bombers detonated IEDs in a police check post. The Taliban acknowledged responsibility for employing this VBIED (vehicle borne improvised explosive device).[95]

For an Indian author, unable to reconcile himself to 26/11, it may be worthwhile to carry forward the story of terrorist outrages inside Pakistan in the month of December 2008, so that Pakistanis (who may happen to read this book) can realise the futility of their government's addiction to employing terrorism as an instrument of state policy against India. The combination of VBIED and a suicide bomber appeared to be an attractive option to Pakistani terrorists. For, on 1 and 5 December 2008, this combination was tried, respectively, on the Charbagh-Mingaora road in the NWFP and at Orakzai in the FATA. On the first occasion, a military checkpoint was the target. Although no group owned responsibility, two soldiers and eleven civilians died, and 64 civilians were injured. At Swat, in NWFP on 13 December 2008, an anti-Taliban priest and his followers were attacked. This priest and eight civilians died, and 25 civilians were kidnapped. Marauders damaged 16 houses by setting them on fire. In two days, at Swat again, two of the kidnapped persons were slaughtered. The Taliban took credit for these incidents. At Shalbandi in the NWFP, on 28 December 2008, a suicide bomber and VBIED destroyed a polling station. Four police officers, four children, and

35 civilians died, and 16 civilians were wounded. Explosions also damaged a mosque, a market and some houses. The TTP acknowledged responsibility.[96]

One can now turn to India where five years after 26/11, Ram Pradhan made some revelations, which should be recorded at this point. He told Priyanka Kakodkar of *The Hindu* that, as the head of an administrative committee (and not a commission of inquiry), he had no authority to compel Maharashtra government officials to offer their evidence. Yet, he received complete cooperation from all officers of the State. But the terms of reference of his committee were narrow and he had to confine the inquiry to State officers. Probably, the Union government did not want that the Pradhan panel should examine testimonies from officers of such Union agencies as the RAW and IB. Ram Pradhan repeatedly solicited the cooperation of Union government officers, who refused to provide any input. He was also disappointed that, despite the passage of five years, the State and Union governments were negligent in identifying the moles in Mumbai, who helped not only Headley, but enabled Kasab and his accomplices to launch the lethal assaults in 2008. Ram Pradhan submitted to the State and Union governments a brief note on these moles, without whose active support, such assaults could not have occurred. In the same year, 2013, Levy and Scott-Clark, authors of *The Siege*, reconfirmed the existence of moles. Ram Pradhan also felt unhappy, as he looked back after five years to 26/11, and the current state of implementation of his committee's recommendations. Pradhan had urged upon the state government to install CCTVs in such places as railway stations and department stores, although paucity of resources did not permit such installations on as massive a scale as in America after 9/11. But, possibly due to the government's tendering system and other usual procedures (as far as Pradhan could ascertain from newspaper reports), the progress of work on this matter was not satisfactory. Finally, what was a matter of consternation to impartial observers, even after the lapse of five years since 26/11, as Pradhan discovered, Mumbai's police constables were still carrying guns as a sort of substitutes for sticks because, as in 2008, so in 2013, due to ammunition shortage, constables had the opportunity for firing practice only once annually.[97]

A few weeks after 26/11—in December 2008—a bipartisan commission, appointed by the United States Congress, brought out a report with the title *World at Risk, The Report of the Commission on the Prevention of Weapons of Mass Destruction Proliferation and Terrorism.*[98] This report devoted one chapter to Pakistan. The title of this chapter was: 'Pakistan: The Intersection of Nuclear Weapons and Terrorism'. This chapter stressed that in the 9/11 event, Al Qaeda used Afghanistan as its safe haven, although hijackers enjoyed all-round facilitation from Pakistan. But, as of 2008, Pakistan itself, especially its FATA, emerged as one safe haven for Al Qaeda, which used this area as a base of operations in vast parts of Africa, Asia, Europe and America. In this base, Al Qaeda also set up expensive facilities for new recruits to terrorist agencies. The chapter on Pakistan in *World at Risk* noted that Al Qaeda was trying to add to its armoury the weapons of mass destruction (WMDs), i.e., the biological, chemical, nuclear and radiological weapons, and that it would not shrink from using them in a future terrorist assault. This danger increased in October 2008, when China agreed to build two nuclear power plants in Pakistan by way of reaction to India-America civil nuclear cooperation accord. Even if one optimistically ruled out the transfer of nuclear materials from civilian to military plants in Pakistan, there was no doubt that agreement with China boosted Pakistan's confidence, and tended to strengthen its determination to increase its stock of nuclear weapons. *World at Risk* noted the assessment of a large majority of American experts on terrorism that in the near future, terrorists in Pakistan were most likely to gain access to nuclear technology. Therefore, the chapter on Pakistan in *World at Risk* contained the grim warning that, although Pakistan was an ally, it could turn out to be the source of terrorists using WMDs against America.[99]

Probably, the worldwide media reaction to 26/11 prompted the Pakistani military and the ISI to advise the LeT not to stage any large scale attack on India for some time. Moreover, the Sheikh Hasina government, which came to power in Bangladesh in January 2009, arrested a number of terrorists belonging to the LeT, HUJI/Bangladesh (HUJI-B), and the ULFA, i.e., the United Liberation Front of Assam (which was a Pakistan-linked Indian militant agency). But India continued to suffer from unabated terrorist threats from LeT, JeM and HUJI-B. On 4 June 2009, New Delhi police arrested an LeT militant. On 7 August 2009, on the eve of Independence Day (15 August), New Delhi police arrested two HUM operatives. In J&K, during January-November 2009, terrorists killed 52 security personnel and 71 civilians, although the number of foreign terrorists came down from 800 to 700 in the course of the year. On 8 October 2009, the Indian Embassy in Kabul suffered from a suicide attack, which caused the death of 17 persons.[100]

Pakistan-sponsored terrorists were thus relentless in targeting India in 2009. No less relentless were they in harming Pakistan, their godfather. As in the past, the NWFP and FATA were exposed most frequently to attacks. A few significant features of militant operations in Pakistan in 2009 (conducted by the Taliban or Al Qaeda) may be highlighted here. There was a rise in the number, frequency and technical complexity of suicide bombings in 2009. Such urban centres as Rawalpindi, Peshawar, Islamabad and Lahore were the targets in nearly fifty per cent of these blasts. Terrorists became more and more self-confident as they attacked the offices of security forces, targeting three of them in Lahore on a single day, viz. 15 October 2009. Even the General Headquarters of the Pakistan Army became a target on 10 October 2009. The ISI offices in Lahore and Peshawar were subjected to suicide bombings. Individuals, including people's representatives, diplomats, journalists, civil and military officers and religious scholars came under attack. Educational institutions, especially schools for girls, were targeted with nearly 100 of them suffering from rocket attacks or blasts in 2009.[101]

In the Malakand Division of the NWFP, the Pakistan government had to launch large scale military action in April 2009. Many innocent persons lost their homes, and became refugees in their own country. But that was apparently an unavoidable collateral damage for arresting, injuring and killing hundreds of terrorists belonging to the Tehrik-i-Nifaz-i-Shariat-i-Mohammadi (TNSM). The Malakand Division began to experience normalcy after successful conclusion of the military operation. Again, in the middle of October 2009, the Pakistan military had to wage full scale operations against the TTP, when, following the death of their leader, Baitullah Mehsud on 4 August 2009 because of an American drone attack, his nephew and successor, Hakimullah Mehsud, escalated the TTP's retaliatory attacks. By early December 2009, the government could gain control over highways and principal towns, but the problem of local refugees persisted. Many terrorists remained active. The government had to resort to air strikes against the TTP in support of ground attacks, especially in the tribal agencies of Orakzai, Bajaur and Mohmand.[102]

A few other terrorist incidents in Pakistan may be noted here. At Dera Gazi Ghan in the Punjab province on 15 December 2009, a VBIED, detonated by a suicide bomber in the residence of a government officer, killed 30 civilians (including some children) and injured 90 civilians. In addition to this residence, several other houses, one mosque, a number of vehicles and shops, two banks and some buildings were damaged. No militant group acknowledged responsibility. Similarly, no group owned responsibility for another suicide bombing by means of a VBIED at Timurgara in the NWFP on 18 December 2009. It took place in the vicinity of a mosque, which was near a police station. Five vehicles and the police enclosure were damaged. Twelve police officers were wounded. The mosque was damaged. Ten civilians were killed and twenty injured. Some children too were killed or wounded.[103]

The Pakistan government, however, could do little to control sectarian violence, especially against Shias. So, on 5 February 2009, at Dera Gazi Khan in the Punjab, there was a bomb explosion in the vicinity of a Shia mosque; thirty people died and twenty got wounded. On 5 April 2009, there was a suicide attack upon a Shia mosque at Chakwal; 24 persons lost their lives and 140 suffered from injuries. A Muharram (Shiite) procession in Karachi became the target of a suicide bomb blast on 28 December 2009; 93 persons died and 75 were wounded.[104]

In 2009, the United Nations Sanctions Committee stamped the terrorist label upon the JUD and some of its leaders, whereas the LeT, the parent body of the JUD, had been so designated even before 26/11. The Pakistan government, more in reaction to international furore on 26/11 than to Indian allegations, banned the JUD and the LeT. Pakistan even ordered a crackdown on a LeT sanctuary in Muzaffarbad. It placed under arrest more than fifty LeT and JUD leaders. But many of them secured their release at a later date.[105] Evidently, Pakistan continued to support these agencies, which had to be allowed to plan and execute terrorist assaults upon India in order to safeguard the interests, not of the ordinary people of Pakistan, but of the narrow interests of the army and ISI.

The Pakistani rulers seemed to suffer from a sort of schizophrenia in simultaneously nurturing Pakistan's terror groups for attacks against India, but trying to restrict their activities inside Pakistan even by strict military measures. Their chief financier and political patron, the Americans, devoted enormous energy and efforts to the collection of data about terrorism, analysis of huge masses of data to explore the comparative roles of a variety of socio-economic stresses in shaping terrorism (in contrast to usual crimes), and then devising a counter-terrorism strategy. Americans drew a sophisticated differentiation between sub-categories of terrorism in terms of types of attacks or weapons used against individuals/masses, and of impact of religious and environmental factors upon moulding extremist thoughts. American experts on terrorism made laudable efforts to develop theoretical models for accomplishing the goal of prevention of terrorism. One of their theories emphasised the availability of potential terrorists, who had the necessary will, of accessible targets and of resources for the pre-emption of terrorist attacks. Another theory went beyond this routine analysis of opportunities to a sort of game theory approach, in which limited counter-terrorism resources were so craftily deployed in terms of the relative significance attached to prospective targets by terrorists that terrorists would tend to suffer from confusion/indecision about the eventual choice of targets.[106] But all these refined American techniques of analysis of counter-terrorism appeared to have little or no effect on restraining the Pakistani rulers or their terrorist protégés.

Therefore, on 13 February 2010, seventeen persons died and 65 were wounded when a mixture of ammonium nitrate, petroleum hydrocarbon oil, ball bearings and RDX in a bomb was exploded (by means of a battery) at the German Bakery in Pune (Maharashtra), which was a favourite haunt of foreigners. Of the non-Indians killed, one was from Iran, one from Italy and two from Sudan. Among the injured foreigners, one was from Germany, three from Iran, two from Nepal, and one from Taiwan. The responsibility for the attack was acknowledged by the Indian Mujahideen Kashmir and Lashkar-e-Taiyaba-al-Alami. The restaurant was naturally wrecked. The man, who carried the bomb inside a backpack while entering into the restaurant, was caught by the police after being identified on the closed-circuit television. Evidently, Pakistani rulers did not bother that the same forces, which harmed India, also debilitated Pakistan. Thus, near about the time of the German Bakery blast in Pune, on 10 February 2010, for example, the TTP accepted responsibility for a VBIED rammed into a military patrol vehicle by a suicide bomber at Wazir Dhand in Pakistan's NWFP. Eleven soldiers died and eight soldiers were wounded. Seven civilians were killed and two (including a journalist) were wounded. In addition to the aforesaid military vehicle, three civilian vehicles were destroyed. Next day, on 11 February 2010, the TTP, again, owned responsibility for vandalising a police compound at Bannu in Pakistan's NWFP. A VBIED was detonated by two suicide bombers. Nine police officers were killed, and eight were wounded. Six civilians died (as also one child) and 15 received injuries (as also two children).[107]

Following the German Bakery attack in Pune, the first terrorist attack took place in April 2010 in Bangalore. The spot was crucial: the entry gates of the Chinnaswamy Cricket Stadium. But the detonation of low-capability IEDs could only injure fifteen persons, while none lost life. The next terrorist incident occurred in September 2010 in New Delhi in the vicinity of Jama Masjid. A tourist bus was targeted by gunmen, but none died. Moreover, an ammonium nitrate bomb, placed near the bus, failed to explode. In December 2010, a prominent place in Varanasi—the Sheetla Ghat, which was close to the most important Ghat, the Dashashwamedh Ghat—witnessed a bomb explosion, which did not kill or wound anyone. To some extent, this might reflect the success of security agencies in enforcing restrictions. Suspicion fell on the IM for planning all these three incidents in April, September and December 2010, especially because of an email sent to media persons after the Sheetla Ghat occurrence.[108]

India appeared to get away somewhat lightly in the matter of assaults by Pakistan-sponsored jihadis from the time of Pune explosion on 13 February 2010 to December 2010. But how did Pakistan fare?

From 22 February to 25 December 2010, Pakistan suffered 27 terrorist attacks. Hundreds of policemen, soldiers and civilians (including women and children) died, hundreds more were injured, numerous vehicles and houses were damaged. Some indications of specific terror targets may be provided here. On five occasions, a police compound, a police station or vehicle were attacked. Military convoys/patrols were attacked twice. A joint military/police convoy was attacked once. A non-Shia civilian convoy was targeted once. Political rallies were attacked on two occasions, relief distribution points for internally displaced persons on three occasions. Hospitals were targeted twice. The following religious places were attacked: two places of worship for Ahmadis (Ahmadiyas) on a single day; one Sufi shrine; one Ahmad Shah Gazi shrine, and one other mosque. How Shias were targeted is worthy of mention: one convoy of Shia civilians; one Shia rally; and two Shia processions. One meeting of government officials with tribal leaders was subjected to an attack; so was a solitary religious preacher departing from a mosque. In eleven of these cases of terrorist outbreaks, no group claimed any specific responsibility. The TTP, significantly, acknowledged responsibility in eight cases; the LeJ in two cases; the TTP and LeJ together in four cases. The Taliban, the LeJ Al Alami and the Baloch Liberation Army (BLA) owned responsibility in one case each. The names of the terror outfits (excepting BLA) could be deliberately or unwittingly designed to create confusion. But there should be no confusion about the Pakistan government (especially the army/ISI) creating such outfits for hurting India, but sometimes hurting itself more than India, as in the year 2010.[109]

Apparently, Pakistani authorities were so obsessed with injuring India, that they did not pay much attention to how, year after year, their terrorist progenies were murdering larger and larger numbers of people their progenitors were expected to protect. Thus, for instance, in 2007, the number of attacks staged by terror groups inside Pakistan stood at 889, and the number of deaths at 1338. The corresponding figures for 2008 were, respectively, 1837 and 2293; for 2009, these were 1916 and 2670; for 2010, 1332 and 2153; and for 2011, these figures stood at 1436 and 2033. The number of injured was excluded from these estimates.[110] It is noteworthy that these figures compiled by different countries/agencies may diverge, but there is undisputed convergence on continuity in large-scale terrorism inside Pakistan. For instance, the Institute of Regional Studies, Islamabad, appears to have accepted an estimate of only 153 terrorist acts inside Pakistan in 2007, 246 acts in 2008, and 398 in 2009. As many as 6715 died in 2008 due to terrorist attacks, 11704 in 2009, 7435 in 2010, and 3658 from January to July 2011.[111]

Pakistani authorities failed also to pay requisite attention to how their relations with their American counterparts deteriorated. This led to an unprecedented incident in the night of 1-2 May 2011 at a house in the Bilal Town of Abbottabad Cantonment, hardly one kilometre away from the Pakistan Military Academy in Kakul. It is to an elaborate examination of this incident (and other matters) that we may now turn.

Endnotes

1. Zahid Hussain, *The Scorpion's Tail*, New York: Free Press, 2010, pp. 24-25.
2. Pervez Musharraf, *In the Line of Fire: A Memoir*, New York: Free Press, 2006, pp. 200-01.
3. Musharraf, *In the Line of Fire*, pp. 201-03; Hussain, *The Scorpion's Tail*, p. 25.
4. Musharraf, *In the Line of Fire*, pp. 202-04; Hussain, *The Scorpion's Tail*, p. 25; Riaz Mohammad Khan, *Afghanistan and Pakistan: Conflict, Extremism and Resistance to Modernity*, New Delhi: Oxford University Press, 2011, pp. 84-85.
5. Hussain, *The Scorpion's Tail*, pp. 26-27.
6. Musharraf, *In the Line of Fire*, pp. 206-07, 213, 216-18, 223; Khan, *Afghanistan and Pakistan*, pp. 101-02.
7. Musharraf, *In the Line of Fire*, p. 223.
8. *Ibid.*, p. 237.
9. *Ibid.*, pp. 227-31.
10. Hussain, *The Scorpion's Tail*, pp. 61-62; Report in *The Indian Express*, 16 September 2013.
11. Ayesha Siddiqa, *Military Inc.*, pp. 39-40; Shibashis Chatterjee, 'Realism and Democracy: Two stories of the American Engagement with Asia', in Priya Singh (ed.), *Democracy in Asia: Discourses and Counter-Discourses*, New Delhi: Knowledge World, pp. 16-17.
12. Khan, *Afghanistan and Pakistan*, pp. 102-05, 108.
13. Ashok K. Behuria, 'The Rise of Pakistani Taliban and the Response of the State,' *Strategic Analysis*, Vol. 31, No. 5, September 2007, pp. 706-07.
14. Hussain, *The Scorpion's Tail*, pp. 68-71, Musharraf, *In the Line of Fire*, p. 267.
15. Ashok K. Behuria, 'The Rise of Pakistani Taliban and the Response of the State', *Strategic Analysis*, Vol. 31, No. 5, September 2007, pp. 707-08; Musharraf, *In the Line of Fire*, pp. 233-36.
16. Behuria, 'The Rise of Pakistani Taliban and the Response of the State', pp. 708-10; Musharraf, *In the Line of Fire*, p. 260.

17. Khan, *Afghanistan and Pakistan*, pp. 113-16. For significant criticisms of American military expenditure for the War on Terror in Afghanistan and elsewhere, see, e.g. Amy Belasco, *CRS Report for Congress: The Cost of Iraq, Afghanistan and other Global Wars on Terror Operations Since 9/11*, Congressional Research Service: The Library of Congress, Washington DC, Updated 14 March 2007, no page number.
18. Dan Caldwell, *Vortex of Conflict: US Policy towards Afghanistan, Pakistan and Iraq*, New Delhi: Cambridge University Press, 2012, pp. 264-65.
19. Peter L. Bergen, *The Longest War: The Enduring Conflict between America and Al-Qaeda*, New York: Free Press, 2011, pp. 160-70.
20. Belasco, *CRS Report for Congress*, Updated 14 March, 2007, no page number.
21. Khan, *Afghanistan and Pakistan*, pp. 118-19.
22. *Ibid.*, pp 119-20.
23. Bergen, *The Longest War*, p. 166.
24. PTI report, *The Statesman*, 21 October 2013.
25. Steve Coll, *Ghost Wars*, London: Penguin, 2004, pp. 552-56.
26. Behuria, 'The Rise of the Pakistani Taliban and the Response of the State', p. 717; Hussain, *The Scorpion's Tail*, pp. 102-04.
27. Musharraf, *In the Line of Fire*, p. 273.
28. Hussain, *The Scorpion's Tail*, pp. 105-07, 112-13; Khan, *Afghanistan and Pakistan*, pp. 253-54.
29. Hussain, *The Scorpion's Tail*, pp. 106-07; Khan, *Afghanistan and Pakistan*, pp. 254-55; Centre for Innovative Research Collaboration and Learning (CIRCLe), *Pakistan since 9/11: A statistical report of a Decade of the War on Terror*, *www.circle.org.pk*, 2011, p. 7.
30. Hussain, *The Scorpion's Tail*, pp 108-11, 116-19; Khan, *Afghanistan and Pakistan*, pp. 255-56; CIRCLe, *Pakistan since 9/11*, p. 7.
31. Behuria, 'The Rise of Pakistani Taliban and the Response of the State', pp. 718-20; CIRCLe, *Pakistan since 9/11*, pp. 6-7.
32. Hussain, *The Scorpion's Tail* pp. 119-21; Pak Institute for Peace Studies, *Pakistan Security Report 2008*, Islamabad, p. 4.
33. Report from Islamabad, *The Times of India*, 5 November 2007; Sheryl Gay Stolberg and Helene Cooper, The New York Times News Service, reproduced in *The Times of India*, 5 November 2007; editorial, *Ibid.*
34. Irfan Husain, *Dawn*, 27 October 2007; Chidanand Rajghatta, *The Times of India*, 4 November 2007; Rajinder Puri, *The Statesman*, 4 November 2007; AFP report, *The Statesman*, 5 November 2007; Ishtiaq Ali Mekhri, *The Times of India*, 5 November 2007; Raju Santhanam, *The Statesman*, 5 November 2007.
35. Neena Gopal, *Gulf News* (Doha), 5 November 2007; Reports in *The Times of India*, 5 and 29 November 2007.
36. Chidanand Rajghatta, *The Times of India*, 23 November 2007 (with references to *The San Fransisco Chronicle*); Sayeed Hasan Khan and

Kurt Jacobsen, *The Statesman*, 30 November 2007; Sumit Ganguly, *The Times of India*, 30 November 2007.

37. Hussain, *The Scorpion's Tail*, pp. 123-24, 131; CIRCLe, *Pakistan since 9/11*, pp. 7, 12; Khan, *Afghanistan and Pakistan*, p. 143.
38. Pak Institute for Peace Studies, *Pakistan Security Report 2008*, p. 4.
39. CIRCLe, *Pakistan since 9/11*, p. 28.
40. *Ibid.*, p. 11.
41. Report, *The New York times*, 19 February 2007; United States Department of State, *Country Reports on Terrorism 2007*, Office of the Coordinator for Counterterrorism, Washington DC, 2008, p. 7.
42. *Ibid.*, p. 8.
43. Chidanand Rajghatta, *The Times of India*, 2 December 2007.
44. G. Parthasarathy, *The Times of India*, 29 November 2007: Wilson John, *The Pioneer*, 29 November 2007; Rajat Pandit, *The Times of India*, 29 November 2007.
45. Amy Belasco, *Congressional Research Service Report for Congress*, Washington DC, updated 8 February 2008, p. 38; Chidanand Rajghatta, The *Times of India*, 29 May 2008.
46. Nikolas J. Koppel, ed., *Combating Islamic Militancy and Terrorism in Pakistan's Border Region*, New York: Nova Science Publishers, 2010, pp. 5-7.
47. *The Washington Post*, 22 April 2008; Hussain, *The Scorpion's Tail*, pp. 39-40; *The Washington Post*, 23 October 2008; *The New York Times*, 24 October and 22 November 2008; Koppel, *Combating Islamic Militancy and Terrorism in Pakistan's Border Region*, pp. 7-11.
48. Hussain, *The Scorpion's Tail*, p. 146; Koppel, *Combating Islamic Militancy and Terrorism in Pakistan's Border Region*, p. 11.
49. Hussain, *The Scorpion's Tail*, pp. 146-47; Khan, *Afghanistan and Pakistan*, p. 146.
50. Koppel, *Combating Islamic Militancy and Terrorism in Pakistan's Border Region*, pp. 13-14; Khan, *Afghanistan and Pakistan*, p. 147.
51. For some insightful observations on this issue, see Ashley J. Tellis, 'Engaging Pakistan—getting the Balance Right', Carnegie Endowment for International Peace, Washington DC, 1 September 2008, pp. 2-5.
52. Khan, *Afghanistan and Pakistan*, pp. 138-39, 146.
53. Ashley J. Tellis, 'Pakistan and the War on Terror: Conflicted Goals, Compromised Performance', Report, Carnegic Endowment for International Peace, Washington D.C., 2008.
54. Khan, *Afghanistan and Pakistan*, p. 148; Hussain, *The Scorpion's Tail*, p. 147; Richard Holbrooke (a former American Ambassador to the United Nations), *The Washington Post*, 31 March 2008; Christophe Jaffrelot, *The Indian Express*, 14 November 2013.
55. Wilson John, *The Pioneer*, 9 April 2008; Haroun Mir, *The Times of India*, 9 April 2008; editorial, *The Pioneer*, 28 May 2008.

56. PTI report, *The Statesman*, 29 June 2008.
57. Swapan Dasgupta, *The Pioneer*, 29 June 2008; Times News Network, *The Times of India*, 29 July 2008.
58. Rajinder Puri, *The Statesman*, 20 May 2008 and 8 October 2008; National Counterterrorism Center, *2008 Report on Terrorism*, Washington DC, 30 April 2009, p. 48.
59. Report in *The Times of India*, 17 May 2008.
60. B. Raman, *The Pioneer*, 27 August 2008.
61. National Counterterrorism Center, *2008 Report on Terrorism*, Washington DC, 30 April 2009, p. 54; editorial, *The Pioneer*, 2 August 2008; Times News Network, *The Times of India*, 29 July 2008.
62. B. Raman, *The Pioneer*, 29 July 2008; S. Kumar Uttam, *The Pioneer*, 28 August 2008.
63. For an incisive and compact analysis of the SIMI phenomenon, see S. Gurumurthy, *The Pioneer*, 27 August 2008.
64. S. Gurumurthy, *Ibid.*
65. Rajiv Deshpande, *The Times of India*, 2 August 2008; Ranjan Roy, *Ibid.*
66. V.P. Malik, *The Indian Express*, 29 August 2008; also see editorial, *The Pioneer*, 31 July 2008.
67. Gagandeep Bakshi, *The Indian Express*, 28 August 2008.
68. Ahmed Rashid, *Descent Into Chaos: How the War against Islamic Extremism is being lost in Pakistan, Afghanistan and Central Asia*, New Delhi: Allen Lane, 2008, p. 401; the entire book merits a thorough study; 'the original Afghan Shura', is a phrase used by Rashid denoting the jihadis, who initiated the anti-Soviet campaign in Afghanistan in the 1980s; Rajat Pandit, *The Times of India*, 23 August 2008, providing excerpts from an exclusive interview with General Deepak Kapoor.
69. National Counterterrorism Center, Washington DC: *2008 Report on Terrorism*, p. 59; Rahul Tripathi, *The Times of India*, 14 September 2008; Reports in *The Indian Express*, 14 September 2008 and *The Hindu*, 15 September 2008.
70. K.P.S. Gill, *The Pioneer*, 24 September 2008.
71. Chidanand Rajghatta, *The Times of India*, 6 September 2008.
72. K. Subrahmanyam, *The Times of India*, 3 September 2009.
73. *The Hindu*, 14 September 2008; *The Asian Age*, 14 September 2008; *The Wall Street Journal*, 15 September 2008.
74. For details, see Ashok Malik, *The Pioneer*, 25 September 2008.
75. The Times News Network, *The Times of India*, 27 August 2008; Rakesh K. Singh, *The Pioneer*, 19 September 2008; Stephen Tankel, *Jihadist violence: The Indian Threat*, Woodrow Wilson International Center for Scholars, Washington DC, 2013, pp. 38-40.
76. Stephen Tankel, *Jihadist Violence*, p. 42.
77. Abhinav Kumar, *The Indian Express*, 2 October 2008.
78. Ajai Sahni, *The Pioneer*, 1 October 2008; chronological report in *The Hindustan Times*, 29 July 2013.

79. PTI report from Islamabad, *The Statesman*, 26 August 2008.
80. See, e.g. an editorial in *The Indian Express*, 18 September 2008, for relevant observations on this issue.
81 See an elaborate report on the NIC meeting by the Times News Network, *The Times of India*, 14 October 2008; also see C.P. Bhambhri, *The Economic Times*, 18 October 2008.
82. Bret Stephens, *The Wall Street Journal*, 4 October 2008; article by Usman Khalid, *The Nation*, reproduced in *The Statesman*, 14 November 2008.
83. Bret Stephens, *The Wall Street Journal*, 4 October 2008; editorial, *The Statesman*, 7 October 2008.
84. Bret Stephens, *The Wall Street Journal*, 4 October 2008; Husain Haqqani's interview to CNN quoted in an article by Usman Khalid, *The Nation*, reproduced in *The Statesman*, 14 November 2008.
85. Paul Richter, *The Los Angeles Times*, 24 October 2008.
86. Stephen Tankel, *The Jihadist Violence*, p. 43; Reports in *The Guardian* (London) 27 and 28 November 2008; National Counterterrorism Center, *2008 Report on Terrorism*, p. 65.
87. Bruce Riedel, *http://afgazad.com/Zabaan-13/112013-Five-Years-on-Mumbai-Terror-Masterminds-Still-at-Large.pdf*. Also see the PTI report from Washington DC, *The Statesman*, 19 November 2013.
88. Adrian Levy and Cathy Scott-Clark, *The Siege: The Attack on the Taj*, New Delhi: Penguin Books India, 2013, esp. pp. 23-26, 45-48, 50-51, 53-56.
89. For amazing details, see Adrian Levy and Cathy Scott-Clark, *The Siege*, pp. 54-55, 57-58.
90. Report from Washington DC including a statement of 8 November 2010 by James R. Clapper, *The Indian Express*, 9 November 2010; Rahul Tripathi, *The Indian Express*, 21 January 2014, quoting M.K. Narayanan.
91. Yogesh Naik and Sanjeev Shivadekar, Times News Network, *The Times of India*, 28 May 2009; Express News Service, *The Indian Express*, 28 May 2009.
92. PTI report, *The Hindu*, 22 December 2009; *The Indian Express*, 1 December 2009.
93. Muhammad Ali Ehsan, *The Express Tribune*, Karachi, 20 July 2013.
94. *http://transcripts.cnn.com/TRANSCRIPTS/0812/02/lkl.01.html*
95. National Counterterrorism Center, *2008 Report on Terrorism*, pp. 63-65.
96. *Ibid.*, pp. 65-68.
97. Priyanka Kakodar, *The Hindu*, 27 November 2013; Levy and Scott-Clark, *The Siege*, p. 57, where as many as sixteen Indian moles of LeT are mentioned.
98. New York: Vintage Books, 2008.
99. *World at Risk*, pp. 65-67.
100. Stephen Tankel, *Jihadist Violence*, pp. 43, 46; United States Department of State, Office of the Coordinator for Counterterrorism, *Country Reports on Terrorism 2009*, Washington D.C., 2010, pp. 148, 150-52.

101. United States Department of State, Office of the Coordinator for Counterterrorism, *Country Reports on Terrorism 2009*, pp. 156-58.
102. *Ibid.*, pp. 158-59.
103. Office of the Director of National Intelligence, National Counterterrorism Center, *2009 Report on Terrorism*, Washington DC, 2010, p. 66.
104. *Ibid.*, p. 159.
105. *Ibid.*, pp. 159-60.
106. Brian Forst, 'Afterword to the State Department's Country Reports on Terrorism, 2010: Challenges, Accomplishments and Prospects in National Counterterrorism Center', *2009 Report on Terrorism*, Washington DC, 2010, no page number.
107. Stephen Tankel, *Jihadist Violence*, p. 47; Office of the Director of National Intelligence, National Counterterrorism Center, *2010 Report on Terrorism*, Washington, DC, 2011, p. 31.
108. Stephen Tankel, *The Jihadist Violence*, pp. 49-50.
109. National Counterterrorism Center, *2010 Report on Terrorism*, Washington, DC, 2011, pp. 31-57.
110. The National Counterterrorism Center, *Report on Terrorism 2011*, Washington, DC, 2012, p. 10.
111. Sajjad Malik, 'Terrorism: Impact on Pakistan's Socio-Political and Economic Security and Strategic Policy', *Regional Studies*, Vol. XXX, No. 2, Spring 2012, p. 44.

Four

Passage to 2014

The National Assembly and the Senate of Pakistan held a joint session on 9 May 2011. It resolved unanimously that the Government of Pakistan should carry out an elaborate probe into the incident of 1-2 May 2011, in which at about 0100 hours, Osama Bin Laden (OBL) was killed by America's Special Forces (known as Navy SEALs). These Special Forces, with authorisation from the CIA and President Barack Obama, used four helicopters, which set out from Jalalabad in Afghanistan. For more than three hours in one late evening of May 2011, they flew over Pakistan's air space, entailing a penetration of more than one hundred kilometres of Pakistani territory. They raided the Abbottabad residence of the Al Qaeda leader, OBL, and killed four other persons, including two males and two ladies (one Pakistani and one Arab), in addition to OBL himself. The Abbottabad operation did not take more than 36-38 minutes, after which the Americans claimed to have taken OBL's body to a ship in the Indian Ocean, and performed Islamic rituals to bury the body in deep waters.[1]

The Pakistani public felt outraged. They thought America owed an explanation. But Pakistan's defence forces, entrusted with the country's security, had a far more profound obligation to explain. There were many questions that agitated the minds of the Pakistani people. They wondered whether Pakistan's intelligence personnel were aware of the presence of OBL (a person whom many countries were trying to hunt down for years) right inside a Pakistani cantonment town. Even Pakistan itself was bound by UN resolutions to look for OBL in order to dispense justice. A related question was why Pakistan did not (or failed to) try to resist the entry or exit of American Navy

Seals. Curiosity about answers to these undoubtedly complex questions was overlaid with anxiety, suspicion and even a sort of helplessness, because a number of foreign countries hurled accusations that Pakistani military/intelligence authorities were in collusion with OBL and/or the CIA. Alternatively, these Pakistani authorities would confront charges of gross dereliction of duty or humiliatingly plain incompetence.[2]

The *Abbottabad Commission Report* invites a comparison with the *9/11 Commission Report*. The latter bristled with super-abundance of hard data (including interviews with easily accessible decision makers at all relevant levels). In contrast, the Abbottabad Commission had to cope with a demonstrable lack of credible information, and a lack of access to political and civil-military leaders, who mattered the most in policy formulation and implementation. Therefore, Justice Javed Iqbal and his colleagues deserve unstinted praise for producing a report that is immensely rich in skillful analysis of probabilities, lucidity, impartiality and objectivity. If the *9/11 Commission Report* is also a model in terms of possession of these characteristics, the *Abbottabad Commission Report* is even more so because of evident infirmities in the flow of information it suffered from. The 9/11 phenomenon was a turning point in the evolution of America's foreign policy. The 1 May 2011 incident, too, was an extraordinarily important episode in Pakistan's foreign policy, especially in the matter of its association with America in the War on Terror since 9/11.

The performance of Justice Javed Iqbal and his colleagues were all the more creditworthy, because they were conscious of some severe limitations from the very beginning. For example, according to the Joint Resolution of Pakistan's National Assembly and the Senate, the Leader of the House and the Leader of the Opposition were to be consulted before the finalisation of the composition and mode of operation of the Inquiry Commission. In all probability, these consultations were avoided. Moreover, there were unpublicised warnings that no Inquiry Commission should be so independent as to find fault with the military in such a manner as to cause demoralisation in the armed forces. Members of the Commission, it is noteworthy, carried out their difficult assignment without availing of any honorarium. They were wise enough to skip the honorarium and attendant controversies, because they knew that the de facto rulers of

Pakistan had no interest in such a Commission, and that these rulers had not acquiesced in its formation without an uncomfortable groundswell of legislative and popular clamour for an Inquiry Commission.[3]

The Abbottabad incident did not happen all of a sudden. It happened because American decision makers had long been frustrated by the duplicitous conduct of Pakistani authorities, especially the ISI. It was indeed a marvel of administrative-military-political chicanery that the same agency, the ISI, could at once support and oppose, protect and punish, shelter and torture, home-grown terrorists (often deployed in anti-Indian campaigns) belonging to a large number of militant outfits. Americans had to ponder whether they should at one stage deal a visibly hard blow to Pakistan, bear some retaliation, and wait for the time when retaliation would give way to the usual pattern of anomalous (almost self-contradictory) cooperation-cum-noncooperation. The advantage of hindsight would prompt the speculation that the impact of the Abbottabad incident would conform to this scenario.[4]

It was a minor mystery as to how, despite several years of OBL's stay in the Abbottabad residence, neighbours told the Commission that they were so thoroughly unaware of his presence that they tended even to disbelieve that he had been living there. Perhaps a feeling of being reduced to fools played a part in shaping this response. Nevertheless, there could be no doubt about OBL's presence and eventual expiry in view of the statement of President Barack Obama on 2 May 2011, and confirmation by Al Qaeda sources on 6 May 2011.[5]

OBL spent nearly six years in Abbottabad out of a total of more than nine years that he resided inside Pakistan since 2002. OBL's house was situated in a civilian locality within the cantonment, where many people had recently settled because of displacement by the earthquake/floods of 2005 or by military operations against terrorists. It was highly unlikely that OBL's house would not attract the attention of civil-military officials and neighbours in the locality. For, its walls were abnormally high, in some places as high as eighteen feet. The top floor had a screen wall of seven feet. Barbed wire was distinctively used. But, despite such unmistakable security measures, there were no security guards, and no telephone/television connection. No cars or outsiders entered into the large compound, not even for the collection of wastes. False documents and wrong identities were used to carry out a lot of illegal procedures without which this OBL residence could not have been constructed. The failure (if any) to detect that this was an OBL hideout was incomprehensible, even though one could easily conjecture that all civil/intelligence military organisations erred comprehensively and collectively. The nature of inefficiency and /or negligence could only throw up a hint of passive (if not active) collusion. For, officials, interviewed by the Abbottabad Commission, did not seem to exhibit even normal curiosity about this unusual house, which had at least 25 inmates including OBL, and yet which, according to one house survey, was vacant.[6]

OBL and his family could not have lived for many years in Abbottabad and other parts of Pakistan, changing residences at some intervals, without a steady and reliable support system. Islamist militants in various parts of Pakistan certainly constituted an important source of such support. But the Abbottabad Commission did not have access to accurate evidence on such non-official—not to speak of official—bases of their support. Nevertheless, when Pakistan's intelligence agencies too appeared to lack such access, the Commission could not but feel perturbed. For, it was widely known that Islamist militants within the Pakistani military itself formed a powerful network. Pakistan's military officials always tended to underrate this network, whereas foreign observers tried to overrate the same. Nevertheless, whatever was known about the circumstances and duration of stay of OBL and his family in a number of places inside Pakistan (including Abbottabad) could not but sustain one possible speculation: sections of Pakistani intelligence personnel extended informal and indirect support to OBL, while exercising abundant care to cover the tracks for the purpose of denial of links with OBL. The Prime Minister's Office (PMO) was legally responsible for the custody of records about an important person like OBL, for, it received relevant reports from the Interior Ministry and Intelligence Bureau (IB). But, because of obvious extra-legal and administrative mandates, the ISI was the inventory of information about OBL. If the ISI attempted to deny this, that would fail the minimum test of plausibility.[7]

Pakistan could have avoided embarrassment (if not ignominy) if it had been able to capture OBL before Americans did in May 2011. The ISI certainly lagged far behind the CIA in technical expertise for surveillance. But this could be arguably more than compensated by the enormous reservoir of local information with the ISI, which the CIA could not match. The CIA used to provide information to the ISI about OBL for a number of years, although this did not lead to OBL's arrest. But around 2005, the CIA stopped exchanging information on OBL with the ISI. For, in the mean time, the CIA developed suspicion about the reliability of the ISI. The CIA even alleged that the ISI sometimes leaked information supplied by the CIA to terrorists, enabling the latter to escape detention. At one stage, therefore, the CIA did not mind receiving information about terrorists from the ISI, but withheld the results of analysis of this information in the light of myriads of data accessible to the CIA. Evidently, when the CIA came to know about OBL's presence in Abbottabad, it decided not to share that vital information with the ISI, even though the two agencies were legally bound to transmit such information to each other. The Abbottabad Commission addressed some questions on this subject to Americans, who, expectedly, did not answer.[8]

Americans lodged numerous complaints with Pakistani authorities about the protection extended to OBL by sections of Pakistani intelligence personnel. These were so serious and frequent that the meetings of three topmost persons in Pakistan—the President, the Prime Minister and the Chief of Army Staff (COAS)—should have considered them. Even assuming that such a consideration took place, no evidence on this matter was made available to the Abbottabad Commission. After all, the relationship between even leading politicians like the Prime Minister and the DG of ISI was so extraordinary that the former asked the latter for a briefing and the latter never cared to provide it. The capture of OBL by Americans in May 2011 amounted to a sort of military intervention, and an actualisation of any incipient military threat that could be inferred from the above noted allegations by America against the Pakistani intelligence establishment. Impartial observers might not be satisfied with levelling merely the charge of incompetence/inattentiveness against Pakistan's intelligence community. They might suspect collusion between some members of this community and OBL's terrorist supporters.[9]

The Abbottabad Commission must be congratulated on probing deeply the circumstances leading to America's raid into the OBL compound in May 2011. The deeper the probe, the greater the number of questions for Pakistan's military intelligence establishment. Most of the questions are nearly unanswerable. As a result, despite the Commission's report being impeccably impartial, sensitive and sanitised, even an uninitiated reader of this report could hint at the dysfunctionalities in America-Pakistan relations, at the consequential failures of America's war on terror, and at ominous scenarios of what could happen in the Pakistan-Afghanistan region in the coming years.

The basic dysfunctionality in Pakistan's relations with America had its roots in Pakistan's India policy. Guidelines on this subject, formulated in the Pakistan government's Defence Policy of 2004 and the Joint Strategic Directive of 2007, were prevalent in May 2011.

According to these guidelines, India was the enemy country—not America—and Pakistan's defence forces were fully prepared to cope with probable combats only in the eastern frontier with India. Even though, in the recent past, due to misunderstandings on the prosecution of the war on terror, Americans created some conflictual situations on Pakistan's western frontier, e.g., by military raids in Pakistan's border areas, Pakistan could not anticipate such a daring and risky military venture by America as the one launched in May 2011 inside the OBL compound. Even if one assumes that this American military move could be anticipated by Pakistanis, they could do practically nothing to bridge the technology gap with America and stop the American incursion into the OBL compound. For, American helicopters possessed capacities of suppression of flight noise, for stealth technology, etc. They had night vision and radar evasion capabilities. Pakistanis, therefore, were unable to detect their intrusion. There was a larger and far more embarrassing question: even if the Pakistan Air Force (PAF) had the power of detection, what should it have done? Should the PAF have launched a military counter measure and risked escalation with incalculable consequences because of the presence of American F-16 fighters and AWACS across the Pakistan-Afghanistan border? The answer was surely in the negative, and the question too was not relevant, because in view of the aforesaid defence guidelines of 2004 and 2007, the PAF's deployment in Pakistan's Afghan frontier was in conformity with the requirements in times of peace.[10]

There was no abnormal occurrence in Abbottabad on the day of OBL's capture, except when one of the American helicopters, which met with an accident, had to be blasted, and the noise was striking. The COAS obviously came to know about it, and alerted the PAF chief. But nothing could be done at that moment to the intruding helicopters, which had already crossed Pakistan's border. True, American AWACS and F-16s were flying along the border for emergency intervention in defence of the American helicopters. But their flights could also be deemed to be a routine activity as on a normal day, although some critics might smell a partial lapse of judgement. There was, again, an unfounded suspicion that America might have dispatched a communication, which sterilised any probable PAF action against trespassing helicopters. Nevertheless, a real complaint against Pakistani political-military leaders was that they ignored past warnings from President Barack Obama about a likely American military move, especially when these warnings came in the wake of deaths of Pakistani civil-military personnel due to American combat operations in defiance of Pakistan's territorial sovereignty. The rather unconvincing answer to this complaint by Pakistan's politicians and military officers was that Obama's warnings were not delivered in writing, and, therefore, could not be treated as a policy message. These could probably be interpreted as Obama's attempts to placate dissenting public opinion in his own country.[11]

Suppose, Obama's warnings were taken seriously by Pakistani authorities, and Pakistani defence forces could even learn in time of the American helicopters approaching the OBL compound. Still, Pakistan, mindful of America's overwhelming military-technological superiority might not have judged it worthwhile to intercept the American helicopters. For, there were American F-16s in the vicinity, and the already fragile America-Pakistan political relations might have plunged immediately into an unacceptable collapse. Pakistan, although unable to exercise any military option against America, had, however, for years an ample number of other options, which, if availed of, might have pre-empted the American raid in Abbottabad. In the period preceding May 2011, Pakistan, for instance, could have dismantled the terrorist infrastructure inside Pakistan. Authorities in Pakistan could have, moreover, prevented militants from using the Pakistani bases for lethal assaults on American and NATO forces in Afghanistan. Such measures might have dissolved (or minimised) American suspicions about Pakistan's chronic collusion with terrorists, enhanced cooperation with America for the capture of High Value Targets (HVTs) including OBL, and thus created a political convergence with America, that could prompt a policy review, and a rethink about plans to stage the May 2011 intrusion into the OBL compound at Abbottabad.[12]

The Abbottabad Commission referred to the incident in May 2011 as a 'national shame', as 'the worst failure since 1971', and as 'a national tragedy'. Yet, according to the Commission, it 'was not a standalone failure', not an 'exception to the rule', but 'the rule'. For, it signified a 'systemic failure': 'The political, military, intelligence and bureaucratic leadership cannot be absolved of their responsibility for the state of governance, policy planning and policy implementation that eventually rendered this national failure almost inevitable.' It was probably the most appropriate and accurate verdict on what was happening in Pakistan for decades.[13]

Nevertheless, while providing this mega verdict on the situation in which the political-military-intelligence elites were merely serving their narrow personal/sectional/institutional interests at the expense of vital national interests, the Commission did not shy away from referring to important sectoral failures. For example, good and responsible governance did not have a chance to emerge in Pakistan for decades, because whenever a new set of political leaders came to power, they resorted to the unfair practice of dismissing and appointing officials for considerations of parochial political jealousies and rivalries, and they did not pay attention to the supply of minimum of essential services to the ordinary people. If, again, a military government came to power by displacing political leaders, they tended to replace high ranking civilian officials by military officials (in service or retired). This only aggravated the problems of governance, including that of provision of training for civil servants. When, for instance, military officials took over the job of the police and the IB, they occupied positions for which they had no training, while the normal needs of training or capacity building for police and IB personnel remained neglected. What is characterised as systemic failure is actually the product of failures of many individuals and organisations permitted to exercise powers wrongfully and discharge duties for which they were not fit. One has to draw a distinction between usurpers and regular deserving incumbents. In the incident at the OBL compound in May 2011, military officials could blame police and IB officials for various shortcomings, whereas police and IB officials could point to the root of these shortcomings, viz. withdrawal of essential resources from them by an over-ambitious military elite.[14]

The Abbottabad Commission had also not lost sight of other institutional failures while rightly harping on the comprehensive and collective failure of the entire ruling circle, i.e., the systemic failure. For instance, there are a large number of intelligence organisations in Pakistan: the IB, FIA, Special Branch, CID, the ISI, Military Intelligence, Air Intelligence, Naval Intelligence, etc. Evidently, there are areas of overlap, which require careful and continuous coordination. As to the coordination of work among intelligence agencies in the armed forces, there are regular meetings of the Joint Intelligence Coordination Committee. But there is no comparable coordination mechanism for various civil intelligence agencies, not to speak of that for civil and military intelligence organisations. True, each agency develops its own agenda and priorities. But, for the purpose of forging an adequate input to policy making, there must be a tradition of sharing of information among a multiplicity of civil-military intelligence agencies at the headquarters as also field levels. But that is deplorably lacking. The lack of coordination between intelligence organisations assumed such a grotesque proportion that the IB, which had normally to play an important part in counter-terror activities, did not bother about exploring the whereabouts of OBL on the specious plea that this was a military matter in which the IB could not interfere. In a way, attempts at avoidance of coordination amounted to evasion of accountability. The ISI, the most powerful intelligence agency of Pakistan, being largely free from the burden of accountability, naturally suffered from degeneration and incompetence. Political leaders could remedy this problem, but they did not have the will to do so. [15]

The 336-page *Abbottabad Commission Report* is a model of dignified writing on extraordinarily complex, diverse, even incendiary, aspects of public and international affairs. Only once probably the Commission appeared to forget its sense of restraint. While referring to the assassination of OBL, it wrote that 'The US acted like a criminal thug'. It is, however, possible to argue that America had to act in this fashion because of multi-faceted thuggery on the part of Pakistan *vis-à-vis* America, Afghanistan, India, and its own people (most of them innocent and poor). For decades, Pakistan's military-intelligence establishment went on doing what it should not have done, and refrained from doing what it should have done. At the root of the problem was the exercise of political predominance by military-intelligence authorities—despite the periodical observance of the formality of elections. 'The legacy of unconstitutional military rule and in particular the dark era of General Zia-ul-Haq left Pakistan with the poisoned legacy of a criminal, violent, ideological and anti-national infrastructure of extremism.' Civilians ceased to exercise legitimate control over the shape, content and fulfilment of a national security policy in tune with the urgent needs of the people of Pakistan. Military-intelligence authorities acquired illegitimate control over the national security policy, and enabled non-state actors to use the name of Islam to practise mindless violence and challenge the foundation of the state of Pakistan. Terrorist agencies (including the one attached to OBL) set up parallel governments as it were, and the Pakistan government appeared to be incapable of taming them. This could have prompted the Americans to plan OBL's assassination in May 2011.[16]

Whether before or after May 2011, Americans also committed other such acts of transgression of Pakistan's sovereignty. Whereas this incident of OBL's assassination was observed to be one of 'national disgrace' and 'national humiliation', Pakistan's military-intelligence establishment made it somewhat inevitable by arranging safe shelters for HVTs, including those belonging to Al Qaeda, and by half-heartedly pursuing a counter-terrorism strategy. This establishment appeared to compensate for its own deficiencies by a sort of outsourcing to Americans, who carried out drone strikes to eliminate HVTs, although these caused untold misery to innocent civilians killed or injured by such strikes. Americans could claim these collateral damages to be unavoidable because HVTs obtained sanctuaries among innocents. If Pakistan had taken determined actions against such terrorist networks as OBL's network, and also captured OBL, Americans would not probably have to launch a venture as risky as the one in May 2011. Pakistan's anti-terror policies appeared to be so counter-productive as to multiply rather than minimise extremism, and contributed to the failure of the government to extend basic human security to common Pakistanis in matters of access to food, education, etc.[17]

The Abbottabad Commission must be congratulated on sharply underlining the grave political-administrative tragedy of Pakistan, of which the OBL incident of May 2011 was only an instance. 'Institutions either failed to discharge responsibilities that legally were theirs or they assumed responsibility for tasks that legally were not part of their duties and for which they were not trained. This reflected the course of civil-military relations and the power balance between them.' Moreover, 'what is undeniable is that the incident [of May 2011] was the outcome over time of a whole series of actions and inactions at very senior decision making levels. Unless this is acknowledged, discussed in the highest political forums of the country and seriously addressed and redressed as a major national priority, there can be no guarantee against future disasters of the kind that have happened before and after the US assassination raid in Abottabad on the night of May 2, 2011. The biggest challenge for the future of Pakistan is the refusal to acknowledge unpleasant facts and the tendency to shy away from addressing fundamental flaws in critical decision making processes that affect the survival interests of Pakistan.'[18]

One paramount message of the *Abbottabad Commission Report*—providing an apt foreground for the projected withdrawal of American and NATO forces from Afghanistan in December 2014—is the dismal state of America-Pakistan relations, and the resultant dysfunctionality of America's war on terror. Both the countries are deeply disappointed with each other's performance. Yet, both try to perpetuate the illusion of a strategic partnership. Meanwhile, the terrorists may find themselves far more powerful in December 2014 than in 2001-02 when America and Pakistan collaborated in commencing the war on terror. The *Abbottabad Commission Report* was submitted on 9 July

2013. Meanwhile, i.e., in the period since 1 May 2011, terrorists in Pakistan continued to add significantly to their strength, and expose the deplorable weaknesses of Pakistan's military-intelligence establishment. For instance, in a few days, 'Later in May, a devastating series of suicide attacks and bomb blasts by the Pakistani Taliban and Al Qaeda killed more than 160 people and wounded 350. The most serious attack was on a naval base in Karachi on May 22, when six suicide fighters held off an entire garrison and destroyed $70 million worth of US-supplied naval reconnaissance aircraft.[19] The suicide attackers used small arms as also rocket-propelled grenades (RPGs), killing about twelve soldiers.[20] In May 2011, again, VBIEDs struck several police stations and suicide attackers used IEDs against a training centre of the Frontier Constabulary of Pakistan. The TTP acknowledged responsibility for these incidents.[21] On 6 May 2011, an attack on a paramilitary training centre occurred, killing more than 90 persons and injuring more than 100 persons. The TTP referred to this attack of 6 May 2011 as the first act of revenge against the killing of OBL. In the same month, the Indian Mujahideen exploded a low-yield bomb outside the High Court of Delhi. But none died and very few were injured.[22]

In order to have a proper appreciation of the brilliant and lucid *Abbottabad Commission Report*, it is essential to review international reports on OBL killing immediately after the event. American Navy SEALs had the authority to fight Pakistani forces in case they faced resistance at any stage of their mission. The same toughness of mood persisted as America ignored the Pakistani demand, and refused to apologise for the OBL incident. America also made preparations for coping with any adverse Pakistani move in reaction to this incident. For instance, if Pakistan obstructed supplies to US-NATO forces in Afghanistan, America would explore non-Pakistani routes of supply. Nevertheless, there were reports that as early as 2001, there was a secret deal between Musharraf and Bush that, if required, America would assassinate OBL on Pakistani territory, that Pakistan would publicly protest against it for the sake of form, and that America would tolerate it. Naturally, after OBL's death, Musharraf denied that there was ever such a secret deal with Bush.[23]

At the time of OBL's death, Musharraf was in Britain, where he was living in self exile since 2008. He observed that when he was the

President of Pakistan, some ISI-military officials, who were low-ranking and roguish, might have information about where OBL was actually residing. America, however, was alert for some years about details of how Pakistan was deceiving America in the war on terror, and hence the CIA maintained a safe house in Abbottabad (till OBL's death) for watching what happened in OBL's compound. After all, since 2005, three successive heads of the ISI—Ashfaq Parvez Kayani, Nadim Taj and Shuja Pasha—extended protection to OBL in Abbottabad where even a command and control centre for terrorists operated regularly under OBL's superintendence. The comment by Pakistan's Prime Minister, Gilani, that all intelligence agencies in the world were guilty of failure in tracking down OBL, was, therefore, hardly realistic.[24]

India's response to the Abbottabad incident was tame, even if typical. So, Prime Minister Manmohan Singh stated in Kabul that India would refrain from launching the type of operation that America carried out in Abbottabad for the purpose of capturing those terrorists, who were living in Pakistan, while India wanted them for trial. P. Chidambaram, India's Home Minister, spoke of arch-terrorist Dawood Ibrahim residing in Pakistan, and added that Pakistan's denial could not negate this hard fact. Terrorists fleeing from India to Pakistan numbered 50, according to a list publicised by India. Chidambaram affirmed that India would carry on a dialogue with Pakistan on a number of issues, but, on the issue of the 2008 terrorist attack in Mumbai, India had to mobilise the support of the international community for exerting pressure on Pakistan, so that the conspirators of this attack (enjoying a sanctuary in Pakistan) could be brought to justice. In America, notably, federal prosecutors charged Major Iqbal (in active service with the Pakistan army), as also some other persons, with plotting the 2008 Mumbai attacks.[25]

Hamid Karzai, the President of Afghanistan, reacted to the OBL episode by sharply criticising American and NATO leaders for not taking seriously Karzai's warnings about Pakistan sheltering the Al Qaeda and Taliban, and about the urgent need for fighting terrorists in their Pakistani sanctuaries rather than in Afghanistan's villages.[26] As days passed, new information and incidents went on embittering America-Pakistan relations, whereas the Pakistan government could not make even any attempt to explain OBL's presence in Abbottabad.

ABC and the *Times,* London reported the discovery of a diary at OBL's Abbottabad compound, which contained a plan for killing Barack Obama and for upsetting the 2012 elections in America.[27]

In June 2011, a police station in Pakistan suffered from a number of deaths and casualties due to the activation of suicide jackets. Moreover, a combined military-police check post was subjected to attacks by small arms, mortars and RPGs. In course of these attacks, 16 police officers were abducted and subsequently murdered. Elsewhere in June 2011, a crowd gathering at the site of an IED detonation confronted a suicide strike on a motorbike.[28] On 13 July 2011, Mumbai suffered from three simultaneous bomb attacks—two at market places and one at a bus stop. Twenty six people died, and around 130 persons were wounded. India's counter-terrorism agencies found out that Pakistan-sponsored operatives were associated with planning these bomb attacks in Saudi Arabia, and manufacturing the explosives in India.[29]

The Taliban successfully fired RPGs to bring down a transport helicopter on 6 August 2011. Thirty-two American military personnel and eight others died. Seventeen SEALs (including some who had raided the OBL compound in Abbottabad) were among the deceased Americans. If this was a Taliban revenge against OBL's assassination, Americans too retaliated soon—in a few weeks—by killing Atiya-abd-al-Rahman by means of a drone strike in Pakistan's North Waziristan. Rahman was the second in command to Ayman-al-Zawahiri, who succeeded OBL as the Al Qaeda chief.[30] Two mosques in Pakistan became targets of suicide strikes in August 2011—one by the detonation of a jacket, and another by that of a VBIED. In September 2011, in addition to targeting Shia attendees in a funeral, Pakistani terrorists attacked the house of a Deputy Inspector General of Frontier Constabulary. A VBIED was exploded outside his house, whereas grenades and IEDs were used by a suicide striker boldly entering into the house. Three children, twelve civilians and thirteen soldiers died. In October 2011, too, fourteen Shias died when a bus was attacked with small arms. In November 2011, ten police officers were injured as a prison van was targeted by a suicide attacker. In December 2011, seven body guards and nine civilians were killed by the BLA detonating a VBIED outside the residence of a former state minister.[31]

Whereas the above noted terrorist incidents inside Pakistan in the year of OBL's assassination were alarming enough for the establishments in Islamabad and Washington DC, probably no less alarming was the seemingly irreversible erosion of mutual trust between the two establishments. After OBL's killing, Pakistan's central legislature warned America against the recurrence of another Abbottabad-type raid; America did not bother. Again after OBL's assassination, America demanded that Pakistan should supply the names of top ISI personnel, who might have had information about OBL's activities in Abbottabad; but Pakistan did not bother. America had sufficient grounds for suspicion of collusive links between OBL and the ISI. Yet, the situation in the Pakistan-Afghanistan region was so complex and sensitive that America did not want to subject its relationship with Pakistan to a complete collapse.[32] That is why America did not react in any visibly adverse manner when Pakistan's Punjab province protested against the OBL episode by an abrogation of as many as six pacts with America for urgently needed assistance in the vital fields of education, health and solid waste management.[33]

The America-Pakistan relationship was as pervasive as it was inscrutable—partially due to Pakistan's domestic compulsions. Pakistani rulers had to make strenuous efforts to impress/mislead the public that they were not as dependent on the US as they actually were. During his campaign for the US presidency in 2008, Barack Obama opposed the Bush government's Iraq war, whereas he not only supported military operations in Afghanistan, but also promised to expand these operations. In March and December 2009, when Obama was the President, these operations were actually enlarged.[34] WikiLeaks brought to light some secret US diplomatic cables, which contradicted repetitive declarations by the Pakistani military that foreign forces would not be allowed to operate inside the Pakistani territory. In accordance with these cables, by the summer of 2009, US special operations forces and the Pakistani military collected intelligence in an integrated manner. By September 2009, moreover, the US and Pakistani forces engaged in combined deployment and operations. On this subject, the Pakistani newspaper *Dawn* quoted US Ambassador to Pakistan Anne Patterson's statement in May, October and November 2009.[35]

What was even more significant, the secret US diplomatic cables, revealed by WikiLeaks and reported in *Dawn*, pointed to the Pakistani military's request for US drone cover for Pakistan's military operations in tribal areas. Pakistan's civilian leaders, however, told US officials that they would publicly denounce, but privately welcome the US drone attacks on the Pakistani soil. The reliability of WikiLeaks disclosures could be tested by references to a meeting between Pakistan's Army Chief, General Ashfaq Parvez Kayani and Admiral William J. Fallon, the US CENTCOM commander, which took place on 22 January 2008. In this meeting, Kayani requested Fallon for systematic drone protection over Pakistan's military actions in North Waziristan. Anne Patterson stated this in a secret cable of 11 February 2008. Moreover, in a secret US cable from Islamabad on 24 March 2008, it was stated that the US Chairman, Joint Chiefs of Staff, Admiral Mike Mullen requested Kayani for consent to operations by US drones in a third restricted zone. The implication was clear: Pakistan had already approved two such zones of operation. Publicly, of course, the Pakistani military persistently asserted that they did not support the CIA's unmanned aircraft strikes inside Pakistan. What Anne Patterson wrote in a confidential cable of 19 February 2009 revealed nearly everything that needed to be known about the drone strikes issue. Kayani was to visit the US in a week, and Patterson had to forward agenda points to Washington DC. She wrote: 'Kayani knows well that the strikes have been precise (creating few civilian casualties) and targeted primarily at foreign fighters in the North and South Waziristan tribal regions.'[36]

The trap of deceptive cooperation laid by Pakistani authorities was so wide as to catch numerous parties: the US, the government and people of Pakistan, as also militants in Pakistan. For instance, AP reporters discovered a village about thirty-five miles from the celebrated OBL compound. This village was endowed with glacial rivers, hills and pine forests. But villagers, in urgent need of firewood, did not have the courage to chop pine trees. For, they were conscious that the hills concealed a training centre for Islamist militants. The Pakistan army was fully aware of, but refused to acknowledge the existence of this secret terrorist enclave. The AP team collected information about another such enclave at the Manshera district in the fateful month of May 2011. All this merely reconfirmed what was an open secret: Pakistan was long playing a game of boundless duplicity. It procured money and arms from the US to fight terrorists, but, simultaneously, patronised some extremist groups for use as its own assets.[37]

America, too, could be accused of playing a double game by other countries, especially India, when the US judiciary recorded (in May 2011 coincidentally) incontestable evidence about the ISI sponsoring and monitoring the 2008 terrorist attack in Mumbai. David Coleman Headley, the US Justice Department's witness in the trial of another terrorist, Tahawwur Hussain Rana, revealed in a Chicago courtroom that a frogman of the Pakistan navy assisted terrorists in landing in Mumbai for the 2008 attack. Headley not only exempted himself from death penalty by plea bargaining with the US government, he also revealed elaborately his links with the ISI, and the ISI's connections with the LET and other terrorist outfits. The US designated these outfits formally as terrorists. Logically, the US should have conferred the same designation on the ISI. But it did not do so, presumably because it wanted to continue to do business with the ISI, although in confidential cables, the US government called the ISI 'a terrorist support entity'. The month of May 2011 heaped further embarrassment on the US as *Dawn* reported WikiLeaks documents, which underlined how high-ranking military officers of Pakistan, on training at Islamabad's National Defence University, received anti-American discourses. These officers, who sent their children to Britain and the US for higher studies, imbibed misperceptions about the US at the National Defence University. Ironically, from 2001 to 2008 (for instance), the US supplied $18 billion of aid to Pakistan.[38]

If OBL was found and slain in a spot about 800 yards from the prestigious military academy of Pakistan in Abbottabad, Mullah Mohammed Omar was still staying near Quetta in an ISI-protected safe house. So, in the month of May 2011 (and afterwards), the glaring question was: who had greater responsibility to take not one (like OBL's assassination), but a series of decisive measures against terrorists in the Pakistan-Afghanistan region—the US or Pakistan. The obvious answer was: the US, which could no longer afford to hibernate and emulate Pakistan in a duplicitous game, especially when the Haqqani terrorist outfit, sponsored by Pakistan, had killed hundreds of Americans in Afghanistan. For quite some time since 9/11, and the near-fiasco in Iraq, the US was not being respected as the sole superpower in the world. After OBL's death, this respect was partially restored and the American people experienced a sense of prestige, unity and security. Therefore, the US should no longer go on trotting out excuses of why they could not alienate Pakistan beyond a certain limit, and should refrain from taking determined steps against terrorists inside Pakistan. After all, the US must not forget, the Pakistan Taliban (and not the Al Qaeda) announced the first revenge call after OBL's demise. As to Pakistani authorities, they did not seem to comprehend that despite their long-practised double game, the Pakistan Taliban did not swerve from their principal aim to displace Pakistan's rulers from their governmental positions. In an interview to the AP, Waliur Rahman, the Pakistan Taliban's Deputy Commander, pointed out that OBL's departure merely incited them to complete OBL's mission with renewed vigour. According to him, the Pakistan government, enslaved by the US, was the principal Taliban target. He also identified the NATO, Jews and Christians as the other enemies of Taliban. According to Salman Rushdie, it was high time to proclaim that Pakistan was a terrorist state, and that the international community should respond adequately.[39]

The US action-inaction syndrome in the Pakistan-Afghanistan region was comprehensible, but not defensible. The US was prepared to overcome the moral dilemma of conducting a war on terror. It received vital clues about OBL's residence from terrorists detained and questioned in a manner not quite consistent with the standards of human rights advocated by the US. Moreover, while Pakistan liked US drone attacks in defence of its own security forces, it could not certainly approve other drone strikes, which affected funeral or marriage assemblies. But the US did not care for Pakistani sentiments on this matter. Pakistan, too, did not bother about the US prodding Pakistan to take steps against those terrorist agencies, like the LET or HUM, which Pakistan tried to reserve for the proxy war against India (although Pakistan was not always successful in keeping these outfits completely off Pakistani targets). If one takes into account the TTP, Pakistan's relationship with indigenous terrorists was becoming unsustainable. So was its relationship with the US. Apparently, the US was getting ready to withdraw its combat force from the Pakistan-

Afghanistan region in the near future. It reconciled itself to the dismal truth that it was failing to win the war on terror in this region. For, it could not resolve the basic contradictions in a situation where it had, invariably, to depend on Pakistan's cooperation in order to win (unless it was prepared to take extreme measures, which might not receive the endorsement of the US Congress), but Pakistani cooperation was at best lukewarm. So, even when the whole of America extended unequivocal emotional support to the US President for the liquidation of a mass murderer like OBL, the President did not appear to be resolute in following it up by other comparably bold measures.[40]

President Obama made two simultaneous declarations in December 2009: first, to escalate US military operations in Afghanistan, and second, to commence military drawdown in July 2011.[41] Obama's political opponents could notice a contradiction in the simultaneity of these two declarations. But such a criticism would be superficial. It would miss the fundamental contradiction in US-Pakistan relations, noticed in the previous paragraph, and thus fail to discover the logic behind Obama's twin declarations of December 2009. This logic was clearly and comprehensively analysed later in the August 2010 *Report of the Afghanistan Study Group*. This report stressed that even the decision to expand military operations in Afghanistan was based on the wrong assumption that Al Qaeda's ability to launch a direct attack on the US homeland would suffer a big blow if the US registered eventually a military triumph in Afghanistan. For, there were only about 400 Al Qaeda operatives in the Pakistan-Afghanistan region, most of them trying to hide themselves in Pakistan's KPK and FATA. However much the US might try military escalation in Afghanistan, the hard core Al Qaeda militants would be able to work in small cells in Pakistan, Afghanistan, and in other parts of the world including Europe.[42]

Afghanistan's annual GNP was estimated at $14 billion in 2010. The annual expenditure of the US in Afghanistan was approximately $100 billion. Thousands of US and NATO soldiers died in the theatre of war, or received deadly injuries. In fact, these deaths and injuries reached such a high level in July 2010 that several NATO allies were compelled to declare their decisions to pull back their troops. Core US interests, according to the Afghanistan Study Group, did not justify expenditure on the above noted scale. These interests were to minimise the possibilities of direct terrorist assaults upon the US homeland, and to ensure that the Pakistan-Afghanistan (or the Afghanistan-Pakistan) area did not provide such safe sanctuaries to terrorists, especially the Al Qaeda, as to facilitate attacks on mainland US. Another dominant US interest was to pre-empt the access of terrorists to Pakistan's nuclear armoury. According to the Afghanistan Study Group, unless the US deescalated its military presence, it might fail to serve these interests. For, the very presence of foreign troops in large numbers added to the unity, strength and recruitment potential of otherwise fractious terrorist groups, conveniently lumped under the name of Taliban. Afghanistan was a site of perpetual strife between tribes and ethnic groups, e.g., Pashtuns, Tajiks, Uzbeks, etc. But, because the US army was denounced as an occupation army, a sort of traditional civil war got transformed into a war between terrorist groups and foreign forces. Whereas the Taliban fighters were known to be cruel and dishonest, no less were the functionaries of the government led by President Hamid Karzai, especially those posted in rural areas. Above all, US troops were bravely fighting the Taliban, which, ironically, received enormous financial and logistical assistance from Pakistan's ISI.[43]

Significantly, Barack Obama revealed, as early as 1 August 2007, in a speech at the Woodrow Wilson Center, Washington DC, his keen awareness that, essentially, Pakistan was itself the problem. Pakistan was so venal that it undermined US efforts to wipe out terrorists. Obama realised that the US had to direct Pakistan firmly to destroy the sanctuaries of terrorists on its own territory. In a year after Obama's insightful Wilson Center address, President Bush, exasperated by Pakistan's persistent perfidy, asked the CIA to cease to provide any advance warning to the Pakistan government about US drone strikes, although information should be transmitted immediately after the launch of the drones. Probably, President Bush repented his early 2005 decision to respect Pakistani sentiments, and cancel a plan (at an advanced stage of implementation) to capture stealthily such prominent terrorist leaders as Ayman-al-Zawahiri. On 22 January 2009, President Obama ordered drone assaults in Pakistan, translating into action his promise of unilateral US measures inside Pakistan aired in the aforesaid Wilson Center speech. Certainly, the Abbottabad compound incident of 1-2 May 2011 marked a great advance in the implementation of this boldly pragmatic promise.[44]

Whereas at long last, the US was trying to tread a realistic path for coping with terrorism and Pakistani treachery, Pakistan itself failed to devise an appropriate policy to take on indigenous terrorists. For example, on 29 May 2011, an eminent Pakistani journalist, Syed Saleem Shahzad, the *Asia Times* Online Bureau Chief for Pakistan, wrote authoritatively on the nexus between Al Qaeda fighters and Pakistan Navy functionaries, which enabled the terrorists to infiltrate the navy base in Karachi, and ravage the base on 22 May. Shahzad afterwards complained of threats by the ISI. But he failed to save himself. He died on 31 May—obviously because of an ISI conspiracy. Notably, navy officers ran the ISI's media wing, and they could not endure Shahzad's truthful exposures. In the past, too, these officers hounded a number of journalists and their family members. Threats were followed on a number of occasions by murders, eight journalists dying in 2010, and another eight in the first seven months of 2011. Therefore, the Committee to Protect Journalists, with headquarters in New York, depicted Pakistan as the world's most dangerous country for journalists. The US government too blamed the Pakistani authorities for Shahzad's death, although the ISI promptly denied its role.[45]

As Pakistan thus remained in collusion with terrorists, it paved the way to further discomfiture for itself. For, the Taliban decided to compel the Pakistan government to terminate its alliance with the US by launching assaults on Pakistan's important civil-military establishments. Maulana Faqir Mohammed, a TTP leader, made the ominous announcement that, unlike in the past when the TTP concentrated on campaigns in Afghanistan, henceforward, it would replicate on a large scale such actions as the daring raid upon the Pakistan naval base in Karachi on 22 May, and throw Pakistan's security agencies off balance. Maulana Faqir also talked of his plan to attack border outposts of Pakistani security forces in KPK. It was not clear whether Pakistani authorities took seriously this TTP threat of a new strategy, the first such formal declaration of its kind. But they certainly had to sit up when the US administration set July 2011 as the deadline before which they had to capture five most powerful Al Qaeda and Taliban leaders by means of military actions in North

Waziristan. These terrorist leaders were Ayman-al-Zawahiri, Mullah Omar, Iliyas Kashmiri, Sirajuddin Haqqani and Atis Abdur Rehman. The July deadline derived significance from the decision of the US and NATO to commence drawdown of their forces from Afghanistan in that month. Pakistan was given the option to launch the military offensive unilaterally or jointly in North Waziristan. Although for long, the US was pressing Pakistani security forces to act in North Waziristan, Pakistan remained hesitant for some vital reasons. North Waziristan was the home of terrorist groups friendly to Pakistan. For instance, the Haqqani militant network acted as the liaison group for Pakistani intelligence authorities in dealing with the Afghan Taliban. Moreover, in North Waziristan, Mullah Nazir and Hafez Gul Bahadur headed terrorist groups, which helped the Pakistan government in successfully counteracting tribal constellations, who were hostile to the Islamabad government.[46]

Eventually, on 3 June 2011, one of the top terrorists mentioned in the previous paragraph, Iliyas Kashmiri, a former officer of Pakistan's Special Service Group (SSG), was killed as a result of two US drone attacks. Next day, on 4 June 2011, whether due to US pressures, or their own threat assessments, Pakistan's security forces killed as many as 26 terrorists moving to Pakistan from across the Afghan border. Pakistani militants exhibited their strength on 5 June 2011, when they killed 25 persons and wounded nearly 50 people by bomb blasts in a bakery (run by the army) and a bus stop. Next day, on 6 June 2011, US drone attacks killed 18 militants in the FATA, which were reputed to be the world's biggest centre of terrorist networks, e.g., the Taliban, Al Qaeda, and other associated groups. Significantly, the US ignored Pakistani protests and demands for cessation of attacks by unmanned aerial vehicles (UAVs), and in the FATA on 8 June 2011, US drone strikes on a training camp resulted in the deaths of not less than 22 militants.[47]

US-Pakistan tensions on the issue of prosecution of the war on terror showed no sign of relaxation. Indigenous anti-government terrorists in Pakistan too were not ready to relent. Despite President Obama's evident preference for an early withdrawal of US soldiers from Afghanistan, there was no possibility of any lessening of pitiless pressure on the Taliban in the immediate future, as US Defence Secretary Robert M. Gates impressed upon NATO partners on 9 June

2011. Such pressure alone might oblige the Taliban to consider a negotiated settlement of the conflict that was nearly a decade old. Anders Fogle Rasmussen, NATO's Secretary General, agreed with Gates that ground realities would determine the pace of withdrawal of combat forces from Afghanistan. In the combative post-Abbottabad mood, the Pakistan military reduced the number of US soldiers posted in Pakistan, even while, as reports published on 10 June 2011 indicated, Pakistani terrorists attacked two check posts and murdered thirty Pakistani soldiers. Moreover, Army Chief General Kayani decided to overrule repeated US advice for a large scale operation in North Waziristan. An important meeting of top Pakistani commanders on 9 June endorsed this decision of Kayani.[48]

Nevertheless, following the eleven Corps Commanders' meeting on 9 June 2011, General Kayani issued a number of clarifications about the role and performance of the Pakistani military, especially in the perspective of relations with the US since 2001, and the use of the Coalition Support Fund. That Kayani restricted the number of US troops stationed in Pakistan and that he did not act upon US pressures for immediate military operations in North Waziristan, have already been noted above. But there were other momentous matters awaiting clarification by Kayani. Pakistan decided to minimise training assistance from the US, limiting the same to the Frontier Corps, and that too only in the case of introduction of new equipment. As to cooperation with the US on intelligence collection and transmission, Pakistan announced zero tolerance for independent secret activities by any foreign agency. Since 2001, Pakistan was to receive \$13 billion in aid from the US. Actually, however, Pakistan received only \$8.6 billion. But the army got, over a ten-year period, only \$1.4 billion from the US, whereas the navy and the air force obtained lower amounts. The Government of Pakistan used \$6 billion of US aid by way of support for budgetary allocations. But the US did not provide the enormous funds needed for families of soldiers, who died or received injuries in the course of anti-terrorist operations. Above all, the entire country suffered terribly and immeasurably on account of infrastructure damages, and the consequent investment famine, caused by reckless terrorist assaults.[49]

The US, however, could not afford complacency. Whereas the Pakistani military was obsessed with overcoming the humiliation of the Abbottabad incident, the US experts (belonging to diverse intelligence agencies) diligently translated and deciphered the mass of documents seized from the Abbottabad compound. These experts were certainly knowledgeable about a substantial number of Al Qaeda militants, their action plans and respective roles inside their organisation. But the Abbottabad documents helped them in gaining a deeper familiarity with the mindsets of these militants. The US counter-terrorist agencies, including the CIA, used the newly available information to probe the activities of especially Al Qaeda operatives, whose actual status was revealed to be more important than previously thought of.[50]

The US success in the Abbottabad raid, however, deflated General Kayani's status. Ordinary Pakistani soldiers, who were all anti-US, interpreted the extraordinary three-year extension of Kayani's tenure as Army Chief in 2010 as a reward for his pro-US stance, and a confirmation of collusion between Pakistani and US governments on this issue. Immediately after the Abbottabad incident, sensing a rebellious attitude among middle ranking officers, Kayani visited a large number of garrisons and other military institutions (including mess halls) in order to pacify the anti-US officers and soldiers. In the course of his visits and speeches, Kayani confronted something, which no other Army Chief had witnessed in the past: he heard openly critical remarks even from battalion commanders. Pakistani troops exhibited a lack of motivation, discipline and efficiency in the matter of fighting the Taliban, largely because they viewed the anti-Taliban war not as Pakistan's but America's war.[51]

Meanwhile, the Al Qaeda appeared to resolve the leadership issue following OBL's assassination. Jihadi sites announced on 16 June 2011 the decision of the General Command of the Qaeda Al Jihad to vest in Sheikh Dr. Abu Muhammad Ayman-al-Zawahiri the responsibility of commanding the Al Qaeda. A surgeon from Egypt, Ayman-al-Zawahiri merely noticed that a de facto position was transformed into a de jure position, because he had not only been OBL's deputy for more than a decade, but also because the world had recognised him as the chief spokesperson of Al Qaeda. Zawahiri, stationed in the Pakistan-Afghanistan border area, continued to conduct Al Qaeda operations as before and sharply announced that OBL would terrorise the US as much after he died as he did when he lived. Zawahiri carried a $25 million reward on his head. The statement of the Al Qaeda General Command appointing him as OBL's successor issued a clear threat that Al Qaeda would pitilessly carry out jihad against the US, Israel and their supporters.[52]

A powerful Al Qaeda affiliate, the Pakistani Taliban, was quick to declare respect for Zawahiri's nomination as the Al Qaeda chief. Normally, the ruling circle of Pakistan should have been worried about this declaration.[53] For, it pointed to the alarming possibility of more vigorous assaults by them on the state of Pakistan. But this ruling circle, including General Kayani, was so overwhelmed by the shock of OBL's death that they toyed with the fanciful (nearly absurd) option of courting China and boycotting the US. China was too pragmatic to encourage this option at a time when China's economic relations with the US were so extensive as to enable China to emerge shortly as a global power enjoying positive attention from the Western powers. Therefore, Kayani's manouevre failed. Worse, the news of failure of overture to China leaked out.[54] America's mistrust of Pakistan, already pronounced, was heightened. A terribly messy relationship became messier. For, around this time, there came reports of the arrest of five Pakistanis by the ISI on the allegation of assisting the CIA to assassinate OBL. These arrests, coincidentally, followed the visit of CIA chief Leon Panetta to Islamabad. Panetta presented satellite video images confirming the ISI's (already familiar) collusion with the Afghan Taliban.[55]

The Pakistani military seemed to be hell-bent upon defying the US in conducting the war on terror. Even when the US was prepared to offer repeated chances to the Pakistani security forces for verification of whether Pakistanis deserved the trust of the US, Pakistan remained obstinate in demonstrating that they were not worthy of US trust. On 18 June 2011, for instance, US officials narrated how the US shared intelligence with Pakistanis about a number of bomb making sites in the terrorist-infested tribal regions, but Pakistanis, instead of launching immediate attacks, leaked information in such a way that militants were able to escape safely, carrying their incriminating baggage, before the attacks took place. Pakistanis offered an extraordinary excuse: they could not launch military operations in the extremely dangerous tribal areas without informing and securing in advance the endorsement of tribal leaders. The truth was that the Pakistani armed forces were not ready to attack the dens of those militants, e.g., the Haqqani group members, who were judged to be friendly to the Government of Pakistan (even though this group operated against the US forces in Afghanistan). In the case of other terrorist networks, known to be hostile to the Pakistan government, the Pakistani military did not hesitate to combine ground and aerial offensives.[56]

On 23 June 2011, President Obama delivered a tough message to Pakistan for the liquidation of safe havens granted by Pakistan to terrorists, while he also announced a process of withdrawal of US troops from Afghanistan, commencing in 2011, and continuing till the end of 2014, when Afghan forces could assume responsibility for the country's security. The Taliban, however, denounced Obama's promise of troop withdrawal as nominal. It demanded immediate and wholesale departure of all foreign forces, and warned that it would carry on military campaigns till such departure occurred. Surprisingly—what indicated the immense complexity in the Pakistan-Afghanistan situation—shortly before Obama's declaration of troop drawdown, President Hamid Karzai labelled US and NATO soldiers as occupation forces serving their selfish purposes in Afghanistan. Karzai obviously went to extreme in denouncing the activities of the US and NATO forces (which he did in the past too in a less trenchant fashion) because of his deep aversion to raids by these forces at night, which resulted in numerous deaths of Afghan civilians. The US, however, began to widen options for a political settlement of the long conflict in Afghanistan, and, without terminating the current military engagements with the Taliban, started peace parleys with these jihadis.[57]

In mid-2011, like the US, President Hamid Karzai too reportedly started negotiations with the Taliban for achieving peace in a war-torn country. But the prospects did not appear to be encouraging. For, the military chief of the Taliban, Mullah Abdul Qayyum Zakir, was fanatically pursuing plans for Operation Badr, i.e., a final military campaign to expel US troops from Afghanistan. He had once been detained at Guantanamo, the notorious US prison for terror suspects. He wanted to avenge this detention. Moreover, Zakir decided to demonstrate to the world that OBL's death did not signal the ruin of the Taliban. Zakir resolutely mobilised Taliban fighters in numerous bases. Under the ISI's supervision, Zakir and his close associates succeeded in establishing a sort of domination over the Pakistani province of Balochistan. Zakir was fond of boasting that he had a large auxiliary corps of suicide attackers with plenty of IEDs. In these circumstances, with Pakistan's unwavering support for the Taliban, which neither Karzai nor the US was in a position to dilute, it was doubtful how the Taliban could eventually be expected to help the Afghan government in welding together numerous clans, tribes and warlords for Afghan unity and nationhood, without which it might not be possible to accomplish lasting peace in Afghanistan.[58]

President Hamid Karzai applauded the announcement of President Obama on 23 June 2011 about the troops' drawdown. Obama said that 10,000 US soldiers would leave Afghanistan by the end of 2011, and another 23,000 in the summer of 2012. Karzai welcomed this measure as good for the US as well as for Afghanistan, because, gradually, the Afghans were to defend their own land. The US maintained the largest number of troops in Afghanistan—99,000. Britain's 9,500 soldiers formed the second largest contingent, Germany's 5,000 forming the third biggest contingent, followed by France's 4,000. The aforesaid announcement by Obama was based on elaborate consultations with the NATO allies. Europeans were naturally worried about the financial crisis rocking their continent, and Britain decided to withdraw 450 soldiers by the end of 2011. Germany too decided to reduce the number of its soldiers for the first time at about the same time, and France said that it would follow the plan of gradual drawdown of troops in a manner comparable to the US mode. All this reflected an improvement, however tenuous and temporary, in the ground situation in Afghanistan, but underlined caution instead of a rush for the exit.[59]

Along with Europe, the US too was passing through a financial crisis, especially since 2008. Moreover, it was possible to argue that, since October 2001, when the US intervened militarily in Afghanistan, the internal strife in Afghanistan registered a rise, and the Taliban, despite occasional setbacks (especially after Obama authorised a military surge in late 2009), regrouped itself and enhanced its strength. There was now a consensus among the US and its NATO allies that there could be no military solution to the infinitely complex problems of Afghanistan, and that a political settlement required some sort of reconciliation with the Taliban. There was also a consensus (although not acknowledged publicly) that Pakistan, much more than Afghanistan, was responsible for the sustenance of terrorism inside Afghanistan. Obama's statement of 23 June 2011 was a belatedly sad acknowledgement of these grim realities, and this acknowledgement could not be postponed any further. The awful experiences, following the invasion of Iraq in March 2003, aggravated the dreadfulness of these realities.[60]

If the US and its NATO allies appeared to forge a realistic posture towards the war on terror in the Pakistan-Afghanistan area, India seemed to adopt a posture that violated its self-interest. India's ruling politicians and security forces remained dormant (if not moribund) while the people of the country were physically and mentally devastated by a series of terrorist outrages planned by Pakistan. 'There is so much talk, and evidence, of the low-intensity conflict (in the garb of terrorism and sponsored insurgency) having replaced full-blown warfare, but on at least two occasions (the terrorist strike on Parliament House and Mumbai's infamous 26/11), the forces were unable to mount the swift, surgical strikes that would have been effective responses. It is not as though new paths have not been identified: just that there has been a reluctance to take them.'[61]

In this perspective, the two-day talks between Foreign Secretaries of India and Pakistan at Islamabad, which ended on 24 June 2011, though paraded as positive, were actually futile. For example, the Indian Foreign Secretary raised the issue of trial in Pakistan of the accused in 26/11 attacks. The Indian Foreign Secretary also said that a resolution of the complex J&K issue required a terror-free environment. The Pakistani Foreign Secretary stressed that terrorism threatened both the countries, which therefore had to collaborate in counteracting terrorism. The only positive feature of these discussions was probably the decision to continue to talk.[62] But India appeared to score a self-goal on the issue of terrorism. For instance, just before the aforesaid talks of Foreign Secretaries commenced, India's NIA hauled Hindu terrorist groups to the court in the case of the Samjhauta Express blast at India's Panipat in February 2007. Moreover, the Foreign Secretaries discussed the blast. But India's court proceedings were in flat contradiction of the report of the 1267 committee of the UN Security Council. This report imposed sanctions on the Al Qaeda and the Taliban, freezing their assets. It also prohibited troubles by and mandated an arms embargo on a businessman of Karachi, Arif Qasmani, who acted as the principal coordinator of the LeT. Qasmani, according to this UN report, supplied money to Al Qaeda, and obtained in exchange the service of operatives for masterminding the Samjhauta Express explosions.[63]

Pakistan's military and intelligence authorities sank low in the esteem of the country's people after the Abbottabad episode. Therefore, in order to show off the capacity for independent action irrespective of US reactions, and thereby enhance the army's reputation, the Pakistan government risked its own security and reduced the number of US trainers and soldiers deployed inside Pakistan.[64] This naturally facilitated likely attacks by terrorists upon the security infrastructure of Pakistan. In this highly sensitive situation, when Admiral Mike Mullen, the US Joint Chiefs of Staff Chairman, declared unambiguously that the Taliban's Haqqani network acted on ISI's behalf to launch terrorist strikes inside Afghanistan, endangering thereby not only Afghanistan's political stability, but also the security of US and NATO forces, Pakistan's army chief Kayani lost his patience. He warned that the US should think ten times before attacking the Haqqani group inside Pakistan, for, Pakistan happened to be a nuclear power.[65] President Asif Ali Zardari lent support to Kayani by writing an article in *The Washington Post*, which argued that the US allegation about Pakistan patronising the Haqqani terrorist group seriously impeded the war on terror.[66]

On 29 September 2011, Yusuf Raza Gilani, the Pakistani Prime Minister, convened a political conference. The undeclared aim of this conference was to provide support to Kayani, and pose a riposte to the above noted comment of Admiral Mike Mullen. One principal message of the conference was that, on the issue of national security, complete political solidarity prevailed in Pakistan.[67] The US, however, pursued its usual anti-terror course. For example, on 30 September 2011, the US took an important action in strife-ridden Yemen, which had serious implications for Pakistan. A CIA drone killed a powerful Al Qaeda leader, Anwar Al Awlaki, in Yemen on that day. Awlaki had an excellent command over the English language, which enabled him to transmit jihadi messages all over the world. He thereby could create/recruit and inspire potential suicide bombers, although he himself did not organise suicide assaults.[68] Pakistan's deep aversions to US drone attacks in the Pakistan-Afghanistan border certainly made Awalaki's assassination look ominous.

Some time after the death of Awlaki, the US assembled a huge number of fresh troops, cannons, etc. in that area of North Waziristan, close to the Pakistan-Afghanistan border, which remained the sanctuary of the Haqqani terror network. Ignoring Pakistan's objections, the US launched drone strikes in this heartland of the Haqqani group. Pakistan's Defence Minister, Ahmed Mukhtar, felt so perturbed that he went as far as to state that the US should realise the limits to Pakistan's patience. Nevertheless, even before this statement was issued, ten terrorists died of drone attacks in North Waziristan, three of them being Egyptian operatives of Al Qaeda.[69] Ahmed Mukhtar's warning failed to influence the US, which, on the contrary, decided very soon to forward a stern message to Pakistan. On 20 October 2011, Hillary Clinton, the US Secretary of State, came to Pakistan. She was accompanied by the CIA Director, General David Petraeus, and the Joint Chiefs of Staff Chairman, General Martin Dempsey. Hillary advised that Pakistan should in no time suppress the Haqqani outfit. For, a serpent, reared in one's backyard, would not only bite a neighbour but also oneself.[70]

An important explanation of why this US outburst against Pakistan's long familiar unsatisfactory role in the war on terror occurred publicly was perhaps Pakistan's recent success in sabotaging the prospects of a lasting settlement in Afghanistan. The Afghan government was trying to pave the way to such a settlement by opening negotiations with the moderate section of the Taliban. A former President of Afghanistan, Burhanuddin Rabbani, was leading these negotiations. But a few terrorists, pretending to be moderate Taliban negotiators, met Rabbani and murdered him on 20 September 2011. One of the murderers happened to be a Pakistani citizen and, like many other Taliban cadets, was normally a resident of Quetta, a safe sanctuary. Hamid Karzai, the President of Afghanistan, made the unequivocal declaration that he had irrefutable evidence/proof of Pakistani complicity in Rabbani's assassination.[71]

When Pakistan adopted a confrontationist posture vis-a-vis the US (as evident from some of the above noted statements and actions), it probably nursed an expectation that China would extend support to Pakistan. But Pakistan's media reports (as noted in Indian newspapers) belied this Pakistani expectation. Notably, China itself was emulating the US in trying to build up its military presence inside Pakistan, especially in the tribal areas. For, Muslim separatists of China's Xinjiang province were maintaining strongholds in these areas for nearly a decade, and organising cross-border militant missions inside Xinjiang.[72] Overall, therefore, Pakistan seemed to face an uncomfortable situation. One wonders whether this explained why, at this juncture, Pakistan began to publicise the possibility of granting the most-favoured-nation (MFN) treatment to India in the matter of trade (whereas India had granted this status to Pakistan in the 1990s). One could wonder further whether this accounted for a statement by Pakistan's former President, General Musharraf, in Washington DC that Pakistan's ISI and India's RAW (Research and Analysis Wing) should collaborate with each other.[73] This appeared to defy all experiences and imagination.

Yet, Pakistan was so crafty and ruthless in the deployment of terrorists in Afghanistan and India that both these countries were sometimes constrained to bypass the truth in order to placate Pakistan. For instance, in the SAARC conference of November 2011, held in Maldives, Hamid Karzai told journalists that India was the only country with which Afghanistan had a strategic partnership. He expressed gratitude to India for handsome contributions to Afghanistan's economic development. Yet, he identified India as a close friend, and Pakistan as the twin brother.[74] This was nearly preposterous, because Pakistan-aided terrorist bands were devastating Afghanistan. Pakistan, of course, argued tamely that although in the past Pakistan had provided assistance to some terrorist agencies, they never bothered to obtain presently Pakistan's permission before they selected the targets of their atrocities.

As to India, its anxiety to reduce the intensity of Pakistan-sponsored terrorist outrages was so deep that on one occasion (as in March 2011) Prime Minister Manmohan Singh invited Prime Minister Yusuf Raza Gilani to India for witnessing a cricket match. On another occasion, as in the Maldives conference of SAARC in November 2011, in the course of discussions on the sideline, Manmohan flattered Gilani by describing Gilani as a man of peace. Pakistan, however, did not swerve a bit from its determination not to punish the perpetrators and planners of 26/11 Mumbai attacks. It went on repeating such unconvincing alibis as that India could not furnish adequate evidence, or that Pakistan had to respect its own judicial system. In spite of all this happening for years, Manmohan told journalists in Maldives that India and Pakistan had long wasted valuable time on peevish debates, and that they should now devote themselves to the construction of a new history of their bilateral relationship. Manmohan further observed that terrorism was an eternal problem, and that Pakistan was also suffering from it. Therefore, according to Manmohan, the two countries should unite to safeguard their bilateral relations against the impact of terrorism.[75] Nevertheless, Manmohan did not have the courage to add that Pakistan itself was the chief architect of this terrorism, and that, not to speak of abolition of terrorist training camps inside its territory, Pakistan was not ready even to take any step towards minimisation of the programmes in these camps.

In this tussle between fearful liberalism and perfidious rigidity, the latter enjoyed an incontestable advantage. So, during the above noted SAARC conference in Maldives on 10 November 2011, Rehman Malik, Pakistan's Home Minister, came out with a startling declaration: Ajmal Kasab, the accused in the 26/11 terrorist attack on Mumbai and imprisoned in India, should be hanged, especially because Kasab did not represent any government institution. It was a miraculous declaration indeed. The Government of India had already submitted to the Governments of Pakistan and the US a mass of documents forming a body of irrefutable evidence on why the 26/11 attacks could not have been staged by Kasab (and his dead accomplices) without comprehensive and direct support of the Government of Pakistan. But Malik did not have to remember all this. For, in Maldives, he had to commit many acts of falsehood. Thus, Malik said that the Pakistan government was not at all aware of OBL's presence inside Pakistan, and that, there being no legally admissible evidence against JUD, it did not figure in the list of terrorist agencies compiled by the Pakistan government. About the JUD founder Hafeez Saiyid, too, according to Malik, there was no proof of terrorist activities.[76] Actually, on this subject, India, the US and the UN had collected a lot of invaluable evidence.[77] As already noted, on 26/11, Pakistan stuck to the bland assertion that information could not be equated to proof. So, however much evidence could be placed before Pakistan on 26/11, it would not show any interest. Yet, not to speak of Pakistan's home minister, even India's Prime Minister Manmohan Singh made certain statements in Maldives (noted above), which indicated that he had forgotten the affirmations on 26/11 by India's Chief of Army Staff, the Home Minister and the Defence Minister.[78] It bears reiteration that since 1947-48, India has been demonstrating a mindset vis-a-vis Pakistan that smacks of defeatism and an addiction to appeasement, which leads to the most amazing example of India trying to equate itself with Pakistan in terms of harbouring terrorists. Despite the verdict of the US State Department and the UN that the LeT was responsible for the Samjhauta Express blasts (as already mentioned in this chapter), India accused Indian terrorists of causing these blasts.[79]

The very announcement by Pakistan's Prime Minister Gilani that Pakistan was considering the grant of MFN status to India seemed to overwhelm a section of India's chattering class.[80] Simultaneously, with the announcement of this proposal, Prime Minister Gilani candidly affirmed that it would take a long time to carry out this proposal, for he merely asked the Commerce Minister to initiate talks with New Delhi, and actual measures could be taken only when this proposal was judged to be conducive to Pakistan's national interest. Thus, what was offered by one hand was nearly taken back by another. There are past precedents of such proposals, offered by the governments of Benazir Bhutto, Nawaz Sharif and Pervez Musharraf, eventually turning out to be fruitless. Moreover, Pakistani leaders had the expertise to speak in variegated voices on the same subject at about the same time. For instance, Gilani's proposal on the extension of MFN status to India was soon followed by a statement of Foreign Minister, Hina Rabbani Khar, which assured that there was no question of sliding back on this matter because the Pakistani Cabinet's approval was already there, and that the two governments would explore ways to build up normal trade relations. The Foreign Minister added, significantly, that even the military did not raise any objection to this proposal of MFN status for India. Actually, this extraordinary observation, attesting to the military's political pre-eminence, would point to the need for an inquiry into the probable interest or lack of interest of the Pakistani military in the grant of MFN status to India. Ordinary Pakistani consumers would undoubtedly benefit from an expansion of trade with India. For, they could purchase many articles, e.g., bicycles, at a much cheaper rate if these were imported not from South Korea, but from India. But a large number of military officers, who, before or after retirement, ran lucrative foreign trade enterprises in their own names or in the names of others, would lose, because lower import prices meant smaller profits. This might explain the repeated failures of government proposals for promotion of Pakistan-India trade ties by the extension of MFN status to India.[81]

It was inestimably difficult for India to persist in carrying on a peace process with a country like Pakistan, where democratically elected politicians had to abide by (the visible or invisible) dictates of the military. But the behaviour of the government in New Delhi appeared sometimes to lend this process a touch of inanity. Thus, at the time of the Maldives conference (mentioned above), the Indian Prime Minister made the observation that, although the Pakistani Prime Minister was prepared to work together with India, any recurrence of the 26/11-type crisis would impede the process of normalising India-Pakistan relations.[82] For, Pakistan did not—and was not in a position to—take credible steps towards punishing the known offenders in the 26/11 episode. Pakistan was in a quagmire of its own creation. On the one hand, as Foreign Minister Khar deplored, terrorism had claimed 50,000 Pakistani lives. On the other hand, Pakistan itself was patronising terrorists, making no attempts to close down the terrorist training camps in the POK, where at least 2000 trained/armed terrorists were reportedly preparing to infiltrate into India.[83] The Home Minister of India stated on 6 November 2011 that on this issue of infiltration from Pakistan, there were many discussions with Pakistan, but Pakistan did practically nothing to curb this menace. On the contrary, Pakistan was ceaselessly engaged in facilitating the infiltration of armed terrorists into India: it made 485 attempts in 2009, for example, and 489 attempts in 2010. Pakistan used to accelerate these attempts, especially before the advent of winter. Moreover, Pakistan was regularly violating the ceasefire pact with India. It did so on 77 occasions in 2008, on 28 occasions in 2009, 44 occasions in 2010, and on 23 occasions up to the month of August in 2011.[84]

In these circumstances, there was only one prop of India-Pakistan amity: the imagination of the Indian government. This amity, however, could materialise only if the Pakistan government liberated itself from its jihadi mindset *vis-à-vis* India. This liberation could not be attained before a prior suppression of the jihad within Pakistan. Signs for the possibility of such suppression were elusive. On 7 November 2011, for example, at an Id prayer ceremony in a place 90 miles away from Peshawar, one National Awami Party (NAP) leader, his son and bodyguard were killed by a human bomb. Seven persons were injured by this suicide attack. There was a precedent in 2007: at an assembly for holy Id, due to the detonation of a human bomb, at least 50 persons died, and 100 suffered injuries. The Taliban did all these, targeting specifically the NAP, which basically subscribed to religious toleration and did not believe in jihad.[85]

In this context, it was worthwhile referring to textbooks prescribed in Pakistani schools. A perusal of these textbooks could make it glaring that friendship with India was something that Pakistan simply ignored. In a 139-page report of a US government-appointed commission to survey global religious freedom, it was stated recently that Pakistani textbooks clearly described Hindus as eternal enemies of militants and of Islam. This message of hate and hostility was broadcast not only by non-official madrasas, but also by government schools. Evidently, the government failed to carry out its pledge (announced in 2006) of syllabus and textbook reforms due to inordinate pressures by militant groups. As a peace loving country, India had to continue efforts to build constructive relations with Pakistan. But the outcome of these efforts was beyond India's control.[86]

There were also certain matters, which were beyond the control of even the super power, the US. This became apparent after twenty-four Pakistani soldiers lost their lives because of a NATO air raid on Pakistan's border with Afghanistan. Domestic compulsions notwithstanding, Pakistan was indeed audacious when, immediately after this incident on 26 November 2011, it suspended the supply through Pakistani territory of oil and other supplies for the ISAF in Afghanistan.[87] Undoubtedly, the ISAF's reservoir of supplies was so large that this Pakistani ban could not affect the ISAF's activities. But it was certainly a classic case of the tail wagging the dog. For, Pakistan even mandated that within fifteen days, the US had to close down completely the Shamsi air base, thirty miles away from Quetta, which was used by US drones. Pakistan refused to accept the US position that the incident on 26 November was unintentional and accidental, and that the day of air raid had been decided in consultation with Pakistan.[88] According to Pakistan, the US did not supply correct information at the time of consultations, and that was the cause of the air raid occurring at the wrong place. The NATO forces started elaborate investigations into this raid. Yet, Pakistan could not be pacified.[89]

Pakistan was not only annoyed with the killing of its soldiers by the NATO forces on 26 November, but was also ready to defy the US and NATO by deciding to boycott the Bonn conference on Afghanistan scheduled for 5 December 2011.[90] Pakistan thus re-attested that it was not interested in stability in Afghanistan. For, convened after a decade, the Bonn conference was to discuss a matter of paramount importance: how to safeguard the security and independence of Afghanistan after the ISAF's planned withdrawal in 2014.[91]

Moreover, in a gesture of near-surrender to the Pakistani dictate, the US wound up the air base in Shamsi (mentioned above), removing all drones, personnel and equipment. Interestingly, the US took over this base after 9/11, whereas the United Arab Emirates (UAE) had obtained it on lease from Pakistan in 1992. Remarkably, in the year 2011 itself, the US had ignored twice the Pakistani directive for withdrawal from Shamsi: once, after a CIA contractor killed two Pakistanis in Lahore, and again, after OBL's assassination.[92] Why, then, did the US agree to abide by the Pakistani directive for leaving Shamsi after the 26 November incident? No accurate answer to this question could possibly be provided. But some plausible speculation was permissible. Perhaps, the US had already succeeded in setting up a drone base in Afghanistan. Probably, there could be additional speculation on whether the US retreat on the issue of the Shamsi base foreshadowed a weakening of long term US commitment to the war on terror in South Asia and other regions, and should arouse grave anxiety (if not alarm) among those countries, which (with or without any formal declaration) depended on the US for confronting terrorism originating from Pakistan.[93]

One disturbing query was whether the US retreat from Shamsi betokened a return to the pre-9/11 era when the US was habituated to pampering Pakistan, so much so that Pakistan engaged in black-marketing nuclear technology in Iran, Libya and North Korea. Moreover, Pakistan utilised US arms and money (available aplenty at the time of anti-Soviet jihad in Afghanistan) for the establishment of terrorist training camps, deploying these terrorists recurrently against India. After 1989, along with the withdrawal of Soviet troops from Afghanistan, the US too abdicated its responsibilities rather suddenly. It almost appeared as if the undeclared objective of the US was to enable Pakistan to gain hegemony over Afghanistan and thus to endow Pakistan with enormous geopolitical influence.[94]

This situation produced a chain reaction of developments leading inevitably to 9/11. The catastrophe of 9/11 could probably have been avoided if the unmatched resources of US defence-state-intelligence agencies had been appropriately utilised. An inappropriate use of these resources meant that the US government failed to realise or anticipate certain developments, which were usually comprehensible to others. Thus, in the 1990s, strikingly obvious developments in the Pakistan-Afghanistan region eluded the grasp of the US.[95] Terrorist agencies like the Al Qaeda and Taliban—nourished by money and arms from the US (at the time of anti-Soviet jihad) and continuing financial-ideological support from West Asian countries, like Saudi Arabia—acquired immense power, especially after they took a giant stride towards economic self-reliance by means of narcotics smuggling.[96] Add to these opportunities thrown to foreign terrorists for training as pilots, misusing the liberal democratic institutions of the US, and 9/11 was only a matter of time.[97] The US retreat from Shamsi in 2011 raised the spectre of consolidation of terrorism in the coming years.

The reality behind the spectre was repeatedly underlined by Afghanistan's President Karzai, who contended that the Taliban terror inside his country could only be stopped by Pakistan, because the Taliban's militant activities originated from and were planned in the territory of Pakistan.[98] The civilian Government of Pakistan, with Gilani as the Prime Minister, was too weak to tackle the Taliban. It was not even sure of its own survival. Rumours abounded that the armed forces wanted to oust the present President of Pakistan, Asif Ali Zardari. In the month of December 2011, thus, Gilani alleged that there was a conspiracy to unseat his government.[99] Although he added that the people of Pakistan had to decide whether the prevalent rule by elected representatives should be replaced by an autocratic arrangement, he did not have the self-confidence even to suggest whether Pakistan's armed forces were interested in installing this autocracy. Army Chief Kayani, however, ruled out any military coup.[100] Pakistan's military-intelligence agencies, it should be reiterated, pursued an enigmatic policy of collusion and confrontation with the Taliban, which perpetuated and aggravated a situation with unpredictably calamitous consequences for Pakistan and South Asia.

Those who apprehended such consequences also had parallel worries about the prospective US role. Would the US remain indifferent to a probable (though not certain) Taliban takeover of the Pakistan government even before 2014?[101] After all, there were alarming precedents for such acts of US short-sightedness. For example, critics pointed to some chronic dysfunctionalities of the US government, especially the wrongful rivalries between the FBI, the CIA and the defence department (occasionally verging on even deception and fraud), which undoubtedly contributed to the rise of the Al Qaeda, and paved the way to 9/11.[102] Even 9/11 could not impart the shock therapy to cure such dysfunctionalities. Hence, leaving vital tasks of the war in Afghanistan incomplete, the US staged an invasion of Iraq.[103] Initially, there were dramatic successes in Iraq, but these were followed by a series of reversals. In Iraq, the US trod 'a path of dubious legality and damaging morality,' and a large number of civilian and military decision makers were responsible for this.[104]

President Obama's announcement of military withdrawal from Afghanistan in 2014 (noted above) raised important questions about the role of China in Afghanistan—past, present and future. China seemed so far to be preoccupied with the procurement of precious minerals from Afghanistan.[105] Remarkably, one Chinese agency was the first to strike oil in Afghanistan.[106] So, China registered a huge success in Afghanistan. But it maintained a studied silence about its success. It was necessary to recall that China already invested $4 billion in the Aynak copper mine of Afghanistan (which ironically was discovered in the days of Soviet hegemony over Afghanistan).[107] China was averse to publicity on this matter. Probably, China was apprehensive that publicity might incite terrorists to stage attacks. Significantly, there being no Chinese soldiers in Afghanistan, China received security in its mining venture from Afghan policemen trained and armed by the ISAF. Although the US and NATO forces were scheduled to leave Afghanistan by 2014-end, China did not mind safeguarding its long term economic-commercial interests in Afghanistan as long as possible with indirect, though obvious, support from these forces.[108] A large number of US and NATO soldiers were killed or injured in Afghanistan. In contrast, not a single Chinese soldier lost his life in Afghanistan.

In the past, whenever the US and NATO requested China for military assistance in Afghanistan, China evaded this request on some pretext or the other. Beijing's rulers apparently did not view with favour the presence of their own troops on the soil of Afghanistan. Yet, at least ten thousand Chinese soldiers were present in the POK and neighbouring places.[109] Chinese rulers, moreover, disapproved the idea of their soldiers fighting under a commander of another country, and that too on a foreign territory. Nevertheless, China was ready to respond appropriately to any request from the UN for participation in an international force.[110] Actually, China suffered from deep anxiety that any presence of Chinese soldiers in Afghanistan would have an adverse impact upon the internal security situation in China's Xinjiang province. For, a large number of Uighur rebels in Xinjiang had taken and were currently taking military support from terrorist leaders in Afghanistan. From time to time, Uighur rebels caused a lot of trouble to China (as in 2009). The Al Qaeda was known to be connected with the military training of Uighurs. Global jihad being the principal goal of Al Qaeda, China had to be extremely careful about deployment of its troops in Afghanistan.[111] Still, in the near future, it may be extremely difficult for China to synergise an expanding economic programme with unavoidable police/military presence, especially after ISAF's departure in 2014. Happy days of riding piggyback on ISAF-aided Afghan policemen would come to an end. China covets not merely copper and oil, but also other valuable minerals in Afghanistan, e.g., gold, iron, cobalt and lithium. The total price of these as-yet-unexplored deposits was estimated at $1trillion. Lithium reserves (to take one example) are so immense in Afghanistan that its salience for the world economy can be judged to be as significant as that of Saudi Arabia's petroleum. For, lithium is essential for the production of a variety of manufactured articles, like computers or high end mobile phones.[112] If China's voracious appetite for minerals in Africa and the inexorable determination to procure them are replicated in Afghanistan after 2014 (when there would be a strictly limited presence of ISAF), thousands of Afghan workers should be engaged in a multiplicity of Chinese economic enterprises (e.g., mines) inside Afghanistan. The security of these enterprises would have to be ensured by Chinese forces.[113] There could be no certainty that some of these Afghan workers would not come under Al Qaeda's influence to stage suicide attacks. Without the effective deployment of Chinese security forces, it might not be feasible to forestall such attacks.

At that stage, China's military-diplomatic abilities would be subjected to a stiff test. In the past, China supplied extensive assistance to the Taliban–initially, in the days of Soviet hegemony over Afghanistan, and, afterwards, till the 9/11 episode. China's Communist Party, moreover, developed intimacy with Jamaat-e-Islami, which was a sort of guardian for the Taliban.[114] Amazingly, the allergy of Chinese communists to religion did not impede these ties with the Jamaat. But the complexities of the internal situation in Pakistan and Afghanistan were rising, so were the tussles between Pakistan and Afghanistan. It was uncertain as to how successfully the Afghan security forces, trained and armed by the ISAF, would be able to confront the Al Qaeda and Taliban after 2014. Nor was it clear how China proposed to deal with the infinite intricacies of this situation in the Pakistan-Afghanistan area.

China would of course try to reach accommodation with the Taliban in order to pre-empt terrorist attacks upon its economic ventures in Afghanistan. But all countries—Afghanistan, Pakistan, the US—were trying (publicly or privately) to cultivate the Taliban. Even here boundless complexities arose, because Pakistan did not want the Kabul government to develop understanding with the Taliban. Pakistan dreamt of reviving the cosy connection with the Taliban for the reestablishment of the situation during 1996-2001, when, under Pakistani patronage, the Taliban controlled a large part of Afghanistan, and Pakistan had the satisfaction of exercising domination (however limited) over Afghanistan. Actually, there was hardly any chance of Pakistan enjoying such domination over Afghanistan once again. For, there were a number of Taliban factions, some of which, far from being loyal to Pakistan, slaughtered Pakistani soldiers from time to time.[115]

Thus, years of Taliban dependence on Pakistan for money and arms, as also linguistic homogeneity, could not immunise Pakistan against periodic assaults by the Taliban. Therefore, it was not clear how China would be able to remove the linguistic barrier and extend so much economic-military aid to the Taliban as to be able to inoculate its economic enterprises against terror strikes. Pakistan, again, was so nervous about Taliban's adverse reaction to the recent ISAF attacks on Pakistani soldiers (even if by mistake) that despite decades of handsome economic-military donations from the US, Pakistan forced the closure of the US drone base at Shamsi (as already mentioned). True, even after this shutdown, the US began to carry out drone strikes upon terrorists from some other base outside Pakistan.[116] Therefore, whatever goodwill was generated among the Taliban by the closure of the Shamsi base, could not but be dissipated soon. Moreover, opposition leaders like Imran Khan added fuel to the fire by openly denouncing the deployment of drones by the US. This only aggravated the alienation of the Taliban from the Islamabad government.[117]

The US, concentrating on self-expulsion from Afghanistan, might probably have no other major objective till 2014-end except to minimise losses before or during the near-complete troops withdrawal by means of partial accommodation with the Taliban.[118] Therefore, China would be obliged to plan military measures to take care of its expanding economic interests. But, to set up military bases in Afghanistan for this purpose was to expose oneself to that sort of tremendous harassment and losses, which scarred the ISAF. For, in Afghanistan there was a multiplicity of militant groups, which, fighting one another as also foreign forces for decades, acquired military skills, which the Chinese troops, divorced from the actualities of war experience for a long time, could not be able to match. So, the soil of the eternal ally, Pakistan, would have to be made available for Chinese military bases. Published reports indicated that in Pakistan's KPK or FATA, as also around the Gwadar part of Balochistan, China was preparing to construct such military bases.[119] Terrorist groups in the Pakistan-Afghanistan area would have a new cause of rage against Pakistan, if it enabled China to build these bases, whereas China was likely to emerge as the terrorists' substitute target for ISAF, even if the ISAF retained after 2014-end a small military presence in Afghanistan for training missions and/or drone operations.

On 29 February 2012, Pakistan's Cabinet decided that trade with India should be liberalised, and that by 2012-end all restrictions would be eliminated. This could be deemed to be a consequence of prolonged discussions with India since April 2011. Annual two-way trade around 2012 amounted to $2.7 billion. But this trade was official or visible. A much greater amount of invisible (or unofficial) trade took place through third countries like Singapore. It was estimated that—in the absence of current restrictions—two-way trade would reach $10 billion by 2015.[120]

One may recall that in 2008, shortly after he came to power, Pakistan's President Asif Ali Zardari declared that he wanted to open up new horizons in relations with India. In 2009, again, Indian Prime Minister Manmohan Singh resolved to resume talks with Pakistan—despite the failure of Pakistan to take appropriate action against Pakistani terrorists responsible for the 2008 Mumbai attacks. In India, Manmohan's decision was certainly a matter of debate. But, no less debatable was the above noted decision of the Pakistani Cabinet for trade liberalisation with India—as far as Pakistanis were concerned. For, apart from the terrorist groups of Pakistan, who were opposed to an expansion of trade ties with India, many business circles in Pakistan were against such expansion for fear of losses due to competition with India.[121]

In spite of such problems, Pakistan was able to prepare a negative list of 1200 articles in replacement of the pre-existing positive list of 1963 articles. Consequently, Indian businessmen were expected to be able to export more than 6800 articles to Pakistan. Moreover, the negative list—comprising clothes, medicines, motor cars, etc.—was likely to be abolished by 2012-end. This was remarkable. For, this contradicted Pakistan's long-held belief that it was not possible to have any constructive engagement with India in the matter of trade or other matters, till the J&K problem was resolved to Pakistan's satisfaction.[122]

A question arose as to how Pakistan could cast aside this belief and opt for a change. Undoubtedly, the civilian government procured the consent of China, long acclaimed as Pakistan's permanent friend, in support of this change. That was apparent on 3 November 2011, when, at a press conference, a representative of China's Foreign Ministry declared that an improvement in India-Pakistan trade would contribute to the cause of peace, stability and development not only in these two countries, but also in the entire South Asian region.[123]

It was worth a serious explanation as to why China came out with such a declaration. Perhaps, China started worrying about Pakistan's economic-political problems. For example, Balochistan offered an important indicator of these problems. A nationalist movement emerged in Balochistan in reaction to political-economic exploitation by Islamabad. A number of violent incidents took place over the years, some of them affecting Chinese individuals and institutions. For, Baloch rebels were fully aware of profound friendship between Pakistan and China. Some Chinese engineers were killed in Balochistan. Chinese business enterprises in Balochistan were even planning to wind up their activities. The basic reason behind such developments, more than six decades after the creation of Pakistan, was that, in the view of the Baloch people, at the time of Pakistan's birth in 1947, Balochistan deserved independence. The Khan of Kalat, who ruled nearly the whole of Balochistan, went to court to persuade Britain to grant independence to Balochistan. The eminent lawyer, who pleaded for the Khan of Kalat at the court, was no less a person than Mohammed Ali Jinnah. But, after Pakistan became independent, and Jinnah became ill, lying on his death bed, the Pakistan armed forces forcibly annexed Balochistan to Pakistan.[124]

A brief discussion of how complex the Baloch situation was and how it posed a threat to authorities in Islamabad is pertinent here. A number of influential Baloch leaders obtained political asylum and resided abroad. They included Mir Suleiman Dawood (recognised as the present Khan of Kalat); Hariyar Maree, son of Nawab Khair Boksh Maree, a senior Baloch nationalist leader; Kachkole Ali Baloch, a former leader of the opposition in Balochistan's legislature; Senate member Sanaullah Baloch, and Sardar Akhter Mengal, the senior-most leaders of the powerful Mengal family. Rehman Malik, Pakistan's Interior Minister, announced a general amnesty for all self-exiled Baloch leaders. But these leaders stipulated a number of stiff preconditions for engaging in talks with the Pakistan government. Some of these preconditions were: all military operations in Balochistan should be immediately stopped; all the 13,000 Baloch youth (who had disappeared) must be traced; a ban should be imposed on the establishment of any new military cantonment in Balochistan;

and Pakistan's intelligence agencies had to cease their activities compulsorily in the province of Balochistan. Even a former Prime Minister of Pakistan, Nawaz Sharif, laid down a precondition for participation in an all-party conference on Balochistan convened by the Pakistan government: he demanded that all the kidnapped Baloch youth had to be rescued.[125]

Obviously, it was beyond the capacity of Pakistan's civilian government to accept the above noted demands of Baloch leaders for trying to solve the problem of Balochistan. True, this government exhibited an image of power, because it was the first incumbent government in Pakistan's history, which would be able to place before the legislature (in May 2012) the fifth consecutive budget.[126] But the image was misleading, for, it was also true that this government confronted an extreme economic-political crisis. For example, on one occasion, the government marketed bonds with a maturity period of only three months. But, there being no purchaser, the government itself had to buy back these bonds in a situation of embarrassment. Remittances by Pakistanis working in foreign countries—especially in West Asia—constituted a principal source of strength for the economy of Pakistan. But questions arose about the durability of this strength, because some West Asian countries like Kuwait or Qatar were expelling Pakistani citizens.

Moreover, the government was facing a perilous political predicament inside the country. Nationalist forces in Pakistan continued to retreat before the onslaughts of Islamist militants. A variety of religio-political clashes created a huge number of internally displaced persons (IDPs) in Pakistan, numbering about 3.5 million. The Taliban could establish its hegemony even in a cosmopolitan city like Karachi. Terrorists easily targeted Shias, not to speak of Ahmadis. But they did not spare even members of the armed forces. In the recent past, for instance, seventeen members of a suicide squad infiltrated into a naval base. Four of them died, but thirteen others, wearing the navy's uniform, managed to find shelter inside the base itself. This incident (mentioned earlier briefly) pointed to the ominous possibility (even if not-too-near) that the Pakistani state, long under the domination of the military, might instead slip under the control of terrorist organisations. Al Jawahiri, the Al Qaeda chief, even called upon the people of Pakistan to launch a rebellion against the Pakistan government and the military.[127]

All this happened despite the ban imposed by the Pakistan government upon nearly forty terrorist organisations, including the LeT, JeM, TTP and Al Qaeda. Many of these organisations, however, persisted in their operations, either by the adoption of new names or with the support of allied agencies. The United Nations, for instance, identified the Jamaat-ud-Dawa (JuD) as the new face of LeT (which had been responsible for the Mumbai massacre of 2008). On 12 March 2012, the Government of Pakistan proposed negotiations with the banned outfits in the interest of promotion of peace. Rehman Malik, Pakistan's Interior Minister, stated that some of these outfits expressed interest in participation in these negotiations. According to Malik, the government was ready to have talks even with the principal leaders of the Taliban, provided the Taliban renounced terror and violence.[128]

At this stage, one can notice a clue to the probable causes of the above noted Pakistani move towards trade liberalisation with India. Distraught by economic decay and terrorist depredations, Pakistan began to consider the option of improving trade relations with India. After all, India had extended the MFN status to Pakistan as early as 1996. One could wonder whether Pakistan would have felt encouraged to develop close trade relations with India if the Pakistani terrorist agencies refrained from murderous activities inside Pakistan, and confined themselves to attacks upon India. In this connection, one has to add that the economy of Pakistan suffered terrible damages on account of heavy expenditure on the maintenance of a vast terrorist infrastructure inside Pakistan for years of proxy war it had launched against India. Even the anti-Indian and pro-Pakistan All Party Hurriyat Conference (APHC) of J&K could not avoid the impact of this damage. For, the Islamabad government was constrained to send a message to the APHC that for some time Pakistan had to suspend stirring up the J&K issue.[129] One Pakistani Minister, again, paraded a conciliatory mood by requesting Indian aid for training in polio vaccination.[130]

One query about India's official policy towards Pakistan, however, became inescapably pertinent. How reasonable was India's decision to resume talks with Pakistan, which had been suspended after the 2008 Mumbai attack. India withdrew the diplomatic pressure on Pakistan (caused by such suspension) even before it obtained any satisfactory response from Pakistan to its legitimate complaints about this attack. Pakistan, on the contrary, refused to take any step towards closing down the terrorist bases on its territory, which were ready to stage attacks against India. Moreover, as A.K. Anthony, India's Defence Minister, affirmed on 14 March 2012, Pakistan ignored Indian protests, and persisted in hostile activities along the border, e.g., by repairing as many as 886 bunkers.[131]

About non-official responses in India to the Pakistani offer for trade liberalisation with India, one comment may be appropriate. The Indian media seemed to be overwhelmed by this offer, whereas caution was imperative. It was natural on the part of a Pakistani newspaper and even a research journal to express profound enthusiasm for the expansion of trade relations with India.[132] For, that might resolve some of the economic problems troubling Pakistanis. But, it was not difficult to guess that the Pakistan government's motivation behind trade expansion with India probably ranged far beyond the quest for relief from an economic crisis. If trade promotion led to a relaxation of restrictions upon travel across the LOC in J&K, it might not be difficult for trained Pakistani militants to disguise themselves as businessmen and infiltrate into India. It was instructive to recall in this context that in some areas of J&K, each family was compelled to ask one of its male progenies to join a jihadi group and visit Pakistan for military training, so that subsequently he could sneak into India for terrorist operations.[133]

President Obama visited Kabul for a few hours in 2012 to observe OBL's death anniversary, as also to deliberate on the sort of military presence maintainable at the end of 2014. President Karzai probably obtained an adequate assurance of military support.[134] But the feasibility of this assurance faded in a few hours when not less than seven Afghan guards died in a terrorist attack at a locality of Kabul enjoying maximum security cover.[135] This was an alarming indicator of the capacity of terrorists (whether belonging to the Taliban, Al Qaeda or the Hakkani group) to stage deadly terrorist attacks at any place of their choice long before the projected withdrawal of US-NATO forces from Afghanistan in 2014. Therefore, it was a plausible fear that even if, after 2014, the US and NATO preserved a limited military presence in Afghanistan for training and drone operations, the most powerful terrorist outfit, the Taliban, might succeed in establishing a sort of hegemony over a large part of Afghanistan.

This hegemony, however, would always face challenges due to acute ethnic or other rivalries, which perpetuated fratricidal conflicts in the country for decades.

It was not easy to predict whether the resultant situation could be deemed to be near-chaotic. But one prediction would partially be risk-averse: the US could be wrong in believing that after 2014, it might succeed in keeping at least a small training/drone base in Afghanistan over a long period of time. For, the Taliban could muster all its resources and bear enormous losses to wipe out this base. The US was not likely to receive any direct assistance from Pakistan in withstanding such a desperate Taliban onslaught. Even in 2012, the US had to endure tremendous tensions in securing Pakistani cooperation for the supply of petrol and other military commodities to Afghanistan by the land route through Pakistan.[136] Moreover, although drones proved to be the most potent US weapon in the war on terror, Pakistan did not currently permit the use of drones from the Pakistani soil. In the past, there was remarkably a vague, though unpublicised, Pakistani concurrence for such use.[137]

In this context, one grave failure of the Pakistan government should be stressed. It never informed the people of vital truths about threats to the country's security. There was no evidence that the Pakistan government ever tried to convince the people that Pakistan's terrorist groups—and not the Indian government and the people—were Pakistan's principal enemy.[138] Consequently, it was far from apparent as to whether the Pakistan government made any serious attempt to alert the public, for example, that the use of drones safeguarded not only the US security, but also Pakistan's sovereignty.[139] For decades the powerful Pakistani armed forces were so infected with religious zealotry that a large number of soldiers tended to imbibe terrorist-friendly attitudes. This might explain—at least partially—why the Pakistani military failed to take effective measures against terrorists on the Pakistan-Afghanistan border. Probably, Pakistani rulers were developing anxieties about the not-easily-measurable spread of the pro-jihadi outlook among the members of the armed forces. Probably, therefore, before the end of 2014, when the terrorists were likely to be more assertive, Pakistani rulers thought of doing something that could economically benefit the ordinary people, and, simultaneously, pave the way to cooperation with India in a foreseeable dangerous time. This might account for Pakistani efforts to extend in 2012-13 those trade facilities to India, which India had granted to Pakistan as early as 1996, although, as already mentioned, the length of the list of sensitive articles (ineligible for normal trade) merely mocked at these efforts.[140]

Some NATO countries, e.g. Germany and Australia, promised substantial economic assistance to Afghanistan annually after 2014.[141] In 2011, NATO provided evidence of joint military action in Libya, and it was reportedly preparing plans for military intervention outside Europe in future.[142] Afghanistan should be a priority in the list of non-European countries eligible for NATO military intervention. Add to this the inevitable (though small) US military presence in Afghanistan after 2014. Yet, the mind-boggling complexity of situation in the Pakistan-Afghanistan area made it realistic to imagine an escalation of violence in the entire area after 2014.[143]

The above noted visit of President Obama to Afghanistan in May 2012 took place at a time when the Secretary of State, Hillary Clinton, came to Kolkata and New Delhi—although for a very short period. These two visits, howsoever brief, could not probably be viewed in isolation from each other or from the larger perspective of the war on terror. For, US legislators were actually aggrieved by Pakistan's role in this war.[144] This was a major reason why the US had to decide to wind up its military operations gradually in Afghanistan. While in New Delhi, Clinton offered some assurances about containing Pakistan-sponsored terrorism. But the hollowness of these assurances continued to remain conspicuous.[145] Clinton demonstrated her farsightedness by paying due attention to terrorist threats to eastern and north-eastern India. For, if, along with a probable deterioration in the security situation in the Pakistan-Afghanistan area after 2014, eastern and north-eastern India too became more vulnerable, China would gain influence and the US tended to lose. Clinton, therefore, expressed a deep interest in the progress of India's counter-terrorist operations in eastern and north-eastern India. Furthermore, when she was in West Bengal, Clinton promised economic aid, which could serve some important purposes. It would strengthen counter-terrorism efforts by contributing to an improvement in India-Bangladesh relations, especially because Bangladesh under Prime Minister Sheikh Hasina helped India by capturing a number of terrorists, who operated in north-east India, but used Bangladesh as a sanctuary. Economic aid could also promote India's relations with Myanmar and Thailand by the use of West Bengal as a gateway.[146]

Success of the war on terror depended greatly on the preservation of political stability in Pakistan. But the principal stakeholders—politicians, judges, soldiers did not mind taking steps to endanger political stability, acting in isolation and/or together. This was witnessed, for instance, in April-June 2012. Prime Minister Yousouf Raza Gilani appointed Rehman Malik as Home Minister at a time when Malik was yet to renounce his British citizenship. When the Supreme Court detected this, Malik lost the position of Home Minister. Malik pleaded before the Supreme Court that he had already applied for renunciation of his British citizenship. Gilani appeared to take advantage of this plea, and made Malik an adviser.[147] But Gilani himself got into trouble. His failure to act upon the Supreme Court's orders to commence action in Switzerland against President Zardari's corrupt conduct led to his conviction for contempt of court and a token punishment of less than one minute's detention on 26 April 2012. Gilani's plea that as the country's President, Zardari enjoyed immunity from prosecution inside or outside the country was not acceptable to Chief Justice Iftikar Chaudhry. On 25 May 2012, however, the National Assembly Speaker Fehmida Mirza gave a five-page ruling that Gilani did not commit any contempt of court, and that Chief Justice Chaudhry's verdict was unwarranted. In a normal democracy, the Speaker's decision was not expected to be challenged by any institution.[148]

But, on 7 June 2012, petitions challenging Speaker Fehmida Mirza's decision were submitted to the Supreme Court. On 19 June, Chief Justice Chaudhry, presiding over a three-judge Bench, dismissed Gilani from the post of Prime Minister. 'The curious part of the judgement is the directive to the President, essentially telling Zardari to sack Gilani for standing by him, and to replace Gilani with a Prime Minister, who would reopen corruption cases against him.'[149] Pakistan's Election Commission carried out the Supreme Court's order and issued a formal notification to disqualify Gilani. Along with Gilani, sixty three members of his Cabinet were denotified. The PPP accepted the Supreme Court's verdict without any protest. The PPP Parliamentary Party proceeded to choose Gilani's successor.[150]

The confrontation between politicians and judges took a dramatic turn on 21 June 2012. Makhdoom Shahbuddin was the choice of the ruling PPP for the post of Pakistan's Prime Minister. But, when Shahbuddin was filing his nomination papers at the National Assembly, an anti-drug court issued a non-bailable warrant against him. The allegation against Shahbuddin was that he once violated government rules, while importing a restricted drug.[151] The timing of issuance of warrant against Shahbuddin was much more than accidental or coincidental. This was done plainly to humiliate the civilian government. Otherwise, this could have been done much earlier. After all, most of the political leaders of the Pakistan government were known to be corrupt.[152] President Zardari himself was fabulously corrupt, and it was remarkable that loyalty to Zardari impelled Gilani to resort to self-destruction.[153]

The military leaders of Pakistan were palpably happy with the discomfiture of politicians and the exit of Gilani, even though this episode signalled an undeclared alliance between the judiciary and the military. Army Chief Kayani and ISI Chief Ahmed Shuja Pasha were thoroughly displeased with Gilani over the Hussain Haqqani-Mansoor Ijaz controversy erupting in the recent past, when Gilani even planned to fire Kayani and Pasha, although eventually he did not. On this issue too, known as the Memogate, the judiciary backed the military. Ijaz was a US businessman of Pakistani origin. Haqqani was the Pakistani Ambassador to the US. Soon after the assassination of Osama Bin Laden, as Ijaz revealed in November 2011 (i.e., a few months before Gilani's dismissal), Ijaz acted upon Haqqani's instruction to hand over to the US Joint Chiefs of Staff Chairman, Mike Mullen a memo in which the Pakistan government solicited US intervention to forestall a military takeover in Pakistan. Whereas the authenticity of Ijaz's memo was in deep doubt, it was widely known that Haqqani had sharp differences of opinion with the military establishment, which would not miss this chance to chastise Haqqani. Chief Justice Iftikhar Mohammed Chaudhry appointed an inquiry commission, which took four months to decide that Haqqani was guilty, although, meanwhile, Haqqani had already resigned from the Ambassador's post. Military leaders were delighted. The collusion between the military and the judiciary became glaring.[154]

The above noted tensions between the executive-legislative, military and judicial establishments—of which the Memogate was only one striking illustration—could not but affect adversely the capability of the Pakistan government to cooperate with the US in the war on terror. So, at a time when the Memogate created ripples in the domestic and international media, the extremists inside Pakistan appeared to achieve new heights of consolidation by means of the formation of Difa-e-Pakistan (DEP), or the Council for the Defence of Pakistan (CDP). Mohammed Hafiz Saeed, the JUD leader, unified by means of the DEP around forty Islamist groups, which represented forces of jihad and religious fundamentalism. Significantly, the government had already branded a large number of these organisations as dangerous. But Hamid Gul, a former ISI chief, joined DEP. Observers suspected the ISI and military to be bestowing patronage on the DEP. The civilian government did not seem to pay much attention to DEP—not to speak of the military. On the contrary, the government witnessed the flow of funds to many organisations within the DEP from previously locked bank accounts, which the government chose to unlock. The DEP depicted the US, Israel and India as anti-Islam. It also looked upon the democratically elected Government of Pakistan as hostile to Islam, because it aligned itself with Western powers and rejected the aim of war against India as a priority. The DEP carried on pugnacious propaganda in a large number of schools/universities, and possessed the capacity to summon thirty-forty thousand people on the streets any time. It held meetings nearly every week in big cities.[155]

As Pakistan seemed to be reluctant to take on terrorists, as evident from the birth and progress of DEP, the Obama administration had no option but to rely more and more on drone strikes upon terrorist targets. Estimates for Pakistanis killed by unmanned US aircrafts from 2004-end to May 2012 ranged from 1819 to 2008, and 80 per cent of these deaths occurred during the period of Obama's presidency.[156] Pakistan complained that drone strikes violated its sovereignty. The US Secretary of State, Hillary Clinton, observed in June 2012 that Pakistanis were 'losing sovereignty' because they had 'large areas', which were 'ungoverned'.[157]

Shortly afterwards, on 7 July 2012, Hillary Clinton made a significant announcement in Kabul, which attested to the launching of serious preparations for the near-complete withdrawal of US-NATO forces from Afghanistan by December 2014. This announcement conferred on Afghanistan the status of a principal non-NATO ally.[158] During the years of Obama administration, no other country earned this status, which extended to Afghanistan the promise of long term cooperation in the fields of defence and security. For instance, this status made it relatively easy for Afghanistan to acquire defence equipment from the US.

On the next day, 8 July 2012, seventy countries issued a declaration in Tokyo. The foremost message of this declaration was that terrorism was the major cause of insecurity and instability in Afghanistan, and that it threatened peace not only in the neighbouring countries, but also in the world as a whole. Therefore, in Tokyo, donor countries (including India) resolved, presumably as a durable prophylactic against terrorism, that till 2015, Afghanistan was to receive non-military assistance worth US$ 16 billion, subject to a few preconditions. For instance, corruption was to be brought under control, administration upgraded and rule of law established. Moreover, it was essential to create economic opportunities for ordinary Afghans, especially women. Donor countries were as much aware as Afghan President Hamid Karzai that it would take quite some time to defeat terrorism in Afghanistan and build prosperity. Thus, on 8 July 2012, the very day of Tokyo declaration, twenty three persons in Kabul lost their lives; sixteen of them were Afghan civilians, five were policemen, and two were members of the US-led ISAF. The reason was easily intelligible: Taliban fighters were trying to recapture some of those spaces from which they had been evicted during the last two years.[159]

Taliban atrocities on Afghan women sometimes crossed all limits of barbarism. In the second week of July 2012, for instance, Afghan authorities started an anti-Taliban expedition on learning about a 22-year-old woman, wife of a Taliban soldier, who was accused of adultery with a Taliban commander, and her so-called trial was concluded in just one hour. The accused was then taken to a village (about 100 kilometres away from Kabul) and shot dead in public, while the crowd lustily cheered this act of cruelty. In other words, despite some progress, reportedly achieved in the protection of womens' rights after 2001-2002, when the Taliban forces were expelled from power in Afghanistan, the situation remained grim, and, following the departure of ISAF from Afghanistan in 2014, sufferings of women were likely to increase. This was the legitimate anxiety of observers—despite the enjoyment by Afghanistan of the status of a major non-NATO ally.[160]

Not to speak of womens' rights, even on other matters, there was no dearth of evidence about the fragility of the security situation in Afghanistan. On 14 July 2012, for instance, at a marriage ceremony in the northern region of Afghanistan, a suicide bomber killed 23 persons of whom three belonged to Afghan security forces, and one was an Uzbek leader, an ex-member of Parliament, who had participated in the anti-Soviet jihad. Undoubtedly, this bombing was carried out by the Taliban, for, in the recent past, the Taliban announced the commencement of their spring offensive. Actually, the murder of an Uzbek leader by the Pashtun Taliban adversely affected the prospects of minimising ethnic strife in Afghanistan for the purpose of achieving long term stability in the country.[161]

The US was certainly aware of such inordinate complexities of the situation in Afghanistan, which it was preparing to leave by 2014-end (even if it maintained a residual presence). While ground realities defied control, access to ultra-modern technology probably created in the minds of the US policy makers a brief illusion of limited success. Take, for instance, the establishment of centres of biometric data or digital documents in Afghanistan. Fingerprints and eye-scan records were preserved. A negligible number of approximately thirty million people in Afghanistan had birth certificates, and the biometric/digital information centres covered only about 2.5 million persons. In one incident at a Kandahar prison, 500 Taliban inmates fled by digging a tunnel and the above noted information was used to recapture thirty of these escapees. What was incalculable was whether this success of arresting terrorists was more than offset by the grievances of ordinary Afghans subjected to biometric/digital exercises, which terrorist recruiters could capitalise. For, even dead Taliban fighters were included in these exercises.[162]

The US took care to sign with Afghanistan an agreement of strategic partnership, which would remain in force for a decade after 2014. At a conference in Chicago in May 2012, NATO countries promised such assistance—along with US aid—as would contribute vitally to the capacity of the Afghan government to deploy an army of 2,50,000 soldiers in the post-2014 period. But Pakistan remained the progenitor of real problems. For, it was determined to continue to use the Taliban and Haqqani outfits—the distinction between the two sometimes fading—as proxies for weakening the Afghan government and maximising Pakistan's sway over Afghanistan. The US was trying long to ensure that opponents of the Kabul regime did not secure any sanctuary inside Pakistan, and that Pakistan would cooperate with the Kabul government for the facilitation of a political settlement with the Taliban. But this effort did not succeed, although some US decision makers continued to nurture an unrealistic expectation that Pakistan's attitude to the Afghan government would switch over to an accommodative mode.[163]

The lack of cooperation between the US and Pakistan sometimes reached disturbing proportions. For example, as already noted, Pakistan had the temerity to blockade the land route through Pakistan for the dispatch of essential military supplies to NATO forces in Afghanistan, following an air raid by the US on a frontier post in the Pakistan-Afghanistan border on 26 November 2011, which resulted in the death of some Pakistani soldiers. Pakistan wanted the US to apologise before it would lift the blockade. But the US did not fully comply. On 3 July 2012, the US Secretary of State, Hillary Clinton, telephoned Pakistan's Foreign Minister to express regrets, and added significantly that Pakistan-Afghanistan cooperation should pre-empt in future those mistakes, which caused recent losses to the Pakistan army.[164] Subsequently, NATO trucks resumed their journeys across the land route through Pakistan. As long as these trucks were using the longer central Asian land route, an avoidable expenditure of US$ 100 million had to be incurred. When the blockade ended, and there was a restoration of the Pakistani route, Pakistan earned two dividends. One, the US agreed to expedite the payment of more than US$ 1 billion for enabling Pakistan to launch military operations in the restive Pakistan-Afghanistan border. Two, the US promised to support Pakistan's loan application to the IMF.[165]

Pakistan, however, wanted to extort other benefits for reopening the NATO supply route through its territory. Pakistan resorted to a lot of bargaining. It demanded five thousand US dollars per truck as transit fee. But this demand was rejected. The old rate of US$ 250 per truck remained in force.[166] Such bargaining illustrated the unhealthy state of US relations with Pakistan. Occasionally, in the US Congress, Pakistan was warned that the US grants to Pakistan could be reduced. One Congressman was so candid as to observe that Pakistan could be compared to Benedict Arnold, a notorious villain of the American War of Independence against Britain. Arnold committed an act of treachery and joined the British against Americans.[167] This was a plain hint at Pakistani collusion with terrorists, the sworn enemies of the US.

Indeed, Pakistan recklessly deployed terrorist groups against Kabul, New Delhi and NATO forces. Hillary Clinton, the US Secretary of State, was right to observe in Tokyo on 8 July 2012 that in the war on terror, the US relationship with Pakistan was essential as also conflictual.[168] Basically, the depraved mindset of the Pakistani military was responsible for this extraordinary situation. The Pakistani military pursued the somewhat unattainable aim of spreading its influence in India and Afghanistan by the use of terrorist groups, whereas the pretence of participation in the war on terror was unavoidable, because US aid remained indispensable to Pakistan. If, thus, the measures adopted by the Pakistani military were partly self-contradictory, these were also partly suicidal. In a sort of vicious tug of war, the Pakistani state became weaker and weaker. Religious fanaticism was on the rise. A few recent instances—far from exceptional—should be noted. On 17 July 2012, one doctor from Ghana and a colleague (who represented the WHO), were attacked in Karachi while administering polio vaccines; the doctor was struck by two bullets.[169] On 21 July 2012 in Lahore, according to government sources, one police constable shot dead his own sister, because she was wearing the dress for men, i.e., jeans.[170]

Amidst these bizarre circumstances in a neighbouring country, India's activities needed some attention. In May 2012—after a lapse of thirty years—India exported bananas to Pakistan. These were so tasteful that in Islamabad one dozen of these bananas fetched a price as high as three hundred rupees.[171] Even the repatriation from Saudi Arabia to India of one of the principal accused in the 26/11 massacre, Abu Zindal, did not appear to spoil the taste of these bananas! Actually, Pakistan was prolonging the farce of trial for the 26/11 accused, and even the farce had a freeze, because since 2009 trial judges were replaced as many as five times.[172] India and the US submitted a mass of hard evidence on the 26/11 terror attack. But the Pakistani habit of denial of facts transformed itself into a crude art. So, the newly appointed Pakistani Ambassador to India, Salman Bashir, had the audacity to announce that any connection between a Pakistani state agency and 26/11 was unbelievable.[173]

As to India, the habit of some political leaders, journalists and cricket administrators (some being political leaders themselves) to appease Pakistan without advancing India's interests was unbelievable. The Board of Control for Cricket in India (BCCI) announced that they were willing to organise three one-day matches and two twenty-over matches with Pakistan in India. The Board at least had the minimum sense to add that, till the security situation improved in Pakistan, it was not possible for Indian cricketers to visit Pakistan.[174] Even India's Home Minister Chidambaram affirmed that there was no argument against the normalisation of India-Pakistan relations in the field of sports, and that he would ensure complete security for Pakistani cricketers touring India.[175] In fact, administrator-politicians associated with the BCCI and players could earn handsome economic rewards from an India-Pakistan cricket tournament. But the benefits to India as a country (in the context of Pakistan's relentless proxy war against India) were far beyond comprehension. Therefore, it was good news indeed that some officials in India's Home Ministry as also the Congress party in Maharashtra were opposed to the India-Pakistan cricket matches. Equally palatable was the news that one of the greatest Indian cricketers, Sunil Gavaskar, opposed these matches. But India had no dearth of advocates of appeasement towards Pakistan. So, an editorial in a national daily bitterly criticised Gavaskar's contention, arguing that this was a mistake on the part of Gavaskar, analogous to the lapses he sometimes committed in the cricket field, and that opposing an India-Pakistan cricket tournament was to be judged as a crime in the world of cricket.[176]

The state of Pakistan continued its glaring servitude to terrorists, for which there were numerous examples over the years. One example of 9 October 2012 caught worldwide attention: at noon (12.15 hours) on that day, jihadis attacked a 14-years old girl, Malala Yousafzai (and two other girls) on a school bus. This incident took place at Mengora, the principal town of the Swat Valley, about 160 kilometres from Islamabad. The assault on Malala was deadly. She was first taken to a local hospital, and then transported by air to a military hospital in Peshawar. Ehsanulla Ehsan, the spokesman of Tehrik-e-Taliban (TeT), informed journalists over the telephone that he accepted responsibility for this attempt at murder. He accused Malala of devotion to the Western countries, as also of considering President Obama to be worthy of worship. Moreover, Ehsan complained that in the past, Malala spoke publicly against the Taliban.[177] Actually, in the past, Malala did not hesitate to affirm openly that everyone in Pakistan must recognise the right of all children, male and female, to go to schools, so that they could realise their potentials fully, and prove their usefulness to the society. If, Malala warned, Pakistani children were not permitted to hold pens in their hands, terrorists could compel them to handle weapons.[178]

The condition of Malala was so alarming that an ambulance aircraft, provided by the royal family of United Arab Emirates, took her to Britain. This information had to be kept secret, because the Taliban had threatened to attack Malala again.[179] In Britain, remarkably, following a major surgical intervention, when physicians became a little hopeful about Malala's recovery, two strangers appeared in the hospital for meeting Malala. The police had suspicions; they questioned these two persons for the collection of necessary information, and compelled them to quit without any opportunity to see Malala.[180]

In Taliban-infested Pakistan, the Malala episode created a stir. In Lahore and some other big cities, there were protest marches and candlelight processions in denunciation of the cowardly Taliban attack on Malala.[181] Army Chief Kayani visited Malala lying unconscious in a Pakistani hospital. He then issued what could be regarded as a platitudinous statement. It was now time, he stated, to struggle unitedly against Malala's attackers (and their sympathisers), who were overpowered by a barbarous mentality.[182] Raja Pervez Ashraf, who became the country's Prime Minister following Gilani's dismissal, declared in a similar vein that the savage attack on Malala underlined the need of unity to eliminate terrorism from Pakistan, and to save the people of the country. The people of Pakistan, especially students, arranged prayer meetings for Malala's recovery.[183]

But all these were temporary, though genuine, outpourings of popular emotions, which did not signal any change in the vicious characteristics of Pakistan's political culture. Some of the major characteristics were: visible/invisible military domination, support for some (if not all) jihadi groups, which was shaped partly by roguish calculations (domestic and international) on the part of the ruling circle, partly by helpless fear on the part of the ordinary people, and partly by acceptance of, or acquiescence in, religious fanaticism. Rehman Malik (entrusted with the duties of the Home Minister) announced the conferment of Sitara-e-Shujat (one of the highest civilian awards of Pakistan) upon Malala.[184] This too could hardly signify any positive transformation of Pakistan's political culture.

The conduct of some political leaders attested to the strength of this political culture, which could not but strike a liberal democrat as perverse. Take, for instance, Imran Khan, the cricketer-turned-politician, who was the leader of Tehrik-e-Insaf. Malala was shot at a time when Imran Khan just concluded his two-day march in support of the Taliban. Imran Khan's political message was that the Pakistan government should refrain from military operations against the Taliban, and that the US must stop drone strikes, which killed the Taliban. In other words, Imran Khan completely supported the pro-jihadi political culture (alluded to in the previous para). Imran Khan argued that drones killed not only militants, but also many ordinary people. It was, therefore, necessary to consult some comparative estimates for deaths of terrorists and ordinary persons, caused by the Taliban and drones, which were available at the time of Imran Khan's pro-Taliban march. Since 2003, the Pakistani Taliban killed 4,670 soldiers/policemen, and 14,427 ordinary persons. In contrast, during the same period, drone strikes liquidated about 3000 persons who were not terrorists.[185]

Imran Khan's reaction to the attempted murder of Malala was significant. Malala was a well-known person in social-political circles, national and international. Three years before the actual murderous attack on her—when Malala was only eleven years old—she revealed in her diary the savage character of Taliban rule in the Swat district. The British Broadcasting Corporation publicised Malala's diary in one of its Urdu programmes. So, Imran Khan, like most political leaders, knew Malala. After her attempted murder, Imran Khan went so far as to comment that Pakistanis voluntarily abdicated the right to criticise terrorists, and vested in a teenager like Malala this obligation to denounce terrorists. All Pakistanis were aware that the activities of terrorists were unjust and Malala was right. But they were all submerged in fear-filled silence.[186]

Imran Khan, after all, was the leader of an opposition party. Let us, therefore, turn to the ruling party. President Zardari recently made a statement, which was eloquent. It was not possible, he stated, to launch military operations anew against terrorists, who were active inside Pakistan and outside. The principal reason for this, according to Zardari, was the lack of will of opposition parties, especially the Pakistan Muslim League (N), led by Nawaz Sharif. It was worth a recall that in the past, when Nawaz Sharif was the Chief Minister of the Punjab province, he donated 35 acres of land in the vicinity of Lahore to the LET headed by Hafiz Saeed. This was in a place named Muridke, which emerged virtually as a jihadi manufacturing hub. The US, incidentally, announced a bounty of one million dollars for the capture of Hafiz Saeed, who moved anywhere and everywhere he desired. But he was an invisible man—to both the Pakistani and US governments. What Zardari did not have the courage to add, when he was criticising opposition parties in the aforesaid statement, was that even the Pakistani armed forces remained reluctant to organise full-scale and systematic campaigns against terrorists in the tribal territories on the Pakistan-Afghanistan border.[187]

Zardari and other leaders of the ruling party had no option but to submit to the authority of the military on any matter considered vital by the military. For example, it became known in the month of October 2012 that Lieutenant General (Retired) Asif Yasin, who replaced a civilian officer, Nargis Sethi, as Pakistan's Defence Secretary, happened to be extremely close to Army Chief Kayani. This case had an interesting background, illustrating the usual state of civil-military relations in Pakistan. Former Pakistani Prime Minister Gilani defied the military by removing Lieutenant General (Retired) Khalid Nayim Lodhi from the post of Defence Secretary and installing Nargis Sethi in that post. But the depraved political culture of Pakistan was not compatible with a civilian officer in the post of Defence Secretary, because the Pakistani military claimed this post as its birth right. So Nargis Sethi's tenure as Defence Secretary did not last long.[188]

Thus, there was hardly any prospect of military domination in Pakistan giving way to civilian supremacy. From time to time, members of the judiciary or media persons tried to take independent moves.[189] On 19 October 2012, for instance, the Supreme Court of Pakistan gave a direction that legal actions should be taken against ex-Army Chief, Aslam Beg and ex-ISI Chief, Asad Durani for undue interference in the 1990 general election. For all advocates of liberal democracy, this was indeed a positive judicial step.[190] But nobody could predict the eventual outcome of the Supreme Court's move. The situation in Pakistan was so unfortunate that many journalists, for instance, were paying severe penalties for telling the truth. They were being kidnapped from homes, work places, hotels, shops, university premises and even from buses.[191] There were some administrators, too, in Pakistan with a liberal disposition. They wanted to rename one roundabout in Lahore as Bhagat Singh Chowk. But extremist groups like the JUD sabotaged this move to honour an Indian freedom fighter of the British colonial era, who was not a Muslim.[192]

Indian policy makers persisted in trying to please Pakistan for the sake of lasting peace. By the end of October 2012, Pakistan decided to make some improvements in commercial ties with India, e.g., by reducing restrictions on visits by Indian businessmen to Pakistan.[193] At about the same time, Indian authorities decided to stage India-Pakistan cricket matches on the Indian soil.[194] Indian authorities probably did not perceive the irony and ignominy in a scenario where country A agreed to host cricket matches with country B, even when B's jihadis were regularly slaying A's citizens inside India. Actually, three cricket matches were held in India, but shortly afterwards, the LOC in J&K witnessed three Indian soldiers being beheaded by Pakistanis.

Probably, Indian policy makers had become optimistic on studying Army Chief Kayani's speech to cadets on 14 August 2012, Pakistan's Independence Day. Kayani stressed that the Pakistani nation as a whole had to fight terrorism and extremism, and that, otherwise, the army's efforts might not succeed, and the country could be engulfed in a 'civil war'. Kayani added that 'religious intolerance, political turmoil and anarchy' posed the greatest dangers to the country, which was passing through a critical phase.' 'Therefore,' Kayani advised, 'all our efforts should be directed at improving and correcting our internal situation.' Kayani went so far as to remind the cadets on Independence Day that 'the purpose behind creating Pakistan was not only to carve out a piece of land but also to establish a welfare Islamic State where the foundation of a tolerant and modern society should be laid...where life and property of minorities were safe and they could freely practise their faith.'[195]

Kyani's advocacy of a moderate, modern Muslim state, emphasis on terrorism and extremism inside Pakistan, as also abstention from laying stress on the threat from India, provided a probably broad hint that he and the military establishment had no objection to an improvement of relations with India. To some extent, Kayani's aforesaid statement was also a signal of approval for the sort of improvement in trade relations that had already taken place. For instance, although Pakistan was yet to accord formally to India an MFN status, a number of significant steps were taken by Pakistan. In the recent past, it bears reiteration, Pakistan imported only 2000 varieties of articles from India. By the end of 2012, Pakistanis could import from India 6,800 items out of a total of 8,000. On its part, India reduced by 30 per cent the list of commodities banned for imports from Pakistan. It was not easy, however, to asses to what extent, as already noted, the financial interests of corporations run by retired military officers were to be promoted by an improvement in India-Pakistan commercial transactions.[196]

Three agreements, signed by India and Pakistan in 2012, promoted trade facilitation in various ways, e.g., in matters of licensing, certification, laboratory tests, settlement of grievances of traders, etc. On 14 December 2012, the two countries agreed to relax visa barriers for travellers. Moreover, both the countries agreed, under the SAFTA arrangement, to restrict the number of sensitive items to 100 by 2017. They examined the prospects of opening a second trade gate at the Wagah-Attari border and a new avenue at the Munabao-Khokrapar border. India and Pakistan, moreover, decided upon the establishment of Amritsar-Lahore grid connectivity, so that, eventually there would take place 500 megawatt of power trade.[197]

Prospects for improvement in India-Pakistan relations appeared to brighten after Nawaz Sharif became Pakistan's Prime Minister as a result of parliamentary elections in May 2013. For, Sharif promised before the elections that he would resume the dialogue with India, which was suspended after the 1999 military coup. Unlike in the case of this Sharif government, no other civilian government in the past succeeded another, completing a full term of office.[198]

Nevertheless, there could be another view—probably more realistic—about whether Sharif was indeed in a position to bring about any significant upgradation of relations with India. For, in order to boost popular support in the 2013 elections, Sharif adopted the dominant Pakistani doctrine of what was the nature of terrorist threat to Pakistan. In accordance with this doctrine, first, Pakistan did not face any threat from Al Qaeda; secondly, the US war on terror was not Pakistan's war; thirdly, the US was guilty of actual terrorism in Afghanistan and Iraq; and fourthly, the terrorist tag should be attached to Indian activities in J&K. This was really the Al Qaeda doctrine. Military and intelligence agencies not only subscribed to this doctrine, but also preached it to ensure that the majority of Pakistani people embraced the same. Whenever terrorists massacred innocent Pakistanis, officers of these agencies tended to attribute the heinous act to the US, Israel and India—sometimes explicitly, sometimes implicitly. Prime Minister Sharif, unable to contest the above noted Al Qaeda doctrine of terrorism, was hardly expected to act effectively to strengthen Pakistan's relations with India.[199]

It is remarkable that, amidst these somewhat forbidding circumstances, Pakistanis and Indians have launched a number of organisations for the promotion of peace, interaction between peoples and even engaged in exercises to explore solutions for such infinitely complex issues as J&K. The examples are: Aman ki Asha (AKA), Pakistan-India Forum for Peace and Democracy (PIFPD), Pakistan Institute for Legislative Development and Transparency (PILDAT), and South Asia Free Media Association (SAFMA). They have not only held conventions, conferences, dialogues, etc. but also published an impressive number of books. Nevertheless, if there is any attempt to identify tangible results from these laudable enterprises, it may not be fruitful. Even on an issue that is profoundly humanitarian, i.e., prevention of repeated detentions of innocent fishermen inadvertently crossing improperly demarcated territorial waters of India and Pakistan, despite a joint survey in 2007, practically nothing could be done.[200]

So, India-Pakistan relations had no grand chance of improvement—despite Sharif being elected as Pakistan's Prime

Minister. Sharif and his Indian counterpart, Singh, were to meet on 29 September 2013 in New York, where they would be attending the United Nations General Assembly (UNGA) session. On 27 September, at the UNGA, Sharif made some combative comments against India on J&K. These might have pleased his countrymen, but were irrelevant because of the Shimla accord of 1972, which obliged both the countries to resolve J&K bilaterally. Even the International Court of Justice (ICJ) once snubbed Pakistan by urging adherence to the 1972 accord, when Pakistan complained against India to the ICJ after India shot down a Pakistani surveillance aircraft in 1999. The ICJ even affirmed that it lacked jurisdiction over this affair. On 28 September, Singh severely rebuked Pakistan in his UNGA speech. The 29 September meeting between Sharif and Singh did not succeed, quite expectedly, especially because, before that meeting, Sharif described Singh as a 'village hag'. It must be stressed, however, that, just before the Sharif-Singh meeting in New York, a Pakistan-sponsored terrorist attack occurred in J&K, and yet Singh was bold enough to affirm that he was ready to carry on talks with Pakistan despite such acts of terror (this certainly did not receive endorsement from many Indians).[201]

Meanwhile, in Islamabad, on 9 September 2013, the All Parties Conference (APC) decided in favour of talks with the Taliban in order to cope with terrorism. This was no surprise, because General Kayani was known to look upon such terrorist networks as the Haqqani outfit as a vital support base for Pakistan after the US withdrawal from Afghanistan.[202] There were, however, disagreements in Pakistan on whether it was advisable to have a dialogue with the Taliban, which was so obscurantist as to have no respect for the penal code of Pakistan, even though Pakistan was itself an Islamic Republic. So, the Taliban, and a large number of Pakistanis with Taliban-type extremist mindsets, advocated punishment, for instance, for not saying prayers (namaz) five times a day. Another point of disagreement was whether it was beneficial for the country to talk to the Taliban from a position of weakness. This query acquired urgency, because, even after Pakistan army's announcement that it was withdrawing from such crucial terrorist-infested regions in the FATA as Dir, Malakand and Swat, on 15 September 2013, i.e., only six days after the APC's recommendation of talks with the Taliban, the latter killed a Major

General and a Lieutenant Colonel as also four soldiers in the region, including North Waziristan.[203]

If, in spite of this aggressive stance of the Taliban, the Pakistan government did not decide to discontinue talks with the Taliban, one could speculate on whether this was more a sign of the government's declining confidence than of the realistic recognition of Taliban's growing strength spelling an urgent need for a compromise. After all, it was evidently this recognition, which prompted (perhaps compelled) the US to forget its pressure in the recent past on Pakistan not to talk to the Taliban, and to commence talks in absolute secrecy with Mullah Muhammad Omar's secretary in November 2010 with German diplomatic assistance. Undoubtedly, the economic crisis in the US and Europe played a major part in forging these talks with the Taliban, which might enable the US and NATO forces to find an orderly way out of Afghanistan. As to Pakistan, it was suffering from an acute economic crisis for years. Therefore, the divergence between Pakistan and the US on whether to talk or not to talk to the Taliban for a peaceful settlement tended to disappear. It was, nevertheless, difficult to predict the actual outcome of such talks.[204]

The uncertainty about the results of these talks could be underlined by, at least, two facts. One was the enthronement of Mullah Fazlullah, who had been associated with the Movement for the Enforcement of Islamic Law, or Tehrik-e-Nifaz-e-Shariat-e-Mohammadi (TNSM), as the TTP Chief on 7 November 2013. The other was the behaviour of TNSM in recent years. Maulana Sufi Mohammad established the TNSM in 1989. Shortly after 9/11, the TNSM was banned, and Sufi Mohammad (trying to fight the ISAF) was sent to prison by Pakistani authorities. In 2008, when the TNSM-TTP alliance used abominable terror and established Sharia courts in the Swat Valley (which was a part of the Malakand Division), compelling at least 500,000 residents to leave the Valley, the government decided to bring Sufi Mohammad out of the jail and use his services for a truce with the militants. This truce became operational in February 2009 and permitted the militants to enforce Sharia lawfully in the Malakand Division on the condition of renunciation of force. Nevertheless, in April 2009, militants repudiated the truce on the pretext that the government did not permit them to appoint the judges of Sharia courts. This time, Sufi Mohammad failed to oblige the government, which approached him for a truce, because there was opposition by the TTP. On 15 September 2013 (as noted in the paragraph preceding the last), two high-ranking military officers were murdered. This was reportedly at the instigation of Mullah Fazlullah, the recently crowned TTP chief with extensive TSNM links, who was the son-in-law of Sufi Mohammad, and who did not favour talks initiated by Prime Minister Nawaz Sharif.[205]

An important reason why the TTP was not in favour of talks aimed at the promotion of peace was that it coveted the opportunities for loot in the Pakistani towns. The Al Qaeda, too, endorsed Fazlullah's aversion to talks with the Pakistan government. The TTP could not afford to alienate the Al Qaeda for, at least, two reasons. One was the assured supply of huge funds from the Gulf countries channelised through the Al Qaeda. The other reason was that Al Qaeda was instrumental in preserving the TTP as a force by keeping its 40 groups together—perhaps again with the lure of money. The Al Qaeda was probably aware that Pakistani opinion was largely against any conflict with the TTP. Therefore, the Al Qaeda and Fazlullah could plan to demoralise Pakistan's security forces by mounting aggression. The Pakistan army, under the outgoing Army Chief Kayani, did not seem to have any determination to take on either the TTP or the Al Qaeda. Kayani and his army were preoccupied with somehow eliminating the Indian presence from Afghanistan before the ISAF's withdrawal in 2014. By the end of November 2013, Raheel Sharif succeeded Kayani as the 15th head of a 600,000 strong army.[206]

Raheel Sharif inherited an unenviable situation, which was bristling with contradictions. He must have been pondering, which would be the correct path in coping with the Al Qaeda and the TTP—not to speak of the constant pressure from the US that Pakistan should do much more about the war on terror than it was actually doing. The new Army Chief was aware that his soldiers—like a large number of Pakistanis—were not enthusiastic about launching full-fledged military strikes against the Al Qaeda and the TTP. There was also the well-known view that, despite the regular slaughter of civil-military persons by these militant outfits, they could be used as strategic assets after the withdrawal of ISAF from Afghanistan in 2014. Yet, when as many as 67 IEDs were used to target military check posts during and after September 2013 in North Waziristan Agency (NWA), and a number of soldiers were killed and injured, the Pakistani military had to retaliate against terrorists. Still, it seemed to suffer from a sort of schizophrenia, and, contrary to what at least a section of Pakistanis desired, the Pakistani military deliberately refrained from full-scale military action against militants, and sheepishly underlined this at the end of the initial round of clashes in NWA. There was even a report that the chance of success of a large scale military assault in the NWA was 40 per cent. Terrorists had four major groups: the Afghan Taliban, the Uzbeks belonging to the Islamic Movement of Uzbekistan (IMU), the Punjabi Taliban and the Haqqanis led by Jalaluddin Haqqani. The Pakistan army was not sure whether it should continue to favour only the Haqqanis for its anti-India strategy after the US-NATO withdrawal from Afghanistan. All the above noted four groups were enjoying the financial patronage of Al Qaeda, and consequently, remained more or less under the control of the Al Qaeda. Therefore, from the standpoint of such countries as the US and India—though not from the Pakistani standpoint—there was little to choose between these four groups. These terrorist groups developed an extraordinary love-hate relationship with the Pakistan army, navy, air force (as also the ISI), and nobody could predict or fully comprehend who would use whom and when. For example, Pakistani military authorities reportedly employed some terrorists to eliminate former Prime Minister Benazir Bhutto. Some terrorists, again, would humiliate these authorities (as already noted) by attacking a naval base in Karachi and freeing colleagues in detention.[207]

The biggest airport of Pakistan in the country's largest city, Karachi, came under terrorist attack on 9 and 10 June 2014. With one sharp blow, this resolved four dilemmas tormenting the Pakistani military establishment for years. These were, first, whether to placate and punish Pakistani terrorists at chosen intervals; secondly, whether to select some terrorist groups (e.g. the Haqqani group) for a favourable treatment; thirdly, whether to distinguish between good Taliban and bad Taliban, and promote talks with the former; and fourthly, whether to continue duplicitous conduct vis-a-vis the US in the matter of carrying out the war on terror, especially with regard to an invasion against terrorist strongholds in the NWA. The terrorist strike on the Karachi airport settled answers in the negative on all these four issues, knocking off past hesitations/prevarications, and the Pakistani military launched the much-delayed all-out attack against the TTP in NWA on 15 June 2014. The determination of the military was apparent from the use of jet bombers and tanks. The Karachi airport attack led to the deaths of about forty persons (including ten Uzbeks), whereas on the first day of the invasion in the NWA, six soldiers died, but 177 Taliban militants (including presumably the good Taliban) were killed. The TTP reacted by declaring a state of war, and warning international airlines, other foreign agencies and individuals that they should suspend all commercial transactions with Pakistan and leave the country.[208]

By launching determined actions against terrorists, the Pakistani military naturally enhanced its public image. Normally, civilian leaders should have openly welcomed it. But Pakistan was not yet a normal state. Therefore, civilian leaders appeared to hesitate to praise the military. One explanation could be the recent civil-military tussle on the attempted murder of a Geo TV journalist, Hamid Mir. He survived but his brother accused the ISI of plotting this unsuccessful murder. Prime Minister Sharif met Hamid Mir. He also went to the ISI headquarters, and expressed admiration for the services of ISI officers. The ISI retaliated. Geo TV's journalists faced harassment. Its broadcasting licence was initially suspended. It had to pay a fine. But the military demonstrated its power by manipulating the eventual closure of the Geo TV station. Prime Minister Sharif was unhappy, but he had to bear it. Sharif did not have the courage to contest the military will at a time when the military was decisively engaged in fighting terrorists.[209]

The Pakistani military took a number of risks while launching a full-scale attack on home-grown terrorists. First, the terrorists always affirmed that they had the support of religious authorities. Whatever the correctness of this affirmation, the Pakistani military could not wish it away, and ignore the probable damage to popular support for the military. Secondly, as the armed forces marched into villages and towns in the tribal belt, ordinary people had to flee, swelling the number of internally displaced persons. This certainly detracted from the popularity of the Pakistani military. Thirdly, the Pakistan army could not be sure of whether those military personnel wedded for long to terrorists (even if secretly) would not try to sabotage the military's counter-terrorist programme. Fourthly, at the initial stage, the government estimates might optimistically stress the losses of terrorists, but, at subsequent stages, nobody could predict the comparative figures of losses on both sides. After all, many terrorists would certainly cross the Durand Line, and afterwards multiply government losses by attacks from sanctuaries in Afghanistan. It was a race against time for the government forces, because they wanted to maximise the opponent's losses before the ISAF withdrawal from Afghanistan, when, obviously, the terrorist militias would gain some advantages.[210]

The middle of 2014 marks a watershed in this study of cross-border terrorism with a focus on Pakistan. For, in the first place, the Pakistani armed forces appeared to shed their inhibitions on dealing with terrorists. Secondly, the longstanding divergence with the US in the matter of drone strikes against militants seemed to disappear. In the past, Pakistani authorities suffered from an ambiguity on this point. Sometimes, they interpreted drone strikes as diluting their sovereignty. On other occasions, they appeared to appreciate the value of drone attacks, even if without much public acknowledgement. In mid-2014, however, there were apparently no protests against the use of drones by the US, when, for instance, it killed twenty terrorists in NWA on 16 July 2014, and again liquidated eleven terrorists in the Pakistan-Afghanistan border on 19 July 2014. Remarkably, many (not all) Pakistanis preferred the targeted attacks on militants by US drones to inaccurate army artillery strikes, which killed a much larger number of civilians than US drone strikes. Thirdly, the middle of 2014 witnessed the emergence of a new government in New Delhi, headed by Prime Minister Narendra Modi, and Prime Minister Nawaz Sharif responded positively to Modi's invitation to attend the inauguration ceremony. This could not but raise expectations about an improvement in India-Pakistan relations not merely on trade issues, but also on the much more sensitive security issues in view of the Pakistani military's decisive intervention against militants. Nevertheless, doubts persisted about whether the Pakistani armed forces could rise above decades of indoctrinating themselves and the people about treating India as an enemy country on account of deep-seated religious fanaticism.[211]

This may be the appropriate terminal point for Chapter Four of this study.

References

1. Justice Javed Iqbal and others, *Abbottabad Commission of Inquiry Report*, Islamabad, 2013, pp. 1-2, 18-19.
2. *Ibid.*, p. 18.
3. *Ibid.*, pp. 19-24.
4. *Ibid.*, pp. 267-68. As late as February 2015, Pervez Musharraf unequivocally confessed to *The Guardian* of London that the ISI employed the Taliban to launch attacks against India: see PTI report from Karachi, *The Statesman*, 16 February 2015.
5. *Abbottabad Commission Report,* pp. 269-71.
6. *Ibid.*, pp. 272, 275-76, 282.
7. *Ibid.*, pp. 278-79.
8. *Ibid.*, pp. 280-81, 283, 285-86.
9. *Ibid.*, pp. 284-88.
10. *Ibid.*, pp. 288-89.
11. *Ibid.*, pp. 289-91.
12. *Ibid.*, p. 290.
13. *Ibid.*, pp. 304-06 for all above noted questions.
14. *Ibid.*, pp. 308-09.
15. *Ibid.*, pp. 309-11.
16. *Ibid.*, pp. 305, 324-25.
17. *Ibid.*, pp. 322, 328, 332-33.
18. *Ibid.*, pp. 334-35.
19. Omer Farooq Khan, *The Times of India*, 13 May 2011; Ahmed Rashid, *Pakistan on the Brink*, London: Allen Lane/Penguin, 2012, p. 10.
20. Office of the Director of National Intelligence, National Counterterrorism Center, *Report on Terrorism, 2011*, Washington DC, 2012, p. 22.
21. *Ibid.*; also see Salman Masood and David E. Sanger (from Islamabad), *The International Herald Tribune*, 22 May 2011.
22. Stephen Tankel, *Jihadist Violence*, p. 50.
23. Chidanand Rajghatta, *The Times of India*, 10 May 2011; Eric Schmitt, Thom Shanker and David E. Sanger, *The International Herald Tribune*, 10.May 2011.
24. News Analysis, *The International Herald Tribune*, 9 May 2011; News Analysis, *The Times of India*, 9 May 2011; Siobhan German and Mathew Rosenburg, *The Wall Street Journal*, 9 May 2011; *The Washington Post*, 9 May 2011; Report from Washington DC, *The Times of India*, 11 May 2011.
25. Reports in *The Indian Express*, 9 and 12 May 2011.
26. Rashid, *Pakistan on the Brink*, p. 10.
27. Reports from Washington DC/London, *The Times of India*, 15 May 2011.
28. National Counterterrorism Center, *Report on Terrorism 2011*, p. 23.
29. Stephen Tankel, *Jihadist Violence,* p 51; National Counterterrorism Center, *Report on Terrorism 2011*, p. 24.

30. Rashid, *Pakistan on the Brink*, p. 11.
31. National Counterterrorism Center, *Report on Terrorism 2011*, pp. 25-28.
32. Helene Cooper and Ismail Khan, *The New York Times*, 7 May 2011; *The Times of India*, 16 and 17 May 2011.
33. *The Times of India*, 21 May 2011.
34. David Cortright, *Ending Obama's War*, Boulder: Paradigm Publications, 2011, p. 9.
35. *The Times of India*, 21 May 2011.
36. Omer Farooq Khan, *The Times of India*, 20 May 2011.
37. *The International Herald Tribune*, 22 May 2011.
38. Chidanand Rajghatta, report from Washington DC, *The Times of India*, 24 May 2011; AFP report from Islamabad, *The Times of India*, 26 May 2011.
39. AP report, *The Washington Post*, 18 May 2011; Stephen L. Carter, *Newsweek*, 16 May 2011, pp. 8, 11; Salman Rushdie, *Newsweek*, 16 May 2011, p. 16.
40. Leslie H Gelb, *Newsweek*, 16 May 2011, pp. 6-7; Stephen L Carter, *Newsweek*, 16 May 2011, p. 11.
41. Cortright, *Ending Obama's War*, p. 6.
42. *A New Way Forward: Rethinking US strategy in Afghanistan, Report of the Afghanistan Study Group*, August 2010, pp. 1, 5.
43. *Report of the Afghanistan Study Group*, 2010, pp. 1, 4, 7.
44. Andrew Romano and Daniel Klaidman, *Newsweek*, 16 May 2011, pp. 26-28.
45. *The Times of India* and *The International Herald Tribune*, 1 June 2011; Rashid, *Pakistan on the Brink*, pp. 10-11.
46. PTI report from Islamabad, *The Times of India*, 3 June 2011.
47. Omer Farooq Khan's report from Islamabad and AP report from Peshawar, *The Times of India*, 5 June 2011; PTI report from Islamabad and AFP report from Peshawar, *The Times of India*, 6 June 2011; PTI report from Islamabad, *The Times of India*, 9 June 2011.
48. *The International Herald Tribune*, 9 June 2011; PTI report from Islamabad, *The Times of India*, 10 June 2011.
49. Faryal Leghari, *Khaleef Times*, Dubai, 11 June 2011.
50. AP report from Washington DC, *The Times of India*, 10 June 2011.
51. PTI report from Washington DC, *The Statesman*, 17 June 2011.
52. PTI report from Cairo, *Ibid.*, 17 June 2011.
53. Editorial, *Ibid.*, 20 June 2011.
54. Rajinder Puri, *Ibid.*, 18 June 2011.
55. Editorial, *Ibid.*, 18 June 2011.
56. AP report from Washington DC, *Ibid.*, 20 June 2011; for a confirmation of amicable relations between the Haqqani group and Islamabad, see Syed Farooq Hasnat, *Global Security Watch*: *Pakistan*, New Delhi: Pentagon Press, 2012, p. 171.

57. AP report from Washington DC, *The Statesman*, 20 June 2011; PTI report from Washington DC, *Ibid.*, 24 June 2011; Editorial, *Ibid.*, 21 June 2011.
58. For relevant information and comments, see an article by M.L. Kotru, *Ibid.*, 24 June 2011.
59. PTI reports from Brussels and Kabul, *Ibid.*, 24 June 2011.
60. For some insightful comments on this issue, see editorial, *Ibid.*, 25 June 2011.
61. Editorial, *Ibid.*, 27 June 2011.
62. PTI report from Islamabad, *Ibid.*, 25 June 2011.
63. For elucidation, see the article by Rajinder Puri, *Ibid.*, 25 June 2011.
64. PTI report, *Ibid.*, 2 October 2011.
65. For implications of Kayani's statement, see an article by Rajinder Puri, *Ibid.*, 20 October 2011.
66. PTI report, *Ibid.*, 2 October 2011.
67. PTI report, *Ibid.*, 3 October 2011.
68. Editorial, *Ibid.*, 4 October 2011, on Awlakis's death.
69. PTI report, *Ibid.*, 18 October 2011.
70. PTI report, *Ibid.*, 22 October 2011; editorial, *Ibid.*, 26 October 2011.
71. AFP report, *Ibid.*, 3 October 2011; report in *The Economist*, 24 September 2011, p. 41.
72. Report from Islamabad, *The Statesman*, 27 October 2011.
73. Report from Washington DC, *Ibid.*, 28 October 2011.
74. Statesman News Service and PTI report, *Ibid.*, 12 November 2011.
75. Simran Sodhi, *Ibid.*, 11 November 2011.
76. Statesman News Service and PTI report, *Ibid.*
77. Article by Rajinder Puri, *Ibid.*, 13 November 2011.
78. See, for instance, the statement by India's former minister for external affairs, Yashwant Sinha, PTI report, *The Indian Express*, 11 November 2011.
79. Article by Rajinder Puri, *The Statesman*, 13 November 2011.
80. Note the false optimism expressed in an editorial in *The Telegraph*, 8 November 2011.
81. PTI reports, *The Statesman*, 4 and 5 November 2011; article by SK Sadar Nayeem, *Ibid.*, 10 November 2011; Article by M L Kotru, *Ibid.*, 14 November 2011; editorial, *The Telegraph*, 16 November 2011.
82. PTI report, *The Statesman*, 13 November 2011.
83. Article by M.L. Kotru, *Ibid.*, 14 November 2011.
84. PTI report, *Ibid.*, 7 November 2011.
85. PTI report, *Ibid.*, 8 November 2011.
86. For shocking details about this and other aspects of religious freedom in Pakistan see *Annual Report of the United States Commission on International Religious Freedom May 2011*, pp. 110-23; also see PTI report, *The Statesman*, 10 November 2011.
87. PTI report, *Ibid.*, 3 December 2011.
88. PTI report, *Ibid.*, 7 December 2011.

89. Article by Matthew Rosenburg and Eric Schmitt, New York Times News Service, reproduced in *The Telegraph*, 5 December 2011.
90. PTI report, *The Statesman*, 30 November 2011.
91. For pertinent observations, see an editorial, *The Telegraph*, 8 December 2011.
92. PTI report, *The Statesman*, 5 December 2011.
93. For relevant observations, see a commentary in *The Independent*, London, reproduced in *The Telegraph*, 30 November 2011.
94. Article by Vinod Saighal, *The Statesman*, 4 December 2011.
95. Jonathan Randal, *Osama: The Making of a Terrorist*, London: I.B. Tauris, 2006, pp 244-47.
96. *Ibid.*, Osama, pp. 248-49.
97. See, e.g., Bill Clinton, *My life*, New York: Alfred A. Knopf, 2004, p. 955.
98. See, e.g. PTI reports, *The Statesman*, 7 and 15 December 2011; AFP report, *Ibid*, 9 December 2011.
99. Report in *The Telegraph*, 23 December 2011.
100. Article by Nasir Jaffry, *Ibid.*, 24 December 2011.
101. See, e.g. comments by a former Foreign Secretary of India, Kanwal Sibal, *Ibid.*, 14 December 2011.
102. See, e.g. Randal, *Osama*, pp. 253, 267.
103. *Ibid.*, pp. 257-59.
104. Bradley Graham, *By His Own Rules: The Ambitions, Successes, and Ultimate Failures of Donald Rumsfeld*, New York: Public Affairs, 2009, p. 675.
105. Raghav Sharma, 'China's Afghanistan Policy: Slow Recalibration', *China Report*, Vol. 46, No. 3, 2010, New Delhi, pp. 203-04.
106. PTI report, *The Statesman*, 28 December 2011.
107. Gunjan Singh, 'China's Afghanistan Policy, http://www.ipcs.org/article/afghanistan/China's%20Afghanistan%20policy-3040.html
108. 'The Chinese Policy Toward Afghanistan: From Military Bases to Industrial Bases,' http://www.turkishweekly.net/op-ed/2863/the-chinese-policy-toward-afghanistan-from-military-bases-to-industrial-bases.html
109. Krishnan Srinivasan, *The Telegraph*, 25 January 2012; Srinivasan happens to be a former Foreign Secretary of India.
110. Jeff Reeves, 'Does China's Afghan Foreign Policy Constitute a Grand Strategy', *Defense Concepts*, Vol. 5, Ed. 4, Washington DC, p. 38.
111. *Ibid.*, pp. 25-27.
112. 'The Chinese Policy Towards Afghanistan: From Military bases to Industrial Bases', *op. cit.*
113. *Ibid.*
114. Raghav Sharma, 'China's Afghanistan Policy: Slow Recalibration', pp. 208-09.
115. Reports in *The Statesman*, 25 December 2011 and 4 January 2012; *The Telegraph*, 9 January 2012.

116. Report in *The Hindu*, 12 January 2012.
117. Eric Schmitt, *The Telegraph*, 27 December 2011.
118. Editorial, *The Statesman*, 5 January 2012; editorial, *The Telegraph*, 6 January 2012; PTI report, *The Statesman*, 13 January 2012.
119. Articles by Rajinder Puri, *Ibid.*, 11, 14 and 24 January 2012.
120. Article by C Raja Mohan, *The Indian Express*, 2 March 2012.
121. See, e.g. an editorial, *Ibid.*, 2 March 2012.
122. See an article by Salman Haidar, *The Statesman,* 6 March 2012.
123. See editorial, *Frontier*, 29 January-4 February 2012, p. 2.
124. See, e.g. an article by Rajinder Puri, *The Statesman*, 29 February 2012.
125. PTI report, *Ibid.*, 25 February 2012.
126. PTI report, *Ibid.*, 4 March 2012.
127. PTI report, *Ibid.*, 18 March 2012.
128. PTI report, *Ibid.*, 13 March 2012.
129. See, e.g. a write-up by M. Saleem Pandit, *The Times of India*, 27 February 2012.
130. See an editorial, *The Statesman*, 4 March 2012.
131. The Statesman News Service, *Ibid.*, 15 March 2012.
132. See, e.g. an editorial in *Dawn*, 3 March 2012; Shaheen Akhter 'Expanding Cross-Loc Interactions: A Conflict Transformation approach to Kashmir', *Regional Studies*, Islamabad, Vol. xxx, No. 1, Winter 2011-12, pp. 3-37.
133. See, e.g. an analysis by Manoj Prasad, *The Indian Express,* 3 March 2012.
134. See an editorial in *The Statesman*, 5 May 2012; also see an article by Salman Haidar, *Ibid.*, 8 May 2012.
135. See, e.g. an editorial, *Ibid.*, 17 May 2012.
136. PTI report from Washington DC, *The Indian Express*, 22 May 2012; also see an editorial, *Ibid.*, 17 May 2012.
137. See an article by Zahid Hussain, *The Statesman,* 17 May 2012.
138. See, e.g. an article by Sayeed Hasan Khan and Kurt Jacobsen, *Ibid.*, 19 May 2012.
139. This is, e.g. the view of Zahid Hussain: see *Ibid.*, 17 May 2012.
140. PTI report, *Ibid.*, 7 May 2012.
141. PTI reports, *Ibid.*, 17 May 2012, and *The Indian Express*, 18 May 2012.
142. Consult an article by Anders Fogh Rasmussen, *The New York Times*, reproduced in *The Indian Express*, 18 May 2012.
143. See, e.g. an AP report from Islamabad, *Ibid.*, 18 May 2012.
144. PTI reports, *Ibid.*, 18 May 2012, and *The Statesman*, 20 May 2012.
145. See, e.g. an article by Salman Masood and Eric Schmitt, *The Indian Express*, 17 May 2012.
146. See articles by Swati Sengupta and Prithvijit Mitra, *The Times of India,* 9 May 2012, and Rajiv Bhatia, *The Indian Express,* 22 May 2012.
147. Article by Ruchika Talwar, *The Indian Express*, 8 June 2012.
148. Statement by PPP leader Usman Salim Malik, *The Statesman*, 21 June 2012.
149. Comment by Suhasini Haidar in an article in *The Indian Express,* 22 June 2012.

150. PTI reports from Islamabad, *The Statesman,* 20 and 21 June 2012.
151. PTI report from Islamabad, *Ibid.*, 22 June 2012.
152. Article by Seema Mustafa, *Ibid.*, 22 June 2012.
153. Article by Kuldip Nayar, *Ibid.*, 21 June 2012; also see an editorial, *Ibid.*
154. Francesca Marino and Benia mino Natale, *Apocalypse Pakistan*, New Delhi: Niyogi Books, 2013, pp 169-170; article by Cyril Almeida, *The Indian Express*, 18 June 2012.
155. Marino and Natale, *Apocalypse Pakistan,* pp. 172-73.
156. J.K. Baral, 'The Afghan Game: Interests and Moves', *Strategic Analysis*, 2013, Vol. 37, No. 6, p. 704.
157. *The Times of India,* 22 June 2012.
158. Report from Kabul, *The Statesman*, 8 July 2012.
159. Reports from Tokyo and Kabul, *Ibid.*, 9 July 2012.
160. AFP report, *Ibid.*, 10 July 2012.
161. Report from Kabul, *Ibid.*, 15 July 2012.
162. Report from Kabul, *The Indian Express,* 13 July 2012.
163. Report from Kabul, *Ibid.*, 10 July 2012.
164. News analysis by Ruchika Talwar, *Ibid.*, 7 July 2012.
165. Report in *The Economist*, London, reprinted in *The Indian Express,* 10 July 2012.
166. *Ibid.*, 18 July 2012.
167. PTI report, *The Statesman,* 21 July 2012.
168. Reuters report, *The Indian Express,* 9 July 2012.
169. PTI report from Karachi, *Ibid.*, 18 July 2012.
170. PTI report from Lahore, *The Statesman,* 22 July 2012.
171. See, e.g. an editorial, *Ibid.*, 17 July 2012.
172. PTI report from Islamabad, *Ibid.*, 18 July 2012.
173. PTI report, *Ibid.*, 16 July 2012.
174. *Ibid.*, 17 July 2012.
175. Commentary by Amitabh Sinha, *The Indian Express,* 18 July 2012.
176. Editorial, *Ibid.*
177. Report from Islamabad, *The Statesman*, 10 October 2012.
178. *The Nation,* Islamabad, 16 October 2012.
179. Report from Islamabad, *The Statesman,* 16 October 2012.
180. Reports from London/Islamabad, *Ibid.*, 17 October 2012.
181. Report from Islamabad, *Ibid.*, 12 October 2012.
182. See an editorial, *Ibid.*
183. PTI report from Islamabad, *Ibid.*, 14 October 2012.
184. Report from Islamabad, *Ibid.*, 17 October 2012.
185. Report in *The Economist*, London, reproduced in *The Indian Express,* 15 October 2012.
186. Imran Khan, Quoted in an article by Firoz Bakht Ahmed, *The Statesman,* 30 October 2012.
187. Article by M L Kotru, *Ibid.*, 30 October 2012.
188. Report from Islamabad, *Ibid.*, 29 October 2012.

189. Interview, Mohammad Ziauddin of *The Express Tribune,* Karachi, by Simran Sodhi, *The Statesman*, 27 October 2012.
190. Report from Nasir Jafffry of the AFP from Islamabad, *Ibid.*, 20 October 2012; also see a PTI report, *Ibid*, 21 October 2012.
191. Article by Firoz Bakht Ahmed, *Ibid.*, 30 October 2012.
192. PTI report from Lahore, *Ibid.*, 1 November 2012.
193. PTI report from Islamabad, *Ibid.*
194. SNS report, *Ibid.*, 31 October 2012.
195. Najam Sethi, editorial, *The Friday Times*, weekly, Islamabad, 17-23 August 2012.
196. Syed Imran Sardar, 'Trade Liberalisation Between India and Pakistan: Focusing Direct and Indirect Barriers,' *Regional Studies*, Vol. xxxii, No. 1, Winter 2013-14, p. 76; Ishtiaq Ahmed and Hannes Ebert, 'Will Pakistan's India Policy under Sharif Shift Strategically?' *Strategic Analysis*, Vol. 137, No. 6, November-December 2013, p. 669.
197. Syed Imran Sardar, 'Trade Liberalisation Between India and Pakistan: Focusing Direct and Indirect Barriers,' p. 77.
198. Ishtiaq Ahmad and Hannes Ebert, 'Will Pakistan's India Policy under Sharif Shift Strategically?' pp. 667-68.
199. Article by Khaled Ahmed, *The Indian Express*, 20 August 2013; also see Ishtiaq Ahmed and Hannes Ebert, 'Will Pakistan's India Policy under Sharif Shift Strategically?'p. 671.
200. Shaheen Akhtar, 'India-Pakistan Cross Border Peace Initiatives: Challenges and Prospects, '*Regional Studies*, Vol. xxxii, No. 1, Winter 2013-14, pp. 3-11.
201. Article by Khaled Ahmed, *The Indian Express,* 2 October 2013.
202. Vali Nasr, *The Dispensable Nation: American Foreign Policy in Retreat*, New York: Doubleday, 2013, p. 86.
203. Article by Khaled Ahmed, *The Indian Express,* 20 September 2013.
204. Ahmed Rashid, *Pakistan on the Brink*, pp. 112-14; Vali Nasr, *The Dispensable Nation*, p. 81.
205. See an excellent article by Christophe Jaffrelot, *The Indian Express,* 14 November 2013.
206. Article by Khaled Ahmed, *Ibid.*, 16 November 2013; PTI report from Islamabad, *The Statesman*, 29 November 2013.
207. Article by Khaled Ahmed, *The Indian Express,* 10 January 2014.
208. PTI report from Islamabad, *The Statesman,* 17 June 2014.
209. Report in *The Economist,* Reproduced in *The Indian Express,* 17 June 2014.
210. Articles by Salman Haidar, *The Statesman*, 15 July 2014, and Christophe Jaffrelot, *The Indian Express*, 16 July 2014.
211. Report in *The Economist*, Reproduced in *The Indian Express*, 23 October 2013; PTI report from Islamabad, *The Statesman*, 17 July 2014; PTI report from Islamabad, *Ibid.*, 22 July 2014; article by Hussain Haqqani, *The Indian Express*, 23 July 2014.

Five

Literature on Islam

There are numerous books on Islam and the Holy Prophet, which may be deemed to be valuable. But this author has chosen to discuss three books in terms of their authenticity, measured by the immense knowledge of their authors, their familiarity with relevant languages/ source materials, and transparent objectivity. These books are:

Anwar Shaikh, *Faith and Deception*, Cardiff: Principality Publishers, 1996; Ali Sina, *Understanding Muhammad: A Psychobiography of Allah's Prophet*, USA (place not mentioned): Felibri. Com, 2008; and M.A. Khan, *Islamic Jihad: A Legacy of Forced Conversion, Imperialism and Slavery*, USA: Felibri.com, 2008. Another recent book is no less authoritative in terms of use of source materials and perceptive analysis than the three above noted books, but cannot be used in detail for lack of space. This book is: Andrew G. Bostom (ed.), The *Legacy of Jihad: Islamic Holy War and the Fate of Non-Muslims*, New York: Prometheus Books, 2008.

Anwar Shaikh contends that Muhammad, the Holy Prophet, had an inestimable urge for dominance. In order to fulfil this urge, Muhammad preached faith in Him as the Saviour, manipulating fear and favour. Ordinary human beings are to look upon Him as the Saviour in order to escape consignment to hell, which is so dreadful, as depicted in the Koran and Hadith, that it may be graceless to describe it in this study. In sharp contrast, the paradise is a place of boundless enjoyment, a few glimpses of which can be presented here. The paradise is a Garden of Bliss reserved for Muslims. A man who secures entry into the paradise will have for himself seventy two young, ageless, extraordinarily pretty women called houris.

Even an old man having entry into paradise will become thirty years old, and gain virility equivalent to that of one hundred men. He will have access to wonderful wine sealed in musk. He will own eighty thousand servants. Muhammad manipulated fear of hell and favour of paradise to attract converts to Islam. According to Anwar Shaikh, Muhammad tarnished his Holy status by recruiting devotees in such a fashion. Anwar Shaikh further observes that faithful Muslims suffer from blissful ignorance so as to believe that they can gain salvation by committing acts of piety to please Allah, when they kill infidels, plunder their wealth, and molest their women. No wonder that William E. Gladstone, Prime Minister of Great Britain, made a highly critical observation about the Koran as he held the book 'in his hand and declared in the House of Commons: "so long as there is this book, there will be no peace in the world".'[1]

Muhammad, as Anwar Shaikh writes, desires to be obeyed, loved and worshipped by human beings. Therefore, he uses revelation as the spiritual instrument to become Godhead, to be at once the servant and viceroy of God, mediating between human beings and God. Mohammad's urge for dominance is so overwhelming that He wants to be permanently adored after death, and He declares that there will be no other Prophet to succeed Him. God has so revealed Himself to the Prophet that he has no option but to obey God, and human beings too should have no other choice but to pay obeisance to the Prophet.[2]

Anwar Shaikh critically examines the contention of the Koran that God creates human beings, because He desires to be worshipped. This desire is so powerful that God does not hesitate to threaten non-believers with banishment to hell, and almost bribes believers with the promise of astonishing rewards in paradise. Anwar Shaikh thus raises the question whether God can undermine his own dignity in this manner. He also raises another crucial question about who really benefits from the phenomenon of revelation: humans or God. For, revelation dictates man to surrender so unreservedly to God that there is no question of man receiving guidance from God. Therefore, revelation indirectly becomes the instrument by which God compels humans to succumb totally to the will of the Prophet, who may be treated as God in disguise.[3] Revelation transforms the word of the Prophet into God's Word. Thus the Prophet's word becomes the Eternal Law, and the believers are bound to abide by it even after

Muhammad leaves this world. The lapse of many centuries has rendered this Law obsolete. Yet the believers even today have to carry out this Law.[4] As Anwar Shaikh puts it, 'This is what is happening in the world of Islam today, and acting as the fountain of regression.'[5] Whatever the faithful Muslim does, must conform to the Koran, and, consequently, he has to emulate Muhammad in everything: eating, drinking, talking, dressing or walking. Anwar Shaikh then scrutinises various provisions of the Koran to find out whether they merely capitalise the basic human propensities to respond to fear or favour. For these provisions are not an objective portrayal of realities, they reduce themselves to myths.[6]

Anwar Shaikh's fundamental criticism against the approach of the Koran is that the Koran pits faith against reason, resorts to a sort of brainwashing, which works magically on especially those people who suffer from apparently incurable deprivation, and dream of justice and delight in the post-death world about which, as already noted, the Koran can bring into play fear or favour, i.e. the fear of hell versus marvellous attractions of heaven. A man who cannot satisfy his desires begins to pray to a supernatural force, i.e. Almighty or God, and his prayer may be successful only when this man knows the proper way to pray to God. Prophethood fills up the gap in this knowledge of an ordinary mortal. The Prophet appears as the Agent/Intercessor/Medium/Viceroy of the Almighty. The Almighty will reward the followers of the Prophet, and amply compensate for their sufferings by assuring them a place in heaven, whereas opponents of the Prophet may find themselves thrown into the hell-fire. After all, the supplicant cannot have any direct access to God. He has to depend on the Prophet, who tends to be treated as the Almighy, even though His words do not produce any concrete evidence of actual action. In this way, faith supplants reason.[7] 'People must believe in the Koran as a command of Allah,' writes Anwar Shaikh, 'otherwise they are Kafirs (infidels), whose life and property are at the mercy of followers of Muhammad.'[8]

Human beings, who are votaries of reason, are not ready to have faith in the supernatural without any acceptable proof. The Koran, however, seeks to regulate man's behaviour by indoctrination. 'It achieves this purpose by demanding complete faith and creating perpetual war between the Muslim and non-Muslim so that nobody should have the chance to think rationally or act as cultured humans', says Anwar Shaikh.[9] Moreover, Anwar Shaikh poses an important question on the character of the Almighty who obviously dominates human beings (though created by Himself) by means of disunity, slaugther, loot and molestation. He can accomplish this only by the substitution of faith for reason.[10]

Anwar Shaikh provides an authentic analysis of the composition of the Koran in order to support his contention that Muhammad, and not Allah, is the author of the Koran (being the receiver of revelations), and that Muhammad is the string puller behind Allah. There is a grave doubt about whether the entire text of the Koran was put to writing in course of Muhammad's life. For, Muhammad affirmed that he was illiterate. As to the period of revelations, 610 AD was the date of the first revelation, and 632 AD was the approximate date of the last, because the Prophet died on 8 June 632. Since the number of revelations rose over a period of 22 years, all sorts of substance were used to record revelations, e.g. ribs and shoulder of camels, palm leaves, leather, parchment or stones, without any chronology, pattern or system. Compilers were many, including the close companions of Muhammad, who were normally around him, and who memorised revelations. But some of these companions died in battles, and their memories of revelations vanished. Around 660 AD, Caliph Uthman, a son-in-law of the Prophet, got scraps of revelations compiled, thereby providing the first authoritative text of the Koran, i.e. revelations. Uthman did what was actually Muhammad's job.[11]

Anwar Shaikh argues that the Koran is full of inconsistencies many of which arise out of the Prophet's illiteracy. The Koran has attested to the loss of some revelations because of Muhammad's forgetfulness. This contradicts a basic Koranic contention that every word of the Koran is permanent. Muhammad, however, affirms that Allah Himself resolves to make Muhammad forget some revelations, which is again a challenge to the doctrine of Koran's permanence. Moreover, this cannot but pour indignity on Allah, who is Perfect and Omniscient.[12] Anwar Shaikh comments:[13] 'A true God cannot do this. Therefore, the Koran is not God's Word but the composition of Muhammad, which he has ascribed to Allah to sustain his prophethood.' If Koran is Allah's work, and exclusively so, no idea or world of a human being should form any part of the Koran. But Anwar Shaikh quotes a Hadith to prove that the Second Caliph, Umar, was the author of about fifty thoughts included in the Koran.[14] Anwar Shaikh also uses the Hadith to demonstrate an amazing point: Muhammad and Allah decide certain matters jointly.[15] With his painstaking research, Anwar Shaikh has discovered a disturbing deficiency in the Koran, which detracts from its status as a Divine Scripture. Due to lack of awareness of the importance of chronology, revelations in Mecca get mixed up with revelations in Medina.[16]

Another disorder of the Koran arises out of the belief of Muslims as clearly expounded by Anwar Shaikh, that the Lord cared so much for providing perennial guidance to the human progeny that he sent 124,000 prophets to the earth. This implies something which may be deemed to be lethal to the Koran's permanance. Many, if not all, of these thousands of prophets probably carried new Holy Books to adapt human needs to evidently changing times. In this context, what one Hadith observes, as noted by Anwar Shaikh, may undermine the sanctity of the Koran and perturb Muslims. The observation is: 'Time will come when Islam will exist in name only and the Koran will be just a collection of words. The mosques will be full but completely unguided. During that period the mullahs shall be the worst of creatures under the sky: they will be the source of mischief.'[17] As of 20156, the relevance of this Hadith to the situations in Pakistan, Afghanistan, Iraq, Nigeria, Somalia or Syria, is unquestionable. It is worth quoting Anwar Shaikh to reinforce this Hadith, especially with reference to the situation in 2016 in the above noted Muslim countries. 'The truth is that Islam has become the biggest business on earth today. It is the source of livelihood and prestige for the mullah and the effective fountain of power for the Muslim politicians. Though contemptuous of each other, they are mutual collaborators for the obvious reasons, and shall go to any length to praise the Koran for exploiting the faithful. The book that was composed 1400 years ago by a person who claimed to be illiterate, cannot stand the test of time without the followers' perjury, pretence and prevarication', writes Anwar Shaikh.[18]

The primary task of any religion or a respectable school of thought is to draw a line between virtuous and vicious deeds. For instance, they consider molestation of women, murder, loot or a detructive use of force as bad. But, quoting copiously from various tenets of the Koran, Anwar Shaikh contends that Islam is a unique religion which depicts these evil acts as aspects of a Holy War or jihad. For, jihad does not target any tyrannical or unjust ruler or institution or individual. It is directed specifically against persons who have no faith in Allah and Muhammad, and are, therefore, judged as infidels. Thus, Islam fails to observe any distinction between virtue and vice.[19]

Muhammad and the Koran adopt a completely determinist view of human actions and destiny. Various provisions of the Koran testify that all actions of human beings have been chalked out by Allah. This leads an avid reader of the Koran to a labyrinth of contradictions. For instance, if everything is predetermined by Allah, why should there be a Day of Judgement on which Allah will assess the virtues and sins of human beings and dispatch them to heaven or hell. None can intercede on this Day. Allah alone will decide, for, He is the most competent judge. But, gradually, there emerges a profound contradiction. There are Koranic tenets which prescribe that, on the Day of Judgement, there can be an intercession with the consent of the Allah. Next, there comes another tenet according to which Allah can permit Muhammad to recommend for even the worst sinner a coveted place in the Next World, where he can amply receive compensation for all his failures and sufferings on this earth. There is one condition: this man has to be a Muslim. The Throne of Justice on the Day of Judgement witnesses Muhammad sitting alongside Allah. The contradiction in the matter of intercession on the Day of Judgement is coupled with another. Muhammad, according to the provisions of the Koran, has to be merciful to all human beings. But the Koranic text makes it abundantly clear that the Prophet can exercise mercy and bestow favours only on Muslims.[20] Taking all these into account, Anwar Shaikh concludes: 'It is a serious misconception that Islam seeks to declare prophethood of Muhammad because, in reality, it allots the highest position to Muhammad in a scheme of divinity where Allah becomes a mere decorative figure to serve the purpose of Muhammad.'[21]

Tenets of the Koran clearly underline that Allah sent the Prophet to this world for the perpetuation of violence and conflict by inculcating in Muslims a perennial hatred towards non-Muslims. The Prophet was to ensure that Muslims would pay homage to Allah by the ceaseless practice of jihad, and kill, loot and subjugate non-Muslims. The supreme divinely ordained goal of the Prophet was to rob non-Muslims of their natural rights to life, liberty and property, as also the dignity of their women.[22]

Ali Sina contends that one can comprehend the behaviour of Muslims in the contemporary world only by comprehending the character of Muhammad. Muslims compose one-fifth of humanity, and they worship Muhammad, who was a 'psychopath'. Contemporary Islamist terrorism is an ancient phenomenon, having its roots in the terrorist practices of Muhammad soon after his arrival in Medina. Since that period, Muslims have been doing exactly what Muhammad was doing when he was alive. Many Muslims today, especially practising terrorists, support suicide bombing, and look upon martyrdom via murder as a supreme act of piety. Muhammad imposed slavery on thousands, himself raped lady prisoners, and allowed his men to do so. He thought he was entitled to do all this. His conscience did not exhibit any sense of guilt.[23]

Ali Sina raises the query of why Muslims are responsible for about ninety per cent of conflicts all over the world, even as they constitute about twenty per cent of world population. The statistical significance is startling: Muslims as a collectivity are thirty six times more violence-prone for conflict settlement than any other group on the earth. Actually, Muslims of the world are fully aware that Muhammad was a mass killer, an assassin, a ruthless gangster, a looter, a paedophile, and a shameless womaniser. Muslims still adore Muhammad without any reservation. According to them, Muhammad cannot be assessed by normal standards of morality. For, Muhammad himself had to set the standards. Muslims suffer from an astounding lack of capacity to question Muhammad or Islam, observes Ali Sina. Muslims think that to raise any question is to fail a test of eligibility for true Muslims.[24] Ali Sina adds: 'to pass this test and to prove their faith, all they have to do is believe in every nonsense and absurdity unquestioningly.'[25]

In Islam, a religion is reduced to a personality cult—that of Muhamad. The Prophet says that the Koran represents the words of God. But (like Anwar Shaikh as noted above) Ali Sina stresses that these words are Muhammad's dictates. Ali Sina advises impartial observers to view Muhammad through the firsthand accounts of his trusted companions and wives. When Muhammad began his career as a preacher, he was little more than a pariah. In a short period he became the virtual sovereign of the vast tract of Arabia. Muhammad achieved this, emphasises Ali Sina, by the adoption of all questionable means one can conceive of, i.e. divide and rule, incitement to seditious activities, fomenting hatred among groups for instigation of violent conflicts, etc. Moreover, Muhammad was known to terrorise his potential victims and subjugate them by assassinations, raids, torture, and rape.[26] Ali Sina writes: 'We will learn about his genocides and his penchant for deception as a strategy, the very strategy used by Muslim terrorists today. After understanding Muhammad you will come to see that the terrorists are doing exactly what their prophet did.'[27]

When in his book Ali Sina develops the points noted above summarily, he reveals a mine of information and insights. Muhammad commenced his career as the preacher of a new religion in Mecca, where the people were apathetic to him. Consequently, even after the passage of thirteen years, he had a few followers of reasonable calibre like Abu Bakr, Uthman, and Omar, as also around seventy persons who were either discontented young men or slaves. Like the majority of non-Muslims in the contemporary world, the inhabitants of Mecca practised religious toleration. They worshipped pagan deities. Persecution on religious grounds was unprecedented. Meccans, therefore, felt annoyed when Muhammad deliberately disparaged their deities. As Muhammad's insults became intolerable, Meccans began to boycott Muhammad and his followers, although they did not persecute Muslims in any manner. Inhabitants of Mecca refused to buy anything from, or sell anything to, Muslims. Meccans were pluralists and polytheists. There were 360 idols in Kaaba, each presiding over a tribe. Christians, Jews, Saleeans, Zoroastrians, and many other religious groups coexisted peacefully for a very long time in Arabia. It was Islam which introduced religious bigotry in Arabia.[28]

Muslims claimed that Meccans oppressed them, simply because Muhammad made this claim, even though this was remote from reality. Muhammad thus sanctified victimhood for himself, even though actually he was victimising others.[29] Today 'Muslims do the same. Everywhere it is Muslims who are killing, oppressing and persecuting, and yet they are the ones who cry loudest claiming to be victims and oppressed. To understand this phenomenon we must understand the psychology of Muhammad and his followers,' writes Ali Sina.[30]

Muhammad began to spread religious bigotry during his days in Mecca. Some liberal Muslims and non-Muslims, however, refer to one Mecca revelation—Sura 109—as signifying religious broad-mindedness. But when one studies the Sura as a whole—and not simply or exclusively the sixth point—the impression is absolutely different, as attested by influential Muslim scholars like Qutb or Maududi. The whole text of the Meccan Sura is as follows

> '1. Say: O ye that reject Faith!
> '2. I worship not that which ye worship,'
> '3. Nor will ye worship that which I worship.
> '4. And I will not worship that which ye have been wont to worship,
> '5. Nor will ye worship that which I worship.
> '6. To you be your Way, and to me mine.

The meaning is clear—despite the apparent distraction caused by the sixth component of Sura 109—Allah directs Muslims to dissociate themselves completely—in all possible ways—from the non-believers, and to remain totally rigid in abstention from compromise with the Faith of non-believers.[31]

There were several contemporaneous prophets in Arabia—including a lady—in addition to Muhammad. Unlike Muhammad, they never preached or practised violence. They were satisfied with wielding authority in their small domains. They were not hegemonists. Women in Arabia commanded abundant respect from the people before the advent of Islam. Muhammad proved himself to be the only Arab prophet who believed in warfare to accomplish domination (and denigrate women). He did not mind using coercion, camouflaged as persuasion, even against his own followers in order to gain supremacy. For instance, when he found the people of Mecca too sophisticated to accept his preaching, he decided to leave Mecca for Medina (formerly called Yathrib). It must be clarified that the people of Mecca did not ask Muslims to leave their town. It was Muhammad who ordered them to proceed to Medina with, as usual, unpractical (if not deceptive) assurances. Although there was no oppression in Mecca, the Koran says that, in order to get rid of oppression, to possess decent homes, and rewards in the Next World, Muhammad asked Muslims to leave Mecca for Medina.[32]

The situation in Medina was full of extraordinary hardships for the believers, who could not repudiate Muhammad's command to depart from Mecca. As hapless immigrants, they had no home or income in Medina (in contrast to Mecca). They had to depend on charitable activities by the people of Medina. Some of them expressed their disaffection privately. Muhammad began to feel that his trustworthiness was being tarnished. Therefore, as before the journey from Mecca, Muhammad used the Koran to bolster himself. The Koran warning was: Muslims must not reduce themselves to the status of non-believers. They should not choose any non-believer as a friend. They should kill those co-religonists, who wanted to leave Medina and return to Mecca, thereby turning against Allah.[33] But Muhammad had to create some means of livelihood for his penury-stricken followers in Medina. He had to rescue himself again by Koranic verses by which he publicised the false claim that Muslims had to leave Mecca because of persecution, and therefore, they were entitled to retaliate against Meccans. Muhammad's specific advice was that his followers should resort to robbery, targeting Meccan caravans. So, Muslims became marauders, while their conscience remained clean. Muhammad's followers themselves commenced hostilities against Meccans, and yet unjustly claimed victimhood. Meccans were not only looted but also killed by Muhammad's followers, whenever they acquired sufficient strength.[34]

Ali Sina's comment is thought provoking 'This is what Muslims do today. They are the ones oppressing non-Muslims, terrorising them and they are the perpetrators of systematic persecution of minorities among them, and yet, they cry victim and portray themselves as the wronged ones. It is through these claims of victimhood that they justify their atrocities on their victims.'[35]

There is an Arabic proverb which talks about a man who himself beat another, began weeping, and then even accused his victim of striking him. According to some scholars, this and its sophisticated versions were the mode of operation of Muhammad himself. Muhammad accomplished stupendous success by this strategy. He set one tribe against another, sons against fathers, brothers against brothers. He disrupted the social bonds. Resorting to such unfair means, Muhammad succeeded in course of time in establishing his hegemony in the whole of Arabia. Strikingly, as Ali Sina underlines, what the Arabs did under Muhammad's directions 1400 years back, by practising hostility against their own people, has been repeated by Western converts to Islam in the late twentieth or early twenty-first century.[36] Ali Sina cites the case of one John Walker Lindh, an American, who became a Muslim, and went to Afghanistan to join the Al Qaeda's war against America. In another case, a British journalist, Yvonne Ridley, went to Afghanistan, and the Taliban made her a captive. She embraced Islam after she was set free, and rated Britain as one of the most hated countries of the world ranking a little behind the US and Israel. She became an advocate of suicide operations, regarded them as missions of martyrdom, and looked upon the activities of Musala Al Zarqawi (a mass murderer in Iraq) as heroic. In the words of Ali Sina, 'Islam is a cult. Cults reduced normal people into zombies and sub-humans.'[37]

Koranic verses have been handy for believers in sanctifying murder and plunder, enabling them to earn rewards not only on this earth but also in the Next World. These verses impelled Muhammad's initially small number of followers in Medina to loot Meccan caravans. These also incited believers to launch expeditions against infidels in the coming centuries. For instance, Amir Timur (also known as Tamerlane) has acknowledged in his autobiographical account of campaigns in India that he had the aims to fight Islam's enemies, grab their earthly possessions, and also secure a coveted place in heaven. In one of his letters to the US, again, Osama Bin Laden quoted a Koranic verse in justification of his declaration of war against the US. There is a powerful thread of continuity between what Muhammad did against Meccan caravans, what Tamerlane did against India, and what Osama Bin Laden did against the US.[38] Ali Sina observers: 'Everything Muslims do today that baffles the world is an imitation of what Muhammad did.'[39]

The number of Muhammad's followers in Medina (who were migrants from Mecca) was small. Therefore, he resorted to proselytisation. Medina's inhabitants began to convert to Islam. But they were shy of subjecting non-Muslims, including the members of Meccan caravans, to loot. For, before Muhammad began practising religious bigotry, there was no tradition of religious conflict in Arabia.[40] So, Allah had to come to Muhammad's rescue by a Koranic verse so that Medina's Muslims would embrace militancy, and swell

Muhammad's bandit army. A Koranic verse emerged, arguing that believers may sometimes be inclined to avoid some steps, e.g. combat, which, according to Allah, are good for them. Similarly, believers may accept certain activities as legitimate without knowing these are bad for them. Only Allah can claim the knowledge to decide what is good and what is bad for the faithful. This sort of innovative (though deceitful) indoctrination proved to be productive. Eventually, Muhammad succeeded in infecting Medina's Muslims with greed. They agreed to participate in plunder. Their lust for booty was reinforced by Muhammad's enticement of enjoying an idyllic haven in the Next World because of conformity to Allah's commands on which actions were virtuous or vicious.[41] Ali Sina offers a resplendent rejoinder: 'As Muhammad's army grew and his ambition soared, the bandit decided to graduate to potentate.'[42]

Muhammad demanded that Muslims should finance his military expeditions. He would invoke the Koran to reprimand those who hesitate to spend adequate money on these expeditions. Muhammad goes so far as to claim that funds so spent were in Allah's way, and Allah would treat it as a loan, and repay many times more than the loan amount. While Muhammad assured believers of due recompense for financing his military expeditions, he urged upon them to remain self-effacing, and treat this effort not as a sacrifice but as a privilege. Muslims should appreciate the opportunity to serve Allah in this manner. Koranic verses require believers to kill non-believers in the name of Allah or collect ransom. What is of extraordinary significance is that Allah can slay non-believers even without the support of the faithful, and yet Allah wants Muslims to do so in order to test their faith. If they pass this test, they will be adequately rewarded by Allah. As to those Muslims who are incapable of fighting, they may contribute to charities, which not only build madrasas and mosques, but also train/finance terrorists to wage jihad against non-believers.[43]

Muhammad's followers often boast of Muhammad's capabilities as a warrior. But these capabilities are more imaginary than real. For, Muhammad developed an expertise in evading battles. 'He preferred ambushes and raids, which allowed him to take his victims by surprise and massacre them while they were unprepared and unarmed.'[44] Muhammad organised 74 raids in course of the last decade of his life. Some of them were indistinguishable from assassinations. Others witnessed thousands launching expeditions. Muhammad took part in 27 of them, called ghazwas because of his participation. Others in which Muhammad did not participate were called sariyyahs. Both the variants—ghazwas and sariyyahs—stood for sudden assaults following raid and ambush. In ghazwas, again, Muhammad always remained at the back, guarded by his special forces. There is no authorised biography which attests to Muhammad fighting in person. 'Physical courage, indeed, and martial daring, are virtues which did not distinguish the prophet at any period of his career.'[45]

Muslim terrorists in the late twentieth and early twenty-first centuries have distinguished themselves by slaughtering innocent civilians who do not possess arms, and these murderers do not even exempt children. Many of them kidnap girls and use them as sex slaves. They seem to be strikingly emulating Muhammad and his followers, who launched surprise attacks on villages and towns, killing men unprepared for the attack, capturing women and children, looting camels, goats and other categories of livestock. Non-Muslim Arab tribes wanted to avoid conflicts with persons whom they considered to be robbers led by Muhammad. Therefore, they tried to appease Muhammad by entering into peace treaties. Nevertheless, as Muhammad accquired more and more power, he did not hesitate to attack non-Muslims in a gross and unwarranted violation of such peace treaties. After a surreptitious victorious assault, again, young widowed women were distributed as prizes among Muhammad's men who treated them as enslaved sex workers, whereas an extraordinarily pretty lady would fall into the lot of Muhammad himself. Rape of women, held captive after a war was permitted by the Koran.[46]

The Koran clearly prescribes terrorisation of non-believers. This may be the prelude to the exilement of infidel communities resulting, eventually, in genocide. In this context, Muhammad's behaviour towards Jews was unbelievably scandalous. Jews were the original settlers in Jerusalem as early as the days of Moses. Subsequently, in 587 BC, the King of Babylon, Nebuchadnezzar, pillaged Jerusalem, compelling Jews to move to different parts of the world, including Yathrib (later called Medina). Arab tribes, victims of a natural calamity in Yemen, first arrived in Yathrib around 450-451 BC—i.e. much later than the Jews. In Yathrib, Jews were artisans, blacksmiths, farmers, goldsmiths, and merchants. Arabs, displaced from Yemen, came to different regions of Arabia, including Yathrib. They were economic refugees, doing various jobs under Jewish employers. The Banu Qainuqa, the Banu Nadir and the Banu Quraiza were the three Jewish tribes residing in and around Yathrib. Muhammad initially thought the Jews would embrace Islam, because they shared with Muhammad (1) the respect for prophets mentioned in the Bible and reiterated in the Koran, as also (2) monotheism. Muhammad became revengeful when, in spite of such convergence in ideas, Jews did not pay much attention to him. Muhammad coveted the riches of the Jews, who manufactured a variety of items, including household furniture and weapons. But Jews themselves were not warlike. Muhammad went so far as to express his exasperation with Jews by means of some Koranic verses, which, strangely, accused Jews of breaking their laws, killing their prophets and forsaking gratitude to Allah. Jews made the blunder of employing Arabs in various jobs, including those of soldiers. Muhammad, therefore, could easily threaten Jews with military action, unless they agreed to convert themselves to Islam. Jews ignored this threat, and confined themselves to their own houses. They failed to anticipate the vengefulness of Muhammad, who stopped water supply to Jewish quarters, and declared that he would butcher all members of the Banu Qainuqa. A Koranic verse was available to affirm the threat.[47]

In two weeks, this Jewish tribe virtually surrendered when they proposed negotiations, which prompted Muhammad to promise not to kill these Jews, provided they left the city. Muhammad took away all the possessions of Jews, including weapons (which the Jews maufactured but did not have the expertise to use in military confrontation), and exiled them. This Jewish tribe went to Syria, where it could not live long. So, this was a sort of genocide, Muhammad-style.[48] No wonder that Ali Sina wrote: 'The Islamic world is sick, and it would be shortsighted to deny that the cause of this sickness is Islam. Almost every crime, every act of inhumanity perpetrated by Muslims is inspired and justified through the words and deeds of Muhammad. This is the painful truth that, sadly, so many would rather not see.'[49]

The Banu Nadir was the second Jewish tribe targeted by Muhammad. The Prophet's design was to slaughter the members of this tribe. But with his usual cunning, he first made a totally arbitrary and unwarranted demand for money from this tribe. He pondered that non-compliance with the demand would give him the pretext to launch an invasion. But the Banu Nadir tribe was so fear-struck that it agreed to meet the financial demand. Therefore, Muhammad had to manufacture a pretext to facilitate a sort of genocide. He and his followers were sitting near a wall as members of the Jewish tribe requested them to wait while they got busy arranging the payment. Muhammad was exceptionally gifted. In any situation that he deemed to be uneasy, he could rely on the availability of a Koranic verse or an inspiration to achieve his aims. All on a sudden, he was found to leave his followers waiting near the aforesaid wall, and went to his residence. Subsequently, when his followers contacted him, Muhammad concocted a totally false story about a plot by Jews to kill him by hurling a rock from the top of the abovenoted wall, and told his companions that he learnt about this plot from Angel Gabriel. In defence of such a recourse to falsehood, there was a Koranic verse that portrayed God as endowed with the greatest capability for deception.[50]

Muhammad decided to avenge the alleged conspiracy of the Banu Nadir by forwarding an ultimatum that called upon this tribe to leave Yathrib in ten days, or face a bloody massacre. The tribe played safe, not only by departing from Yathrib within the stipulated time, but also leaving all their possessions intact for Muhammad. There was of course a Koranic verse to ordain deportation for non-believers as an alternative to punishment by sword in this world as also by consignment to hell in the next world. The non-Muslim Arabs, despite their being primitive, shunned such barbaric practices as destroying trees in a desert. But Muhammad had the benefit of a Koranic verse to justify such savage practices against the Banu Nadir tribe before their banishment.[51] Ali Sina makes a trenchant observation: 'Muslims do what their prophet did. They consider burning and looting properties of non-Muslims legitimate acts of war, as they were practiced and sanctioned by him. Based on the actions of Muhammad, it is fair to conclude that Islamic violence is unfortunately not a deviation from true Islam. Murdering, plundering, raping and assassinating are Islamic practices. Nothing is off limits when it comes to promoting the religion of Allah.'[52]

Muhammad next turned to the last surviving Jewish tribe in Yathrib, the Banu Quraiza. Evidently, Muhammad's desire to wipe out this tribe was known to Archangel Gabriel, who for the fulfilment of this desire, visited Muhammad and recommended that he should draw out his sword to punish the Banu Quraiza tribe, because it was guilty of sedition. Gabriel promised to take an assembly of angels to where this tribe lived even before Muhammad would launch his invasion. Gabriel and his angels would instill fear in the minds of members of this tribe, and cause tremors in their citadels. Muhammad, without any delay, directed the muezzin to announce the call for military action against the Banu Quraiza on the occasion of the usual call to faithful for prayer. Remarkably, the Muslims treat the call for prayer as also a call for hostilities. No less a person than Ayatollah Khomeini, in a speech of 1981 in commemoration of Muhammad's Birth, stated unequivocally that a mosque (mehrab) denoted a place of war, and any war, like the early wars of Islam, should commence from mosques, whose Holy Imams were all militant fighters.[53] Ali Sina writes: 'Muslims' riots and hooliganism always initiate from the mosques after they offer their prayers. They are most vicious during the holy month of Ramadan and on Fridays.'[54]

After arranging the call from a mosque for hostilities against the Banu Quraiza, Muhammad and his followers besieged the habitation of this tribe. At the end of a 25-day siege, the tribe was forced to surrender. Muhammad then massacred all the men, imprisoned women and children, and distributed the possessions of the tribe among his soldiers. There was no specific evidence of any alleged crime of sedition committed by the Banu Quraiza tribe. The genocide against them was, thus, unjustified. But, strikingly, there was a Koranic verse to rationalise the slaughter of men of the Banu Quraiza tribe as also the incarceration of their women and children. Moreover, in compliance with Muhammad's wish pronounced on the deathbed, the second Caliph, Omar, committed a genocide on those Jews, Christians and pagans who rejected conversion to Islam or deportation.[55]

All this happening 1400 years ago was only a small, though ominous, beginning. Anwar Shaikh has written a number of books, using numerous Koranic verses and Hadiths, proving thereby that the struggle against non-believers, commencing in the days of

Muhammad, has continued in the twentyfirst century. This struggle, depicted throughout history as a holy war, and christened as jihad, merely supplies a religious garb to the fanatical adventures for domination, which started in Muhammad's Arabia on a small scale, but in the twentyfirst century has assumed global dimensions. The evolution of jihad is extraordinarily interesting, having its roots in the economy of Muhammad's Arabia. Bedwin tribes formed the majority of the people. They moved from place to place to find grazing grounds for their animals. But living conditions were obviously difficult. Bedwins, therefore, had to depend on a subsidiary, though lucrative, occupation. They were looting caravans carrying commercial articles as also the habitations of settled tribes. Such brigandage, called razzia or ghazwa, did not carry any stigma. It developed into an accepted custom long before Muhammad's arrival on the scene. As the verses of Al Qutami, a celebrated Unayyad poet put it: 'Our business is to make raids on the enemy, on our neighbours and on our brother, in case we find none to raid but a brother.'[56]

Robbery/brigandage, an honoured symbol of masculine bravery, became a sort of national characteristic of Arabs. Muhammad recognised its place in Arab history, and had the political skill to comprehend its potentials for his vital design, viz. the establishment of an empire for Arabs. Like any other empire, the Arab empire also implied exploitation of the less powerful by the more powerful. But Muhammad endowed this with a divine appearance as he equated the Arab empire to an empire of Allah, the Most Compassionate. There was an unavoidable criticism and a contradiction in this equation, which might not have bothered Muhammad and his companions. In the name of Allah, the most ungodly acts of slaughter of non-Arabs for the sake of domination by Arabs was sanctified. And yet God, who is omniscient and omnicompetent, seemed to depend on his own creation for the establishment of His empire! In the twenty-first century, however, the jihad of Muslims against non-Muslims has posed a challenge to the spiritual dignity of mankind. For, the practitioners of jihad appear to renounce all moral norms endorsed by civilised people throughout the world. They approve a perpetual hostility between Muslims and non-Muslims, and annihilation of non-Muslims as a virtuous act prescribed by God.[57]

There are some perplexing questions arising out of it. How can a Merciful Allah issue this prescription, and how can a man with the minimum of rationality submit to such a prescription? The answer, derived from a variety of Koranic verses and Hadiths, can only add to perplexity. The non-believers belong to the Satan's party, whereas believers (Muslims) belong to the God's party, and if a believer agrees to practise jihad, i.e. kill a non-believer or gets killed, he will receive a unique reward from God. He will secure entry into the paradise where all good things, including luxuries, are freely enjoyable without any drudgery of labour. Unending sexual orgies with pretty girls (and handsome boys) seem to be the foremost attraction of the paradise. Massacre of non-believers ennobles Allah and Muhammad. The jihadi, however, may have to kill his closest relatives if they refuse to obey Allah and Muhammad, and remain infidels.

In the twenty-first century, one can witness a number of jihadi organisations in different parts of the world, who have accepted the permanent division of humanity between God's party and Satan's party, whereas murdering/torturing or collecting booties from non-believers is accepted as a Godly act and a tribute to Allah. The age-old Arab custom of brigandage thus gets transmuted into international terrorism practised by Muslims against non-Muslims. Moreover, if believers can collect regular and permanent tributes or taxes (jaziyas) from non-believers, brigandage can mature into an approximate imperialist conduct.

A number of Hadiths attest to Muhammad's profound intention to establish an Arab empire. According to him, this was the will of Allah, and Arabs must establish a vast empire to gratify God. Imperialist activities thus acquired a Divine majesty. Hadiths can be interpreted as Muhammad's commands to Muslims. Some Hadiths dictated clearly that Jews, Iranians, Turks and Romans were to be liquidated. Muhammad himself predicted that the Arab empire could come into being only after the Arabs decimated Jews and Turks, and destroyed the Iranian and Roman empires. In the words of Anwar Shaikh, 'This is exactly what happened, enabling the Arabs to set up within twenty years of the Prophet's death an empire, which was larger than the Roman Empire that had required centuries to build.'[58] By 751, to carry further the story of Arab imperialism, Arabs conquered the whole of Central Asia, where the people were

Buddhists, and there were Buddhist monasteries in such places as Bokhara and Samarkhand. Arabs destroyed all these monasteries, because, according to their thinking, Islam was the only true religion, and other religions had no place in Islam's territory.[59]

This chapter—the author of this book must stress—represents the estimates of dissident Muslims about Islam. In order to obtain a more balanced view of Islam, readers of this book are to study the observations of one of the greatest scholars on Islam, Maulana Abul Kalam Azad, narrated in the Preface to this book. Moreover, readers have to note some important comments in Chapter Six.

Endnotes

1. *Faith and Deception*, pp. 21-38. Quoted in Rafiq Zakaria, *Muhammad and the Quran,* New Delhi: Penguin, 1991, p. 59.
2. Shaikh*, Faith and Deception*, pp. 47-48.
3. *Ibid.*, pp. 49-51.
4. *Ibid.*, pp. 58-59.
5. *Ibid.*, p. 59.
6. *Ibid.*
7. *Ibid.*, pp. 60-63.
8. *Ibid.*, p. 63.
9. *Ibid.*, p. 64.
10. *Ibid.*, p. 65.
11. *Ibid.*, pp. 67-69.
12. *Ibid.*, pp. 69-71.
13. *Ibid.*, p. 71.
14. *Ibid.*, p. 73.
15. *Ibid.*, p. 74.
16. *Ibid.*, p. 75.
17. *Ibid.*, p. 77.
18. *Ibid.*, pp. 74-75.
19. *Ibid.*, pp. 85-86.
20. *Ibid.*, pp. 89-93.
21. *Ibid.*, p. 90.
22. *Ibid.*, pp. 94-96; Also see Khan, *Islamic Jihad*, p. 52.
23. Ali Sina, *Understanding Muhammad*, Synopsis, no page number.
24. *Ibid.*, Introduction, No page Number.
25. *Ibid*
26. *Ibid.*, p. 1.
27. *Ibid.*, pp. 1-2.

28. *Ibid.*, pp. 11-13; Also see Khan, *Islamic Jihad*, p. 12.
29. Sina, *Understanding Muhammad*, pp. 13-14.
30. *Ibid.*, p. 14.
31. *Ibid.*
32. *Ibid.*, pp. 16-18.
33. *Ibid.*, p. 18.
34. *Ibid.*, pp. 19-20.
35. *Ibid.*, p. 20.
36. *Ibid.*, pp. 20-21.
37. *Ibid.*, p. 21.
38. *Ibid.*, pp. 21-22.
39. *Ibid.*, p. 22.
40. See, e.g. Ziauddin Sardar, *Mecca: The Sacred City*, New Delhi: Bloomsbury India, 2014, for an elaborate and interesting account of pre-Islamic Mecca.
41. Sina, *Understanding Muhammad*, pp. 22-23.
42. *Ibid.*, p. 23.
43. *Ibid.*, pp. 23-26.
44. *Ibid.*, p. 28.
45. William Muir, *Life of Muhammad*, Vol. II, chapter 2, p. 6.
46. The abduction of two hundred seventy six school girls in Nigeria by Boko Haram prompted the UN Security Council to designate Boko Haram formally as an Al Qaeda-linked terrorist group: see PTI report, *The Indian Express*, 24 May 2014; these girls were aged 12-15, and they were not returned even after a famous Nigerian Singer, aged 23 years, offered her virginity in exchange for the release of these girls: see Jenn Selby, *The Times of India*, 27 June 2014; Ali Sina, *Understanding Muhammad*, pp. 28-35.
47. Ali Sina, *Understanding Muhammad*, pp. 38-41.
48. *Ibid.*, pp. 41-42. Also See M.A. Khan, *Islamic Jihad*, pp. 33-34.
49. Ali Sina, *Understanding Muhammad*, p. 39.
50. Ali Sina, *Ibid.*, pp. 42-44. Also see Khan, *Islamic Jihad*, pp. 34-35.
51. Ali Sina, *Ibid.*, pp. 44-45.
52. *Ibid.*, p. 46.
53. *Ibid.*, pp. 46-47.
54. *Ibid.*, p. 47.
55. *Ibid.*, pp. 47-50. Also see Khan, *Islamic Jihad*, pp. 35-36.
56. Anwar Shaikh, *This is Jehad*! Houston: Publisher Amitava Ghosh, 1999, p. 24.
57. *Ibid.*, pp. 24-25.
58. *Ibid.*, p. 50.
59. *Ibid.*, p. 51. Also see Khan, *Islamic Jihad*, p. 129.

Six

Concluding Observations

The planned departure of US forces and ISAF as a whole from Afghanistan by December 2014 (even if less than total)—as announced by President Barack Obama as early as 22 June 2011—did not signify an accomplishment of declared objectives, not to speak of any triumph. On the contrary, it would mark the climax to an unending and unsuccessful contest with failures. The process of troop drawdown had a symbol of planning: 5000 US soldiers by July 2011; another 5000 by December 2011; 33,000 by September 2012. There should be no US combat troops in Afghanistan by the end of 2014, although for an indefinite period, some soldiers would stay on for offering support in diverse ways, e.g. training. In 2011, when Obama made the aforesaid announcement of troop withdrawal, the ISAF totalled about 132,381 soldiers in Afghanistan, including 90,000 US forces. Other NATO countries, like the US, had their own projections for troop withdrawal. But an uncomfortable question lingered: did the US and NATO ever plan for success or stalemate (if not worse) in their counterterrorism operations in Afghanistan? For, effective—not to speak of successful—counterterrorism operations in Afghanistan required a much larger number of ISAF than were ever present in Afghanistan.[1]

Actually, 2011 was not probably an auspicious year for the announcement of troop drawdown. For, since 2001, when the war on terror commenced in Afghanistan, 2011 happened to be the year of most violent disturbances. Although the strength of ISAF as also the amount of military-civilian aid rose significantly in Afghanistan since 2010, in the first six months of 2011, in contrast to 2009, insurgent attacks increased by 119 per cent, and by 42 per cent in contrast to 2010. Moreover, terrorists began to spread their activities in a number of regions which previously remained immune from such activities. Deaths of civilians (mostly due to IEDs) increased in 2011 by 8 per cent in contrast to 2010—causing internal displacement, movement of people from rural to urban areas, and rise in asylum petitions by Afghans in foreign countries. Quite logically, there was a decline in the number of Afghan refugees returning from abroad to their home country. The speculation was that, in preparation for 2014-end, various insurgent groups were trying to occupy new positions which would add to their strength. Thus, the announcement of troop drawdown could be interpreted as counterproductive, because it created greater insecurity among ordinary Afghans.[2]

Insurgent groups in Afghanistan, broadly known as the Afghan Taliban, comprised a few major groups demonstrating various degrees of cooperation. In 2001, with the US invasion, the Taliban leaders escaped to Pakistan, and formed a council in exile under the name of the Quetta Shura. Jalaluddin Haqqani headed one important network; Gulbuddin Hekmatyar was the chief of Hezab I Islami; there were smaller groups too. The total strength of the Afghan Taliban was estimated to vary from 25,000 to 35,000. Leaders of insurgent groups were not only known to reside in Pakistan, but also to receive patronage from the Pakistan government and intelligence agencies. Moreover, the Pakistan government resolved to remain an opponent of the government of the Islamic Republic of Afghanistan, and therefore built up close connections with the Afghan Taliban. Again, there were other minor groups in Afghanistan, which multiplied insecurity in the country, although they were not in league with the Taliban. Their principal motive was to make money from the narcotics trade, and together with the Taliban, they carried on this trade with an annual turnover of about US$ 150 million.[3]

The relationship of the Afghan Taliban with one Pakistan-based insurgent group, i.e. the TTP, was somewhat complex, whereas the connections between the TTP and the Pakistan government were almost mystifying. The Pakistan government affirmed that about 1500 TTP fighters had bases in Afghanistan, which lay opposite to some districts in Pakistan's KP and FATA. TTP cadres were known to fight foreigners in Afghanistan, whereas the Afghan Taliban was known to have battles with Pakistan's security forces. What was not easily perceptible was to what extent the TTP was ready to fight Pakistan's security agencies. For, sections of the TTP used to enjoy the Pakistan government's patronage. The US drones, however, did not spare the TTP leaders and cadres located in Afghanistan. US air strikes killed a few top ranking TTP leaders in Afghanistan on, for instance, 10 December 2010, and not less than 35 TTP cadres on 23 July 2011. But the Pakistan government complained that the TTP launched attacks from Afghan territory, killing a large number of Pakistan's security forces. Therefore, Pakistan launched artillery and missile attacks in Afghanistan in pursuit of TTP militants escaping to Afghanistan. But the Afghan government contested this Pakistani claim, and deplored that Pakistani attacks killed a large number of Afghan civilians in different parts of Afghanistan. The relative truth/ falsity of Afghan and Pakistani contentions on this issue had one valuable test: Pakistani attacks on Afghan territory failed to target even one TTP cadre.[4]

It was a surprise, because, in 2011 for instance, one TTP militant detained by the police confessed to the killing of Shahbaz Bhatti, the minister for minority affairs of the central government of Pakistan.[5] In fact, throughout 2013, the TTP engaged in bomb attacks, including suicide missions, and killed hundreds (injuring thousands) of civilians (including community workers), journalists, law enforcement personnel, security officials. It also targeted schools. The TTP (and other militant groups) frequently assaulted religious minorities, e.g. Christians and Shia Muslims. Schools for girls were the special targets of the TTP, and, in 2012, Maulvi Fazlullah, the leader of Tehrek E Nafaz E Sharia Mohammadi, allegedly shot Malala Yousafzai, a 14-year-old girl, in her head, but due to national and international support, she escaped death, and attracted worldwide attention as a human rights campaigner. The TTP became so bold and adventurous that it occasionally abducted and beheaded the government's security agents, and even publicised the video footage of the gruesome incident. The TTP sometimes abducted government employees, and released them after the collection of huge sums as ransom. It hurt Pakistan's tourism industry by killing as many as nine mountaineers.[6]

Perhaps the most atrocious component of terrorism-related human rights situation in Pakistan was the recruitment of child soldiers.

Militant groups made deceptive promises to parents, and compelled them to part with boys and girls (aged 11 to 18). Or, they could be abducted, and then indoctrinated to act as spies, throwers of bombs/ explosives, and even suicide bombers. For one simple act of bombing, a teenager could receive a payment of 2000-5000 rupees. Moreover, they would be subjected to physical abuses, including sexual abuse. Occasionally, terrorist groups made payments to the parents of child soldiers, who happened to be mostly poor.[7]

Another important aspect of terrorism-related violence concerned Pakistani media persons. Journalists, their family members, as also their organisations, became targets of harassment, retribution, abduction and violence. In course of 2013, seven journalists were killed, and one imprisoned. Moreover, the Pakistan government did not bother much to try to punish persons committing fatal attacks against media persons. Therefore, the Committee to Protect Journalists incorporated Pakistan in its annual 'impunity index'. The government, again, employed the multipurpose security argument to curb internet freedom. It put in place a mechanism to erase objectionable matters from internet sites, and even banned some of them, e.g. You Tube. Subsequently, Pakistanis found it inaccessible even after the government claimed it removed the ban on You Tube.[8]

We may keep in mind the situations in Afghanistan and Pakistan, as depicted summarily in the few preceding paragraphs, and then turn to consider how NATO interprets its role in the war on terror, the outcome of its efforts on the eve of its departure in 2014, and afterwards. Afghan national security forces, according to NATO, demonstrated a growing capability in 2013. With a strength of 352,000 troops and policemen, the Afghan forces would take over responsibility gradually for the security of their country. Therefore, ISAF could have the confidence that, by 2014-end, they would successfully complete their combat mission, and then assume various functions of support. This would be an extremely important role, and include advice, aid and training for the Afghan security forces. A proper performance of this role would attest to the positive transformation of capabilities of ISAF comprising personnel from 28 NATO allies and 22 partner countries. This grand coalition had to continue to ensure that Afghanistan would never again become a sanctuary for terrorists working on a global scale.[9]

ISAF began to reduce its presence in Afghanistan in 2013, while Afghan forces began to occupy leadership roles in security operations. In 2001, when ISAF commenced its activities, there was no integrated Afghan National Security Forces (ANSF). In the year of ISAF's departure, the ANSF could have a strength of about 352,000. During 2013, ISAF concentrated on capacity-building in the ANSF by the establishment of 375 Security Assistance Teams. They purveyed advice and training to Afghan policemen and soldiers. At the commencement of 2013, ISAF had 184 bases in Afghanistan with 185,000 soldiers. At the end of 2013, ISAF maintained 88 bases, and the number of personnel correspondingly went down to 75,000. NATO had earlier set up Provincial Reconstruction Teams (PRTs) for the supply of development assistance to various provinces of Afghanistan. As local authorities began to assume responsibilities for the tasks assigned to PRTs, their number came down from twenty two to four in course of 2013. These four PRTs would be wound up in 2014.[10]

Possibly, the most important query staring at researchers in 2014 on the matter of cross border terrorism, emanating from Pakistan and victimising India, is whether one can envisage any permanent solution to this acute problem. Such a solution postulates a peaceful coexistence between Islam and other religions, notably Hinduism, which happens to be the religion of a majority of Indians. There is plenty of literature on how Hinduism can not only coexist with, but gradually accommodate, other religions, including Islam. It is not necessary here to refer to this literature. But one specific instance may be deemed to be remarkably relevant for this study. This instance relates to seventeenth century India, and its relevance stems from the striking fact of collaboration between a Muslim prince and Hindu scholars towards accomplishing a philosophical dialogue between the two religions, and use knowledge to transcend sectarian religious identities. The prince was no less a person than Dara Shikoh (a pious brother whom emperor Aurangzeb got assassinated). He worked with Hindu scholars in Varanasi in order not only to translate the Upanishads into Persian but also use the knowledge of Upanishads to analyse the truth of the Koran.[11]

The optimistic perspective on Islam, indicated above, is seldom shared by others. Take, for instance, the assessment by one who is regarded as one of the greatest scholars of the twentieth century:

Bertrand Russell. Russell wrote:' Among religions, Bolshevism [Communism] is to be reckoned with Mohammedanism rather than with Christianity, Buddhism and Hinduism. Christianity, Buddhism and Hinduism are primarily personal religions, with mystical doctrines and a love of contemplation. Mohammedanism and Bolshevism are practical, social, unspiritual, concerned to win the empire of the world.'[12] Take, again, the comment by Ibn Warraq that 'very useful analogies' could be drawn between Communism and Islam,' between the mindset of communists of the 1930s and the Islamists of the 1990s and 21st century.'[13]

In the twentyfirst century, jihadists in different parts of the world are determined to prove that they cannot permit any religion to exist—except Islam. But, they cannot match the power of Arab empire builders of the seventh and eighth centuries. Yet, what they are doing is menacing enough.

Take, for instance, the Boko Haram with headquarters in Nigeria. Just a few kilometers from Chibok, a place from where more than 200 school girls were kidnapped by Boko Haram terrorists, as already noted, as many as four churches were set on fire by Boko Haram on 29 June 2014. After attacking worshippers, the terrorists torched houses and killed dozens of people. One of the church buildings decimated was established as early as the 1920s. Remarkably, security personnel were not only slow to respond to the terrorist assault, but did not have the guts to take on terrorists in a frontal assault, and fired at them from a convenient distance.[14] To carry forward the Boko Haram story, on 23 July 2014, at a city in northern Nigeria, a suicide bomber tried, but failed to murder a moderate religious leader in a crowded business district. But he could kill 32 of the people attending prayers led by this cleric. On the same day, in a market place, the extremists murdered at least 50 persons.[15] On 27 July 2014, again, Boko Haram terrorists kidnapped the wife of the Vice Prime Minister of Cameroon, and, in doing that they murdered an unknown number of persons.[16] Boko Haram is trying to establish an Islamist state in Nigeria, and, for this purpose, does not hesitate to employ female suicide bombers. On 27 July 2014, one female suicide bomber tried unsuccessfully to murder police officers, but succeeded only in killing herself. Next day, two female suicide bombers killed themselves at a petrol station and a trade show in Kano, the biggest town in northern

Nigeria. On 29 July 2014, in a northeastern town of Nigeria, again, two female suicide bombers attacked two mosques and killed 13 persons. Next day, one female suicide bomber killed 6 persons and wounded 6 others, at a college in Kano.[17]

Boko Haram, like a number of other Islamist extremist groups, can flourish mainly because of acute problems of governance in the countries of Central Africa, e.g. those around Lake Chad—Cameroon, Chad, Niger and Nigeria. Poverty and unemployment create opportunities for organisations like Boko Haram. Youths without jobs are not always oriented towards religious extremism, but they may join a terrorist group, especially one that is visibly becoming more and more powerful, when they are left without any worthwhile option. Malgovernance impedes resistance to terrorist agencies, especially in a very poor country like Niger. But, like Chad, Niger at any rate permits troops from neighbouring countries to exercise the right of hot pursuit against extremists. But Cameroon does not, and it also remains guilty of negligence in dealing with religious terrorism. One reason behind Cameroon's non-cooperation with Nigeria in coping with religious extremists may be the long-standing dispute over the 2100 km border with Nigeria defying for years the UN attempts to resolve it. Chad, however, has a powerful army. It is also rich in oil. By regional standards, Chad possesses sophisticated weapons, procured from Russia and Ukraine, e.g. combat helicopters and Mig-29 Jets.[18]

Nevertheless, in May 2014, Cameroon revised its earlier policy and mobilised troops in the border, killing 40 terrorists working with Boko Haram. Heads of states of the Central African region had a meeting in the same month in France. They discussed how to enhance, with the support of Western powers, cooperation in counterterrorist military and intelligence activities. Such cooperation, as also its impact on terrorism, were hindered by such factors as language barriers between soldiers with British and French connections, historic hostilities and hatreds, as also by inefficiency laced with corruption. One was reminded of the situation in Iraq, where, despite assistance from the US and Iran, the army could not properly cope with the jihadis. In the month of May 2014, again, in Cameroon's northern region, Boko Haram became bold enough to hold ten Chinese workers as captives. Instability in the Central African Republic (CAR) rose because, for quite some time, Islamist extremists looted weapons from state military depots, and magnified the strength of Boko Haram. Cameroon and Chad had to accommodate more than 100,000 refugees from the CAR. Living in filthy camps, they were potential targets of Boko Haram for the recruitment of new cadres. On 17 September 2014, Boko Haram gave anew a vivid demonstration of its growing strength when two suicide bombers raided a college in northern Nigeria's Kano, massacring at least 15 students. Western countries have been naturally worried that Al Qaeda affiliates in Libya and Somalia can join Boko Haram to form a formidable network.[19] The most disturbing matter for Nigerian authorities is Boko Haram's occasional change-over from guerrilla tactics to territorial possessions in the manner of ISIS (Islamic State of Iraq and Syria). The Nigerian army prefers a retreat to a fight with Boko Haram when the latter overruns a town. Boko Haram kills the residents of a town under its control if they do not obey Sharia in the most orthodox fashion.[20]

Islamist networks are spreading their activities in a large number of countries as also several continents. There is no dearth of new names for terrorist groups even when they are allied with such well-known agencies as Al Qaeda. Thus, in Somalia, Al Shabab (tied to Al Qaeda) posed such a challenge to authorities that African Union soldiers expelled Al Shabab from Mogadishu, Somalia's capital, forcing Al Shabab to confine itself to rural areas. The US has been carrying out lethal air strikes, killing, for instance, the Al Shabab's explosives specialist in October 2013, and a topranking intelligence official in January 2014. On 1 September 2014, the US launched a number of unmanned as also manned aerial strikes, which succeeded in killing a dozen high ranking commanders of Al Shabab as also its emir, Ahmed Abdi Godane also known as Mukhtar Abu Zubeyr. But under his successor, Ahmad Umar Abu Ubaidah, an adviser and cousin of Godane, Al Shabab (which was responsible in 2013 for killing 67 persons by an attack on the Westgate shopping mall in Nairobi, the capital of Kenya, an ally of Somalia, is determined to continue its ravages.[21]

Take, again, Libya. Islamist radicals here call themselves the Benghazi Revolutionary Shura Council. Clashes between this extremist group and the group led by General Khalifa Hifter are frequent, and the number of casualties quite high. These are really climaxing the bouts of violence regularly erupting in Libya since the fall of Muammar Gadhafi in 2011. On 2 September 2014, for instance, fighting between the Benghazi Revolutionary Shura Council and General Hifter's group killed 31 persons, 20 on Hifter's side and 11 on the side of extremists. Moreover, 36 persons were injured.[22] Even Australia, far away from the terrorist storm centres of West Asia and Africa, is not spared by jihadis. Only one instance of a gruesome conspiracy of random public beheadings in Sydney and Brisbane will be noted here to illustrate the zeal of jihadis to coerce Australians by the perpetration of shocks and horror. Mohammad Ali Baryabi, an Australian presently occupying a senior position in the ISIL (Islamic State of Iraq and Levant) which is the same as ISIS, launched the remotely handled conspiracy in Australia. The macabre plan was to kidnap some persons in Sydney and Brisbane, use video cameras while murdering them, and forward the videos to the media branch of ISIL for widespread publicity. Australian authorities got scent of the plot in May 2014. But they waited for compelling evidence of a clear and present danger till 18 September 2014 when they smashed the plot by arresting 15 persons. The degree of fanaticism of these jihadis was to be deeply deplored, because, despite experiencing the Australian standard of living and political culture, they were prepared to cause a terrible blow to innocent Australians. Baryabi's exhortations for random executions to his Australian co-conspirators were crudely straightforward. One was reminded of Lee Rigby, a British soldier, who was murdered in 2013 by two Muslim militants, both converts, in a random assault on an English road.[23] Furthermore, Australian authorities prevented an IS attack on the parliament, which targeted the Prime Minister and top officials.[24]

All the abovenoted jihadi pursuits are in accordance with the original design of bold pioneers in the early days of Islam. What, however, these pioneers pardonably failed to foresee is the emergence of an acute Shia-Sunni conflict as also a sort of fratricidal contest among Arabs in the twentyfirst century. An eminent Muslim scholar, Maulana Salman Husain Nadvi, has advocated the establishment of a caliphate by Saudi Arabia. According to Nadvi, the noble cause of jihad was to be realised by a confederation of jihadi organisations sponsoring a world Islamic army. Nadvi is confident that the Ahle-Sunnah youth of the Indian subcontinent can supply five million soldiers for this army. This prescription of Nadvi, if carried out in practice, can only aggravate Shia-Sunni differences, which have already reached a dangerous point in Iraq and Syria, especially in view of the rising power of ISIS. These differences, if allowed to fester, can only retard the much-needed endeavour to cope with the problems of peace, stability, democratic development, gender justice, etc. not only in India and Pakistan, but in the entire Muslim world. In the words of a Pakistani writer, I.A. Rehman, Pakistan 'is in no position to bear the cost, in lives and material resources, of the intra-religious conflict that is being extracted from the Arab family.'[25]

It is worthwhile distinguishing between Sunni and Shia terror groups. Sunni groups believe in a perpetual war against apostates and infidels. Shia groups concentrate on ensuring the survival of Iran and Hezbollah.[26]

The Shia-Sunni conflict is being exacerbated in alarming ways, IS (i.e. the shorter depiction of ISIL or ISIS), for instance, has declared that it will wipe out all holy places of Shias. This has incited All India Shia Husaini Fund (AISHF) to retaliate by announcing a bounty of one crore of rupees for elimination of the head of each of the principal Sunni extremist organisations, e.g. Al Qaeda, Taliban, Harkat Ul Mujahideen (HUM) and, of course, IS. The secretary general of AISHF, Syed Hasan Mehdi, has issued an explanation for this bellicose announcement. He says his organisation, a charity, has been trying to make people aware of the evils of terrorism for as long as twentyfive years, but this has been fruitless. For, the Sunni extremist outfits have been slaughtering innocent persons for years, treating them as inferior to animals. Cities like Bangalore, Chennai, Delhi, Hyderabad and Lucknow (the headquarters of AISHF) have advertised the abovenoted bounty by means of posters. In reply to a question on how he is going to procure the enormous bounty amount, Mehdi affirms that after one of the Sunni terrorist chiefs is put to death, sixty million Shias in India will be ready to pour the money.[27]

To take again the instance of Yemen, Houthis (Shias based in Yemen's northern part) present an exceedingly complex case of Shia-Sunni tussle baffling the Muslim world. Houthis fought a more or less successful guerrilla war against Ali Abdullah Saleh, Yemen's president for three decades. Saleh had to depart in November 2011. But Al Qaeda in the Arabian Penninsula (AQAP) used the opportunity thrown up by Saleh's discomfiture in the face of mass agitations and street fights for a year, and took possession of some territory in Yemen's southern part. Leading AQAP personnel in Yemen, despite being jailed, are famous for escaping from prisons, as the authorities are notoriously lax.[28] Saleh's successor, Abd Rabbo Mannsour Hadi, confronts the double predicament of fighting AQAP as also Houthis, who virtually laid a siege on Yemen's capital Sanaa by means of huge demonstrations and effective roadblocks since the middle of August 2014. Hadi is not a Sunni extremist, but has natural symapathies for Sunnis of Yemen whose demands he has to weigh against the concessions Houthis plead for. Houthis stepped up their agitation, and assembled on one occasion in front of the prime minister's offices provoking security forces on 9 September 2014, for instance, to shoot and kill not less than seven Houthis. In July 2014, the fund-starved government in Sanaa had to introduce some stern measures like the withdrawal of fuel subsidies offered long by the government. But Houthis demanded a complete restoration of the subsidies, and were not pacified by the concession offered by the government, i.e. a reduction of fuel prices by thirteen percent. Houthis also clamour for a greater share in government, and Hadi's promise to set up a Cabinet with members whom Houthis may like does not satisfy Houthis. So, there seemed to be a repetition of the near-chaotic street battles of 2010-11 in Sanaa. Houthis have become more ambitious and confident since 2011 because of their military success against Islamist and tribal extremists. Instability in Yemen is all too glaring.[29]

A few preceding paragraphs, providing a brief account of world-wide Islamist terrorism, points to a multiplicity of terrorist organisations. A distinction emerges between Shia and Sunni terror groups. Shias (Houthis) in Yemen, for instance, seem to form a unique category, having no apparent connection with Iran or Hezbollah. Houthis, by the fourth week of September 2014, after fighting about seven days in Sanaa (the Yemeni capital), appeared almost to subjugate the military (under Sunni control) as also the allied Islamist tribes. Houthis occupied military bases/offices/houses of Sunnis. A large number of Sunnis were compelled to leave Sanaa.[30] As to Sunni terror groups, there are some operating under the central control of Al Qaeda, even though they may be active in places far away from the Al Qaeda headquarters in Afghanistan. Moreover, there are autonomous groups deriving their moral guidance, but not specific instructions, from Afghanistan-based Al Qaeda. The number of these autonomous terrorist groups may be proliferating in years to come, signalling a sort of decentralisation of the jihadi apparatus. One can speculate whether this may increase the chances of terrorist outrages on the European soil, which may no longer be treated (as in the past) as a place of recuperation (after jihadi actions in, say, remote Afghanistan), but as targets of attack. Germany, for instance, has earned eligibility as a target due to its active role (even if under the NATO auspices) in the war on terror in Afghanistan, as also its programme to train Iraq's military and police officers.[31]

Belgium, a much smaller country than Germany, has emerged as a target of IS, not merely because it is the headquarters of European Comission, but because 400 Belgians have fought in Syria along with jihadis, and 90 of them have returned, with one in nine reportedly intending to carry out terrorist attacks. Belgian police have, according to recent media reports, arrested a number of returnees (including two from the Netherlands), planning to attack the European Commission building in Brussels, although there is no report of any Commissioner being personally targeted. The aim has been to kill as many persons as possible in a building where thousands of officials from 28 European countries work daily. This planned attack (though preempted) can be compared to an assault in May 2014 on the Jewish museum at Brussels (which witnessed the death of four persons). Several European countries, including Belgium, are apprehensive that their nationals, hardened by active participation in jihad in Syria and Iraq, will threaten their security after they return home.[32]

A crucial question that emerges at this stage is: why does Europe produce jihadis? What is the deficiency of the Western/European societies contributing to the emergence of jihadis? After all, Mohammed Atta (of 9/11 notoriety) studied for a Master's degree at a university in a suburb of Hamburg, noted for toleration and liberalism. His Master's thesis on urban planning was a scathing attack on Western architectural forms, e.g. skyscrapers, which tended to supplant traditional Muslim spaces, e.g. maze-like lanes. In fact, Atta's will and testament[33] reveals that he is undefinably yet terribly resentful of everything modern/Western, although he has enjoyed the ease of

Western/European living standards. Atta and other jihadis appear to resemble *The Rebel* of Albert Camus,[34] and reflect a sort of climactic culmination of alienation and skeptisicm characterising a number of Europeans. A jihadi, unlike a liberal democrat, does not accept limits to freedom. He believes in absolute control, whereas a liberal democrat promotes pluralism. Unlike a liberal democrat, again, a jihadi considers cosmopolitanism as impure. To a liberal democrat, reason is a virtue. To a jihadi, it is not; for him a man is virtuous when he is fearless and self-sacrificing, so much so that, in defence of his dogma, he does not hesitate to kill someone who does not subscribe to his dogma.[35] A jihadi reminds one of that pedagogue in Thomas Mann's *The Magic Mountain* who exclaims: 'What our age needs, what it demands, what it will create for itself, is terror.'[36]

The IS, which deserves some attention in the final chapter of this book, is as brutal as it is ambitious. One of its leaders has declared himself as the Caliph. Raqqa is a town in eastern Syria. IS uses it as its headquarters. IS has carried out thousands of death sentences. It has either demolished non-Sunni mosques and churches in areas under its control, or used them for other purposes. IS beheads foreign journalists, and circulates widely the videos of beheadings. All these have prompted a number of Muslim countries to denounce the IS, even though they are not friendly with one another. Boko Haram in Nigeria has also announced the formation of a Caliphate in the territory under its control, but that has not attracted as much of Western attention as the IS-declared Caliphate. IS rules a territory in Iraq and Syria, which is as big as Jordan. By the end of May 2014, it could attract from 81 countries as many as twelve thousand operatives (and the number kept growing), of whom three thousand happened to be from Western countries. Remarkably, Western jiahdis did not hesitate to kill not only Shias but also moderate Sunnis, who were all deemed to be non-believers and infidels. Western fighters acted even as suicide bombers.[37]

On 5 September 2014, defence and diplomatic officials of Australia, Britain, Canada, Denmark, France, Germany, Italy, Poland, Turkey and the US met on the sidelines of a NATO summit, and considered a strategy to destroy—and not merely to contain—the IS. First, they would strengthen allies in Iraq and Syria, who were combating the jihadis on the ground. Secondly, they would strike at

Islamists from the air. The US and its allies would not supply ground combat troops, which were to be deployed by the Iraqi government, the Kurdish Peshmerga and moderate rebel groups in Syria. Moreover, the US expected to receive funds and assistance from Saudi Arabia for moderate Syrian rebels, as also unpublicised intelligence about jihadis from Jordan. In addition, at the NATO summit, Canada affirmed that it would send advisers to Iraq, who would coordinate their work with US advisers.[38]

The US was interested in forming a broad anti-IS coalition. On 15 September 2014, at a ministerial level conference, twentysix countries, including China, Russia and ten Arab countries, agreed to combat IS by all possible measures. They pledged to provide, on request, military aid to Iraq. IS threatened the entire world that the IS would kill whoever refused to join them. Thus, countries attending the aforesaid conference of ministers expressed their determination to fight the IS. In addition, twelve states, who were not represented by their ministers, announced that they would try to stop the flow of new recruits and funds to IS, which seemed to be able to procure enormous amounts of money. A significant feature of the aforesaid conference was the pledge by Qatar and Saudi Arabia to combat the IS, for, these two countries financed Islamist militants in Syria before the IS emerged as a dangerous foe. The fact that Iran did not have the opportunity to participate in this anti-IS coalition-building endeavour due to opposition by Saudi Arabia and the US detracted from the success of this endeavour.[39]

The IS started functioning as a part of Al Qaeda. But, in June 2014, it detached itself from Al Qaeda, while its leader, Abu Bakr Al Baghdadi, declared himself the Caliph. Unlike Al Qaeda, which is often invisible, and does not show any intention to possess and administer territories, IS has declared itself a state in approximately a third of Iraqi-Syrian territory under its control. Within a short period of time, it has been able to establish institutions of government, running banks, courts, mosques, schools, etc. as also distributing electricity and water. Residents in IS territory, including some who do not subscribe to IS ideology, but have to adjust to Islamic laws introduced by IS, admit that IS officials run the administration efficiently. Baghdadi has maintained a distinction between civil and military administration, although military men have manned the police force. He runs a pragmatic system, and, for instance, permits, in his own interest, trading with businessmen paying allegiance to his arch-enemy, i.e. Syria's Assad. IS is known to be history's most well-financed terrorist agency. It has made a lot of money from a variety of sources, e.g. sale of oil from Iraqi and Syrian oil fields (under IS control) to businessmen in Iraq and Turkey, loot of money and gold from the central bank of Mosul (when it was captured by IS), sale of 8000 years old antiquities, and extortion of ransom for hostages. Baghdadi takes good care of his safety, moving between Deir Al Zor, Mosul and Raqqa (depending on the extent of his control over these towns). He, however, does not shy away from providing leadership in actual battles.[40]

IS suffered the first US air raid in Iraq on 8 August 2014, and in ten days, Iraqi security forces and the Kurdish Peshmerga soldiers, thanks to continuing US military support, registered some remarkable successes. For instance, they reestablished control over Iraq's largest dam (ousting the IS), which was near Iraq's second biggest city, viz. Mosul. Four hundred US advisers and repeated US air strikes thus not only strengthened the Kurdish Peshmerga but also significantly enhanced the morale of Iraqi government soldiers, which had simply and strangely vanished immediately after the IS attack. The Kurdish capital, Erbil, became safe. So became tens of thousands of Yazidis fleeing to the hills in August 2014 after the IS offensive against their towns and presently rescued from the hills. Another significant development is the transformation of anti-US Iraqi Shias (led by Muqtada Al Sadr) into enthusiastic advocates of US attacks against IS. But IS is far from being contained, not to speak of being decimated. On the contrary, the number of IS followers rose not only in Iraq/Syria but also in places such as Lebanon and Morocco. Inside Syria, notably, a number of moderate anti-Assad rebels began to join IS or became too weak to remain relevant.[41]

Military measures alone will not suffice to subjugate the IS. In Iraq, for instance, Sunnis have to be won over by the Shia-led government. During 8 years till 14 August 2014, the Iraqi prime minister, Nuri Al Maliki, forfeited the trust of Sunnis by a policy of repression. Actually, chiefs of Sunni tribes affirm that they can easily tackle the IS, but the precondition is that Sunnis must be given an adequate share in decisionmaking on security and other important issues. Kurds, too, have a similar demand. On 14 August 2014, Maliki took a decisive step by yielding place to a new Iraqi prime minister, Haider Al Abadi. This, hopefully, can pave the way to the formation of a more inclusive government in Baghdad, and facilitate a victory in the battle against IS by detaching Iraqi Sunnis from IS influence.[42]

On 15 August 2014, the UN passed a resolution, which authorised sanctions against anyone supporting the IS in matters of recruitment, funds, weapons, or actual participation in jihad. On 17 August 2014, the British prime minister, David Cameron, stressed in a write-up how the streets of Britain were facing a threat from IS. On 19 August 2014, James Foley, a US journalist captured in 2012 in Syria, was beheaded by someone who spoke in British accent, and the video of decapitation was globally circulated.[43] On 24 September 2014, President Barack Obama addressed the UN General Assembly (UNGA), underlining the menace of the cancer of IS-bred terrorism, and assuring that, along with a coalition of 40 countries, the US would decimate the IS. Obama urged upon the Muslim countries, especially the Arab countries, to resolve the sectarian conflicts plaguing the Muslim world, as also to attend to the aspirations of the youth.[44]

On 24 September 2014, moreover, Obama presided over a UN Security Council (UNSC) meeting, which adopted a landmark resolution—Resolution 2178—which deserved as much importance as the earlier Resolution 1267 on the Al Qaeda and the Taliban, and Resolution 1373 passed after 9/11. Resolution 2178 outlined a worldwide counterterrorism strategy directed against IS, advocating regional and global actions against the funding and mobility of foreign terrorist fighters (FTFs) flocking to the IS. Deplorably, IS could boast of a large number of fighters from Arab regimes which were close US allies. These regimes ignored how their policies of repression and apathy to unemployment pushed the youths to the IS brand of extremism. Saudi Arabia, for instance, is known to carry out a substantial number of beheadings even for minor offences, and tries to impress the conservatives in the country that it is truly Islamic. It wrongly believes that in this manner it can throw a religious challenge to the IS.[45]

The UNSC passed on 25 September 2014 a unanimous resolution, which required countries to take measures to stop the migration of their nationals for participation in the IS-sponsored jihad. This resolution obliged countries to adopt laws for prosecution of their nationals and others leaving their countries to prepare, plan, perpetrate or participate in jihadi onslaughts launched by the IS, the ANF (Al Nusrah Front) or any other agency affiliated, presently or in the past, to Al Qaeda. Next day (i.e. 26 September 2014), in pursuit of the UNSC resolution of the previous day, the British parliament gave unequivocal support to British air strikes against IS. On 25 September 2014, for the first time in more than one month of air campaign, the US hit three oil fields and four oil installations under IS possession since the early part of 2014, and located in Deir Al Zour of Syria. This could not but severely hurt the IS, which was earning a lot by smuggling and selling oil in the black market. As air raids targeted Syria's borders with Iraq and Syria along the Euphrates river, around twenty extremists died, and IS vehicles, training grounds, etc. were damaged. The US struck at IS-held oil sites for the second day on 26 September 2014.[46]

Since there are other important matters to be analysed in this chapter on concluding observations of this book, it may be advisable to terminate here the discussion on the US-led coalition campaign against IS, which is likely to last an undefinable number of years. Nevertheless, a few broad comments on the prospects of success or failure of this campaign may be in order.

The anti-IS campaign of the US-led coalition suffers from a multiplicity of handicaps, some of them curiously interlocked. The coalition leader has to decide what is its principal aim, whether it is the degradation and destruction of IS. If so, it has to forget any other aim, e.g. weakening the rule of Bashar Al Assad over Syria. The US cannot win the war against IS without the support of Shias in Iraq and Syria. To try to oppose Assad, because it runs a regime that suppresses Sunnis, is now irrelevant because of the severe threat posed by IS. The IS is the principal enemy not simply because it is brutal, and circulates videos of beheading of US nationals. There may be degrees of difference (not easily or exactly measurable) in the repression practised by IS, Assad, Iran, Iraq or Saudi Arabia. But the IS, or an Al Qaeda associate, Khorashan, has created a mortal danger to the entire region as also to the US homeland. Khorashan, for instance, has reportedly mastered the expertise to develop bombs/ explosives, which may be non-metallic, and evade security checks in airports. US air raids against IS or Khorashan (covering oil sites)—joined by Australia, France, Britain and even some Arab Sunni countries in the latter part of September 2014 (which spoilt the daily earning of US$ 3 million from oil sales)—may impel the IS to depict the US as the monitor of an anti-Sunni coalition. If the US is not in a position to overlook this charge, it has to suspend the anti-IS campaign. Similarly, if it is unable to overcome its reluctance to include Iran (as recommended by Russia) in the anti-IS coalition, it cannot hope to degrade/destroy IS even in the remote future, assuming that Obama's successor in the White House after the next US presidential election will embrace the counter-IS mission. Suspicion and name-calling may persist, and the counter-IS campaigners have to disregard these. After all, there have been differences between Sunni Arab countries on vital matters. For example, their attitude to, or policy towards, the Muslim Brotherhood is not uniform or static. Nor is their support for the IS. Whether for fear of retaliatory strikes by the IS, or executions of hostages, Turkey, a Muslim NATO country, can offer only silent acquiescence in the NATO's fight against the IS. Simultaneously, Turkey grants IS the access to its border, which is substantially helpful. Kurds are playing a leading part in the anti-IS campaign, and receiving ample US support. But Turkey is cautious and suspicious, for, it has a history of war against Kurds. Inside Iraq, again, although they are themselves Sunnis, Kurds (jealous about their autonomy) are not exactly favourites of other Iraqi Sunnis, whereas the anti-IS campaign exhibits cooperation between Kurds and Iraqi Shias. Jordan provides silent support to the counter-IS campaign, although it permits the use of its territory for the dispatch of military supplies to anti-Assad rebel groups. There are, moreover, hundreds of these rebel groups, some of which fought the IS in the past, but presently they are hardly in a position to do so. Above all, these anti-Assad rebel groups, even though they are not as barbarous, powerful or ruthless as the IS, also happen to be Islamists, and not really averse to being jihadis. In an ideal situation, where there are no Shia-Sunni conflicts and no tussles between Iran (the protector of Shias) and Saudi Arabia (the patron of Sunnis), the IS can be subjugated with relative ease. But this inter-country and inter-sect reconciliation cannot be achieved in the foreseeable future.[47]

Significantly, IS is expanding its activities in south Asia. It has circulated flags and pamphlets, including one with the title *Victory* (Fatah) in Pakistan and India. Apparently, militants in the Al Qaeda-Taliban belt have come under the influence of IS. In fact, Jamat Ul Ahrar, a breakaway segment of Pakistani Taliban, has affirmed its solidarity with IS. Young jihadis are naturally impressed by the tough stance of IS, for instance, the declaration of a Caliphate and executions for violation of Sharia, and its ability to govern a territory, whereas they find the aged Al Qaeda leaders (in contrast) vegetating and hiding in the Pakistan-Afghanistan border. IS has reportedly established a local cell in Peshawar known as Islam Khalifat, and has circulated the abovenoted pamphlet, *Victory* in Pashto and Dari languages, taking care to distribute it in the outskirts of Peshawar among Afghan refugees living in camps. In late January 2015, IS signalled its determination to extend its authority to Pakistan (and South Asia) as Hafiz Saeed Khan, a former spokesperson of, and defector from, Pakistan's Tehreek E Taliban, got appointed by IS as the Amir (chief) of Khorashan, a territory sanctified by history as comprising Afghanistan, Pakistan and parts of India. So, the discussion on IS in this chapter, especially the expansion of IS network in Pakistan, sets an appropriate stage for a renewed analysis on developments in Pakistan on the eve of near-exit of ISAF from Afghanistan in the latter part of 2014, an analytically convenient terminal point for this book.[48]

Any discussion on Pakistan (the focus of this book) cannot but emphasise terrorism inside Pakistan, Pakistan's relations with the US, and with Afghanistan. In 2013, the newly elected Sharif regime inherited two valuable anti-terrorism measures from its predecessor (led by the PPP). First, the latter passed an Anti-Terrorism Amendment Bill in 2012, which made it a criminal offence to finance terrorists. Secondly, it passed another Anti-Terrorism Amendment Bill in 2013 (whereas it was lying with the national legislature for more than three years). Consequently, it became permissible to carry out the preventive detention of terror suspects for three months, and a National Counter-Terrorism Authority came into existence to facilitate coordination among several security agencies. Whereas Pakistan's objections to the US deployment of drones against terrorists persisted, relations between the two improved a little, because the US formulated rigid conditions for drone use, and concentrated on important terror targets. Thus, for instance, US drones succeeded in eliminating a TTP leader in North Waziristan, viz. Waliur Rehman, and a Haqqani network leader, viz. Badruddin Haqqani, in addition to some notable leaders of the TTP, the Afghan Taliban and Al Qaeda.[49]

In 2013, Pakistan's relations with Afghanistan registered a little though temporary improvement, when the two governments agreed to install a hotline between their intelligence/military establishments in order to facilitate a systematic interaction. Pakistan, moreover, abandoned its previous opposition to talks between the Afghan government and the Taliban. Yet, Afghanistan and Pakistan soon lapsed into accusations and counter-accusations. President Hamid Karzai denounced Pakistan's ISI for granting sanctuaries to Taliban leaders in Karachi and Quetta, as also for subverting the peace process. Karzai even complained that Pakistan killed those members of the Afghan Taliban who were in favour of peace (although Pakistan denied the charge). Pakistan on its part criticised Karzai for permitting Maulana Fazlullah, a TTP leader, to utilise facilities in Afghanistan's border provinces, Paktika and Nuristan, to launch attacks on Pakistani soldiers. There were clashes on the Pakistan-Afghanistan border. The people and media of Afghanistan exhibited a deep distrust towards Pakistan.[50]

Whereas Pakistan-Afghanistan relations exhibited no sign of improvement in the latter half of 2014 (the terminal point of this book), the threat of the Taliban to Afghanistan's socio-economic-political stability appeared to rise. The Taliban expectedly took advantage of the long-lasting crisis over the result of the presidential election held to replace Hamid Karzai, who served two terms and was constitutionally ineligible for a third term. Abdullah Abdullah, a former foreign minister, secured a larger number of votes than his rival, Ashraf Ghani, a former finance minister. Yet, the percentage of votes won by Abdullah fell short of the constitutional prescription, necessitating a second round of election on 14 June 2014. This was won by Ghani. But Abdullah insisted that the scale of fraud in this run-off election was gigantic. Curiously, in the presidential election of 2009, too, Abdullah thought he had lost on account of such cheating. This political stalemate could not be resolved till a comprehensive vote audit was carried out, and it was found by the election commission that supporters of both the contestants used fraudulent tactics. John Kerry, the US Secretary of State, initiated and worked out a compromise between Ghani and Abdullah, which in a way was an affront to voters who risked Taliban retaliation to cast their votes. The compromise was a sloppy allocation of power and spoils. In late September 2014, Ghani and Abdullah signed the compromise document running into four pages. It stipulated that Ghani would be the President, and Abdullah the chief executive officer (CEO) or Prime Minister, although accountable to the President. This was certainly a messy arrangement which made sense only in the near-chaotic Afghan situation. The US and Western powers were happy because of the end of Karzai's thirteen-year rule. The major characteristic of this period was the emergence of a coterie, loyal to Karzai, and proficient in practising corruption. Division of power between Ghani and Abdullah is likely to generate friction. But that may be preferable to monopolisation of patronage by an all-powerful president, as illustrated by Karzai.[51]

While the presidential election result was in cold storage, the Taliban could probably enhance its usual aggressiveness by gaining a sort of political confidence. So, on 16 September 2014, for instance, the Taliban used a car (loaded with explosives) for a suicide attack upon an ISAF convoy. The Taliban had the audacity to stage the suicide bombing when morning traffic was at its peak in a spot on an important street that led to the US embassy known for ample fortification, and that spot was contiguous to the Supreme Court. Thirteen civilians suffered injuries, three soldiers died, and seventeen civilian vehicles as also one military vehicle sustained damages, whereas nearby buildings were shaken. The Taliban did not hesitate to declare responsibility for the massive blast, attesting to their consciousness of political clout. On 17 September, again, the Taliban trapped a number of Afghan policemen, killing six of them, although losing eight of their own operatives. As the ISAF continued to draw down their contingents, Afghan security forces confronted increasingly severe assaults by the Taliban, which resulted in rising casualties. During a six-month period, April-September 2014, the Taliban killed as many as 1500 Afghan policemen. According to another estimate, on an average, one hundred Afghan soldiers and policemen were losing their lives every week. Civilian casualties too reached the highest level, keeping into consideration the entire period of thirteen years of war on terror in Afghanistan. Ashraf Ghani, immediately after he assumed the country's presidency on 29 September 2014, invited terrorist outfits like the Taliban and Hizb E Islami for political parleys with the government. But the prospects for success of such parleys did not appear to be bright in view of what happened in the midst of such talks during the Karzai regime, which had to stop talks when the Taliban established an office in Qatar, and publicised it as being an embassy of their government-in-exile.[52]

In a farewell address on 23 September 2014, Hamid Karzai, the retiring Afghan president, made some trenchant observations on US policy whose relevance and justification are hard to deny. According to him, the incoming Afghan government should be cautious in dealing with the US and Western powers. For, their policy objectives did not synergise with Afghanistan's requirements. The US on its part could assert that not less than 2350 of its soldiers died in the war in Afghanistan since 2001. But Karzai, who has been refusing to sign the bilateral security agreement (BSA) with the US since December 2013, can claim that his allegation against the US has been proved (at least substantially) by the contents of the BSA signed by the new Afghan President with the US on 30 September 2014. Despite the persistence of instability caused by the terrorist threat to the new Afghan government illustrated by, for instance, a substantial number of Afghan soldiers and policemen leaving their jobs due to frequent Taliban assaults, the US president rejected some valuable recommendations of his military advisers. Thus, he decided upon keeping only 9,800 soldiers after 2014, and not 15,000 as suggested by his military advisers. Moreover, according to these advisers, it was essential to continue to support ANSF by US air power which (let it be stressed) enabled the ANSF to achieve much of the success credited to it for some years. The completion of training and equipping of the Afghan air force would take four additional years after 2014. Meanwhile, as the US president planned, all US troops would return home by the end of 2016. But President Obama refused to carry on the assistance to the ANSF by means of air transport for special forces, air surveillance and close air support after 2014. This merely confirmed that the US president refused to learn from the experiences in Iraq, where the untimely termination of US military support laid the foundation for the emergence of a gigantic terrorist threat from IS against which the US and its allies are compelled to apply airpower in 2014.[53]

One severe limitation of the power sharing arrangement between Ghani and Abdullah is that it does not have any constitutional or legal foundation. This arrangement, moreover, may face several other challenges, e.g. competition between ambitious warlords or power brokers in different regions of the country, pressures from rival coteries eager to occupy official posts meant to be shared by Ghani and Abdullah, etc. The crucial requirement of an authentic and self-sustaining dialogue between the authorities in Kabul and the Taliban—essential for long-term peace in the country—cannot be fulfilled easily or soon because of the Taliban assessment that Kabul's rulers—Ghani and Abdullah—are merely stooges of the US, and because the Taliban fighters have a poor opinion of the probable performance of the ANSF, following the ISAF withdrawal. This withdrawal not only poses a threat to Afghanistan's military security but also to economic development due to an inevitable decrease in Western economic aid. By way of a gesture of compensation, three countries—China, India and Iran—have promised to scale up their development assistance. But they are not likely to match the erstwhile contribution from Western donors. In the field of military security, moreover, in view of divergent policy goals of the three countries vis-à-vis Pakistan and Afghanistan, their contributions can even be much less than in the field of economic development. Nevertheless, the real predicament for Afghanistan arises out of Pakistan's long-standing policy of interference in Afghan affairs. This policy will prevail as long as the Pakistan army plays the dominant part in running the country's foreign policy, in spite of the existence of an elected civilian government, which, as under Nawaz Sharif, for instance, may be oriented towards non-interference in Afghanistan's domestic sphere—but that flatly contradicts the army's desire.[54]

Constitutionally, Prime Minister Nawaz Sharif is the commander-in-chief of the armed forces. But he has very little influence, not to speak of control, over the military. Nor can one forget that in the 1990s, the military manipulated his dismissal from the post of prime minister (not once but twice), because Nawaz Sharif made some feeble efforts to correct the gross imbalance in civil-military relations. In the latter half of 2014, he may have toyed again with attempting this correction, especially for the improvement of relations with India, thereby arresting the Pakistan economy's downward plunge. But his attempt (if any) was nipped in the bud by manoeuvres on the part of the armed forces which saw opposition party leaders like Imran Khan and Tahirul Qadri creating a sort of chaos on the streets of Islamabad for the declared purpose of overthrowing Nawaz Sharif on the specious plea of vote rigging in the 2013 general election. Nawaz Sharif could retain his prime ministerial position, but only at the cost of implicit acknowledgement that the military had to take care of any political paralysis caused by quarrelling politicians. In the 1990s, Nawaz Sharif was palpably guilty of malgovernance. He is so even in 2014, as he persists in nurturing corruption, incompetence and nepotism. He has confirmed even a lack of capability for selecting efficient cabinet ministers. Nawaz Sharif's government, to take another example of the prevalent underperformance, has established a national security division packed with a coterie of intelligence and security officers in service, who have distinguished themselves by their failure to register any achievement. Home-grown terrorism, again, is deemed to be a principal threat to Pakistani state and society. But the National Counter Terrorism Authority (NCTA) wallows in inaction since 2009, partly because of a turf war between the prime minister (who is the legal authority) and the interior minister. In a damning indictment of this Authority, the armed forces have set up their own counterterrorism centre to take on terrorists (who have not hesitated to challenge the military authorities). The civilian government has failed to take proper care of even the equipment needs of policemen, who consequently remain victims of a large number of casualties. The civilian government has been able to do very little to raise its stature by means of good governance.[55]

This does not mean that military leaders, present or past, have much interest in good governance. They are focused on maximising their unwarranted privileges by keeping alive, and occasionally (as in the latter half of 2014) stirring up, anti-Indian and other populist sensitivities. For this purpose, they or their ISI counterparts do not feel shy of floating weird international conspiracy theories, and what is much easier, maligning Pakistan's pitiable civilian government. On 21 September 2014, for example, General Aslam Beg, an ex-army chief, made a television (TV) presentation in which he praised General Raheel Sharif, the present army chief, for his ability to checkmate conspirators in an incredible variety of countries—USA, UK, Canada and Iran—who, according to Aslam Beg, helped Imran Khan and Tahirul Qadri in their endeavour to destabilise Pakistan (in the latter half of 2014). Curiously, one of Imran Khan's party colleagues disclosed that a retired official of the ISI even prepared a scenario for the removal of Nawaz Sharif's government. Remarkably, Aslam Beg revealed in the TV interview (almost throwing the cat out of the bag) that, when he was the army chief, Iran was so close to Pakistan, that Aslam Beg executed a secret transaction whereby Iran received from Pakistan valuable nuclear technology. This confidential deal enabled Iran to gain billions of US dollars. But Iran of 2014, deplored Aslam Beg, was rather different from Iran in Aslam Beg's time. This analysis of Aslam Beg could not evidently stand any test of rationality. But Pakistanis, including Imran Khan, got somewhat addicted to irrationality because of persistent propaganda by the government, especially the military and intelligence agencies. Therefore, in the recent past, some time before he and his party descended upon Islamabad, Imran Khan, with tacit military backing, had prevented the movement of NATO military resources to Afghanistan through the province of KPK, which was under his political control. Imran Khan shared and spread the thoughts of normal Pakistanis when he denounced the US, especially its drone strikes on terrorists inside Pakistan. As to Aslam Beg's TV presentation, whereas a naughty interpretation was, he tried to placate Raheel Sharif for a probable rescue operation in favour of Aslam Beg fighting a corruption case in the Supreme Court, another interpretation could be that such irrational TV presentations were agreeable to the military mindset as also to the Pakistani public's mind.[56]

The irrationality in the Pakistani mind (obvious exceptions notwithstanding) is tragically and collectively revealed in the case of girls fighting for their right to education, freedom and choice. Some of them, e.g. Malala Yousafzai, may gain more of international than domestic attention and publicity in a constellation of circumstances conducive to the award of a Nobel Peace Prize in 2014. But nobody can exactly calculate how much of this achievement is due to Malala's personal talents, and how much to justified decision of some Western countries to extend comprehensive support to her in education and other matters. There are, however, many other cases like that of Mehrin Kauser, who deserve nearly as much attention and patronage as Malala. Mehrin has not received it. Yet, her courageous struggle is a beacon to other unlucky girls whose quest for education and other human rights remains utterly frustrated. In January 2014, Mehrin (a student of zoology at the Women's University in her hometown, Quetta) and her family members were returning by bus from Iran to Quetta. Inside her own province, Balochistan, the Lashkar E Jhangvi (LEJ) launched a vicious bomb attack on Mehrin's bus. Twentynine persons including her mother and sister were killed. Severely wounded, Mehrin, belonging to the Hazara tribe of the Shia community (a special target of LEJ, a Sunni outfit), gradually recovered (with the active assistance of a civil society group), and wanted to resume her studies. But, unlike in the case of Malala, there was no national or international group to support Mehrin's studies, and her university, on the ground of security, stopped sending its bus to the area where Mehrin and other Hazaras resided. Pakistanis (barring exceptions) do not remember Mehrin. In their closet of irrationality Pakistanis do not also recall Malala, unless there is a resplendent event like the Nobel Peace Prize award. What was much more deplorable, in the recent past, Pakistanis in general tended to accept as correct all the ugly, false and malicious propaganda about Malala broadcast by religious fanatics.[57]

Malala represents the creed of universal human rights, especially for girls in Pakistan. But those who hate Malala, notably the Taliban, subscribe to a different creed altogether. The Taliban represents terrorism, a negation of basic human rights. Taliban's ideas seem to have captivated the Pakistan government, especially the military authorities. True, Taliban's militant conduct is hurting Pakistan too, and, in 2014, Pakistani security forces appear to be taking seriously the domestic threat from the Taliban and other terrorist agencies. On 18 October, in one of a series of instances in course of recent months, it was reported that in the tribal areas at the Pakistan-Afghanistan border, Pakistan armed forces eliminated eleven terrorists, and injured ten. But there can be an endless debate on whether Pakistan has greater interest in carrying on a proxy war against India, or in taking on the Taliban. There can also be an interminable discussion on which terrorist agencies (or factions in one agency) are regarded as strategic assets by Pakistani authorities, and which agencies are regarded as so hostile as to become the targets of armed attacks. In this context, Pakistani shelling (on 8-9 October 2014) of more than 130 Indian border villages and 60 border outposts (BOPs), in complete violation of the 2003 ceasefire, offers just an example of how much importance Pakistan attaches to the proxy war against India. For, under cover of heavy mortar fire, Pakistan has been trying to pour (for decades) armed infiltrators into India. Actually, between 1 and 9 October, Pakistan's cross-border firing killed 8 Indians and injured 80 persons, including security personnel. In addition, more than 30,000 Indians got displaced, as 113 villages lay deserted. India, of course, retaliated in a proper way this time (which was not done in the days of UPA rule in New Delhi). One can argue that, in this way, Pakistan wants to test the will of the new NDA government led by Prime Minister Narendra Modi, that Pakistan wants to attract international attention anew to J&K, and that the growing power of IS may have impelled Pakistan terror groups to multiply their anti-Indian depredations.[58]

On 9 October 2014, India's response to unprovoked Pakistani onslaughts came into a sharp focus. The Indian prime minister warned that Pakistan's adventurist moves could carry an unbearable cost. The prime minister underlined the difference between the responses of the UPA and NDA regimes to Pakistan's aggressive deeds, and affirmed that Pakistan realised this difference, and that India would not now tolerate Pakistan's mischievous cross-border raids. Defence Minister Arun Jaitley said, Pakistan was not only violating the LOC in J&K, but also the international border, which was above any controversy. Jaitley argued that, in the midst of such cross-border firing, the prospect for talks between the two countries became obviously uncertain. That New Delhi advocated and implemented stern action against Pakistani misconduct was evident from Pakistan's distress signal to the UN, even though that was irrelevant. In India, however, there is a lobby that consistently opposes strong action against Pakistan. The arguments of this lobby are counterproductive, and highly damaging to India's interests, if one keeps in view Pakistani behaviour since 1947-48, and India's indefensively weak responses. It is argued, for example, that tough actions by India against Pakistan may nullify the 2003 ceasefire, missing the vital point that Pakistan has been repeatedly violating this ceasefire for pushing armed infiltrators into India. It is further argued that decisive actions by India will add to the strength and legitimacy of Pakistan's armed forces, which use the hostility of India to maximise its privileges at the expense of the civilian sector. This argument is nearly meaningless, because, over many decades, Pakistan's armed forces have exercised, and can acquire, whatever power they covet, in not only the designated military field, but also in procuring lucrative civilian jobs, and owning industrial or agricultural estates. Some opponents of powerful retaliatory action by India against Pakistan openly advocate a switchover from hostile rhetoric and action to peaceful dialogue, especially to safeguard the economic interests of the masses who remain poor in both India and Pakistan (partly because of high military budgets). Theoretically, this argument is valuable, but, in practice, it unabashedly ignores the mindsets of Pakistanis, especially of military officials.[59]

Subsequently, the Indian prime minister sang another tune at the Combined Commanders Conference, which attracted the appreciation of those Indians who did not approve India's firm actions against Pakistan's combative conduct. At this conference, Modi did not harp on taking Pakistan to task, and focused on such larger issues as improvement of higher defence management, integration of defence-diplomatic-economic policies, coordination among and modernisation of various defence departments, etc. The Indian prime minister affirmed at the Combined Commanders Conference that he would make it a regular practice to meet the chiefs of three armed services every month. This would hopefully free the defence forces from bureaucratic shackles, and promote essential re-equipment. Prime Minister Narendra Modi thus marked a way out of the stranglehold on upgradation of defence forces designed by the babudom (the daftarshahi or bureaucracy) as also by a top ranking political leader like the UPA's Defence Minister A.K. Antony.[60]

In order to advocate peace with Pakistan one does not have to relax one's guard, or mistakenly deny a terrorist threat to India emanating from Pakistan. But it is this dangerous game that some powerful politicians (and others including journalists and self-styled intellectuals) have been playing repeatedly. In the 1980s, for instance, armed militants appeared in J&K, preaching Islamist fundamentalism.

Farooq Abdullah's government in J&K ignored it; so did the prime minister of India, Rajiv Gandhi. In course of the decade, these militants raised not only the jihadi banner but also a violent movement for separation of J&K from India. In the latter half of 2014, Chief Minister Omar Abdullah (son of Farooq Abdullah) appears to be toeing the same suicidal line, while learning of not less than three occasions when IS (ISIS/ISIL) black flags are unfurled in Srinagar. Initially, Omar describes these incidents as being staged by idiots. Subsequently, he goes further and, fortified by J&K police reports, he asserts that militants are not connected with these incidents. This tendency to underplay what is widely recognised to be a mortal terrorist threat, which is part of a global threat, is self-defeating. The J&K police is notorious for its incompetence in coping with Pakistan-sponsored terrorism, which has made it inevitable for central government's security forces to play a major part in counter-terrorism operations in J&K. To downplay the IS threat is to give the J&K police a pretext to evade their urgent duty to pay due attention to this threat, and allow it to grow relatively unhindered.[61]

In contrast, Lt. Gen. Subrata Saha, GOC 15 Corps (with Srinagar as headquarters), and J.N. Choudhury, National Security Guards (NSG) Director General, have put the IS threat in a proper perspective. Saha has affirmed that all the security forces should exercise their vigilance in a coordinated fashion to counteract the IS threat. Moreover, efforts should be launched to prevent the youth in J&K from being tempted to join the terrorists (who, reportedly, have plenty of funds). Choudhury has buttressed Saha's observations by pointing out that organisations like the Indian Mujahideen, as also HUM, JEM, LET, which are active in India, may join the IS to stage a terrorist strike targeting several Indian cities at a time. This warning appears to gain urgency because of the recent Al Qaeda declaration, as highlighted by Choudhury, that it is bent upon attacking India.[62]

For an appreciably long period of time, jihadi modules have been present (though not always overly active) in various parts of eastern India, e.g. West Bengal and Assam. From time to time, serious undeniable incidents bring them to the fore. On 21 October 2014, for example, at an explosives factory at Khagragarh of Bardhaman district in West Bengal, two terrorists, Shakil Gazi and Sobhan Mandal died of a blast in course of preparation of IEDs. One person was severely injured. Normally, for many years, ruling parties in West Bengal and Assam are known to suppress reports of such incidents because of the obvious preoccupation with vote bank politics. They have also been using the shortsighted but misleading argument that counter-terror measures must not be permitted to damage communal unity. But the blast in Khagragarh has been too powerful to brook any evasion, and the state government has found no option but to make some arrests, notably of two female militants, the wives of two deceased persons (mentioned above). In a few days, there takes place another blast at the Bhatpara village, which is judged to have an important location. It is contiguous to Shimulia village which has a madrasa, where Gulshan Gazi and Alima Bibi (the wives of the Khagragarh deceased) have received training as JUMB cadres. Their trainer is Abul Kalam, an associate of Sheikh Kauser, a JUMB leader and absconder from Bangladesh. The West Bengal government has set up a composite task force (CTF). The police have discovered at Bhatpara the shell of a bomb that is empty but fitted with tell-tale cables. At Khagragarh, however, the recoveries have been much more alarming, viz. jihadi literature, including a primer on how to carry out explosions, a map of some prominent places in Bardhaman district, a jihadi training video, chemicals used in preparing explosives, live grenades, as also tools such as watch dials, etc. The police have raided on 8 October 2014 a cyber café at Bardhaman's Sartikor, and got hold of a hard disc drive. Kauser Ali, Shakil Gazi and Sobhan Mandal have used this cyber café not only to contact one another but also other JUMB operatives in various parts of India and Bangladesh. The Assam police have subsequently arrested six persons from the Barpeta district in connection with the Khagragarh incident. All the detainees being Muslims, a legislator of Assam, Abdur Rahim Khan, has made the stereotyped accusation that there is a conspiracy to harass young Muslims. National/international implications of the Khagragarh incident are evident. Yet, the West Bengal police have not duly cooperated with NIA personnel. For example, the Bardhaman S.P., S.M.H. Meerza, has not granted the NIA functionaries the permission to visit the Khagragarh blast site. Eventually, on 10 October 2014, the central government has declared formally that the NIA is to take charge of the Khagragarh case. But the Bardhaman SP, in a sort of retaliatory move, has overseen the destruction of explosives detected in Khagragarh even before the NIA has had the opportunity to examine them, obviously to shield ruling party cadres. Leaders of the ruling party in West Bengal have trotted out the hackneyed excuses of unwarranted central interference in a State's affairs, and of the failure of the central government to combat infiltration from Bangladesh. These leaders are, however, silent on how infiltrators can gain sanctuaries in West Bengal for a long period, and why the land for some much-needed outposts on the India-Bangladesh border is not made available to the central government.[63]

Infiltration from Bangladesh is an old and perennial problem, whereas for decades ruling parties in West Bengal have consistently looked away for creation and preservation of vote banks. Therefore, government functionaries in West Bengal, even when their attention has been drawn to such phenomena as the presence of thousands of infiltrators in a district or an unusual rise in the number of voters, have refrained from taking necessary action. Moreover, in collusion with political masters, they have facilitated the issuance of ration cards, PAN cards, voter identity documents, etc. to infiltrators, and even enabled some of them, including JUMB, LET operatives, to obtain passports and move between two countries to maintain regular communications between branches of the terror outfits in two countries as also deliveries of IEDs and bomb materials. When, however, an incident like the Khagragarh blast occurs, and they are reminded of another blast in Lalgola of Murshdabad district in the immediate past, they become a little alert. For, they cannot but notice that samples of explosive substances recovered in Lalgola are remarkably similar to those found in Khagragarh. Moreover, the number plate of a motorcycle in Lalgola is found to be identical with that of a Tata-Nano car in Bardhaman. Nevertheless, presently, there is not much hope of such shattering evidence impelling state government functionaries to take appropriate countermeasures. Alarmingly, though not unexpectedly, infiltrators find it relatively easy to expand their networks from border to interior districts.[64]

In this context, the last point to be touched in the final chapter of this book relates to madrasas. This, too, like infiltration, is an old and familiar problem, becoming more and more dangerous over the years but ignored by government functionaries in collusion with ruling politicians in successive regimes of West Bengal. The recent

Bardhaman incident and its aftermath have brought this problem into limelight. So, the well-known aspects of the problem are showered with attention by the electronic and print media. The people of West Bengal are enlightened anew that there are two categories of madrasas. The West Bengal government recognises and provides aid to 614 madrasas, which belong to the first category. The second category comprises madrasas without any affiliation with the government. These have registered a phenomenal growth, and their number, spread over the entire state from the border to the interior locations, has reached 5,000. Some madrasas, receiving government aid, have adopted modern syllabi. But others have not. Some of these madrasas, without any recognition or assistance from the government, appear to have cast off all pretensions to being educational institutions. They have specialised in indoctrinating students and turning them into potential jihadis. One can speculate whether their locations away from the border may have been planned to evade detection by security/ intelligence agencies operating in border areas. If the West Bengal government cares to compile the list of managing committee members of such madrasas, a sordid political picture may become public. Leaders/cadres of some political parties in the State may come to be identified as associated with jihad factories labelled as madrasas.[65]

Pakistani armed forces have been continuing (as late as October 2014) with their (much-delayed) onslaughts on militants in the Pakistan-Afghanistan border. In one tribal district on 26 October 2014 (for instance), combat aircraft destroyed five hideouts of terrorists, killing twenty of them, and wounding a few others. Nevertheless, such counter-terrorist actions are barely scratching the surface. For, the roots of terrorism are not only deep but an integral part of military domination over the polity, direct or indirect. That may explain why there is not much of a serious discussion on the most important issue facing the country, viz. terrorism, which has an adverse impact on the economy, and remarkably reduces, among other things, the opportunities of Pakistanis to visit foreign countries—not to speak of procuring jobs there. Yet, Pakistanis, especially the military elite, appear to be living in a world of denial, self-deception, and international isolation. There has not been any appreciable change from the time of capture/slaughter of Osama Bin Laden in May 2011 to late 2014. In May 2011, Pakistanis, most of all military officials, denounced the US instead of praising the US for killing the most dreaded terrorist on the globe. Even in late 2014, Pakistanis (barring some exceptions) persist in shunning realities. No wonder thus that Pakistan goes on aggravating international isolation, of which there can be no more glaring evidence than the results of a recent Pew Global Attitudes Survey in China, a country regarded as Pakistan's principal and eternal ally. Merely 30 per cent of respondents expressed a favourable attitude towards Pakistan. Therefore, when, on 26 October 2014, Britain terminated its 13-year engagement in Afghanistan, which has witnessed the death of 453 British soldiers, Pakistan may not look upon this as a danger to itself. On the contrary, living in an unreal world, it may seize British withdrawal (which has coincided with the withdrawal of the last component of US marines) as an opportunity to step up proxy war against India and the ongoing efforts to expand its influence in Afghanistan, to the detriment of authorities in Kabul.[66]

So, Pakistan persists in wallowing in a surrealistic world, in which the Taliban terrorism is not an existential threat. When the US disagrees, it is shoved into the category of enemies, the oldest being India. In this situation, the Pakistani military elite nurtures illusions, which further debilitate the state of Pakistan. For instance, it fondly believes that some Arab countries and China may remain steadfast in their support for Pakistan. But it forgets that some militant groups enjoying Pakistani patronage have already targeted Arab countries and China too. Another illusion of the Pakistani military leaders is that, unable to tackle fully the non-state armed groups in Balochistan or Sind, they should encourage feudal landlords in Punjab to establish armed groups of their own to cope with jihadi elements in Punjab, even though these elements are themselves indebted to the Pakistani military-intelligence agencies for support. Once again, one has to reiterate that it is a surrealistic surrounding of anomalies engraved with ironies, in which, for example, young men can feel it legitimate to look for remunerative jobs as jihadis, whereas the state fails to provide opportunities for employment, as also minimum health/ education services for the masses. Militant chiefs are stepping into these areas sometimes to facilitate recruitment of jihadis. Certainly, Al Qaeda gave a big boost to actual and potential jihadis in Pakistan, affiliated to a variety of outfits with disturbing (even if confusing) nomenclature. Nevertheless, a jihadi basically dehumanises himself by accepting the need for unquestioning obedience to the leader of a militant agency. Otherwise, he cannot, for instance, engage in suicide missions.[67]

The Pakistan army is the self-appointed guardian of the country. It does not accept democracy as a supreme value and the collateral norm of civilian supremacy over the military. The Pakistan army does not shrink from exercising guardianship in not only defence policy but also in domestic as also foreign policies. It subordinates foreign policy to defence policy, which are together so designed as to maximise self-aggrandisement by the military. Politicians, deprived of real powers, seek refuge in corruption, favouritism and frauds, whether by evading taxes or refusing to repay bank loans. Of course, they do all these in collusion with bureaucrats. They have furthermore developed a proficiency in rigging elections. In the competition for election frauds, one political group may succeed and form the government. Others feel deprived, and try to unsettle the incumbent government by means of street protests with the ill-concealed support of the army (which always looks for an opportunity to humiliate ruling politicians in order to keep them in leash). In case street protests succeed, and new elections are held, there will once again be a repetition of competitive rigging, and when a new government takes office, it will also be a fearful vassal of the army. The prerogatives of a near-hegemonic authority have so intoxicated the army (and the ISI) that they have tried to multiply and perpetuate their powers by the adventurous step of raising jihadi forces (wrapping them unconvincingly under the cover of non-state actors) to add to their domestic political authority as also their capacity to intimidate neighbouring countries like India and Afghanistan by means of proxy wars, which sometimes remain indistinguishable (as in the case of Afghanistan) from conventional wars of varying magnitudes. But, unlike Pakistan's political actors, jihadi groups can bite back the patron and destabilise the state of Pakistan. In the latter half of 2014, on the eve of ISAF's exit from Afghanistan, this instability appears to be glaringly acute. Moreover, the jihadi mindset has so infected the ordinary Pakistanis, that they indulge, for instance, in a rampant misuse of the country's notorious blasphemy laws, murdering blasphemy convicts in prison. To take another instance, if anyone at any stage of his life has been associated with peace committees opposed to the Taliban, he too cannot escape slaughter.[68]

Jihadis thus have produced a bellicose society. The Taliban belief is, change can only result from slaughter. On an average, Talibanis kill ten persons a day in Karachi. Jihad has preempted the emergence of social trust. The civil society cannot perform its normal function of moderating the use of coercion in society. The women are the worst sufferers in this situation. Males beat them, even throw acid. If they gather courage to visit a police station for lodging complaints, policemen themselves may repeat the violence these unfortunate women have already suffered. Rich Pakistanis deploy goons to murder their competitors, there being no faith in peaceful negotiations, which presuppose a certain level of trust. No wonder that the government's attempts to use peaceful dialogue as a component of counter-insurgency measures do not succeed. Talibanis actually have used such a dialogue, starting (for instance) in February 2014, to plan the recruitment, training and arming of jihadis. Even the pledge of a cease-fire by the Taliban for a month, offered in March 2014 and accepted by the government, collapsed by mid-April 2014, because a number of Taliban factions did not agree with the leaders, and carried on hostilities. In the past, when the Pakistani military had yet to earn some experience in counter-terrorist operations, it relied on operations by heavy artillery, helicopter gunships, and combat aircraft. These operations could earn a lot of publicity on television channels, but mainly displaced ordinary tribals in KPK and FATA, while failing to wipe out terrorists many of whom moved beyond the Durand Line to gain shelters in two provinces of Afghanistan: Khost and Paktika. By mid-June 2014 (as already noted in this book), the Pakistani military changed its mode of operation, and commenced infantry offensives against terrorists, killing hundreds of them in a short time. But the record of terrorists—killing 50,000 Pakistanis (including 5,000 soldiers) since 2001—cannot be matched. Nor is it possible to predict the time to be required for effective elimination of terrorists, and whether Pakistan's palpably acute instability will not lead to an inevitable disaster in the foreseeable future.[69]

In this context, an irony was, instability in the country and especially in the minds of a large number of Pakistanis might have increased if government-Taliban talks had succeeded. Not to speak of minorities like Ahmadis, Hindus, Ismailis and Shias, even a substantial number of liberally oriented Sunni Muslims (who formed the majority of Muslims and of the whole Pakistani population) would have felt frightened that the Taliban, encouraged by the success of talks with the government, might step up their attacks on them in a selective fashion. At least one section of the ISI (which had, for example, never assaulted the militants, and sheltered Osama Bin Laden in Abbottabad) might have supported the Talibani mission of such selective targeting of a vast number of Pakistanis. After all, captains of fanatics like Hafiz Saeed of the JUD not only enjoyed the patronage of some influentials in the ISI, but also commanded enormous financial might to contribute to this murderous mission of the Taliban. It must be added, however, that in spite of the failure of Taliban-government talks and the apparent success of Pakistani armed forces in their strikes against the Taliban in 2014, a huge number of Muslims continue to be hated and killed by other Muslims, who are religious bigots, and who have no specific defensible cause to hate their victims.[70]

Whereas Pakistan military's actions against terrorists go on, killings of Muslims by fellow-Muslims also go on. To take one among numerous examples in the latter half of 2014, on one single day (1 November 2014), in Afghanistan, three soldiers and six policemen died, whereas in Pakistan on the same day, seven soldiers and twenty rebels lost their lives. On 2 November, again, 55 persons, including members of security forces, as also men, women and children died of suicide bombing in Pakistan, and 200 persons were wounded. If this is interpreted as a blowback from Pakistani military action against terrorists in the Pakistan-Afghanistan borderlands, one wonders what can be the nature of such retaliation by Pakistani terrorists if the Pakistan government displays the same determination as the Bangladesh government in sentencing three top ranking Jamaat E Islami leaders in course of a single week in October-November 2014 for war crimes committed in 1971, when a successful liberation struggle led to the emergence of the independent country of Bangladesh (former East Pakistan) separated from Pakistan. Actually, the Interior Minister of Pakistan has made some adverse comments on the death penalty awarded to the Jamaat chief in Bangladesh. The Pakistani envoy has been summoned to the Bangladesh Foreign

Office, which has issued a statement protesting against the Pakistani Interior Minister's comments. It sternly accuses Pakistan of interfering in the internal matters of Bangladesh, correctly identifies vested interests in Pakistan as the inspiration behind such comments, and advises Pakistan to mind its own business. Pakistan has to try to appease the Jamaat in the country. Pakistan has long adhered to Jamaat's theory and practice (accounting for the jihadi genocide and war crimes in East Pakistan in 1971). So, the abovenoted instances of slaughter on the Pakistan-Afghanistan borderland are merely a sort of epilogue to what has been going on for years throughout Pakistan, i.e. the slaughter of non-Sunni Muslims (not to speak of Hindus/Christians/Sikhs). Not only Ahmadis but even Shias have been declared by law as non-Muslims, and ineligible for any high public office. Any reminder of Mohammed Ali Jinnah (the founder of Pakistan) being a Shia seems to be of no relevance to Pakistan today. The Pakistan government—to reiterate what has been substantiated in this book—has itself sponsored Sunni belligerence and hegemony. But when this grows into a threat to the government itself, and the latter takes military action, the TTP retaliates severely. For, it has been noticed that the TTP's allegiance to Al Qaeda is far stronger than that of the Afghan Taliban.[71]

One should remember that, throughout 2013-14, there have been discussions on alarming realities of the Pakistan-Afghanistan situation as ISAF prepares to depart from Afghanistan. Pakistan (as already discussed in this book) has long been living in a castle in the air remote from realities. Sometimes, however, the US seems to match Pakistan's immunity from realism as the day of exit from Afghanistan draws near. So, it nearly challenges the Kabul government's sovereignty as it holds talks with the Afghan Taliban in Doha, and not (as it should be) on the Afghan soil with due respect for the Constitution of Afghanistan. Actually, in Doha, the Taliban office has used the banner of Islamic Emirate of Afghanistan. The US self-inoculation from harsh experience becomes starkly clear on the day the Afghan Taliban's office is opened in Doha, for, on that day, four US soldiers are massacred quite close to their base in Afghanistan. Kabul's Ambassador to the UN reveals the blunt truth when at a Security Council deliberation he stresses that there can be no peace in the region, including Afghanistan, as long as Pakistan sticks to its use of terrorism as a foreign policy tool, as also of safe havens for terrorists on its own territories. The Pakistani Ambassador to the UN, however, denies patent realities, i.e. the existence of terrorist bases in Pakistan. But the US too has to answer the unsavoury query of whether it is prepared to allow Pakistan to exercise significant control over post-2014 Afghanistan as in pre-9/11 days, and whether that is the best way to preserve US security or prevent another 9/11.[72]

One wonders which skeletons will roll out from the US cupboard on the eve of ISAF's departure from Afghanistan. For, the domination of the biggest American companies over the web is obvious, and their connection with terrorist groups has also become evident. Robert Hannigan, the director of Britain's Government Communications Headquarters (GCHQ), has made some disturbing observations about these US companies in an article in *The Financial Times* appearing on 4 November 2014. As a top ranking intelligence official of UK, Hannigan has stressed that terrorist organisations, especially the IS, are misusing the services of these companies, although the companies try to seek refuge in denial. Terrorist agencies have conveniently chosen these companies to set up extensive networks for command and control operations. This poses an enormous challenge to governments. For, their intelligence organisations have to depend on cooperation from private companies. The urgency of this cooperation is apparent from the fact that the IS utilises the internet for radicalisation of operatives, intimidation of opponents, and the larger aim of self-promotion. This is quite unlike how Al Qaeda uses the web, i.e. for anonymous circulation of terrorist literature. There is of course a parallel debate on how far intelligence organisations should use Google and Facebook to gain entry into data about individuals. In 2013, Edward Snowden underlined this debate when he made public the US intelligence data on surveillance of phone conversations and internet. Hannigan recommends that governments in democracies have to safeguard the vital rights of citizens by working out a sort of a new social compact with technology companies. Hannigan emphasizes that there can be no unrestricted right to privacy. It must be added, however, that the British government has been fairly active in combating terrorist propaganda in unlawful websites through the Counter Terrorism Internet Referral Unit (CTIRU). For example, during the last three years, the CTIRU has wiped out about 30,000 items of such propaganda. But there are expert media handlers among jihadis, who can somehow reach their prospective clients (despite the abolition of some of their websites) by changing names of their sites, and utilising the social media as also the Diaspora, a private platform.[73]

Better late than never. What India and Afghanistan have been complaining about Pakistan's use of proxy terrorist agencies to endanger stability in the region has at last been openly confirmed by the Pentagon in early November 2014 by a report of more than one hundred pages submitted to the US Congress. From the standpoint of an Indian (or Afghan) analyst, this report (coming as it does from the Pentagon) is incredibly and unprecedentedly candid. The report acknowledges that the Pakistani terrorist agencies (officially depicted as non-state but actually state-sponsored) have been the major cause of tension between Afghanistan and Pakistan, which thus violates Pakistan's public pledge to assist Afghanistan in achieving political reconciliation in the war-torn country. The Pentagon report has also frankly admitted that in May 2014, only three days before the swearing-in ceremony of the newly elected Prime Minister of India, Narendra Modi, terrorists attacked the Indian Consulate in Afghanistan's Herat province. The then Afghan President, Hamid Karzai, condemned this attack and strongly reaffirmed his interest in Indo-Afghan amity. In June 2014, the US State Department declared that LET was to be held responsible for this attack on India's Herat Consulate. The Pentagon report has further acknowledged that India's support for Afghanistan aims at security and stability of Afghanistan, which will help the whole region by promotion of economic ties with Central Asian countries.[74]

The abovenoted Pentagon report may be a consolation prize for India, but not a real prize as a prelude to tough US action against Pakistan leading to a containment of such agencies as the LET carrying on the proxy war against India. The US has a number of alibis for not taking any such action against Pakistan, and the weakening of the Obama Administration because of the results of US elections on 4 November 2014 may be judged to provide the least important alibi. Even if Barack Obama has been the winner rather than the loser in these elections, the US Administration is not expected to take any significant action against Pakistan in the foreseeable future, which may lessen cross-border terrorism against India. Although Pakistani security forces go on killing/injuring a varied number of militants in FATA almost daily, they significantly ignore information about probable suicide bombing that appears even in newspapers long in advance, when the bomber is to operate at the border with India (as on 2 November 2014), and there is a clear danger of spillover into India. This does not seem to bother the US, because, in the prevalent US view, Pakistan is a large state occupying a strategic position. Its help is necessary for the preparations towards a near-complete departure of ISAF from Afghanistan in 2014. The use of an alternative route for transport of ISAF's weapons, stores, etc. through Central Asia has become uncertain on account of NATO-Russia dispute over Ukraine. So, Pakistan's utility/status goes up in US view, even if there is mounting evidence of persistent social-political malaise in Pakistan. Thus, if poor Christian brick kiln workers (to take one of numerous instances) want to quit the kiln because of continual non-payment of remuneration, the kiln owner may get these Christians massacred on the totally false allegation of desecration of Koran. To take next an example of corruption of politicians, Nawaz Sharif's family has been ordered by the Lahore High Court to repay a loan of Rs. 350 crore to eight banks. But corruption can be a deadly threat to the prospects for emergence of a liberal democratic culture when it is combined with concentration of power at the top and suppression of dissent in leading political parties, viz. the present ruling party PML (N), the former ruling party PPP, and Imran Khan's Pakistan Tehreek I Insaf (PTI). So, Pakistan may remain a failing state for years, and satisfy the US conscience that it cannot fail.[75]

As the Obama Administration attaches a priority to quitting Afghanistan, it is facing a far more acute security problem than the one in Pakistan-Afghanistan: the global threat from IS. The US, furthermore, cannot avoid the embarrassing query of whether, as in the case of Taliban in Pakistan-Afghanistan, in West Asia too, the US has in the past been responsible for propping up extremists whom later it has to fight. Interestingly, Turkey, a NATO partner of US, confronts a situation comparable to that of Pakistan, a non-NATO ally of US. In the Afghan civil war, Pakistan has supported the Taliban and faced a backlash in the form of (among other things) attacks on Shias and their mosques. Turkey has patronised Sunni jihadis in Syria, and witnessed Shia shrines in Istanbul being subjected to criminal attacks. Syrian refugees, numbering about 1.3 million, inhabit Turkey. The IS may find it relatively easy to recruit cadres from among these refugees. The IS has registered its presence, and is expanding its influence, in the Pakistan-Afghanistan region. In October 2014, six commanders of the TTP have declared their loyalty to the IS. On 8 November 2014, *Dawn* has narrated the contents of a confidential report by the Balochistan government's home and tribal affairs department. This report of 31 October 2014 notes the IS claim that it has recruited not less than 10,000 cadres from two districts in KPK. The Balochistan government's report adds that the IS is cementing an alliance between two anti-Shia militant groups in Pakistan, viz. Lashkar E Jhangvi (LEJ) and Ahl E Sunnat Wal Jamat (ASWJ). The report warns that the IS plans to retaliate against Pakistani actions in North Waziristan by attacks on government establishments in KPK, including military ones. This expansion of the IS threatens the regions of Persian Gulf as also South Asia.[76]

The ideas and practices of IS are so barbaric as to have repelled Osama Bin Laden, and caused the dissociation of Al Qaeda from IS. (As already noted in this book), Abu Bakr Al Baghdadi is the Caliph of IS. His Caliphate covers not only Iraq and Syria (parts of whose territories are already under IS rule) but also Afghanistan, Pakistan, eastern Iran and the Central Asian Republics. He designates this whole area as the Islamic State of Khorasan. Baghdadi thus redraws the frontiers drawn by Western imperial powers after the First World War, when the Ottoman empire was dismantled. Baghdadi, significantly, reserves his ultimate war for the annexation of India. Muhsin Al Fadhli heads the IS branch for the Indian subcontinent, its headquarters being situated in an unknown location on Pakistani territory. From time to time IS flags have flown in Srinagar, whereas Afghan leaders feel that IS threatens the security of their country. Estimates for the number of fighters with Baghdadi vary from 20,000 to 30,000. According to some critics, IS may be deemed to be a creature of the US, which has used the IS for replacement of the regime of Bashar Al Assad in Syria. But, with the passage of time, this creature has become a threat to the US and the world. So, on the eve of the 13th anniversary of 9/11, on 10 September 2014, the US President has outlined a counter-IS strategy. Essentials of this strategy are to rely on air strikes but rule out any ground offensive by US forces against the IS; the formation of an anti-IS coalition, including some Muslim countries in West Asia; the training and arming of Iraqi soldiers, of Kurdish Peshmerga militias, as also of moderate rebels in Syria. Some observers may contend that the unstated essentials of this strategy are to make Muslims fight Muslims, to avoid the arrival of bodybags in the American homeland, and to use petrodollars of Muslim states to finance a war that is likely to last quite long. Americans may feel happy that they do not have to receive bodybags at home, but their happiness may be shortlived if they discover that their health/education services will inevitably suffer from reduction, because in course of US air strikes against the IS, some of the missiles being deployed can cost us much as UK£ 105,000.[77]

But this is only a part of the problem of the abovenoted counter-IS strategy of the US. There are other far too complex problems. West Asian countries (and other countries like Pakistan) are witnessing acute Shia-Sunni conflicts. Yet, the US is using the funds and forces of both Shias and Sunnis against the IS. This is likely to create contradictions which are hard to resolve. Probably, the best way to beat back the IS is to encourage the emergence of an autonomous and militarily powerful Kurdish territory. But this is acceptable neither to Turkey's Sunni rulers nor to Iraq's Shia rulers. Turkey, a NATO ally of the US, wants the US to carry on strikes against the Assad regime. But the US, focused on IS, will not agree. The US should be aware that Sunni militants from such diverse places as Chechnya, Libya, and Yemen are crossing the Turkish border to join the IS. As to the so-called moderate Syrian rebels (themselves divided into rival groups and militarily/organisationally weaker than the IS or Al Qaeda-linked Jabhat Al Nusra), nobody can guess when the moderates turn into Sunni extremists. Moreover, there is no evidence that several thousand moderate rebels, trained in Turkey, have been able to register much success in containing the IS or Jabhat Al Nusra, while the bloody conflict rages in Syria. So, in the absence of US troops on the ground, the anti-IS war is likely to last indefinitely. Who will benefit? Some analysts may provide the naughty answer that the US military-industrial complex will be the biggest beneficiary, and the US may remain the unchallenged merchant of death.[78]

How should India cope with the threat of cross-border terrorism from Pakistan when this threat, as of 2014-end (the terminal point of this book), appears to be compounded by, and merging with, the threat from the IS. Since the mindset of the Pakistani military elite is well-known, one legitimate speculation is that the Pakistani armed forces may welcome the IS plan to expand the Caliphate into India. The military manpower of the IS is negligible in contrast to that of Pakistan. Therefore, the IS may welcome Pakistani participation in actualisation of the hegemonic design of the IS. A section of the Pakistani military may possibly be reluctant to embrace the ultra-radicalism of the IS. But this can be overcome by the willing section, especially because the non-state terrorist actors, who are virulent Sunni fanatics, are ready accomplices. At such a stage India may confront so cataclysmic a situation that the US may shed its decades-old fixation with Pakistan, and commence air strikes at the India-Pakistan border (hopefully within the territory under Pakistani control). In anticipation of such a scenario, should India contemplate cooperation with the US (as desired by the US) and its allies in the anti-IS battles by 2014-end or in early 2016? The answer to this question is not easy. For, many Indians, including women, work in West Asian countries. In the recent past, IS captured some Indian nurses, but subsequently released them. A few Indian Muslims have reportedly joined the IS. But a large number may become IS fighters if India formally joins the US-led coalition against the IS. Since Pakistan-IS collaboration against India may take a few years to assume menacing proportions, presently, India may confine its cooperation with the US in the counter-IS strategy to mutually beneficial transmission of intelligence. This may be a sort of paying back the US in its own coin in the post-2014 Pakistan-Afghanistan situation, when the proxy war by Pakistan against India is likely to become exceedingly dangerous, and yet the US may not be willing to abandon its consistently duplicitous ally to make even the gesture of strong action, and only offer intelligence cooperation with India. Nevertheless, even in the near future, there is not much scope of complacency if one reads the English summary of an Arabic document, viz. the IS Manifesto, which elucidates in a highly systematic manner the 100-year plan for establishment of a World Caliphate. This is not the usual propaganda material. It offers a vivid (though disturbing) view of the aims and objectives of IS leaders.[79]

In the immediate future, how should India act *vis-à-vis* Pakistan? There are important areas where for decades—not quite honourably—India has stuck to complete inaction, even though in a corresponding situation, Pakistan would give hell to India in international forums, and win convincingly a publicity war. For instance, in Pakistan every year nearly one thousand Christian and Hindu girls are coerced to convert to Islam and marry Muslims. India has not raised this issue even in domestic platforms, not to speak of international platforms. One also wonders why Pakistani atrocities on Christians and Hindus, including murders on false blasphemy charges, are virtually ignored by the international press, especially the US press. In contrast, when Boko Haram kills only three persons in Nigeria (not to speak of kidnapping a few hundred girls), there is widespread international publicity. Does it indicate that the US government's long-practised acquiescence in Pakistan's unwarranted treatment of matters of India's legitimate concern somehow infects the US press so much as to ignore atrocities on Christians or Hindus, although, admirably, sections of the Pakistani print media do not hesitate to write about these atrocities.[80]

India has observed near-complete silence for decades in the matter of persistent and gross violation of human rights in Gilgit and Baltistan, which are after all parts of J&K, which lawfully belong to India. India has not also publicised its claim with appropriate cartographic data which Pakistan may not be able to match. Next, an area where present jingoistic gestures should be replaced by a pleasant ceremony relates to the lowering of national flag every day at the India-Pakistan border. The joint drill of today is needlessly aggressive, and merely exacerbates the overall atmosphere of hostility. One can do with far less. There is no harm if India takes the initiative, even though the other side is reluctant to reciprocate. Notably, the new government that has come to power in New Delhi in May 2014 has taken a few unprecedentedly resolute steps *vis-à-vis* Pakistan. One, belligerent activities by Pakistani forces at the LOC and international border have been properly counteracted to compel Pakistan to temper its belligerence. If Pakistan has tried to test the will of the newly established government in New Delhi, the strength of this will remains manifest. Two, the new government in New Delhi, in a further demonstration of its will, has cancelled the pre-scheduled Secretary-level talks, because the Pakistani High Commissioner in New Delhi has, in conformity to what has been practised for a long time and tolerated by India, held talks with the Huriyat of J&K, despite clear warnings by the new government against holding such talks.[81]

Pakistani writers, it should be noted in this context, do not tire of elucidating how, because India's new government has suspended comprehensive dialogue with Pakistan for not stopping violence, and because there are a variety of reasons which have contributed to a lowering of nuclear threshold between the two countries, the unresolved J&K issue may act as a nuclear flashpoint. Pakistan thus resorts to an ill-concealed nuclear blackmail. Some of these reasons (far from convincing, if not absurd to an Indian observer) are: India's civil nuclear cooperation pact with the US and the resultant easing of acquisition of nuclear fuel and plants from abroad can enlarge India's nuclear armoury; India's collusion with the Baloch Liberation Army and TTP for the aggravation of domestic instability in Pakistan; growing disparity in the conventional capabilities of the two countries because of ceaseless acquisition/deployment of improved weapons systems by India's army, navy and air force; and indifference of the US and other major powers to attempts at a solution of India-Pakistan disputes, etc.[82]

Some Indian analysts go much further than New Delhi's present government in the advocacy of a tough posture towards Pakistan, which has been carrying proxy attacks against India for more than three decades and, in that process, caused immense harm also to ordinary Pakistanis and to the prospects for emergence of liberal democracy in the country. In such an Indian assessment, there is no alternative for India to the suspension of all cultural and economic transactions with Pakistan, including even contacts in the realm of sports. Pakistan regularly resorts to smuggling dangerous narcotics and fake Indian currency to India, in addition to carrying out savage terrorist attacks. Actually, a suspension of all normal relations with Pakistan may give some relief to the Indian soldiers in J&K by minimising the inflow of armed militants into India. Indian soldiers can then acquire confidence, overcome nervous strain, and avoid accidental killing of innocent persons in J&K, where they have to work in nerve-wracking proximity to the civil population. The need for a tough posture towards Pakistan has become all the more urgent in the last quarter of 2014 because of Pakistan-inspired militant activities in India's eastern State of West Bengal (whereas in Assam such activities have been going on for a long time). Noticeably, the most extensive coverage on these activities by terrorists, belonging to Bangladesh's Jamaat E Islami and JUM and moving to West Bengal (acquiring even places in the Voters' List), has been provided by *Anandabazar Patrika* deploying a large number of reporters—and this has not been matched by all English newspapers in India taken together. For example, on 10 November 2014, there are elaborate reports by Kuddus Afrad, Shivaji Dey Sarkar, Kuntak Chattopadhyay, Rajibaksha Rakshit, Anamitra Chattopadhyay and an unnamed 'our correspondent'. They reveal in detail the links between infiltration, arms-narcotics-currency smuggling and terrorism, as also highlight a crucial role by ladies, who are so highly trained and motivated as to defeat police investigators by a monotonous reply of 'I don't know' to all sensitive queries. The fact (speculated upon for some years) that terrorists seek refuge in India—escaping the clutches of Bangladesh authorities—is underlined in these reports. Remarkably, according to some commentators, whereas Indian authorities do not hesitate to slaughter Maoists at will, they have not as yet showed the guts to kill Muslim terrorists similarly for a probable fear of an unmanageable communal backlash.[83]

The end of 2014—if one examines all the facts stated in the concluding chapter—confronts a grim situation indeed. Pakistan is regularly killing militants, eliminating 27 on 16 November 2014, for example, while losing five soldiers. But it is far from bringing under control the anti-government terrorists, who even attack a convoy of opposition leader Imran Khan's PTI on the eve of a party rally. In order to subdue terrorists, the government and the society of Pakistan have to come out of the clutches of falsehoods enthralling them for at least three decades. Otherwise, one cannot explain why the most prosperous and populous province of Pakistan, Punjab, has emerged as the capital of terrorists. There is no national security policy properly so called. Consequently, terrorists can practise ugly sectarianism, divisive regionalism, and then acquire the confidence to challenge the state by launching insurgency.[84]

The Pakistani military establishment, however, appears to be blind to realities, and does not seem to realise the dangerous fact of emergence of IS inside Pakistan, even though it may not be as powerful as the Taliban or Al Qaeda for the present. For, there are reports that IS may have in possession a nuclear weapon manufactured by the use of radioactive uranium robbed from the University in Mosul, following the city's takeover by IS in June 2014.[85] The military establishment in Pakistan queerly ignores the reality that the situation in Pakistan is such that it can easily attract any religious group with extremist orientation. This reality can be easily perceived by, e.g. references to the perennial persecution of minorities. Not to speak of horrendous atrocities on Christians, which evidently enjoy the backing of a large majority of Pakistanis, even the anti-terrorist leaders of the Shia sect of Muslims are not spared. Take, for instance, the case of Allama Nawaz Irfani, a Shia Imam of Parachinar in the notoriously terror-ridden Kurram Agency of FATA. He is credited with combating the Taliban with visible success for as long as 14 years. Yet, Irfani has been forced by the government to leave Parachinar, kept without any protection, and eventually he is murdered in broad daylight in Islamabad, the capital city. This is only one of many instances to confirm the conclusion of an eminent Pakistani journalist, Abbas Nasir, that even when we know well what ails us, we do nothing, and, therefore, Pakistanis continue to live with a variety of 'existential threats' to security.[86] Probably, one of the best conceivable year-end gift from the Pakistan government to the creators of such threats is the operation of two special trains by Pakistan Railways to carry supporters of the terrorist organisation, JUD, headed by Hafiz Saeed, to a two-day assembly commencing on 4 December 2014. Opposition leader Imran Khan's PTI cannot lag behind the government in placating the arch-terrorist, the planner of 26/11 Mumbai attack. It has postponed its 4 December programme of a Lahore blockade.[87] How then can Pakistan safeguard its security?

It is one thing to propound a National Internal Security Policy (as in early 2014), but quite another to carry out the same. Pakistan has a National Counter Terrorism Authority (as already noted in this book), but, like the National Internal Security Policy, this Authority too is a sort of an orphan or anchorless. Pakistan has also a National Security Committee, but it has never declared unambiguously that no government body should extend secret support to proxy terrorist agencies. The biggest lie Pakistan has to discard is the military-ISI-patronised lie that these non-government terrorist agencies strengthen Pakistan's security. The counter terrorism machinery should have two components: the ISI and the police-IB-CID apparatus. The former should focus on arresting and questioning the TTP operatives, with special emphasis on terrorists having foreign links. The latter should take on militants carrying out sectarian attacks. Amazingly, the Anti-Terrorist Act has not been applied to restrict the mobility of personnel associated with proscribed agencies like LEJ. Evidently, their official guardians have not been warned against assisting them. Policemen in various localities know the whereabouts of the cadres of these agencies (including some common criminals). They can, if permitted by their bosses in the police (and the military) carry out a nationwide swoop, and arrest these terrorist cadres. Policemen can regulate the use of loudspeakers to limit the impact of speeches (from mosques, for instance) preaching hatred of faiths other than one's own. Policemen, moreover, have to be empowered to recover weapons in unlawful possession in order to restrict violence by members of non-state militant agencies.[88]

The prolonged reliance of the Pakistani authorities, especially the military-ISI combine, upon terrorist proxies, may eventually turn out to be self-defeating. For, despite initial recruitment as stooges, the non-state terrorist agencies, notwithstanding occasional convergence of interests (e.g. in the matter of attacks against India) may gradually prefer the role of independent actors. One glaring evidence of this is that neither the chief of the Afghan Taliban, Mullah Omar, nor the Haqqani group, has made any attempt to curb terrorist atrocities inside Pakistan. Simultaneously, continuance of such atrocities on foreign soil (e.g. against New Delhi/Kabul) has robbed Islamabad of the normal option of a proper management of intricate relationships with neighbouring countries by means of conventional diplomatic channels. This is evident from the suspension of composite dialogue with Pakistan by the new government taking office in New Delhi in 2014. Thus, terrorist proxies, not amenable to manipulation at will, have ceased to be strategic assets for the Pakistan government. Moreover, in a post-2014 scenario, a highly probable Afghan Taliban takeover of Kabul may spell a two-fold disaster for Pakistan—in the matter of use of Afghanistan as an imagined security cushion against India, and the coveted exercise of diplomatic leverage over Afghanistan. So, if Pakistan intends to develop an effective counterterrorism strategy, it has to factor in the independence (if not rationality) of terrorist stooges.[89]

Terrorist atrocities are likely to increase in the near future inside Pakistan because of the deep discontent caused by the order of security forces to tens of thousands of tribals in Pakistan's northern region to vacate their homes in quest of safer places, so that they can avoid the deaths/injuries due to military operations. For, such discontent can facilitate recruitment of new cadres for militant activities. The entire environment in the tribal region has become so vitiated by the fear of espionage by security forces that militants sometimes behead a person on a mere suspicion of espionage. Militants do not hesitate to kill/injure boys travelling in a school van in Pakistan's tribal region by means of some explosive device planted on the road. If the prospects for Pakistan thus appear to be grim in 2014, no less so are those in Afghanistan, where the situation has hardly improved since 2013. The Taliban there can sometimes pretend to exhibit its faith in a dialogue with the US, but, actually, it is just waiting for the day when most US troops leave. At that point it is extremely likely that the average monthly slaughter by terrorists of poorly equipped and trained members of the ANF will much exceed the 2013 rate of 250.[90]

The situation in Pakistan and Afghanistan cannot, as of 2014-end, be viewed in isolation from what is happening in other parts of the world, notably in West Asia. An Australian research group, the Institute for Economics and Peace, has published the 2014 Global Terrorism Index. In accordance with this report, the year 2013 has witnessed nearly a 44 per cent rise in terrorist attacks in contrast to 2012, the total number in 2013 being about 10,000. The number of deaths stands at 11,133 in 2012 and 17,958 in 2013. Afghanistan, Iraq, Nigeria, Pakistan and Syria account for more than 80 per cent of the fatalities in 2013. IS, Boko Haram, Al Qaeda and the Taliban have been responsible for 66 per cent of all deaths. Iraq has registered 6,362 deaths in 2013, an increase of 164 per cent over 2012. The IS has to be held accountable for the maximum number of these fatalities. According to this report of the Australian Institute, the spread of violent theologies of militant Islamists explains the rise in terrorism.

The gravity of the situation can be further gauged by the warning in a UN Security Council report published in London's *Guardian* on 31 October 2014. The report notes that 15,000 jihadis (including 2,000 westerners) have moved to Iraq and Syria from more than 80 countries. They have joined the IS and other terrorist groups. The US air strikes in West Asia have not deterred jihadis in other countries, 1,000 of whom are leaving for Iraq and Syria every month. Some French-speaking IS fighters have even called upon Muslims in France to terrorise the country. The UN Security Council report has also drawn attention to the fact that Al Qaeda and IS are parts of the same strategic ideological movement, although on issues of leadership and tactics there may be a lack of congruence.[91]

The IS reportedly is much more violent than other terror groups. In mid-November 2014, for example, it has publicised a video of beheading Peter Edward Kassig, a US citizen (providing medical treatment to victims of civil war in Syria), as also 18 other persons depicted as members of the Syrian military. The IS believes in mass executions. As to Kassig, the IS maintains that he has been buried in a historic battle site, Dabiq, where, in the 16th century, the Ottomans vanquished the Mamluks. This victory was followed by the establishment in various stages of the vast Ottoman empire. In the IS view, this has been the last Caliphate. According to IS, Cassig is the first American crusader to be buried, and it is expectantly waiting for other crusaders who will be disposed of in a similar fashion. It should be added that, since June 2014, the IS has murdered hundreds of tribals in Iraq and Syria for being its political opponents. It has committed atrocities on ethnic/religious minorities, sold women into slavery, and beheaded on camera a large number of Iraqi military personnel.[92]

This author proposes to end his book on a mildly optimistic tone by stressing certain data (although there can be a barrage of contrary data). The Shia-Sunni conflict is as old as 1400 years. Throughout history, Shias have been an underprivileged group. It is only since 1979, with the victory of the Shia-led Islamic revolution in Iran, that Shias have gained some authority. This, however, has provoked rivalry with Sunni-ruled Saudi Arabia. This rivalry, again, has been aggravated since 2004 due to the Jordanian King Abdullah's declaration of suspicion towards Shias as the fifth column of Iran, especially after the replacement of Sunnis by Shias as rulers in Iraq in 2003. The 2011 Arab rebellions, again, have witnessed beleaguered rulers in Bahrain, Syria and Yemen adopting the tactics of divide-and-rule and highlighting Shia-Sunni tensions. Yet, there is silver-lining amidst dark clouds. Al Azhar of Egypt is the greatest theological centre of Sunnis, and its supremo has denounced Salafists for exacerbation of Shia-Sunni rivalries. Moreover, Egypt's security forces have acted firmly against Sunni extremists. Kuwait has a substantial number of Shias although they are in a minority, and its parliament has denounced attempts to bank on the Syrian civil war to foment Shia-Sunni tensions. Hezbollah, basically a Shia militia, provides a classic example of how to promote inter-faith harmony, because a number of Sunnis support Hezbollah. Finally, to clutch another possibility of such harmony, one can cite the cases of some Shia leaders, especially Ayatollah Ali Al Sistani of Iraq, who earnestly try to moderate sectarian rivalries.[93]

Steps taken by Afghanistan's new president, Ashraf Ghani Ahmadzai, inspire some hope about prospects for peace in the Pakistan-Afghanistan region. At a conference on peace and reconstruction in Afghanistan, held in Beijing, the Afghan president has made an overture to Taliban insurgents in his country, inviting them for a dialogue. He has also requested Afghanistan's international partners to sustain a peace process owned and led by Afghans, so that no Afghan terror group can act as a menace to the domestic or international system. Much more importantly, in course of his visit to Pakistan (when the Pakistani prime minister happens to be away), with obvious support from the Foreign Office of Pakistan, Ghani has ignored protocol, and met the Pakistan army chief at the military headquarters. Ghani has thus demonstrated that improvement of relations with Pakistan is his priority. He wants to impress upon Pakistan's real rulers (the military) that the people of Afghanistan and their elected government are Pakistan's genuine and permanent friends—and not the Taliban. Ashraf Jehangir Qazi, a former Pakistani Ambassador to the US, India and China, and Head of UN Missions in Iraq and Sudan, has made some important observations on this matter. 'The arrogance and parochialism of Pakistan's Afghan policy—which within a few years forfeited the enormous goodwill towards Pakistan that was generated in every Afghan home during the Soviet occupation,' observes Qazi in a *Dawn* article—'must be replaced by a more enlightened and generous approach.' Qazi pleads that Pakistan must dehypenate its policy towards Afghanistan and its policy towards India. 'Positive feedback is what matters. Not self-defeating zero-sum games,' Qazi significantly adds.[94]

China and India may try to collaborate in counteracting terrorism in the Pakistan-Afghanistan region. Muslim Uygurs in China's Xinjiang province, affiliated to Al Qaeda-sponsored East Turkestan Islamic Movement, have committed violence not only in Xinjiang but in other parts of China, so much so that some of them have been sentenced to death. This may be viewed as one of the entry points for facilitation of India-China collaboration. If the India-China border problem becomes a stumbling block to the optimisation of such collaboration, a solution can be attempted by a revival of the old formula of Zhou En Lai and Deng Hsiao Ping. Nevertheless, without waiting for this solution to materialise, India may consider it wise to promote peace and economic progress in south and southeast Asia (this being the ultimate deterrent to terrorism) by cooperation with China's efforts to expedite the activation of ancient land and maritime silk routes, along with the Trilateral Highway project connecting India, Myanmar and Thailand. China's maritime silk route (MSR) plan is especially ambitious. It consecrates links, which are six hundred years old, for trade in porcelain ware, silk, tea, etc. Currently, many other items of export and import are planned to link China with Vietnam, Malaysia, Indonesia, Sri Lanka, Maldives and Kenya. Southeast Asian countries will undoubtedly welcome India's participation in this MSR plan, especially because of close connections between Southeast Asia and India in the first 1500 years of the Christian Era.[95]

Actually, in addition to MSR, any revival of even a section of the ancient Silk Route, e.g. Tamu-Mandalay-Lashio-Bhamo-Ruili-Kunming link, can benefit the people in States of India's North East. At any rate, the result of a public attitude survey conducted by the Centre for Environment Social and Policy Research (CESPR) is revealing. More than 80 per cent of the respondents have reacted favourably to the proposal for an economic corridor stretching from India to China through Bangladesh and Myanmar, and wanted not only tourism but also manufacturing facilities created along the corridor passing through their States. They have further observed that trans-border movement of people and goods can promote multilateral trade by means of improved market access, as also enable an easier resolution of such problems as smuggling of arms and narcotics due, hopefully, to economic growth and shared prosperity.[96] For Pakistan, too, the new Silk Routes conceived by China, viz. from China to Pakistan, and China to Central Asian Republics (CARs), can bring into being economic corridors, which are expected to create regional prosperity with the prospect of maturing into a long-term deterrent to terrorism.[97] Remarkably, the four-lane project of a China-Pakistan economic corridor, passing through Pakistan-occupied Kashmir (claimed by India) is moving forward, and prime minister Sharif has already performed ground-breaking.[98]

India's prime minister Modi appears to be deeply interested in building an economic corridor in South Asia. At the 18th SAARC summit in Kathmandu, on 26 November 2014, he has pleaded for connectivity by rail and road in order to promote movement of goods and people-to-people contacts in the region. But, due to Pakistan's obstructionism, the SAARC conference has been able to sign only one agreement, i.e. on energy cooperation. Pakistan has thus acted as the spoiler. Modi has announced at the SAARC summit that India will grant 3-5 years' business visas and immediate visa for medical purposes to citizens of SAARC countries. Moreover, Modi has stressed health as an important sector of cooperation among these countries. He has declared that India will monitor the situation in, e.g. polio-free countries, supplying vaccines to such countries which happen to suffer from renewed polio outbreaks. Mainly on account of Pakistan's negative attitude, SAARC has not been able to achieve a consensus on goals (including the supreme goal of counter-terrorism) in course of three decades. Significantly, Pakistan's avoidance of any talk on terrorism—in sharp contrast to what India, Afghanistan and Sri Lanka have stated—may have preempted any exchange of pleasantries between India and Pakistan on the first day of the Kathmandu summit. On the second day, they have engaged in a ritual of handshake, but without any meeting of hearts. Cross-border trade and intra-regional trade in general (which are important ways to generate prosperity through cooperation) have remained insignificant among SAARC countries.[99]

Countries of the size and influence of China and India have to achieve a proper blend of cooperation and competition. Presently, however, the balance appears to be in favour of cooperation. While China takes initiatives on the MSR, and both China and India do so on cooperation with Indian Ocean Rim (IOR) countries, for instance, both exhibit some areas of convergence. Both pursue regional economic integration, globalisation, a multilateral system of trade, as also a just and inclusive world economic order. Since the end of the second world war, such institutions as the World Bank and the International Monetary Fund have been largely run to serve the interests of rich countries and secure their hegemony. Consequently, Bank-Fund aid to poor countries have been provided under such obligatory conditions as to produce income inequalities and economic exclusion of large sections of the people. In 2014, Brazil, Russia, India, China and South Africa (BRICS) have taken decisive measures towards global financial restructuring by the establishment of a New Development Bank. This Bank will commence lending operations in 2016. The presence of Russia, currently somewhat isolated in Europe because of the acute crisis over Ukraine, is significant, especially in view of the terror-ridden situation in the Pakistan-Afghanistan region, the central theme of this book. It may be pertinent to look forward optimistically to India-China-Russia collaboration to cope with this situation in the post-2014 years.

Hopefully, the US, too, jarred by the IS, will strengthen this collaborative venture, dissolving the decades-old mesmerisation by Pakistan. For, with the spread of the IS network in Pakistan in the near future, the US may discover, that 12,500 US and allied troops (whatever the sophistication of their equipment)—to be stationed in terms of the two agreements signed by the Ghani government of Afghanistan with the US (Bilateral Security Agreement) and with the NATO (Status of Forces Agreement)—may not suffice post-2014 to preempt a new terrorist attack on the US homeland. Such an attack looks plausible partly because India evidently hesitates to supply adequate arms to the Ghani government. Pakistan, too, may indirectly contribute to such an attack by spoiling relations with Afghanistan. Pakistan has been busy digging at the border with Afghanistan a 10 feet wide and 8 feet deep trench with a length of 300 miles, of which, as of early December 2014, 110 miles have already been constructed.

Pakistan argues that this will act as a barrier to the cross-border movement of separatists, smugglers and terrorists. Afghanistan contends that Pakistan is thus trying to make a long-disputed Pakistan-Afghanistan border even more contentious, and that Pakistan has to refrain from generating terrorists for the purpose of combating terrorism. But such Pakistani manoeuvres must not be allowed to impede collective efforts towards counteracting post-2014 terrorism (as noted above).[100]

This author thus ends the book in a mildly optimistic tone. Optimism is blended with a vision for inclusive regional and world orders.[101] An ironic prop for this optimism was provided on 16 December 2014 by the attack of six terrorists (including four suicide bombers) on a Peshawar army school, which initially killed 139 children, one female teacher, a watchman, and injured 245, some of whom were dying. This was a horrible signal for united regional/international assault on terrorism as also planning for a more equitable regional/world order, especially when there was a report from Beijing on the same fateful day of 16 December 2014 that nearly 300 Chinese (presumably from Xinjiang) had joined the IS. In tune with this urgent need for solidarity in response to a national/international tragedy of unspeakable dimensions, prime minister Modi of India requested all the country's schools to observe two minutes of silence on 17 December 2014. Schools in India acted on 17 December 2014 in accordance with this appeal of the prime minister. The Indian Parliament denounced on the same day the dastardly massacre of school children in Pakistan, and passed a unanimous resolution expressing condolences, solidarity and the determination to fight terrorists. India has thus taken steps in the right direction. Will Pakistan follow suit? Can prime minister Sharif of Pakistan act upon his announcement to eradicate all terrorists from Pakistani territory? Will it also mean that his government will stop proxy wars against India by the use of terror agencies?[102]

The success of Sharif's efforts in wiping out the Taliban (whether by the formation of military courts for trial of terrorists or otherwise), and thus shaping a new regional/world order, will depend much on the response of the entire Muslim world towards counterterrorism. After all, it is the conclusion of the Global Terrorism Index that, as in the five years before 2013, so in 2013, Muslims died of attacks by co-religionists in Muslim countries in eighty per cent of terrorist attacks. Therefore, Muslim countries (including of course Pakistan) have no excuse to shrink from a collective endeavour to dismantle barbarism and obscurantism by tough measures, and not confine themselves to mere engagement and negotiations. Whereas such postponement of hard decisions/actions may be deemed to be opportunistic and impermissible, any exclusive reliance on force against terrorists with a religious label may prove to be counterproductive. Muslim countries have to devise an appropriate blend of force with political, social and ideational measures in order to overcome the grave challenge of extremism and violence. One can only hope that these countries will prove themselves equal to this existential challenge.[103]

This optimism can be sustained if—only if—governments and civil societies in Muslim countries try to promote free and critical thought among Muslims. This may bridge the gap between Islam and reason as analysed and elaborated by Anwar Shaikh, Ali Sina or M.A. Khan, who figure prominently in the fifth chapter of this book. These authors (and others whose names are not mentioned because of lack of space) have deftly illustrated, on a thorough study of Koran and Hadith, some logically irrefutable and factually valid (though terrifying) links between events in the early years of Islam and contemporary episodes of Islamist terrorism. These links, wherever they exist in the thought processes of Muslims (young and old), can be snapped by Muslim writers and publicists today--provided they determinedly and systematically emulate a number of Muslim free thinkers and satirists writing in the ninth and tenth centuries. They can also derive profound inspiration from medieval geniuses like Abul Rayhan Al Biruni and Ibn Rushd in order to promote critical analysis of all subjects and doctrines embracing history, philosophy and religion.[104] Changes in thought patterns can hopefully create in the long term the possibility of preempting thoughtless (i.e. terrorist) activities.

Endnotes

1. Ajai Sahni, '*Afghanistan-Pakistan-USA: The Noise Before Defeat*,' http://www.satp.org/satp.org/satporgtp/sair/Archives/sair 10/10–5 htm
2. United Kingdom, House of Commons, International Development Committee, *Afghanistan: Development progress and prospects after 2014*, Vol. I, London, 2012, p. 16.
3. *Ibid.*, p. 17.
4. Ajai Sahni, http://www.satp.org/satporgtp/sair/10/10–5 htm
5. United States Department of State, *Country Reports on Human Rights Practices for 2013: Pakistan*, Washington DC, p. 4.
6. *Ibid.*, pp. 4, 23-25, 27.
7. *Ibid.*, pp. 25-26.
8. *Ibid.*, pp. 28-30.
9. NATO, *Secretary General's Annual Report 2013*, Brussels, pp. 1-2.
10. *Ibid.*, pp. 2-3.
11. For details, see Jonardon Ganeri, *The Lost Age of Reason*, New York: Oxford University Press, 2011, p. 24.
12. Bertrand Russell, *The Practice and Theory of Bolshevism*, London: Allen & Unwin, 1920, pp. 5, 29, 114.
13. Ibn Warraq, *Leaving Islam: Apostates Speak Out*, Amherst: Promethus Books, 2003, p. 136.
14. AP report from Banchi, *The Times of India*, 30 June 2014.
15. Reuters report, *The Indian Express*, 24 July 2014.
16. AP report, *Ibid.*, 28 July 2014.
17. Reuters report, *Ibid.*, 31 July 2014.
18. Report in *The Economist*, reproduced in *The Indian Express*, 1 August 2014.
19. *Ibid.*, also see AP report from Kano, *The Indian Express*, 18 September 2014.
20. Report in *The Economist*, reproduced in *The Indian Express*, 10 September 2014.
21. Report in *The Indian Express*, 2 September 2014; report in *The Economist*, reproduced in *The Indian Express*, 15 September 2014.
22. AP report, *The Statesman*, 3 September 2014.
23. PTI report from Melbourne, *Ibid.*, 19 September 2014.
24. PTI report from Melbourne, *Ibid.*, 20 September 2014.
25. I.A. Rehman, article reproduced from *Dawn* in *The Statesman*, 8 August 2014.
26. COL Thomas F. Lynch III, *Sunni and Shia Terrorism: Differences that Matter*, West Point: Combating Terrorism Center, 29 December 2008, p. 7.
27. Article by Mohammad Hamza Khan, *The Indian Express*, 9 September 2014.

28. Leading AQAP personnel in Yemen, despite being jailed are famous for escaping from prisons, as the authorities are notoriously lax. Bruce Riedel, 'Terrorism's New Avatars', *Yale Global Online Magazine* (*http://yaleglobal.yale.edu*), 7 January 2010.
29. Report in *The Economist*, reproduced in *The Indian Express*, 18 September 2014. In Bahrain, to take another instance, nine Shias have been jailed for attempts to dislodge the Sunni monarch: PTI report, *The Indian Express*, 22. September 2014.
30. AP report, *The Statesman*, 24 September 2014.
31. Olaf Farschid, 'Jihadism—Communication Impact', in *Islamic Extremism: Ideology and Modes of Dissemination*, Vienna: Federal Ministry of the Interior, Republic of Austria, Vol. II, 2008, p. 28.
32. PTI report, *The Indian Express*, 22 September 2014.
33. http:www.werimyki.com/artcls/atta–will.html
34. New York: Knopf, 1954, translation by Anthony Bower, p. 273.
35. Sean M. McIntyre, 'Mohammed Atta on the Magic Mountain', *Telos*, Vol. 144, Fall 2008, pp. 41-42: www. Telospres.com
36. New York: Knopf, 1995, translation by John E. Woods, p. 393.
37. Report in *The Economist*, reproduced in *The Indian Express*, 2 September 2014; article by Seema Chisti, *The Indian Express,* 9 September 2014; editorial, *The Statesman*, 12 September 2014.
38. Report by Helene Cooper, *The New York Times*, reproduced in *The Indian Express*, 6 September 2014; AP report, *Ibid.*
39. Report from Paris by John Lichfield, *The Statesman*, 17 September 2014.
40. Report by Mariam Karouny, *The Indian Express*, 9 September 2014.
41. Report in *The Economist*, reproduced in *The Indian Express*, 29 August 2014.
42. *Ibid.*
43. *Ibid.*
44. Article by Hardeep S. Puri, *The Indian Express*, 26 September 2014.
45. Report in *The Economist*, reproduced in *The Indian Express*, 25 September 2014; article by Hardeep S. Puri, *The Indian Express*, 26 September 2014.
46. PTI report, *The Statesman*, 25 September 2014; AP reports from Beirut, *Ibid.*, 26 and 27 September 2014; report by Andrew Grice and Nigel Morris, *Ibid.*, 27 September 2014.
47. AFP reports from Baghdad/Canberra, *The Statesman*, 31 August 2014; report in *The Economist*, reproduced in *The Indian Express*, 10 September 2014; article by Thomas L. Friedman, *The Indian Express*, 16 September 2014; Leader in *The Independent*, reproduced in *The Indian Express*, 19 September 2014; article by Rajendra Abhyankar, *The Indian Express*, 22 September 2014; report in *The Economist*, reproduced in *The Indian Express*, 22 September 2014; AFP report from Damascus and PTI report from London, *The Statesman*, 24 September 2014; report in *The New York Times*, reproduced in *The Indian Express*, 24 September 2014; report by Heather Sol, *The Statesman*, 25 September 2014; Leader in *The*

Guardian, reproduced in *The Indian Express*, 25 September 2014; AFP report from Beirut, *The Statesman*, 29 September 2014.

48. Reuters report from Peshawar, *The Indian Express*, 8 September 2014; PTI report from Islamabad, *The Statesman*, 29 January 2015.
49. 'South Asia and Afghanistan,' *Strategic Survey*, Vol. 113, No. 1, 13 September 2013, London, pp. 203-204 (DOI: 10.1080/04597230.2013.830465).
50. *Ibid.*, p. 307.
51. AFP report from Kabul, *The Statesman*, 22 September 2014; commentary in *The Statesman*, 23 September 2014; PTI report, *Ibid.*; report in *The Economist*, reproduced in *The Indian Express*, 29 September 2014.
52. AFP report from Kabul, *The Statesman*, 17 September 2014; report from Kabul, *Ibid.*, 18 September 2014; report in *The Economist*, reproduced in *The Indian Express*, 29 September 2014; report from Kabul, *The Statesman*, 30 September 2014.
53. Report from Kabul, *The Statesman*, 24 September 2014; Express New Service, *The Indian Express*, 24 September 2014; report in *The Economist*, reproduced in *The Indian Express*, 8 October 2014.
54. Article by Aryaman Bhatnagar, *The Indian Express*, 8 October 2014.
55. Article by Tariq Khosa, *Dawn*, reproduced in *The Statesman*, 11 October 2014.
56. Article by Khaled Ahmed, *The Indian Express*, 10 October 2014.
57. Article by Abbas Nasir in *Dawn*, reproduced in *The Statesman*, 12 October 2014.
58. PTI report from Jammu, *The Statesman*, 10 October 2014; article by Cyril Almeida in *Dawn*, reproduced in *The Statesman*, 14 October 2014; *Ibid.*, 13 October 2014; PTI report, *Ibid.*, 18 October 2014.
59. Statesman News Service Report from New Delhi, *The Statesman*, 10 October 2014; commentary by the Express News Service, *The Indian Express*, 10 October 2014; article by Seema Mustafa, *The Statesman*, 10 October 2014.
60. For pertinent facts and observations, see, e.g. an editorial, *The Statesman*, 19 October 2014.
61. For relevant data and comments, see, e.g. an editorial, *The Statesman*, 17 October 2014; PTI report from Srinagar, *Ibid.*, 22 October 2014.
62. PTI report, *The Statesman*, 17 October 2014.
63. Statesman News Service reports from New Delhi, Kolkata and Bardhaman, *The Statesman*, 10 October 2014; an additional report, *Ibid.*, 11 October 2014; Statesman News Service report from Guwahati, *Ibid.*, 13 October 2014; report by Kanchan Siddiqui from Bardhaman, 13 October 2014; report by Uday Basu from Kolkata, *Ibid.*
64. Statesman News Service reports from Malda, Kolkata and Murshidabad, *The Statesman*, 15 and 25 October 2014.
65. For some pertinent facts and comments, see, e.g. an editorial, *The Statesman*, 23 October 2014.

66. AFP report from Yaounde, *The Statesman*, 27 October 2014; for a lot of sensitive data and perceptive comments, see, e.g. an article by Husain Haqqani, *The Indian Express*, 8 August 2014; PTI report from London, *The Statesman*, 27 October 2014.
67. For some insightful observations, see an article by Khaled Ahmed, *The Indian Express*, 11 September 2014.
68. PTI report from Islamabad, *The Statesman*, 29 October 2014; for pertinent comments, see articles by Christophe Jaffrelot, *The Indian Express*, 13 September 2014, Babar Sattar, *The Statesman*, 30 September 2014, and Mohammad Tahirul Qadri, *The Indian Express*, 30 September 2014; for a report from Islamabad on an ex-prime minister's corruption, see *Ibid.*, 30 October 2014; for a PTI report from Islamabad on the Pakistan Supreme Court's rejection of petitions to declare 2013 election results invalid, see *Ibid.*
69. For relevant commentaries, see articles by Gurmeet Kanwal, *The Statesman*, 9 July 2014; Khaled Ahmed, *The Indian Express*, 12 July 2014; Khaled Ahmed, *Ibid.*, 24 September 2014.
70. For some persuasive though disturbing accounts, see articles by Khaled Ahmed, *The Indian Express*, 6 and 11 April 2014, 30 May and 3 July 2014.
71. AP and PTI reports, *The Statesman*, 2 November 2014; PTI report from Lahore, *Ibid.*, 3 November 2014; PTI report from Dhaka, *Ibid.*, reports by Anisur Rahman, *Ibid.*, 4 and 7 November 2014; for pertinent observations, see, for instance, an article by Rajinder Puri, *Ibid.*, 2 August 2013.
72. For a relevant commentary, see article by M.L. Kotru, *The Statesman*, 27 June 2013.
73. Article by Robert Hannigan quoted in the PTI report from London, *The Statesman*, 5 November 2014; article by Kim Sengupta in *The Independent*, reproduced *Ibid.*, 6 November 2014.
74. PTI report from Washington, with quotes from the Pentagon report, *The Statesman*, 5 November 2014.
75. Article by Babar Sattar in *Dawn*, reproduced in *The Statesman*, 4 November 2014; PTI report from Lahore, *Ibid.*, 5 November 2014; article by Farhan Bokhari in *Dawn*, reproduced *Ibid.*, 6 November 2014; editorial, *Ibid.*, 7 November 2014; PTI report from Lahore on Nawaz Sharif's family, *Ibid.*, 8 November 2014; PTI report on the killing of militants by the army, *Ibid.*, article by Asha'ar Rehman, *Ibid.*, PTI report from Lahore about Nawaz Sharif's nepotism, *Ibid.*, 14 November 2014.
76. Report in *The New York Times*, reproduced in *The Indian Express*, 7 October 2014; PTI report from Islamabad, with quotes from *Dawn*, *The Statesman*, 9 November 2014.
77. Article by Kim Sengupta, in *The Independent*, reproduced in *The Statesman*, 15 October 2014; articles by the editor and by M.K.

Bhadrakumar, *Frontier*, 19-25 October 2014, pp. 1-2, 8-10; article by Gurmeet Kanwal, *The Statesman*, 6 November 2014.

78. *Ibid.*—all the sources mentioned at the end of the last paragraph.
79. English Summary of IS Manifesto issued by Veryan Khan *vkhan@tracterrorism.org*, 13 October 2014; article by Gurmeet Kanwal, *The Statesman*, 6 November 2014; editorial, *The Statesman*, 10 November 2014, on India's External Affairs Minister seeking cooperation for release of Indian construction workers detained in IS-controlled Mosul; PTI report from Islamabad about IS flags near Pakistani capital, *Ibid.*, 14 November 2014.
80. Articles by Abbas Nasir and Babar Sattar, in *Dawn*, reproduced in *The Statesman*, 10 and 11 November 2014; PTI report from Islamabad, referring to a plea for support to Pakistani prime minister for stopping atrocities against religious minorities, *Ibid.*; AFP report, *The Statesman*, 12 November 2014, on Boko Haram killing three persons in Nigeria; another PTI report from Lahore on death threats to Christians, *Ibid.*, 14 November 2014; article by Pakistan Human Rights Commission Chairman, Zohra Yusuf, in *Dawn*, reproduced *Ibid.*, 18 November 2014.
81. Swasti Vardhan Mishra, *Cartographic Contestation Between India and Pakistan—With Regard to Pakistan Occupied Kashmir*, Calcutta University and Knowledge World, New Delhi, 2014, esp. pp. 3, 16-18; editorial, *The Statesman*, 10 November 2014; Ashok Malik, 'Decoding India-Pakistan Relations', Ananta Aspen Centre, *www.anataaspencentre.in* 10 November 2014.
82. Article by Munir Akram in *Dawn*, reproduced in *The Statesman*, 28 October 2014; Akram, a former Pakistani Ambassador to the UN, talks about a probable nuclear showdown over J&K, but not about daily slaughter of innocents by state-patronised terror networks.
83. Article by Raja Murthy, *The Statesman*, 11 November 2014; editorial, *The Statesman*, 8 November 2014, on jihadis in Assam; Statesman News Service report, *Ibid.*, 9 November 2014; reports on women terrorists in West Bengal and Assam in *Anandabazar Patrika*, 9 November 2014; article by the editor of *The Shillong Times*, Patricia Mukhim, in *The Statesman*, 10 November 2014; article by Abdul Gaffar Choudhury on the export of terror from Bangladesh to India's West Bengal, in *Dainik Statesman*, Kolkata, 2 November 2014, article by Uday Basu confirming this export of terror and its facilitation by successive ruling parties in West Bengal, viz. the CPI (M) and the Trinamul Congress (TMC), in *The Statesman*, 17 November 2014; editorial, *Frontier*, 9-15 November 2014, pp. 1-2.
84. Two PTI reports from Lahore, *The Statesman*, 17 November 2014.
85. PTI report from London, *The Statesman,* 2 December 2014.
86. Article by Abbas Nasir in *Dawn*, reproduced in *The Statesman*, 1 December 2014.
87. PTI report from Lahore, *The Statesman*, 3 December 2014.

88. Article by Tariq Khosa, a retired policeman, in *Dawn*, reproduced in *The Statesman*, 30 October 2014.
89. See a brilliant article by Muhammad Amir Rana, in *Dawn,* reproduced in *The Statesman*, 17 November 2014.
90. Articles by Seema Mustafa, *The Statesman*, 28 June 2013, and Husain Haqqani, *The Indian Express*, 29 June 2013; PTI report from Islamabad, *The Statesman*, 16 November 2014; PTI report from Islamabad, *Ibid*., 19 November 2014; AFP report from Kabul on the shooting of a NATO soldier, *Ibid*., 16 November 2014.
91. AFP report from London, quoting the report of the Institute for Economics and Peace, *The Statesman*, 19 November 2014; report in *The Guardian* quoted extensively in the AFP dispatch from London, *The Statesman*, 1 November 2014; PTI report from London, *Ibid*., 21 November 2014.
92. AFP report from Beirut, *The Statesman*, 17 November 2014.
93. See a valuable report in *The Economist*, reproduced in *The Indian Express*, 5 July 2013.
94. AP report from Beijing, *The Statesman*, 1 November 2014; Ashraf Jehangir Qazi, article in *Dawn*, reproduced in *The Statesman*, 20 November 2014.
95. PTI report from Beijing on Uygur terrorists, *The Statesman*, 1 November 2014; for elucidation of the feasibility of the Zhou-Deng formula for the India-China border settlement, see the chapter on relations with China in Jayanta Kumar Ray, *India's Foreign Relations 1947-2007*, New Delhi: Routledge, 2011; article of Vinod Saihgal, *The Statesman,* 20 November 2014; *The Star-Asia News Network* report on MSR, reproduced *Ibid*., 22 November 2014; for an authentic analysis of how the operationalisation of MSR can benefit, e.g. a country like Myanmar, see Wang Lin, Shi Guanglin & Zhao Yuning, 'Starting Anew and Revisiting the Zngho—Initiated MSR'; *Link Times*, Kunming, esp. pp. 16, 21-22.
96. Article by J.B. Lama, *The Statesman*, 1 December 2014.
97. Aarish U. Khan, 'China goes West: Reviving the Silk Route', *Regional Studies*, Vol. XXXII, No. 3, Summer 2014, esp. pp. 85-87.
98. PTI report from Beijing, *The Statesman*, 1 December 2014.
99. PTI report from Kathmandu, *The Statesman*, 27 November 2014; report in *The Kathmandu Post*, reproduced *Ibid*.; article by Kalyani Shankar, *Ibid*., 30 November 2014.
100. For some comments on the complexities of IS-generated situation in West Asia, resulting in the departure of Chuck Hagel from the position of US Secretary of Defence, see editorial, *The Statesman*, 27 November 2014; for an instance, among innumerable ones, of daily slaughter of Iraqis by terrorists in Baghdad, see AP report from Baghdad, *Ibid*., 29 November 2014; Varsha Singh, 'What will Withdrawal of NATO forces from Afghanistan mean for India', *Business Economics*, Kolkata, 16-30 November 2014, pp. 10-11; PTI report from Kandahar on delay in supply of Indian arms to Afghanistan, *The Statesman*, 30 November 2014; for

one among numerous instances of persistent attempts by Pakistani terrorists to set off IED blasts around the LOC in J&K, see a PTI report from Jammu, *Ibid.*, 2 December 2014; for an example of US tenacity to use drones for wiping out terrorists in Pakistan, including a top Al Qaeda kingpin, see PTI report from Islamabad, *Ibid.*, 8 December 2014 and *The Times of India*, 8 December 2014; Pakistani manoeuvres include unsuccessful efforts by Pakistan-sponsored terrorists to destabilise Indian democracy by a disruption of elections in J&K, where in 2014 the voter turnout has been exceedingly high—a humiliating blow to terrorists who threaten citizens not to vote—PTI reports, *The Statesman*, 7 and 8 December 2014; the incorrigible Pakistani mindset is amply revealed when, e.g. former Pakistani military ruler, Pervez Musharraf, is not shy of affirming even in December 2014 that his 1999 Kargil adventure was a retaliation against India's role in Bangladesh in 1971—PTI report, *The Times of India*, 11 December 2014; as to IS outreach in India, including West Bengal, see report by Saikat Datta, *The Hindustan Times*, 13 December 2014, and SNS report in *The Statesman*, 14 December 2014.

101. *China Daily* article on MSR and China-launched Asian Infrastructure Investment Bank, reproduced in *The Statesman*, 18 November 2014; for an elaborate analysis of Chinese and Indian initiatives in the IOR, see Jagannath P. Panda, 'China's Tryst with the IORA: Factoring India and the Indian Ocean', *Strategic Analysis*, Vol. 38, No. 5, September-October 2014, pp. 668-702; for a thoughtful account on the probable impact of BRICS on the emergence of a new and more equitable international economic order, see Gobind Bhattacharjee's article in *The Statesman*, 20 October 2014; on the isolation of Russia in Europe, see editorial, *Ibid.*, 18 November 2014; for an in-depth analysis of how China's current efforts in rebuilding age-old land/sea silk routes can strengthen Chinese and regional economies, by use of the BRICS Bank and the Asian Infrastructure Investment Bank, see an article by Andrew Sheng, *The Statesman*, 8 December 2014; on the need for a change in Pakistani policy towards Afghanistan for coping with the post-2014 situation, especially in view of the IS threat, see article by Huma Yusuf in *Dawn*, reproduced in *The Statesman*, 9 December 2014; for an incisive analysis of persistent Pakistani ambivalence in the war against terrorists, see an article by Abbas Nasir in *Dawn*, reprinted in *The Statesman*, 14 December 2014; but Pakistan should renounce this ambivalence, because, according to an American think tank, Pakistan is the eighth most dangerous country in the world, Iraq being the first—see PTI report, *The Times of India*, 11 December 2014.

102. APP/ANN/PTI reports from Peshawar, Islamabad and Beijing, *The Statesman*, 17 December 2014; PTI reports from New Delhi and Peshawar, *Dawn*/ANN reports from Peshawar and Islamabad, editorial expressing anguish over the attacks on Pakistani children, an article by Christopher

Bluth (of the *Straits Times*/ANN) on the failure of Pakistan government to contain the jihad launched by the Taliban and other terrorist groups, *Ibid.*, 18 December 2014; for an admirably comprehensive and perceptive analysis by a Pakistani scholar of the post-2014 sceanrio, see Lubna Sunawar, 'The 2014 US Withdrawal—An Unsettled Quagmire for Pakistan', *Regional Studies*, Vol. XXXII, No. 4, Autumn 2014, pp. 98-122—the scholar concludes on page 116: 'Afghanistan's unrelenting political instability could drag the region into a proxy war that would again place still greater pressure on Pakistan, weaken fragile energy rich Central Asian states, and aggravate tensions between New Delhi and Islamabad'; on 28 December 2014, the ISAF officially terminated its 13-year-old combat mission in Afghanistan, and assured the continued functioning of about 12,500 soldiers on a 'training and support' mission in Afghanistan—AFP report from Kabul, *The Statesman*, 29 December 2014; for pertinent comments on this 'Operation Resolute Support', which may hopefully build an enduring NATO-Kabul partnership post 2014, see an editorial, *Ibid.*, 1 January 2015.

103. For facts and comments on Pakistan's tough anti-terror measures, following the recent massacre of school children in Peshawar, see PTI report from Lahore, and an editorial, *The Statesman*, 27 December 2014; an important voice from West Asia/Middle East on this issue is that of an eminent writer, Aijaz Zaka Syed—*aijaz.syed@hotmail.com*—there can be no better place for a reference to Syed's perceptive article than a paragraph near the end of this book: *Ibid.*, 26 December 2014.

104. See, e.g. an article by Ziauddin Sardar in *The Independent*, reproduced in *The Statesman*, 26 January 2015.

Index